Family Caregiving in Chronic Illness

FAMILY CAREGIVER APPLICATIONS SERIES

Series Editors

David E. Biegel, *Case Western Reserve University*
Richard Schulz, *University of Pittsburgh*

The **Family Caregiver Applications Series** is an interdisciplinary book series focusing on the application of knowledge about family caregiving, both within and across dependent populations, extending into the practice and policy arenas. The volumes are well-grounded theoretically and empirically, advance existing knowledge in the field, and are state-of-the-art works designed to fill existing gaps in the literature.

Family Caregiver Applications Series
Volume 1

Family Caregiving in Chronic Illness

*Alzheimer's Disease, Cancer,
Heart Disease, Mental Illness, and Stroke*

David E. Biegel
Esther Sales
Richard Schulz

Published in cooperation with the
Mandel School of Applied Social Sciences,
Case Western Reserve University

SAGE PUBLICATIONS
The International Professional Publishers
Newbury Park London New Delhi

For information address:

SAGE Publications, Inc.
2455 Teller Road
Newbury Park, California 91320

SAGE Publications Ltd.
6 Bonhill Street
London EC2A 4PU
United Kingdom

SAGE Publications India Pvt. Ltd.
M-32 Market
Greater Kailash I
New Delhi 110 048 India

Printed in the United States of America

Library of Congress Cataloging-in-Publication Data

Biegel, David E.
    Family caregiving in chronic illness: Alzheimer's disease, cancer, heart disease, mental illness, and stroke / by David E. Biegel, Esther Sales, Richard Schulz.
        p. cm.
    Includes bibliographical references and index.
    ISBN 0-8039-3213-8. — ISBN 0-8039-3214-6 (pbk.)
    1. Chronically ill—Home care. 2. Caregivers. 3. Chronically ill—Family relationships. I. Sales, Esther. II. Schulz, Richard, 1947-   . III. Title.
RC108.B54   1991
362.1—dc20   90-43952
                                                             CIP

FIRST PRINTING, 1991

Sage Production Editor: Diane S. Foster

Contents

4/23/91

83362

Acknowledgments

The development and publication of this volume would not have been possible without the combined assistance of a number of individuals. We wish to thank our respective adminstrators, Richard L. Edwards, Dean, Mandel School of Applied Social Sciences; David E. Epperson, Dean, School of Social Work, University of Pittsburgh; and Vijai Singh, Associate Provost, and Director, University Center for Social and Urban Research, University of Pittsburgh, for their support and encouragement of our work. Judy Simpson, Project Officer, The George Gund Foundation, was instrumental in helping to secure the resources necessary to make this project a reality. Jackie Goodin provided extensive research assistance in locating and reviewing caregiver intervention materials. Additional research and administrative support was provided by Doris Chandler, Ken Corvo, Judy Knapp, and Charlotte Rath. Finally, we would like to thank Marquita Flemming, our editor at Sage Publications, Inc., for her guidance, feedback, and assistance. Preparation of this manuscript was supported in part by grants from the George Gund Foundation, the National Institute on Aging (AGO5444), the National Institute of Mental Health (MH41887), and the Practice Demonstration Program, Mandel School of Applied Social Sciences, Case Western Reserve University.

David E. Biegel
Esther Sales
Richard Schulz

1

Overview of Family Caregiving

INTRODUCTION AND PURPOSE

During the past two decades, there has been increasing awareness of the significant and substantial roles that families play in providing care for adult family members who become dependent due to chronic mental and physical illnesses. Informal service providers, like the family, have always been the primary source of human service care to individuals in need. In fact, if such informal service providers were unavailable, professional agencies would be so inundated with service demands that they could not function.

More recently, researchers have recognized that family caregiving, although having positive aspects for the caregiver, is often stressful as well. Research on the effects of caregiving shows very clearly that caregiving is not without costs to the caregiver. Many families report caregiving to be an emotional, physical, and at times, financial burden. Significant caregiving problems identified by researchers include: coping with increased needs of the dependent family member caused by physical and/or mental illnesses; coping with disruptive behaviors, especially those associated with cognitive disorders or mental illness such as dementia or schizophrenia; restrictions on social and leisure activities; infringement of privacy; disruption of household and work routines; conflicting multiple role demands (spouse, parent, worker, and caregiver of spouse, parent, or in-law); lack of support and assistance from other family members; disruption of family relationships; and lack of sufficient assistance from human service agencies and agency professionals.

Knowledge concerning caregiving needs has led to the development of several service and policy initiatives designed to reduce caregiver burden and provide supportive assistance so that families can continue their caregiving roles. There is now a growing body of literature pertaining to family caregiving of a variety of dependent population groups such as Alzheimer's disease patients, stroke victims, the mentally ill and mentally retarded, cancer patients, heart disease patients, and the frail elderly.

The purpose of this book is to provide a comprehensive analysis of the role and function of family caregiving both within and across adult populations with dependency needs because of chronic disease. We will examine five specific diseases in this volume—cancer, heart disease, stroke, Alzheimer's disease, and chronic mental illness—and will develop a conceptual framework for presenting and assessing current research and practice relating to family caregiving. More specifically, we will provide a synthesis of existing research knowledge about family caregiving of dependent adult populations. We will also review literature on the effects and impacts of intervention models developed in a variety of settings to assist family caregivers of dependent adults. This effort should result in a better understanding of the similarities and differences in providing care to family members with different types of dependency and need. Thus a major contribution of this volume will be its dual level of analysis. It will use empirical research findings pertaining to specific problem populations to tease out commonalities and differences in caregiving issues, and suggest new directions for research and practice.

We will limit our analysis to caregiving of dependent adult populations, and exclude caregiving of children. An examination of caregiving of both adults and children could not be realistically conducted in a single volume, offering depth as well as breadth, because there are fundamental differences in the issues confronting each age group. Chronically ill children often have unique developmental problems if their physical capacities inhibit normal interpersonal experiences. Providing care to children who are developing organisms is a normal role expected of parents, but caregiving by spouses of disabled partners and by adult children of parents with disabilities have not traditionally been roles that individuals prepared for or expected to assume. Caregivers of the adult populations examined in this volume are, for the most part, middle-aged to elderly. Because our focus is on the family caregiver rather than the patient, our analysis omits a large literature addressing patient outcomes.

This first chapter examines demographic, economic, social, and technological trends leading to the emergence of caregiving as a major societal issue; provides an overview of the nature and extent of family caregiving; discusses the meaning and impact of chronic illness; analyzes the status of caregiving research from an historical perspective; and reviews the organization of the rest of the volume.

TRENDS AND ISSUES IN CAREGIVING

The provision of care by some family members to other family members who become dependent due to the physical and/or mental effects of chronic illness is not a new phenomenon. Families in the United States, as well as in other parts of the world, have always provided care to their dependent members. There is now growing recognition among service providers and researchers that caregiving will become a more salient public policy issue in the future because of a number of recent (and anticipated) demographic, economic, and social changes. Key changes include the following:

- Life expectancy and the aging of the population have increased dramatically during this century.

Life expectancy has increased substantially since 1900, regardless of race or gender, between 1900 and 1985 this increase ranged from 25 years for white males to 40 years for black females (National Center for Health Statistics, 1989). In 1986 the average life expectancy for women was 78.5 years, and 71.5 years for men. By 2005 life expectancy will increase to 81 years for women and 74.1 for men (Older Women's League, 1989). The death rate for the elderly has been falling steadily over the past 40 years, with the age-adjusted death rate for individuals 65 years of age or over falling 29% from 1950 to 1982. The death rate for women fell considerably faster than that for men. A consequence of the changing demography of the population has been an increase in the number of elderly persons with chronic impairments and functional disabilities.

The increase in life expectancy of the elderly coupled with other demographic and social trends has led to a large increase in the elderly population. The number of elderly persons in the United States is growing faster in proportion to the total population than are younger age groups. In 1900, only 4% of the population was aged 65 and over. By 1980 the percentage of elderly had risen to 11%. It is estimated that by the year 2000, 13% of the population in the United States will be 65 years and over, and by the year 2050, one out of every five persons in the United States will be elderly (U.S. House of Representatives, 1987). In the 30 year period from 1950 to 1980, there was a doubling of the elderly population from 12.3 million in 1950 to 25.5 million in 1980 (Taeuber, 1983).

The oldest cohort, those aged 85 years and over, who are at greatest risk for chronic illness, who have the most functional dependency, and who have the greatest needs for health and social services, is growing the fastest. Between 1950 and 1980, the population 85 years and older rose 165%. Between 1980 and 2050, this subgroup of the elderly is expected to increase from 2.2 million persons (1% of the total U.S. population) to 16.1 million persons (5.2% of the total U.S. population) (Taeuber, 1983).

There are more elderly women than elderly men requiring caregiving assistance because women live significantly longer than men. In 1980 there were 10.2 million men aged 65 years and over and 15.2 million elderly women, a ratio of 68 men to 100 women. This ratio declines rapidly with age. Whereas for the elderly aged 65 to 69 years there are 80 males to every 100 females, there are only 44 males to every 100 females aged 85 years and older. Elderly women are also more likely to have lower incomes than elderly males, to live alone, and to experience multiple chronic health problems (Biegel, Shore, & Gordon, 1984; Rix, 1984).

- There has been a shift in the epidemiology of disease from acute to chronic diseases as well as a decrease in accidental deaths, resulting in an increase in the number of persons with limitations on functional activity and mobility.

There has been a large decrease in mortality from communicable and other acute diseases due to advances in public health, immunology, pharmacology, and bacteriology. In 1950, 2 out of 10 persons died from infectious diseases and 6 out of 10 from noninfectious diseases. By 1985 the infectious disease rate had dropped by half, so that 1 out of 10 persons died of infectious disease and 7 out of 10 died from noninfectious disease. The decreased mortality from acute illnesses has led to an increase in the life span and greater vulnerability to accidents and diseases that can lead to chronic illness. Concomitant advances in medicine and medical technology have combined to increase the numbers of individuals who survive serious trauma and chronic illness. For example, in 1950 there were 57.5 accidental deaths per 100,000 population; by 1986 the rate had dropped to 35.2 accidental deaths per 100,000 with many of the survivors requiring lifelong assistance in daily living tasks (Lubkin, 1986; National Center for Health Statistics, 1989). The combined results of these changes is a large increase in the number of individuals with activity and mobility restrictions.

Almost one quarter (24%) of persons aged 45 to 64 years, and nearly half of all noninstitutionalized elderly persons aged 65 years and older, are limited by at least one chronic condition (U.S. Department of Commerce, 1980). In 1987, data from the National Health Interview Survey indicated that 12.9% of the population, almost 31 million individuals, have some limitations of activity caused by chronic conditions. This percentage increases with age, so that 22.3% of those between the ages of 45 and 64 and 37.5% of individuals 65 years and older have such activity restrictions. Focusing on inability to carry on activity, 3.7% of the U.S. population, almost 9 million individuals, were unable to carry on major activity (work; housekeeping; school activities; participation in social, civic, or church activities; etc.) because of chronic conditions. This percentage increases with age, so that 8.5% of individuals aged 45 to 64 and 10% of elderly persons aged 65 years and over were unable to carry on major activity. An additional 5.2% of the total population, over 12 million persons (8.2% of those 45 to 64 years and 12.9% of those aged 65 years and over), were limited in the amount or kind of major activity they could undertake (National Center for Health Statistics, 1989).

Data concerning mobility indicate that 1.4 million Americans are confined to their houses except for emergencies, and another 1.8 million need the help of others or some special aid such as cane, crutches, or wheel chair to move about. An additional 3 million persons have some trouble in "getting around freely" (Strauss et al., 1984).

The above changes have had a direct impact on the demands placed on family caregivers. Depending upon the disease, family caregivers provide significant amounts of assistance to family members with activities of daily living (ADL) tasks as well as in vigilance, monitoring of medications, and the provision of social supports.

• There have been decreased death rates for heart disease and stroke, and five year cancer survival rates have increased.

Although heart disease is still the number one cause of death in the United States, and the United States still has the highest death rate from heart disease in the world, the U.S. heart disease death rate has been falling steadily for the last 35 years.

In 1950, the age-adjusted death rate from heart disease was 307.6 deaths per 100,000 population in the United States. By 1986 the rate had decreased 43% to 175. The age-adjusted death rate from cerebrovascular diseases decreased by an even greater percentage during this period. In 1950 there were 88.8 deaths per 100,000 population. This rate decreased almost two thirds by 1986 to 31 deaths per 100,000 population (National Center for Health Statistics, 1989). The success of our efforts to prevent heart disease and cerebrovascular disease has led to a paradox. The decrease in death rates has increased the likelihood of individuals developing late life chronic disabling conditions such as Alzheimer's disease or arthritis.

The overall death rates for cancer, on the other hand, increased by 6% over this same time period, going from a rate of 125.4 deaths per 100,000 in 1950 to 133.2 in 1986. As might be expected, there were considerable differences in this rate by types of cancer. Colorectal cancer deaths decreased by 24% during this period, while breast cancer deaths increased by 5%, prostate cancer deaths increased by 12%, and respiratory system cancer deaths increased by 205%. Overall, the five year cancer survival rate had increased from 20% in 1930 to 33% in 1960. At present, almost half (49%) of all cancer patients survive five years after diagnosis (National Center for Health Statistics, 1989; U.S. National Institutes of Health, 1988). These decreases in mortality and increases in survival rates have led to a large increase in the number of persons with chronic impairments and functional disabilities who require the assistance of family caregivers.

• There has been an increase in multigenerational families resulting in a growing number of elderly caregivers.

One consequence of the increase in life expectancy and growth in the number and percentage of the elderly population is a shift toward multigenerational families. One fifth of the elderly in their early 60s has a surviving parent, as do 10% in their late 60s and 3% in their 70s (Hooyman & Lustbader, 1986; U.S. House of Representatives, 1987). Thus the elderly are caregivers as well as care recipients. Data from the Informal Caregivers Study (ICS) of the 1982 National Long-Term Care Survey indicates that over one third of the caregiver sample was age 65 and older (25.4% were between 65-74 years and 10.1% were 75 years and older) (Stone, Cafferata, & Sangl, 1987). In a 1988 nationwide telephone survey of caregivers who provided care to a family member aged 50 years and older, the American Association of Retired Persons (AARP) found that 15% of all caregivers were age 65 and older. Of those who identified themselves as primary caregivers, 20% were age 65 and older (AARP, 1989).

- Family structures are changing due to declining fertility rates and the increasing divorce rate.

Fertility rates declined 44% between 1955 and 1975 (National Center for Health Statistics, 1989). The total number of births in the United States is expected to decrease by 9.2% during the 1990s, while the elderly population is expected to increase by over 10% (Older Women's League, 1989). Reduced fertility rates mean there will be fewer children and siblings to share the burden of care for future generations of elderly persons (Treas, 1977, 1981). The combination of declining fertility rates and increasing life expectancy has led to a reversal in traditional caregiving patterns. The average woman now spends 18 years of her life helping a parent as compared to 17 years of her adult life caring for a dependent child. Married couples now have more parents than children (Preston, 1984; U.S. House of Representatives, 1987).

Divorce rates have also increased over the past 25 years. From 1960 to 1984 the percentage of divorced males increased from 2% to 6.1% while the percentage of divorced females increased from 2.9% to 8.3% (Rosen, Fanshel, & Lutz, 1987). This increase in divorces together with an increase in remarriages has led to a growing number of "reconstituted families." As Hooyman and Lustbader (1986) point out, these developments have had a significant impact on caregiving. One consequence is that adult children now may be providing care for former parents-in-law as well as for parents and current parents-in-law. Another consequence is that divorced adult children may have less time or emotional energy left for caregiving.

• Greater numbers of women, the traditional caregivers, are in the labor force.

It is estimated that almost three quarters (72%) of caregivers of the functionally impaired elderly are women (U.S. House of Representatives, 1987). Whether by choice or economic necessity, women (wives, daughters, or daughters-in-law), the traditional caregivers, are also working in increasing numbers. There is concern about the impact of this trend on the ability of these caregivers to continue to meet the needs of their dependent relatives in the future (Biegel et al., 1984; Doty, 1986; U.S. House of Representatives, 1987). In 1960 slightly over one third (37.7%) of women were members of the civilian labor force. By 1986 this percentage had increased to 55.3% (U.S. Bureau of the Census, 1987). Three quarters of all women who work outside the home do so on a full-time basis (U.S. Department of Labor, 1984). The largest category of working women is middle-aged married women. Sixty percent of married women between the ages of 45 and 54 and 42% of married women between the ages of 55 and 64 are in the labor force (U.S. Department of Labor, 1984). These are also likely to be the years when caring for ill family members occurs.

Doty's (1986) review of studies that examined caregiving and work indicates conflicting evidence on the actual impact of women's employment on family caregiving. Some studies find diminished ability to provide home care for relatives because of caregiver employment, and other studies find no difference in the likelihood of providing care or in the amounts of hours of care provided by working and nonworking caregivers. Data collected in 1982 from the Informal Caregivers Survey indicate that one fifth of the employed caregivers reported conflicts between work and caregiving that required some alterations in caregiving schedules (Stone et al., 1987). In a recent nationwide telephone survey of caregivers who provide care to a family member who is 50 years and older, one third (33%) of caregivers who worked full time reported losing time from work due to caregiving, and 9% reported having to take a leave of absence (AARP, 1989).

Concern has been expressed by Brody (1981), Hooyman and Lustbader (1986), and others about the so called "sandwich generation," women in the middle generation with multiple role responsibilities as wife, mother, and caregiver to a parent or in-law. If the caregiver is employed, work is another responsibility to be managed at the same time. Such multiple roles are often managed only at considerable personal cost to women who are expected to naturally assume caregiving responsibilities because of the social expectation of women as nurturers. Unresolved issues include how women manage work and caregiving, the impact of work on the purchase of caregiving services, and the impact of the increase in the percentage of women caregivers who work on the roles and responsibilities of male caregivers.

• Concern about the increasing costs of institutional care for the elderly has led to the development of a number of state level initiatives to support caregivers that are aimed at delaying or preventing institutionalization.

Public and private expenditures for nursing home care have been increasing at a rapid rate. In 1970 total expenditures for nursing home care were 4.7 billion dollars and by 1984 the total had risen 581% to 32 billion dollars. Four years later, in 1988, the total had grown by an additional 47% to 47 billion dollars, representing 10.9% of all health care expenditures. Total expenditures for nursing home care were expected to grow to 56 billion dollars by 1990. From 1970 to 1985 Medicare costs for nursing home care doubled, from 300 million dollars to 600 million dollars, while Medicaid costs increased by 950%, from 1.4 billion dollars to 14.7 billion dollars (Arnett, McKusick, Sonnefeld, & Cowell, 1986; Marcus, 1987; Waldo, Levit, & Lazenby, 1986).

Historically, there has been little public support for long-term care services in the home. Home care especially has been episodic, short-term, and responsive to acute conditions, not chronic diseases (Berkman, 1978; Shanas & Maddox, 1976). Traditionally, government has not supported families' caregiving efforts or functions. Indeed, families who care for the functionally dependent aged are often penalized because the state traditionally withholds services and income benefits when the family retains the caregiving role (Moroney, 1976; Oktay & Palley, 1981). It is only when families are perceived as being unable to provide care or when family resources are non-existent that the government has stepped in to make up the deficit. Now, because of the rising costs of institutional care, some states have responded with policies to address support for home health care as well as with direct support for family caregivers.

Findings from a national survey of state departments of aging show that 34 states offer some type of economic support for family caregivers: 14 have tax supports only, 10 have direct payment programs only (payments to caregivers for services rendered), and 10 states have both tax and direct payment programs. Despite the rapid growth of state programs, which differ considerably from each other, few state level evaluations have been conducted (Biegel, Shore, Morycz, & Schulz, 1989; Linsk, Keigher, & Osterbusch, 1988).

- Changes in health care reimbursement and medical technology have increased responsibilities of family caregivers.

Economic pressures have led to a number of changes in the health and social services system that have put additional pressure on family caregivers. The prospective payment system (PPS) for hospital care under Medicare has led to shorter hospital stays resulting in families having to provide more care than in the past. At the same time, advances in medical technology have increased the numbers of patients who are being sent home to family caregivers who must administer drugs and monitor the patient's medical regime. Although there have been no definitive studies of the impacts of these trends on family caregivers, Coulton (1988) identifies several problems, such as the inability to identify correctly patient needs and the difficulty of assessing caregivers' abilities to provide care, that make it difficult for hospitals to provide adequate support to patients and caregivers after discharge. In addition, as Coulton points out, the very nature of PPS creates incentives for hospitals to presume that family members can manage care at discharge, because the alternative presumption may delay discharge and mean additional costs for the hospital.

NATURE AND EXTENT
OF FAMILY CAREGIVING

Caregiving has become such a ubiquitous term that its meaning is taken for granted, yet the definitions and boundaries of what is included in the term *caregiving* are not always that clear. The provision of assistance and support by one family member to another is a regular and usual part of family interactions, and is in fact a normative and pervasive activity. Thus when a wife provides care for a husband with Alzheimer's disease, cancer, or mental illness, it can be asked whether that caregiving is any different from "normal care." In fact, caregiving due to chronic illness and disability represents something that, in principle, is not very different from traditional tasks and activities rendered to family members. The difference in real terms, however, is that caregiving in this situation represents the *increment of extraordinary care* that goes beyond the bounds of normal or usual care. It is this extraordinary care that can be so burdensome. The provision of care to a family member who has a chronic illness involves a significant expenditure of time and energy over potentially long periods of time, involves tasks that may be unpleasant and uncomfortable, is likely to be nonsymmetrical, and is often a role that had not been anticipated. Actual caregiving tasks vary considerably with the type and stage of illness. Thus caregiving as used in this volume is illness and disability related.

Research studies about family caregiving have burgeoned over the past two decades. These studies provide valuable information about the nature of the caregiving process and the effects of caregiving on perceived stress and health status of the caregiver. However, as Stone et al. (1987) indicate, most studies are based on small, nonrepresentative samples of caregivers selected from a particular geographic region, income level, or living arrangement. In addition, many studies focus on a particular age group or disability, and study samples are often restricted to users of social and/or health care services. As a result it is difficult to obtain a comprehensive profile of who caregivers are, what they do, what needs they have, and what supportive services they utilize.

Two national surveys of caregiving to older adults do provide helpful information about the nature and extent of caregiving in the United States. The first survey (Stone et al., 1987) uses data from the 1982 National Long-Term Care Survey to examine caregiving to the elderly. The second survey, conducted in 1987-1988 by the Opinion Research Corporation for the American Association of Retired Persons and The Travelers Companies Foundation (1988), examines caregiving to dependent adults aged 50 years and older.

Stone et al. (1987) report on data from the Informal Caregivers Survey (ICS), part of the 1982 National Long-Term Care Survey. Survey results show that caregivers are predominantly female, middle-aged, white, and married. Over one third of the caregivers were themselves elderly, aged 65 years and older. Over one third of caregivers were children, a slightly lower percentage were spouses, and the remaining one quarter of the caregivers were other relatives and nonrelatives.

Almost one third of the entire sample indicated that they were primary caregivers who did not receive any assistance from other informal or formal caregivers, and almost three quarters of them lived with the disabled person for whom they were providing care. Caregivers were more likely to have lower income and lower self-reported health than the population at large. Almost half of the caregivers had been providing assistance for between one and four years, with one fifth having provided care for at least five years. Over three quarters of the sample provided care seven days a week, with the majority of the sample providing more than three hours a day of caregiving assistance. Over four fifths of the sample reported providing assistance with shopping and/or transportation, a similar percentage assisted with household tasks, two thirds assisted with personal hygiene, and over half assisted with the administration of medication (Stone et al., 1987).

The survey also examined competing demands on caregivers, such as other caregiving and work. Over one fifth of the sample reported children under 18 years of age in the household, almost one third worked, and about one in 11 reported quitting work to become a caregiver. Of the employed caregivers, one in five reported work conflicts because of caregiving, almost one third reported rearranging work schedules, and almost a fifth of the respondents worked fewer hours and took time off without pay (Stone et al., 1987).

The American Association of Retired Persons (AARP) and The Travelers Companies Foundation survey (1988) defined caregivers as persons who provided unpaid assistance, for either two Instrumental Activities of Daily Living (IADL), or one Activity of Daily Living, to a person 50 years or older within 12 months of the time of the interview. Seven hundred fifty-four caregivers were interviewed by telephone using a random sample of U.S. households with telephones and screening for the presence of a caregiver meeting the above definition. Although the definition of caregiving and the age limit of the care recipient (50 years versus 65 years) was somewhat different from that of the ICS reported above, it is nevertheless helpful to compare the findings of these two studies. Although there were large differences in the average age of caregivers in the two studies, the mean age of the care recipients were almost identical.

Findings show that almost 7 million households, or almost 8% of all U.S. households, contained a caregiver. Almost 4 million households contained caregivers who were giving care at the time of the interview. Similar to the ICS, caregivers were predominantly female, married, and were primary caregivers. Compared to the ICS sample, caregivers were considerably younger, more likely to have children in the household, more likely to work, much less likely to share a household, and more likely to be providing care for a spouse. Caregivers reported providing care for 12 hours per week for the past two years, a lesser amount of care for a shorter average time period than in the ICS sample. Instrumental Activities of Daily Living caregiving tasks were remarkably similar in the two studies. Over three quarters of the caregivers in the AARP sample provided assistance with grocery shopping, transportation, and housework, two thirds assisted with preparing meals and managing finances. Concerning caregiving and work, almost two fifths of caregivers in the AARP sample who worked reported either losing time from work or coming in late due to caregiving responsibilities and one fifth of the caregivers lost benefits as a result of caregiving. These figures show an effect of caregiving on work, but due to the differences in survey questions, it is hard to judge if there were any differences between the two samples in this relationship (AARP & The Travelers Companies Foundation, 1988).

Caregivers in the AARP sample were also asked about service use and unmet needs. Although almost two thirds of caregivers reported using at least one service, generally less than a fifth of the caregivers used any one particular service. When asked why they did not use services, the most frequent response was lack of need, with the second most frequent reason cited as lack of awareness of available services. This latter finding has been substantiated in a number of other studies as well. Caregivers were also asked what types of assistance or services they felt they needed. The most frequent responses, reported by over one third of the caregivers, related to the need for information concerning medicine and health care, information and/or assistance in obtaining services, and information on legislative developments impacting on caregiving. Almost one third of caregivers also expressed needs for emotional support and respite—someone to talk to, free time for vacation, and someone with whom to share coping strategies (AARP & The Travelers Companies Foundation, 1988).

Findings from both national surveys show that family caregivers provide significant amounts of assistance to dependent family members while managing competing demands. Caregivers' responsibilities coupled with their lower incomes and lower self-reported health than the population as a whole suggest the need for supportive services. However, as the AARP survey and others have shown, a variety of institutional and personal obstacles may make it difficult for caregivers to obtain needed assistance.

THE MEANING AND IMPACT
OF CHRONIC ILLNESS

This volume focuses on caregivers of dependent adults with chronic illness. Chronic illness, defined as "the irreversible presence, accumulation, or latency of disease states or impairments that involve the total human environment for supportive care and self-care, maintenance of function, and prevention of further disability" (Lubkin, 1986, p.6), can cause severe stresses for patients and their families. A number of variables affect the impact of chronic illness upon adults. Key variables identified in the literature include: the type of disease and natural history of particular diseases; the stage of the illness—prediagnostic, diagnostic, treatment, rehabilitation, and recurrence; the structure of the family; the role of the ill individual (child, mother, husband); the life cycle stage of the ill individual; and the life cycle stage of the family (Leventhal, Leventhal, & Nguyen, 1985).

Chronic illness affects a patient's entire life—physically, psychologically, socially, and economically. Typical interrelated problems faced by patients include restrictions in life-style and activities, negative body perception, sexual stress, intrafamily conflicts, increased dependency and decreased self-sufficiency, economic pressures, work restrictions or termination from work, and social stigma. These problems can lead to withdrawal from family and friends, lessened participation in social activities, lowered self-esteem, and depression (Bruhn, 1977; Levy, 1979; Lubkin, 1986; Strauss et al., 1984).

More central to the focus of this book, chronic illness also affects the family system. Normal patterns of interaction are disrupted, and there are often reassignments in tasks and roles assumed by particular family members. Leventhal et al. (1985) note that chronic illness alters the relationships not only of family members to the person who is ill but to one another as well. Changes in relationship can occur around problem-focused activities such as work, household tasks, or provision of family income, or in interpersonal areas such as solidarity and belonging, sexuality, and love. These role changes may lead an ill family member to become "sicker," or "well" family members might become "sick" to gain attention (Bruhn, 1977).

Strauss et al. (1984) identify eight social and psychological problems that patients and families face in coping with chronic illness:

(1) the prevention of medical crises and their management once they occur

(2) the control of symptoms

(3) the carrying out of prescribed regimens and the management of problems attendant on carrying out the regimens

(4) the prevention of, or living with, social isolation caused by lessened contact with others

(5) the adjustment to changes in the course of the disease, whether it moves downward or has remissions

(6) the attempts at normalizing both interaction with others and style of life

(7) funding—finding the necessary money—to pay for treatments or to survive despite partial or complete loss of employment

(8) confronting attendant psychological, marital, and familial problems (p. 16).

Family caregivers often shoulder the principal responsibility for maintaining the ill family member at home. Goldetz, as cited by Lubkin (1986), makes clear the wide ranging responsibilities of family caregivers. The roles family caregivers may have to provide for their ill family member include the following: cook, maid, janitor, launderer, nursing assistant, transportation provider, mobility supervisor, overseer/administrator of medications, supervisor of special medical equipment, and provider of personal hygiene such as toileting and incontinence care, as well as manager of transfers, exercises, feeding, and watching.

There are a number of variables pertaining to the nature of chronic illness that affect both patient and family performance. Rolland (1988) believes that the degrees of diversity and commonality among chronic illnesses have not been adequately examined. He presents a psychosocial categorization of chronic illness using four major variables—onset, course, outcome, and degree of incapacitation. These variables are useful in analyzing the similarities and differences of the five chronic illnesses discussed in this volume (see Table 1.1).

Onset of disease can be either gradual or acute. As can be seen in Table 1.1, diseases with acute onset include stroke and myocardial infarction; Alzheimer's disease, cancer, and chronic mental illness have gradual onsets. Rolland notes that although both gradual and acute onset diseases require major readjustments by the total family system, acute illnesses require families to make both affective and instrumental changes in short periods of time. Gradual onset diseases allow a longer

	INCAPACITATING		NONCAPACITATING	
	ACUTE	GRADUAL	ACUTE	GRADUAL
FATAL				
PROGRESSIVE		Lung cancer with CNS metastases	Pancreatic cancer Metastatic breast cancer Malignant melanoma Lung cancer Liver cancer	
RELAPSING			Cancers in remission, etc.	
POSSIBLY FATAL SHORTENED LIFE SPAN				
PROGRESSIVE		Alzheimer's disease Multi-infarct dementia		
RELAPSING	Angina			
CONSTANT	Stroke Mod/severe myocardial infarction		Mild myocardial infarction Cardiac arrhythmia	
NONFATAL				
PROGRESSIVE				
RELAPSING		Chronic mental illness		
CONSTANT			Benign arrhythmia Congenital heart disease	

Figure 1.1 Categorization of Chronic Illness by Psychosocial Type
Source: Adapted from Rolland (1988)

time period for adjustment but can also lead to greater anxiety before a diagnosis is given (Rolland, 1988).

Disease course can be progressive, constant, or relapsing/episodic. In progressive diseases such as Alzheimer's disease or cancer, disability increases over time such that there are minimal periods of relief from the disease and continual adaptations and role changes are required. Family caregivers face increased strain from the risk of exhaustion and the continual need to assume additional caregiving roles as the patient's functioning declines. It should be noted that Alzheimer's disease patients can decline in one dimension but improve in another, causing caregiver demands to shift over time. For example, behavioral problems may disappear over time while ADL disability increases. In a constant course disease an initial medical event occurs and then stabilizes, such as with stroke and single-episode myocardial infarction. The disease may leave a disability in movement, speech, or cognitive functioning. Although relapses can occur, the patient and family experience semi-permanent change that is stable and predictable. There is less need for the constant assumption of new caregiver roles over time, but caregiver exhaustion is still a risk. Relapsing or episodic diseases such as cancer in remission or chronic mental illness are characterized by stable, low-symptom periods followed by disease flare-ups and reoccurrence of symptoms. Although family caregivers of patients with relapsing illnesses provide lower levels of ongoing care and do not need to make as great role reallocations over time as with progressive illness, families are strained by the movement in and out of crisis and the uncertainty as to when the next crisis will occur (Rolland, 1988).

Focusing on outcome, chronic diseases can be characterized as fatal, shortening the life span, or nonfatal. Alzheimer's disease and metastic cancer are fatal, whereas chronic mental illness is nonfatal. The middle category of potentially life shortening disease includes heart disease and stroke. Heart disease and stroke can both shorten the life span as well as increase the risk of sudden death through an additional myocardial infarction or stroke. Rolland believes that a critical factor in adaptation is the initial expectation of whether a disease is likely to be fatal, since both patients and family members may experience anticipatory grief. Families often experience the dual emotion of wanting to be closer to the ill family member on one hand, and on the other hand wanting to pull away (Rolland, 1988).

Chronic illness can be incapacitating due to problems of cognition (Alzheimer's disease), reality disturbance and social stigma (chronic mental illness), movement (stroke), reduced levels of energy (cancer, heart disease), or the demands of the treatment regimen (cancer). Different incapacitation patterns may result in differential impacts on patients and family. For example, diseases with both cognitive and motor deficits require greater role changes within the family than diseases with only one of these deficits. Incapacitation and onset also combine to produce different effects in families. Incapacitation with stroke, for example, is greatest at time of onset, whereas with Alzheimer's disease incapacitation increases over time giving families more time for adjustment and planning (Rolland, 1988).

THE STATUS OF CAREGIVING RESEARCH

Over the past decade the needs of caregivers have become a prominent focus of researchers in a variety of academic and applied disciplines because societal trends have made clear the increasing and complex demands being placed on family caregivers of adults with chronic illness. In recent years there has been a large increase in the number of papers on this subject presented at professional meetings and published in professional journals. There has also been a concomitant increase in funding of caregiver research by the National Institute on Aging and the National Institute of Mental Health, as well as support of caregiver research by numerous private foundations.

Before reviewing the status of current research, we should remind ourselves of some factors contributing to limitations in our current knowledge. Study of the mental health implications of disease has emerged relatively recently. Until the 1960s neither physicians nor social scientists took much research interest in psychosocial factors in illness. Early studies focused on the patient whose distress was both more visible and more accessible to research inquiry. Thus studies of the reactions of patients to such illnesses as cancer and heart disease were the first to emerge from a psychosocial perspective. (It is noteworthy that illnesses characterized by cognitive or affective disturbances, such as mental illness, stroke, and Alzheimer's disease, have had little parallel inquiry into patient distress.) Given the concern with patient problems and stresses, it is not surprising that family caregivers were initially discussed in their role as crucial facilitators of patient well-being. These discussions of what caregivers could do to relieve the strains on patients omitted any recognition of the emotional, economic, or family role consequences of the patient's illness. In short, the early literature did not address the needs and burdens of caregivers themselves.

Not surprisingly, concern about the strains of caregiving emerged first in health areas that placed heaviest demands on family members. Specifically, initial attention focused on patients with diagnoses of mental retardation, mental illness, and, more recently, Alzheimer's disease, illnesses characterized as ones in which patients are incapable of looking after themselves. Family members responsible for these patients' home care were brought into continued contact with health care professionals who, perhaps as a consequence of regular meetings, became sensitized to issues of family burden. The powerful family themes of emotional distress and physical exhaustion that plagued some caregivers did much to sensitize professionals to the personal costs of giving care. Such domestic dramas as caregivers' own deteriorating health or the disruption of their ability to continue caring for the patient were impossible to ignore.

It took longer for health care providers to recognize that less extended, less demanding health problems also took their toll on families. Perhaps such tolls were less dramatic or were merely beyond the purview of the health care establishment. In any event, investigations of the family burdens of caregiving in most chronic illnesses have been slower to emerge.

In addition to problem visibility, other factors have affected the speed of knowledge emergence in each health area. Sociopolitical factors, as well as biomedical urgency, have influenced public funding of health research. As a consequence, research is more likely to be undertaken in some health areas than in others. Although it is outside the scope of this presentation to explore the factors that fuel such differential funding for research, we must recognize its impact. For example, emphasis on cancer research in recent years has led to more research reports on family stress due to cancer than to heart disease, even though coronary research started earlier. Many of the best studies of both heart disease and mental illness were carried out in Great Britain, perhaps because these arenas have received more research funding there.

Caregiving research has developed along two major streams. The first focused on the caregiving process itself, with major emphasis on the effects of caregiving on the caregiver. The second stream of research focused on interventions to address caregiver and patient needs.

Research on the effects of caregiving on the caregiver has gone through a predictable pattern common to new research in the social sciences. Early caregiver research studies were action and advocacy oriented. They attempted to describe the roles, needs, and burdens of family caregivers, often in the words of the caregivers themselves and often without the utilization of any theoretical framework. These studies served an important role by focusing attention on the nature of the problem—the needs of family caregivers.

There was then an attempt to develop better conceptualizations and quantitative measures of the concept of burden itself. Various burden scales were developed and burden was correlated with a variety of caregiver and care recipient demographic and socioeconomic characteristics, as well as such caregiver variables as personality, coping style, social support, and health and mental health outcomes. These studies also began to use various theoretical frameworks to guide analysis. Major limitations were that these studies were cross-sectional in nature so researchers could not make causal inferences, and that the study samples were small and not representative. At the same time these small, conceptually guided studies were being conducted, several large, national studies were also undertaken to help determine the extent, nature, and scope of family caregiving. Thus for example, a major national study of caregivers of elderly who were at risk for institutionalization was undertaken, providing data on caregiver and care recipient characteristics; the nature and extent of caregiving roles; and caregiver satisfaction and emotional, financial, and physical strain (Stephens & Christianson, 1986). Such studies helped bring national attention to caregiving as a public policy issue and helped place caregiving research in the limelight.

To address a concern that caregiving research in aging was proceeding in isolation from caregiving research with other populations, several years ago the federal government organized a conference of researchers from various disciplines who were principal investigators on federal research grants studying caregiving with a wide range of populations. Soon after this conference, the first federal grants were funded that examined caregiving across various dependent population groups to begin to identify the similarities and differences of caregiving needs, processes, and outcomes. A number of such studies are currently in progress. Other studies during this period were based primarily on stress-coping theoretical frameworks and used more sophisticated longitudinal designs, were characterized by greater attention to measurement issues, and utilized multivariate data analysis techniques.

Recent caregiver research has begun to shift the focus of caregiver outcomes from caregiver stress or burden to the "harder" outcomes of caregiver psychiatric and physical morbidity. Part of this shift includes a focus on the search for mediating mechanisms, both physical and psychosocial, that affect caregiver morbidity outcomes.

A parallel stream to research on the effects of caregiving on the caregiver focused on the effects of interventions designed to ameliorate caregiver burden. This stream of research, which began through government and private foundation support, developed separately from the research on caregiver burden and morbidity. The two research streams have recently begun to merge, with intervention research focusing on an examination of process as well as on outcome issues. Intervention research is important because it provides a mechanism for testing causal hypotheses of caregiver outcomes. Caregiving research continues to undergo further development, refinement, and expansion, as this volume makes clear.

ORGANIZATION OF THE BOOK

This book consists of ten chapters. Chapter 2 presents a theoretical basis for caregiving and a conceptual framework for examining family caregiving across diverse dependent population groups, identifying key variables that will be utilized for analysis in the rest of the volume. Chapters 3 through 7 focus on each of the diseases examined. These chapters follow a common outline, discussing the nature of the disease, psychosocial reactions of patients and their caregivers, a brief summary of available services to patients and caregivers, and summarizing existing research on caregiver stress and outcome. This last section of each chapter uses the variables identified in the conceptual framework in Chapter 2 to summarize both existing knowledge and gaps in the literature. Research knowledge for each of the five diseases is then synthesized in Chapter 8 to identify general similarities and differences in caregiving roles and relationships. Chapter 9 examines intervention models for the five population groups, with separate discussions of support groups, educational interventions, and the provision of direct services. Once again, the analysis is both within and across population groups. Research findings pertaining to the effectiveness of particular interventions are examined and synthesized. Chapter 10 discusses directions for future research and policy.

2

Theoretical Perspectives on Caregiving

The goal of this chapter is to introduce a number of relevant theoretical perspectives useful in understanding caregiving. While our attention primarily will be focused on theories concerning the impact of caregiving on the caregiver, we also explore a number of conceptual systems that sheds light on other aspects of caregiving. We will begin by asking a question that has not been addressed directly by researchers in this area, namely: Why do people help? Next, we present Family Systems Theory as a perspective for understanding the impact of chronic illness on the family. This is followed by a discussion of both generic and caregiver specific models of stress-coping that attempt to predict the impact of chronic illness at the individual level. Finally, we present the central features of a stress-coping approach to caregiving, review the literature relevant to each component, identify problems in the existing literature, and make recommendations for the future.

WHY DO PEOPLE HELP?

Much of the literature on caregiving is aimed at dispelling the "illusion of the Golden Past" (Brody, 1985; Kent, 1965), the myth of the idyllic three generation household in which, in contrast to current practice, the oldest generation was diligently cared for by younger generations. As Brody (1985, p. 21) points out in her review of this literature, it is ironic that this myth persists despite the fact that "nowadays adult children provide more care and more difficult care to more parents over much longer periods of time than they did in the good old days."

Although abundant data document the validity of Brody's analysis few researchers have attempted to answer the appropriate follow-up question: Why do people provide such large quantities of help, particularly in view of the apparent personal costs often associated with providing care? To some, the answer to this question may be self-evident. As the demand for care changes so does the amount of care provided because there exist strong normative expectations in our culture to help our kin. This explanation obviously tells us little of psychological significance in understanding caregiving and invites further speculation about the motives of caregivers. The purpose of this section is to address this question from a psychological perspective.

For almost two decades experimental social psychologists have been interested in developing theory and a data base to answer the questions of why and when people help. Interest in these questions was kindled by the tragic stabbing death of Kitty Genovese in 1964, who was repeatedly attacked over a period of 37 minutes in the presence of 38 witnesses, none of whom helped and only one of whom finally called the police. Many experts and members of the press blamed the onlookers for their failure to get involved, suggesting that they were cruel and selfish; others suggested they lacked moral compunction, or were cowards. Still other social scientists had no ready explanation for the behavior of the onlookers and decided to investigate systematically the giving and receiving of help as a form of social behavior.

Because of the circumstances surrounding the murder of Kitty Genovese, much of the early research in this area was focused on finding out why and when people are willing to help strangers in emergency situations. This is obviously far removed from a family caregiving situation, but some of the findings of this research may be relevant nevertheless. For example, one phenomenon documented in a series of studies (Latane & Darley, 1970) was the bystander effect: the more people present, the less likely a given individual is to help. The presence of others may result in the diffusion of responsibility and cause individuals to feel that others will take care of the problem, or it may make individuals feel apprehensive because others will be evaluating their performance as helpers. When applied to a family caregiving situation the bystander effect raises some interesting questions that have not yet been addressed in the caregiver literature. For example, although we know that eldest daughters and wives are most often cast in the caregiving role, we know little about how caregiving responsibilities are negotiated and shared as a function of family size, how this process affects satisfaction with the caregiving role, and how caregiving behavior and satisfaction are affected by the caregivers' concerns regarding evaluations of their performance by others.

Another series of studies showed that victims' personal attributes are powerful determinants of helping. Individuals are more willing to help people in need if they are physically attractive (Harrell, 1978), dressed attractively (Kleinke, 1977), and if they possess no stigmatizing physical characteristics such as unattractive birthmarks (Piliavin, Piliavin, & Rodin, 1975), eye patches, or scars (Samorette & Harris, 1976). People are also more willing to help others who are similar to themselves on such attributes as attitudes, political beliefs, nationality, race, and the way they dress (Dovidio, 1984). Applied to the family caregiving context, these findings point to another set of variables that have been neglected in the caregiving literature. To date, the patient characteristics most frequently studied include physical functioning, cognitive abilities, and perceived personality changes but little attention has been paid to changes in physical appearance associated with a debilitating illness.

Motives for Helping

Attempts to identify specific motives for helping have yielded two types of explanations. One assumes that helping serves an egoistic or self-serving motive while the other centers on empathy and altruism (Batson & Coke, 1983). The egoistic explanation argues that helping is motivated by the anticipation of rewards for helping and punishment for not helping. Individuals may help for obvious reasons such as the expectation of payment, gaining social approval (Baumann, Cialdini, & Kendrick, 1981), avoiding censure (Reis & Gruzen, 1976), receiving esteem in exchange for helping (Hatfield, Walster, & Piliavin, 1978), complying with social norms (Berkowitz, 1972), seeing oneself as a good person (Bandura, 1977), or avoiding guilt (Hoffman, 1982). For example, caring for a relative in order to prevent institutionalization can be interpreted in terms of avoiding censure, complying with social norms, and/or seeing oneself as a good person (Brody, Poulshock, & Masciocchi, 1978).

Guilt and indebtedness are the motives alluded to by the often heard comment made by caregivers, "I know I'm doing everything I can for my mother, but somehow I still feel guilty" (Brody, 1985, p. 26), or in the idea that providing care is a repayment in kind for care provided by the parent at an earlier age. Feelings of guilt may also be the motivating force for individuals who feel they must atone for past sins (e.g., neglect, bad treatment) against their spouse or parent.

A theoretical basis for indebtedness as a motive is provided by Greenberg (1980) who states that feeling indebted has motivational properties, such that the greater its magnitude, the greater the resultant arousal and discomfort, and hence, the stronger the ensuing attempts to deal with or reduce it. Feelings of indebtedness should be higher to the extent that individuals feel the help provided them was based on altruistic motives on the part of the helper, help was given in response to requests or pleas for help from the recipients, and the helper incurred costs in providing the help. All of these factors apply to spousal and parent-child relationships and may be factors worthy of attention in our efforts to understand who becomes the caregiver, the magnitude of the costs the caregiver is willing to incur in providing help to a relative, and the amount of residual guilt experienced by the caregiver.

A substantially different perspective on human nature is provided by a theory of helping that is based on purely altruistic motivation. According to this view, individuals help others because they are able to adopt the perspective of the other, experience an emotional response—empathy—congruent with the other's welfare, and empathic emotion evokes a motivation aimed at reducing the other's needs. The magnitude of the altruistic motivation is assumed to be a direct function of the magnitude of the empathic emotion. Unlike the egoistic perspective described earlier, the primary goal of empathically-evoked altruism is to benefit the other and not the self, even though benefits to oneself may be a consequence of helping (see Batson & Coke, 1983, for a review of the relevant literature). It seems reasonable to assume, although it has not been demonstrated empirically, that the ability to empathize may be based on such variables as kinship, similarity, prior interaction, attachment, or some combination of these, all of which are relevant to the intrafamilial caregiving situation. This suggests that higher levels of similarity, attachment, and prior positive interaction should result in greater levels of caregiving, although they may also lead to higher levels of distress among caregivers (Cantor, 1983; Horowitz, 1985).

Although helping an elderly relative is likely to be based on both altruistic and egoistic motivations, it would be interesting to know whether the two motives differentially affect caregiver well-being. Since emotions are a central feature of altruistically motivated helping, one might hypothesize that the emotional status of the patient plays an important role in determining the amount of help provided and the affect of the helper. Moreover, the nature of the cognitive declines associated with a disease such as Alzheimer's suggests that altruistic motivation may be more relevant to the early stages of the disease when cognitive function is still more or less intact and the caregiver can readily empathize with the patient, and that egoistically motivated helping is the driving force in later stages of the disease when cognitive function is debilitated.

Social Norms and Helping

Sociological explanations for why people help frequently emphasize the role of social norms, such as reciprocity, equity, or social responsibility. The reciprocity norm enjoins us to pay back what others give to us, and the equity norm underscores the importance of costs and rewards in a relationship. Simply stated, a relationship is equitable if those involved receive a return from it proportional to what they have invested in it. According to the social responsibility norm, helping others in need—the sick, infirm, or very young—is a duty that should not be shirked, although the manner in which and how much we help another may depend on our beliefs about who or what is responsible for the cause and solution of the recipient's problem (see Brickman et al., 1982).

Social norms are obviously relevant to understanding caregiver behavior. For example, they may be useful in predicting caregiving behavior among successive cohorts of caregivers, but the existence of norms does not in itself explain why people adhere to them. We still need to answer the questions: Why do these norms exist? Where do they come from? To address these questions we need to examine some underlying characteristics about the nature of human beings.

Sociobiology of Helping

The social-psychological theories of helping described above are based on the notion that social behavior in humans is developed through experience and learning, rather than through instinct. A new theoretical approach that can have direct relevance for understanding the helping process, sociobiology, challenges this orthodoxy. Sociobiology suggests that the fundamental goal of the organism is not mere survival or survival of its offspring, but "inclusive fitness," to pass on the maximum number of genes to the next generation (Hamilton, 1964). Sociobiology believes that human helping can only be understood in terms of the human evolutionary past—close relatives help each other, even at risk of their lives, in order to increase the chance that their genes will survive in their relatives (Forsyth, 1987). Sociobiology thus takes a positive view of human nature, believing that human beings are innately helpful to each other albeit for a "selfish" purpose, the preservation of the gene pool.

To date, tests of this theory, which have relied on research with nonhumans only, indicate that helping is much more common among close relatives than among strangers and in dense rather than dispersed communities (Barash, 1982). Applying this theory to family caregiving, it can be argued that, in general, intrafamily helping behaviors enhance the survival of the familial gene pool. Thus intrafamilial helping of all types is desirable—old helping young as well as the young helping the old. This general rule, however, has at least one qualification: When resource constraints demand that priorities be set among those who can be helped, we would predict that resources will be allocated to the young rather than the old.

Our discussion of why people help raises a number of important questions regarding the instigation and perpetuation of intrafamilial helping, but it does not directly address questions concerning patient and family outcomes associated with caregiving. In order to address this issue, we will describe *family systems theory*, which attempts to understand chronic illness in the context of the entire family. This will be followed by discussion of how humans cope with stressors like caregiving at the individual level.

THE COSTS AND BENEFITS
OF PROVIDING CARE

Impact on the Family

An overarching perspective on family caregiving may be found in theories that view the family unit itself as the object of analysis. These theories are explicitly discipline-spanning, since they stem from the premises of general systems theory (von Bertalanffy, 1968). *General systems theory* sees units at all levels of analysis as containing interacting components that function in a coordinated way to deal with the environment. The pattern of interactions among components is established as the system attempts to adapt to the demands of the external environment. When an effective and efficient adaptation is achieved the system is in balance, or equilibrium. Systems seek such homeostasis because they demand the least effort from each component. These basic assumptions of systems theory lead to the premise that one can understand the actions of any system element only by examining the relationships that exist within all components of a system.

The family has been analyzed extensively from a systems perspective. Family members are viewed as interacting elements in a *family system* that attempts to synchronize its efforts to deal with its social environment. Each family, over time, develops a stable pattern of interaction that permits it to meet environmental demands in an effective and efficient manner. From a systems perspective, the behaviors of one family member can be understood only by examining his or her interrelationships with other family members. This framework emphasizes such system variables as role relationships and communication patterns that emerge and stabilize in the family's efforts to best fulfill its needs (Parsons & Bales, 1955). Once the family system of defined role patterns attains a functional equilibrium, it tends to be perpetuated until an external change serves as a stimulus for a new adaptation (Bowen, 1966).

Another related theoretical framework is found in *crisis theory*. Because systems tend to freeze into stable patterns of interaction, any situational change may represent a potential crisis, requiring restructuring of all family interaction patterns. Such crises create severe stress on family members as they react to the disequilibrium created by the life event. Because stress is a threat to the ongoing functioning of the system, members mobilize energy to establish a new equilibrium as quickly as possible (Selye, 1956).

We can distinguish between two types of family crises, maturational and situational (Gray-Price & Seczesny, 1985). Maturational family crises are associated with normal developmental stages, occurring at such major life transitions as childbirth, school entry, children leaving home, and retirement (Haley & Ransom 1976; Minuchin, 1974). Because these predictable life-stage events inevitably require major restructuring of family interactions, adaptation is facilitated by the prior awareness that most people have of these transition points. Thus such transitions can be anticipated and prepared for, thereby softening their impact.

In contrast, unpredictable crises, such as the illness of a family member, may be viewed as sudden major disruptions to the entire family system. Its ability to maintain itself in achieving its goals is undermined (Cassileth & Hamilton, 1979). The inevitable immediate consequence of such a crisis is anxiety and disequilibrium, not only to the patient but to all other members of the family system. Family systems theory focuses on how the entire family copes with the crisis of illness of one family member. It analyzes the ways the family adapts to the task demands of different stages of this crisis (Giacquinta, 1977; Kaplan, 1982; Leventhal et al., 1985; Mailick, 1979). For example, family members must quickly learn to negotiate with the medical system in order to gain needed information and mediate for the patient. These demands occur while family members are also confronting their own initial fears regarding the overall impact of the patient's illness on their lives, as well as the possibility of losing their loved one. Another task demand involves the need to figure out a mode of dealing with the patient as he or she reacts to the illness, which may involve withdrawal from normal family patterns of interaction (Singer, 1983).

Giacquinta (1977), for example, has developed a model that identifies ten phases of family functioning during four different stages of cancer and its aftermath. Her model begins with the initial disorganizing impact that a cancer diagnosis has on family functioning, and proceeds through the patient's decline and death to the family's postbereavement efforts to establish a new equilibrium. Giacquinta also identifies specific hurdles that the family must overcome at each phase, from despair over the initial diagnosis to alienation for families who cannot expand their social networks again after bereavement.

In summary, since chronic illnesses such as those discussed in this book involve long-term changes in the family members' abilities to perform expected family roles, new role patterns need to be established within the family system (Bruhn, 1977; Mailick, 1979). Wellisch (1985) suggests that an illness such as cancer has impact on marital processes relating to the independence of each spouse, their intimacy and communication patterns, and their sexual relationship. Such role realignments are often accompanied by resentment, in part because of the need to take on additional and unfamiliar role behaviors (Singer, 1983; Vettese, 1981). And because family roles vary at different stages of the family life cycle, adaptation problems and resolutions will also differ (Gray-Price & Szczesny, 1985; Herz & McGoldrick, 1980: Leventhal et al., 1985).

Because of the extensive demands on families dealing with serious illness, it is not surprising that some families of the chronically ill fail to adapt, experiencing severe disruption and breakdown (Bruhn, 1977; Giacquinta, 1977; Kaplan, 1982; Vettese, 1981). The level of family functioning prior to the crisis appears to be a factor central to its ability to cope with the crisis of illness. Families with better communication, better problem-solving skills, and flexible role relationships are viewed as having better ability to cope realistically with the crisis. In contrast, families that have more rigid interaction styles may experience more difficulty (Quinn & Herndon, 1986). Even normal families, however, may need help in dealing with the crisis of serious illness (Gray-Price & Szczesny, 1985; Kaplan, 1982; Mailick, 1979; Singer, 1983; Vettese, 1981).

The family systems perspective summarized here has provided a central theoretical framework for many therapeutic interventions and analyses of family reactions to illness. Unfortunately, empirical research derived from this perspective has been limited. Research based on a family systems perspective would require data from all members of the family, rather than from a single informant. It would need to focus on the dynamics of family interaction, which are hard to measure under any circumstances. Furthermore, the study of family reactions to the crisis of illness requires a longitudinal design in order to monitor the process of coping and adaptation (Kerns & Turk, 1985; Leventhal et al., 1985). Examples of the limited research emerging from a family systems perspective include studies that focus on role reallocations and role problems of family members (primarily spouses) or on the discrepancies in perceptions among family members regarding adaptation problems (seen to be the result of communication disruptions). Thus far empirical research derived from systems theory perspectives has been rare in all social science arenas. Therefore, its scarcity in the recently emerging research literature on family caregiving, although regrettable, is not surprising.

Impact on the Individual

Much of the literature on caregiving can be characterized as an attempt to link some antecedent variables to outcomes assessing the well-being of individuals who provide support to ill relatives. A typical independent variable in this conceptualization might be the functional or behavioral status of the patient, and a representative dependent variable any one of a number of measures assessing the psychosocial status or physical and mental health of the caregiver, such as morale, life-satisfaction, depression, or perceived strain or burden. Sandwiched between the independent and dependent variables is a large number of individual and situational conditioning variables characteristic of all stress-coping models, such as age, gender, socioeconomic status, type and quality of relationship between caregiver and patient, social support, and a number of personality characteristics of the caregiver such as self-esteem and locus of control. The need for conditioning or intervening variables is justified by data demonstrating only moderate relationships between independent variables such as patient impairment (e.g., ability to perform ADL tasks) and caregiver outcomes, such as mental health (Coppel, Burton, Becker, & Fiore, 1985; Pagel, Becker, & Coppel, 1985). This basic model has been elaborated on by a number of researchers (e.g., Cohler et al., 1989; Haley, Levine, Brown, & Bartolucci, 1987; Montgomery, Stull, & Borgatta, 1985; Schulz, Tompkins, Wood, & Decker, 1987; Schulz, Tompkins, & Rau, 1988). On the whole, these models provide a convenient framework for organizing the large number of variables relevant to understanding the caregiving process.

THE BASIC STRESS-COPING MODEL

Probably the most basic way of conceptualizing the caregiving experience is in terms of a framework for interactions between the individual and the environment (Elliott & Eisdorfer, 1982). This model, illustrated in Figure 2.1, has three primary elements: a potential activator (x), an individual's reaction (y) to the activator, and the consequences (z) or sequaele to the reactions. Mediators are thought to be the filters and modifiers that act on each stage of the x-y-z sequence to produce individual variations. In the laboratory, specifying the x-y-z sequence can be relatively straightforward. For example, injecting an antigenic substance (x) under the skin of a healthy individual results in an immunologic response (y) that produces local swelling, redness, and tenderness (z) (Elliott & Eisdorfer, 1982). Few nonlaboratory situations, however, are as easy to characterize or understand. A given activator may elicit a strong reaction in one person and none at all in another, or it may result in a response at one point in time but not another. Moreover, distinctions between reactions and consequences

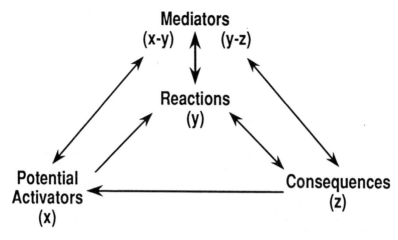

Figure 2.1. The x-y-z Stress Model: A Framework for Interaction Between the Individual
and the Environment
SOURCE: Elliot & Eisdorfer (1982)

are often difficult to make. One way of minimizing this confusion is to
define as carefully as possible the meaning of each component of this
model.

Potential activators are events or conditions that "are empirically
known to change an individual's state under some circumstances. A
potential activator can be defined independently of its actual effects; it
must have only the potential to produce a change" (Elliott & Eisdorfer,
1982, p. 20). Thus a falling tree is not an activator unless it happens to
nearly hit someone and arouses fear. Within this framework, stressors
can be viewed as a subset of potential activators capable of producing
a significant physical or psychosocial reaction.

Reactions, according to this model, are the biological or psychosocial
responses of an individual to an activator. They may be transient and
produce no significant consequences or intense enough to produce
important consequences. They may also change dramatically over time.
An inappropriate emotional outburst from a stroke patient may elicit a
very strong reaction the first time it occurs but may have little impact
on subsequent occasions.

Although it is often difficult to distinguish between reactions and
consequences, it is generally thought that reactions are the transient
responses to specific activators, and consequences are the prolonged or

cumulative effects of those reactions. Consequences can be biological such as a physical illness like infectious disease, or psychological such as depression resulting from bereavement. They can occur at all levels of complexity from the molecular to the social and can vary in intensity, quantity, and temporal pattern. In addition, a consequence usually has an evaluative component: It is desirable or undesirable relative to some social or personal standard. Thus some stressors may result in undesirable reactions but bring about positive consequences. For example, the caregiver of a stroke patient may come to feel very burdened by the challenges of caring for a disabled person but enjoy enhanced feelings of competence and higher self-esteem as a result of this experience.

The final components of the model are the biological and psychological mediators, which may alter the impact of a potential activator and affect the translation of an individual's reaction into long-term consequences. Mediators help to explain why many people experience potential stressors without any apparent consequences, but others react markedly and have many consequences. For example, a number of studies have shown that caregivers with a strong support network suffer fewer long-term negative consequences (e.g., depression) than caregivers with few supporters in their network (Schulz & Decker, 1985; Schulz et al., 1988).

Although our focus here has been on discrete components of the x-y-z sequence, it is important to appreciate that all elements of this model interact with and modify each other:

> Usually, an individual is exposed continuously to large numbers of potential activators, and the resulting reactions interact with one another to produce change. Each element in the sequence also continually modifies and is modified by the other components. Mediators help to pattern each x-y-z sequence for a specific individual and are themselves modified by the cumulative effects of past reactions and consequences. Suppose, for example, that a series of reactions has resulted in damage to the heart. That damaged heart then becomes an important mediator that might enable the potential stressor of intense anger to lead to a cardiac arrhythmia and death. Such an ever-changing, interlinking system is not only difficult to describe but also impossible to study in its entirety. For this reason, investigators inevitable try to simplify the system as much as possible by studying one small portion at a time. It is vital to remember that such studies are only partial approximations of what actually occurs. (Elliott & Eisdorfer, 1982, p. 23)

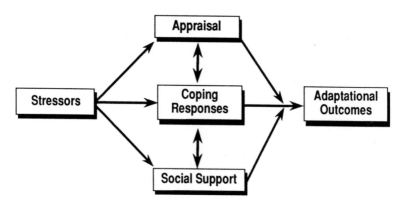

Figure 2.2. A Model of Stress and Coping Among Caregivers
SOURCE: Haley, Levine, Brown, & Bartolucci (1987)

Variations of this general model have been applied to a number of caregiving contexts, including caregivers of spinal cord injured persons, stroke victims, dementia patients, the chronically mentally ill, cardiac patients, and cancer patients. In the remaining pages of this chapter a number of specific caregiving models will be described and evaluated.

Stress, Appraisal, Coping and Adaptational Outcomes

Haley, Levine, Brown, and Bartolucci (1987) used a variation of an earlier model developed by Lazarus and Folkman (1984) to study coping among caregivers of dementia patients. Figure 2.2 shows that the Haley et al. model bears a strong resemblance to the x-y-z model described above. Its key components are stressors, coping responses, and adaptational outcomes, although it treats coping responses along with appraisals and social support as mediating variables. In fact, it could be argued that this model is even simpler than the generic model described earlier because it does not include the reaction component and identifies only a limited number of the possible links between the mediating variables. For example, we would expect that the appraisal of a stressor is influenced by and interacts with the social support available to the individual, but the model does not specify such relationships.

Another difficulty posed by models such as this is the exclusion of structural variables such as socioeconomic status, relationship between patient and caregiver, and gender, as well as health status. A strong case can be made for the inclusion of these variables in the model, both conceptually and analytically. An example of a model that incorporates this approach is presented next.

ABCX Model

The model was developed by Hill and associates (Hill, 1949; Hansen & Hill, 1964) to describe the impact of a stressor on family systems. According to this view, an external event (A) interacts with the family's ability to cope with that event (B) and with the family's perception of the stressor (C). This in turn, can result in crisis and mental health problems (X). A simplified illustration of this model applied to caregivers is presented in Figure 2.3. This model obviously bears a strong resemblance to both of the models described above, and differs primarily in its emphasis on the family as a conceptual unit.

Examples of variables representing each of the four components of the model are presented in Figure 2.3. Typical caregiving stressors (A) would include the health, cognitive functioning, ADL status, and symptomatology of the patient, as well as other contemporaneous life events to which the caregiver may be exposed. Coping with these events is facilitated by the resources (B) the caregiver can bring to bear on these challenges. These would include the caregiver's socioeconomic status, health, and coping skills, as well as the availability of a number of social resources such as a confidant, assistance from other family members, and number of, proximity to, and contact with family and friends. The perception of the caregiving situation (C) can be assessed in terms of role strain, burden, and mastery. These three factors combine to create a mental health crisis, which can be measured by using self-report instruments or through diagnostic assessment.

One advantage of this model is that it helps focus on the many family relationship variables that very likely affect the caregiving process. In addition, it makes explicit the fact that the caregiver may be exposed to life stressors independent of caregiving responsibilities, which may negatively impact on caregiver well-being. On the negative side, the model has been criticized as being too static (McCubbin & Patterson, 1982), making it difficult to study change over time. In response to this criticism, researchers have proposed the "double" ABCX model, which

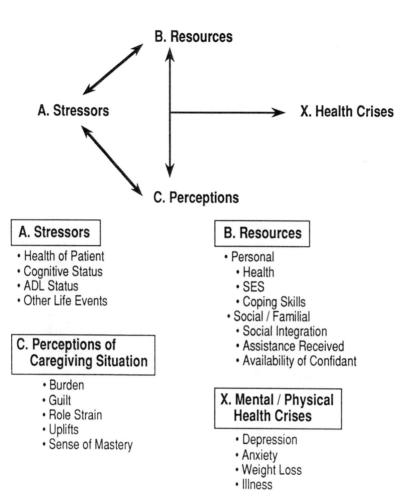

Figure 2.3. The ABCX Model Applied to Caregiving

allows for the study of change (Cohler, in press), although to date there exist no empirical demonstrations of the double model. Another problem concerns the vagueness of conceptual distinctions made by the model. For example, it is not clear how resources (e.g., the availability of a confidant) are distinct from appraisals or perceptions of the caregiving situation.

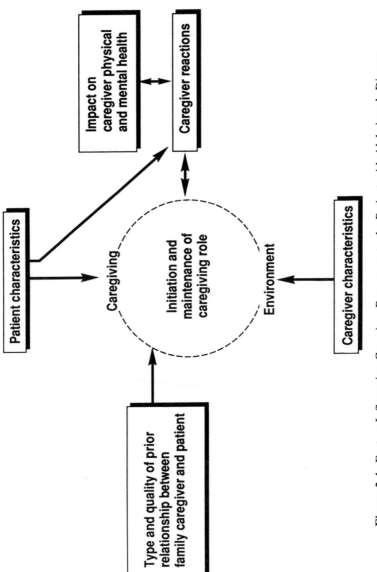

Figure 2.4. Factors Influencing Caregiver Responses to the Patient with Alzheimer's Disease
SOURCE: Given, Collins, & Given (1988)

Patient characteristics

Impact on caregiver physical and mental health

Caregiver reactions

Caregiving

Initiation and maintenance of caregiving role

Environment

Caregiver characteristics

Type and quality of prior relationship between family caregiver and patient

Although the geometric configuration is slightly different, a quick inspection of the model proposed by Given, Collins, and Given (1988) shows it to be a close relative of previously described stress-coping models (see Figure 2.4). It differs slightly in emphasis by focusing attention on the type and quality of the prior relationship between family caregiver and patient as an important influence on the dynamics of caregiving.

Finally, our own work falls squarely within this tradition as well. In studies of caregivers of elderly spinal cord injured persons (Schulz et al., 1987), stroke patients (Schulz et al., 1988; Tompkins, Schulz, & Rau, 1988) and Alzheimer's disease patients (Schulz, Biegel, Morycz, & Visintainer, 1989), we have adapted a model developed by House (1974) and elaborated by George (1980) to organize and demonstrate the relationships between major classes of variables thought to be important in understanding caregiving. Figure 2.5 illustrates five categories of variables incorporated in the model: (a) objective conditions conducive to stress, (b) individual perceptions of stress, (c) short-term responses to perceived stress, (d) enduring outcomes, and (e) individual and situational conditioning variables that affect the relations among the other four sets of factors. Examples of specific variables representing each category are also provided in Figure 2.5.

Focused Outcome Models

The models presented thus far can be best viewed as global outcome models in which the ultimate goal is to understand a relatively long-term enduring caregiver outcome such as psychological well-being, depression, or physical health. Instead of attempting to explain these relatively global outcomes, a number of researchers have focused on specific decision points in the caregiving process. Two good examples of this approach are the work of Morycz (1985) on the desire to institutionalize and Montgomery et al. (1985) on the measurement of burden and its impact on the length of caregiving and the living arrangements of the caregivers. In short, both models are aimed at determining the circumstances under which caregivers no longer are willing or able to take care of their patient relatives in a home setting. Although the decision to institutionalize may be strongly related to caregivers' affective state, it is a very different outcome, both conceptually and from a measurement point of view, than an outcome such as caregiver depressive symptoms.

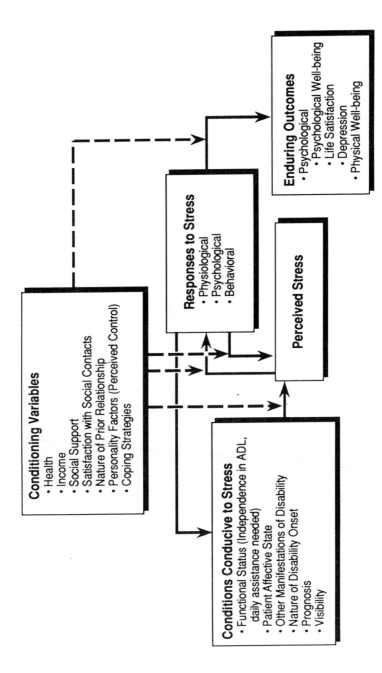

Figure 2.5. Caregiver Stress-Coping Model
SOURCE: Adapted from House (1974) and George (1980).

Morycz's model is empirically based. He interviewed 80 families of Alzheimer's patients and focused on patient, caregiver, and environmental variables as predictors of strain and the desire to institutionalize. Given the strong focus on an important decision point in the caregiving process, it is not surprising that the range of variables examined are centered on patient care issues and the availability of support.

Montgomery's model, presented in Figure 2.6, is conceptually based. Although the outcome of the model is very similar to that of Morycz's, the range of predictive variables identified is substantially different. Instead of focusing on caregiving tasks, this model is concerned with basic structural variables and the orientation of both caregiver and patient on such issues as affection and obligation. The two models are similar, however, in that they both view burden or strain as an intervening variable that directly and importantly contributes to the decision to institutionalize the patient. In addition, Montgomery is careful to distinguish between objective and subjective measures of burden.

THE IMPACT OF CAREGIVING— ANALYSIS OF KEY CONCEPTS

Due to the common origin of the caregiving models described above, considerable consensus exists regarding the central variables relevant to understanding caregiving outcomes. There are differences, to be sure, but they are primarily differences in emphasis, reflecting the disciplinary orientation of the investigator, rather than fundamental disagreements about the nature of the phenomenon being studied. Presumably, a study incorporating measures of all of the variables we have identified, carried out prospectively with a sufficiently large population, and with appropriate analytic strategies applied, would provide us with a thorough understanding of the determinants of caregiving endpoints. Unfortunately, such a study doesn't exist. We can, however, examine the existing literature and ask the following questions:

(1) What components of these models have been tested?
(2) How well was the testing done?
(3) What do the data tell us?
(4) What questions have been neglected?

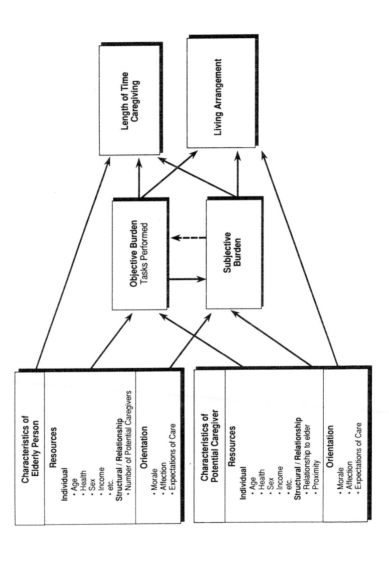

Figure 2.6. Model Predicting Length of Time in the Caregiving Role and Institutionalization of the Elderly Person
SOURCE: Montgomery, Stull & Borgatta (1985)

Because the extensive literature on caregiving is reviewed elsewhere in this book, our goal here is to examine this literature broadly from the theoretical perspective described above. The discussion that follows is organized in terms of the major caregiving variables identified above.

Objective Stressors—Patient Characteristics

Our interest in and concern about caregiving is based on the underlying assumption that patient illness and disability represent an objective stressor to family members. The illness or disability is typically characterized on a number of dimensions including disability in self-care, cognitive impairment, behavior problems, and catastrophic emotional reactions. For example, among Alzheimer's patients, the most frequently identified stressors include memory problems, disability in self-care, and disruptive behaviors such as night waking or daytime wandering. For the chronically mentally ill, intrusive and disturbing behavior, such as unusual eating and sleeping patterns, are frequently cited stressors together with behaviors relating to poor task functions. If the patient is an elderly spinal cord injured person, the emphasis is more likely to be on the level of disability in self-care.

On the whole, the existing literature on the relationship between patient status or symptomatology and caregiver outcomes suggest that the two are moderately related. Studies carried out with diverse populations consistently show that level of physical and cognitive disability is negatively related to caregiver outcomes. In addition to patient disabilities, it seems important for us to consider as well other illness-related factors that are likely to play a role in caregiver response to disability. The visibility of patient disability may have large impacts on the social life of caregivers. Patient behaviors that are disruptive and cause embarrassment may result in a constricted social network as caregivers try to limit contact with network members. Thus illnesses such as dementia and chronic mental illness are likely to be more visible and may be perceived as more stigmatizing than illnesses such as heart disease.

Other factors likely to affect impact on caregivers are the nature of illness onset (sudden or insidious) and prognosis (recuperative, stable, degenerative, or terminal). In sum, it is important to assess not only the biological and behavioral consequences of a disease but also its perceived natural history and the stage of illness in which patients are located—for example, prediagnostic, diagnostic and treatment, rehabilitation and control, recurrence, or terminal (Leventhal et al., 1985). It seems likely that equivalent levels of functional disability will impact differently on caregivers caring for a declining, as opposed to a stable or recovering, patient. As Callahan (1988) eloquently puts it:

> All things may be endurable if the demands are finite in depth and time. But a future that offers no exit at all, even if the burden on a daily basis is not utterly overwhelming, can be an obvious source of sadness and depression. . . . No burden can be greater than trying to imagine how one can cope with a future that promises no relief. (p. 325)

To study the symbolic significance or meaning attached to different illnesses, it is essential that we carry out comparative studies of illnesses. For example, if we wish to assess the role the perceived prognosis of an illness plays in affecting caregiver outcomes, it is necessary that we have sufficient range on that variable in a given study population. This is frequently difficult to achieve in studies of single diseases such as Alzheimer's disease, in which the prognosis is always further decline with eventual death. What is needed is a comparative study of diseases that would allow the researcher to hold constant certain disease attributes, such as functional disability, and systematically vary others, such as prognosis. At minimum, researchers need to recognize the unique trajectories characteristic of different diseases (upward, downward, cyclical, stable, or uncertain) and the fact that there are substantial individual differences in the rate at which individuals travel a disease path.

One of the major shortcomings of the caregiving literature is that individuals in different stages of the disease process are combined and treated as a homogeneous group. Because there are large individual differences in the rate of disease progression, this strategy is likely to create confusion regarding the underlying causes of caregiver distress as well as distort the consequences of caregiving. For example, in the immediate postdiagnostic phase of a terminal illness such as cancer or Alzheimer's disease, the primary stressor may be the anticipated loss of a loved relative; in the late terminal stages of an illness the primary stressors are more likely to include the sheer physical demands of providing care to an extremely disabled relative. Unless outcome measures are sensitive to both types of stressors and their unique consequences, the effects of caregiving are likely to be underestimated and/or distorted. We are not aware of any studies that directly attempt to distinguish among the effects of anticipatory bereavement, feelings of empathy and sympathy for the disabled relative, and the physical/behavioral demands of caregiving.

Perceived Stress/Burden

The central feature of virtually all caregiving studies is the measurement of burden. It is frequently treated as the primary outcome measure or as a predictor of other outcomes such as depression or institutionalization. Some researchers take a narrow perspective in conceptualizing burden, focusing on the tasks associated with taking care of a relative, while others view it broadly and assess burden in terms of general well-being or in terms of a number of multiple dimensions assessing caregiver status. Finally, researchers have also attempted to distinguish between objective and subjective measures of burden.

Because the concept of burden lies at the heart of caregiving, it is essential that we achieve some clarity on the notion of burden at both the conceptual and measurement levels. Dictionary definitions of burden refer to the load borne or carried. Applied to caregiving this translates to the time and effort required for one person to attend to the needs of another. Thus a very rudimentary and relatively objective measure of burden might be a summary score reflecting the amount of time spent, types of services provided, and financial resources expended on behalf of the patient. Presumably, such a measure would be reliably related to objective measures of patient disability.

If we add questions regarding the inconvenience and discomfort associated with performing specific caregiving tasks to this rudimentary measure of burden, our measure becomes both more complex and more subjective. We may wish to assess burden even more broadly by asking questions about the extent to which caregiving causes strain with regard to work, finances, and emotional and physical status (Cantor, 1983; Robinson, 1983), by assessing caregiving related feelings about health, well-being, family relationships, and social life (Zarit, Reever, & Bach-Peterson, 1980), or by measuring emotional impact (Horowitz & Shindelman, 1983) or emotional distress (Gilleard, Belford, Gilleard, Whittick, & Gledhill, 1984) associated with caregiving. Poulshock and Deimling (1984) advocate further refinement by suggesting that burden be viewed as a multidimensional concept in which specific burdens are linked to specific types of impairment. Finally, the literature contains one additional type of burden measure, namely, general measures of psychological well-being, health status, or social activities.

Given the lack of consensus in the conceptualization and measurement of burden, it should not surprise us that the literature presents a confusing picture regarding the correlates and causes of burden. If we hope to achieve some clarity in this domain it is essential that we develop a consensus regarding the conceptual status of burden as well as a consistent approach to its measurement.

First, most researchers would agree that burden is a subjective state reflecting perceptions of individual caregivers. It follows, therefore, that caregivers are the appropriate source of data concerning felt burden. To the extent that one is interested in distinguishing between objective and subjective aspects of burden it would be useful to measure both the tasks carried out by caregivers to assist disabled relatives and the extent to which carrying out these tasks results in inconvenience and discomfort.

Second, measures of burden should assess specific problems experienced in relation to caring for impaired relatives. Researchers should attempt to distinguish between care-related problems and the many other sources of distress that characterize the caregiving context. For example, being upset about the physical decline of a loved one is different from being upset about the time and effort expended to care for that relative, but no existing burden scales attempt to make this distinction.

Third, as suggested by Poulshock and Deimling (1984), burden should be treated as an intervening measure between impairment and other indicators of caregiving effects. Thus global measures of psychological well-being, physical health, or depression should be viewed as being affected by burden as well as many other factors, but should not be viewed as measures of burden. Moreover, efforts should be made to achieve more specificity in linking patient status to particular aspects of felt burden and linking burden to specific outcomes.

Contextual Variables/Mediators

All models of caregiving recognize that contextual or situational variables contribute to caregiving outcomes. This category of variables is broadly defined to include the social networks and support systems of caregivers; characteristics of caregivers including socioeconomic status, health, gender, and relationship to patients; as well as personality attributes such as orientation toward control and attitudes about helping others. It also includes factors characterizing the environment such as the availability and utilization of professional services.

The large number of studies focused on these variables has paid off in a significant body of reliable findings (e.g., see Horowitz, 1985; U.S. House of Representatives, 1987, for excellent reviews). At the descriptive level investigators have characterized the caregiving population in terms of gender, age, race, ethnicity, marital status, employment, economic status, health status, and living arrangements. Thus for example we know that (a) most caregivers are female; (b) their average age is about 57 years; (c) about 70% of all caregivers are married, with female caregivers twice as likely to be widowed as their male counterparts; (d) one third of informal caregivers are employed, although as a group both men and women caregivers are less likely to be employed than similarly aged counterparts; (e) compared to their age peers in the general population, male and female caregivers are more likely to report adjusted family incomes below the poverty line; (f) their self-assessed health is lower than their age peers; and (g) approximately three quarters of caregivers live with the disabled family member or friend.

A second body of research examines these variables in terms of their direct relationship to caregiving impact. As one would expect, living arrangements between caregivers and care recipients are major predictors of caregiver involvement, behavior, and burden. Caregivers who live with the impaired elderly are more involved with the daily care of patients and experience greater limitations on their personal lives. Employed caregivers frequently experience conflict between the demands of work and the needs of patients. Caregivers with a great deal of social support cope better with the demands of caregiving than those with little support.

A third body of research, still relatively undeveloped, treats these variables as interactive conditioning factors that mediate the relationships between stressors and their impact on caregivers. One example of this approach is the stress-buffering hypothesis applied to social support. According to this view, individuals exposed to high levels of caregiving stress benefit from support received from others, but individuals who are not stressed or who experience low levels of stress as a result of caregiving exhibit no beneficial effects attributable to social support.

One of the important contributions of research on social support is its emphasis on the search for mechanisms through which caregiving stressors exert their impact on caregiver outcomes. For example, support may play a role at two different points in the causal chain linking stress to illness. It may intervene between the stressor and a stress reaction by attenuating or preventing a stress appraisal response, or it may intervene after the stress is experienced and prevent the onset of pathological outcomes by reducing the emotional reaction, dampening physiologic processes, or altering maladaptive behavior responses (Cohen, 1988). Thus knowing that others will be available to help care for patients when necessary may prevent caregivers from feeling burdened or stressed. Alternatively, the availability of social support may dampen the impact of a perceived stressor by providing helpful information or assistance or by facilitating healthful behaviors. To date we know relatively little about psychosocial and pathogenic processes through which social support exerts its positive impact. Not only should future research identify where in the stress-coping process support exerts its effects, it should also identify how this is accomplished. In order to achieve the latter, it will be necessary to assess the impact of support on behavior and psychological states such as control and self-esteem, as well as on biological processes.

Enduring Outcomes—Caregiving Endpoints

Caregiving endpoints are the prolonged or cumulative consequences of being exposed to the stresses of caregiving. The types of endpoints reported in the literature include (a) the decision to institutionalize the patient, (b) caregiver role changes, and (c) psychiatric and physical morbidity. Each of these outcomes is examined separately below, although we recognize that in many cases they are likely to be highly interrelated.

Deciding to Institutionalize the Patient.

Both socio-demographic and patient health status characteristics are predictors of institutionalization. Individuals who are older, unmarried, living alone, or who have no children are more likely to enter a nursing home (Palmore, 1976; Vincente, Wiley, & Carrington, 1979). Individuals who are physically disabled or mentally disoriented and require assistance to perform basic ADL tasks are also more likely to be institutionalized (Branch, 1984; Branch & Jette, 1982). In general, these findings indicate that the availability of informal support may delay institutionalization, but they tell us little about factors associated with caregivers' decisions to institutionalize disabled relatives. To address this question we can examine two types of data: One focuses directly on the decision to institutionalize patients and the other focuses on the other side of that coin, namely, predictors of satisfaction with the caregiving role.

A study carried out by Colerick and George (1986) examined patient and caregiver characteristics as a predictor of the decision to institutionalize the patient. They studied a relatively large group of caregivers (N = 209) and found a number of significant differences between caregivers who institutionalized their patients and those who did not. Caregivers exercising the institutional option were most often female, employed, and were among the youngest in the sample. They also reported above average incomes, high levels of stress, and dissatisfaction with time spent in recreational pursuits. A multivariate analysis of their data showed that one caregiver well-being indicator, psychotropic drug use, more than doubled the chances of institutionalizing the patient and that being the spouse of the patient and requiring less outside help to care for the patient reduced the chances of institutional placement. The picture that emerges from these data is that elderly spouses who live with patients are less likely to opt for institutionalization and be more satisfied with their role as caregivers while younger, employed daughters of patients, experiencing high levels of stress, are more likely to institutionalize their parent.

This study is notable also for what it didn't show, namely that patient variables such as severity and frequency of symptoms did not emerge as predictors of institutionalization. The latter finding is inconsistent with the results of Morycz (1985) showing that functional disability of patients was strongly related to the experience of caregiver stress, which in turn predicted caregiver desire to institutionalize patients. The desire to institutionalize was moderately related ($r = .55$) to actual institutionalization.

An indirect way of answering the institutionalization question is to identify factors associated with being satisfied or effective in the caregiving role. Presumably, caregivers who enjoy taking care of a disabled relative are less likely to opt for institutionalization than those who are dissatisfied and unhappy about their responsibilities. Noelker and Townsend (1987) found that among adult children caregivers, the severity of patient disability was negatively related to caregiver satisfaction and that the use of informal and formal support services was positively related to caregiver satisfaction. In addition, the perception among caregivers that everyone involved cooperated to care for the elder also contributed to increased satisfaction. These data suggest that institutional placement may be delayed to the extent that the care needs of the patient are not too great and to the extent that caregivers perceive that a smoothly functioning, cooperative support system is readily available.

Although existing findings on institutionalization are somewhat mixed, it seems reasonable to conclude that patient functioning, the availability of informal and formal support to patients and the caregivers, and the relationship between caregivers and patients (child vs. spouse) all play a role in determining institutional placement. We know little, however, about how these variables interact with each other or how they interact with other important outcomes such as the health status of careproviders. Finally, none of the available data addresses the temporal process that leads to a decision to seek institutional placement. Answers to these questions are needed for the development of informed health care policy.

Role Changes

The demands of providing care to disabled relatives for prolonged periods of time can affect the roles of caregivers in a number of ways. The wife of a disabled husband may have to readopt a role that she relinquished several years earlier when her children became independent. The adult daughter with young children of her own may have to expand her caregiving role to include both children and parents; and males, both husbands and sons, may have to enlarge their repertoire of supportive behaviors to include tasks that traditionally have been associated with the female role.

Because caregiving is normatively considered a female occupation, it is not surprising that the majority of caregivers are females. Despite the prior socialization of women to this role, the literature consistently shows that women exhibit greater adverse effects than male caregivers (Pruchno & Resch, 1989b). There are a number of possible explanation for these gender differences.

Women may be more adversely affected by caregiving because they are forced to readopt a role they only recently relinquished. After spending many of their adult years caring for children, most older women look forward to being free from these responsibilities. To be recast in the caregiving role at a time when their energies and coping resources are diminished may be particularly devastating to older women. An alternative explanation is that the control associated with raising children provides little preparation or anticipatory socialization for assuming authority over an adult male. According to this view, men are more accustomed to taking charge of situations involving another person. Caregiving is therefore an extension of the traditionally male role as authority figure at home and at work. Viewed from this perspective, the dependency of an impaired wife is a difference in degree rather than a qualitative change in roles.

A third possibility is that there are important qualitative differences in the way assistance is provided by men and women. Women may spend more time working with the patient and, because of prior experiences as caregivers, recognize that one could always do more. Men, on the other hand, may be better able to set limits on the amount of help they provide and/or organize others to provide, and not feel guilty about doing so. This suggests that there are important differences in the way caregiving roles are adopted by men and by women that have consequences for their well-being. Unfortunately, little research is currently available on how individuals adopt and carry out their caregiving responsibilities.

Psychiatric Morbidity

The most frequently studied symptoms among caregivers are those indicating depression or demoralization. Thus Schulz et al. (1988) found that the prevalence of individuals at risk for depression as assessed by the Center for Epidemiologic Studies Depression Inventory (CES-D) was almost three times higher than rates found in population samples of similar age. Using the Beck Depression Inventory, Haley et al. (1987) also found that caregivers reported significantly more depressive symptoms than did matched controls. These findings are consistent with case reports showing that some caregivers seek medical attention because of caregiving stress (Lezak, 1978a), and that depression can be severe enough to require hospitalization (Goldman & Luchins, 1984).

On the whole, there is good evidence that caregivers exhibit higher levels of psychiatric symptomatology when compared to appropriate comparison groups. Yet, one must exercise caution when interpreting rates of psychiatric symptomatology as estimates of clinical diagnoses because psychiatric screening instruments are limited in sensitivity and specificity. It is important to remember that the CES-D, for example, does not yield a clinical diagnosis of depression; it identifies individuals who are at risk for depression. Similarly, the General Health Questionnaire (GHQ) yields an estimate of the probability that an individual would be clinically identified as a psychiatric case.

General psychiatric screening instruments are more appropriately considered measures of general psychological distress, since many of the items are not specific to any psychiatric disorder (Roberts & Vernon, 1983). Symptom inventories usually assess psychiatric illnesses on a continuum of severity, rather than as distinct diagnostic entities. Fitting, Rabins, Lucas, and Eastham (1986) suggest that the depressive symptomatology characteristic of caregivers may be more appropriately termed "transient dysphoric mood" or despair arising from their inability to alter or affect patients' outcome. This characterization is similar to the psychological state of "demoralization" that is the general response of individuals who cannot meet the demands of, nor remove themselves from, a stressful environmental situation.

Physical Morbidity

Three types of outcomes have been examined among caregivers as indicators of illness effects. The most frequently used measures are self-reports of physical health status, illness, and illness-related symptoms. A few studies have examined health care utilization as an indicator of physical morbidity and one study examined immune function as an indicator of the susceptibility to disease.

Self-report data related to physical morbidity consistently show negative effects among caregivers, although reported results are frequently open to alternative explanations. For example, Satariano, Minkler, and Langhauser (1984) surveyed 678 elderly individuals and found that the ill health of an individual was a strong predictor of poor health in the spouse. Respondents whose spouses were recently ill were more likely to report ill health when compared to respondents of healthy spouses. These findings could be attributable to the stresses of caregiving but also could be due to other factors such as selective mating, shared environment, or contagion. Snyder and Keefe (1985) reported that approximately 70% of the caregivers they polled reported a decline in physical health because of their support role. They also noted weak but significant positive correlations between the level of disability of patients and the occurrence of health problems in caregivers, as well as between the length of time in the caregiving role and likelihood of reporting health problems. Chenoweth and Spencer (1986) and Haley, Levine, Brown, Berry, & Hughes (1987) also report negative health effects attributable to caregiving.

Although these data are suggestive of morbidity effects, they do not provide conclusive evidence. First, studies without appropriate comparison groups do not tell us whether the self-reported symptoms or illnesses are higher among caregivers when compared to noncaregivers. Second, it is not clear why effects are found on one measure within a study (e.g., overall health ratings) and not others (e.g., physical illness symptoms). Third, the relationship between self-reports of physical health and objective measures of physical health are moderate at best (Maddox & Douglass, 1973), and the rates of concordance decrease as the complexity of the diagnoses increase (Colditz et al., 1986). Finally, it has been established that emotional distress exerts a significant influence on self-reports of physical illness and use of health care facilities (Katon, 1985). Those suffering from mental distress are initially more likely to seek medical rather than mental health services (Houpt, Orleans, George, & Brodie, 1979; Schulberg, McClelland, & Burns, 1987), and present with somatic complaints (Katon, 1985). This suggests that self-reports of physical symptoms, illnesses, and medical care utilization data must be viewed cautiously. These measures may be an indication of psychological distress as opposed to physical illness.

Why Morbidity Effects are Difficult to Obtain

Even if the definitive study assessing caregiving effects on illness were carried out, there are a number of reasons to expect that the observed effects would be minimal. First, the majority of caregivers are married which is, in itself, a selection factor for better health (Kasl & Berkman, 1981). Horowitz (1985) points out, for example, that spouses will be selected as caregivers over adult children, if possible. Second, the caregiving literature indicates that good health is an important selection factor determining who caregivers will be (Brody, 1985; Cantor, 1983; Horowitz, 1985). In families where multiple caregivers potentially are available, health status is likely to be an important selection factor in determining who takes on the majority of the caregiving responsibilities. Moreover, the amount of help designated caregivers receive from other relatives is likely to increase when the health of primary caregivers is threatened. Third, institutionalization of patients is likely to serve as a safety valve for caregivers. When the stresses of caregiving become too great, caregivers can achieve some relief by institutionalizing patients either permanently or temporarily, or by turning over the caregiving responsibilities to another family member. The safety valve hypothesis should be systematically examined in future studies of caregiving. Finally, as indicated earlier, we may be looking for illness effects at the wrong point in time in the caregiving history of individuals. Since the caregiving role may limit or discourage access to professional health care services, it would be difficult to detect illness effects if the primary outcome measure is utilization of health care services among active caregivers. It may be easier to detect such effects after the caregiving role has been relinquished because caregivers feel they can now attend to some of their own needs or because the effects of caregiving stress are lagged.

We have raised a number of questions and have made recommendations regarding the search for links between caregiving and morbidity. The recommendations that follow reiterate and elaborate on some of the major issues related to the health effects of caregiving.

The assessment of psychiatric illness has been limited primarily to responses on self-administered inventories. These instruments can provide estimates of emotional disturbance, but they rarely provide the information regarding frequency and duration of symptoms that is required for clinical diagnoses. It would be a valuable addition to the literature to assess the mental health of caregivers using the Diagnostic Interview Schedule (DIS) and the Schedule for Affective Disorders and Schizophrenia (SADS), two structured interviews for assessing mental disorders. Population estimates are available for both DIS and SADS diagnoses, which would serve as comparison rates for those derived from caregiver samples. Studies now underway will provide these valuable data (see Schulz, Visintainer, & Williams, 1990).

Self-report measures of physical health should also be complemented with more objective measures such as ICD classifications, health care utilization data, and medication use. Moreover, attempts should be made to assess whether illness effects are the result of existing conditions, defined in terms of prior illness or risk factors being exacerbated, or are new conditions unrelated to prior medical history or risk factors.

It seems likely that illness effects are more likely to be found among individuals with increased risk factors for illness.

It would also be useful to determine whether the illness risk of caregivers varies by the predominant type of patient disability; in other words, to find out whether there is a link between type of stressor (e.g., physical disability vs. cognitive disability in the patient) and type of caregiver health problem.

Finally, to the extent that illness effects are observed, it will be important to determine the mechanisms that account for these effects, keeping in mind that mechanisms accounting for symptom reporting, health care utilization, and disease processes may all be different from each other (Cohen, 1988).

CONCLUSIONS

Our goal in this chapter was to provide a framework for examining the vast literature on caregiving and to identify some of the key issues that need to be considered in evaluating the many findings that have been reported in the literature. Although we would not claim to be exhaustive in presenting existing perspectives on caregiving, we have described the dominant themes and issues that are of concern to researchers and practitioners. No doubt new perspectives and even more challenging issues will emerge as research in this area progresses.

3

Caregiving in Cancer

INTRODUCTION

Each year, almost one million new patients and their families must deal with the diagnosis of cancer. This diagnosis is the start, for many, of a long and often difficult journey. It is the arduous nature of this journey, as well as its uncertain outcome, that sustain the fear most of us have of this illness striking our loved ones or ourselves.

Unfortunately, most of us will have to confront such feelings. It is estimated that one in five of us will experience cancer ourselves, while three in four will have someone in our family with this illness (American Cancer Society, 1987; Fobair & Cordoba, 1982; Northouse, 1984). And even if we are lucky enough to avoid this personal confrontation, we are likely to know others who are struggling with the disease (Burish & Lyles, 1983). During the 1980s, it was estimated that 6.5 million new cases of cancer would be diagnosed, with 10 million cases receiving medical care at any one time. During that same decade, 3.5 million people in the United States were expected to die of cancer, making it the second highest cause of death in this country as well as in other industrial countries. (In less developed countries it ranks lower, as the fifth or sixth cause of death [Fobair & Cordoba, 1982].) In 1982, 21.9% of all deaths in the United States were due to cancer (Kerson, 1985a). This translates to nearly half a million cancer deaths a year.

While the number of cancer cases and the number of deaths from the disease have been climbing steadily over the years, overall prognoses and life expectancies have shown modest improvements. In 1930, only one in five cancer patients had a five-year survival rate. By 1960, one in three survived this period. Currently, 40% are alive five years after diagnosis. More encouragingly, mortality rates are declining among younger people and among certain categories of cancer that used to be considered incurable, such as Hodgkin's disease, childhood leukemia, and ovarian and testicular tumors (American Cancer Society, 1987; Burish & Lyles, 1983; Kerson, 1985a; Martin, 1982). Overall, however, 60% of cancer patients die within five years of diagnosis.

Most cancer is detected in middle age or later. It is equally likely to strike men and women, although its form will differ by sex. Morra and Potts (1980) report that 66% of men and 63% of women with cancer are over age 55. Although the incidence of cancer did not differ by race in the past, blacks now have a higher incidence than whites. A study comparing relative incidence rates over 30 years revealed that cancer in blacks has increased 27%, compared to a 12% increase for whites. In that same 30-year period, cancer deaths showed an almost 50% rate increase for blacks, with the death rate for whites increasing 10% (American Cancer Society, 1987).

Thus far we have discussed cancer as if it were a unitary disease; this is not the case. All cancers share the common definition of being an uncontrolled growth of abnormal cells that can metastasize and travel throughout the body in blood or lymphatic systems. They are viewed medically, however, as a group of diseases that differ by type of tissue and by site. Because the prognoses, patterns of treatment, and problems for patients with cancer vary most directly with type of cancer and its stage of development (Mages & Mendelsohn, 1979), we will discuss these variations briefly before exploring cancer's impact on patients and their caregivers.

TYPES OF CANCER

There are five common forms of cancer cells, which tend to locate in different parts of the body and grow at different rates. Carcinoma arises in the surface layer of the skin, in glands, or in linings of body organs. Melanoma is a specific form of carcinoma that lodges in cells producing skin pigment. Sarcoma emerges in connective or supporting tissues, such as bones, cartilage, or fat. Lymphoma originates in the lymph nodes, and leukemia results in transformations of white blood cells.

Five general stages of cancer also can be differentiated. Stage 0 is a precancerous condition, evidenced by abnormal cells that have not yet grown. Stage I designates a tumor or growth that is still self-contained. A localized tumor that has begun to invade underlying tissue would be considered Stage II. Stage III indicates that cancer cells have metatasized and spread to regional lymph nodes, and Stage IV describes cancer that has invaded distant parts of the body. Treatment of cancer, as well as its prognosis, is largely dependent on its stage of development. Consequently, there are more refined classifications of cancer stages that relate to rates of growth, size, and site (Kerson, 1985a; Morra & Potts, 1980). Surprisingly, faster growing tumors are likely to be detected at earlier stages of growth and are more responsive to treatment, thereby making them more treatable.

The most common sites of cancer are the lungs, colon or rectum, and breast or prostate. As may be seen in Table 3.1, lung cancer not only has the highest incidence rate, but by far the highest death rate. Lung cancer has recently surpassed breast cancer as the main cancer killer in women as well as in men. Ironically, this most fatal site of cancer is also the most preventable. Smoking is linked to 83% of all lung cancers and, consequently, 30% of all cancer deaths. Because the other common sites of cancer have dramatically better survival rates, the steady increase in cancer incidence and deaths appears to be driven mainly by lung cancer patterns. The devastating consequences of this cancer seem due to the silent, slow growing nature of lung cancer, with symptoms appearing only when the cancer is in its advanced stages (American Cancer Society, 1987; Kerson, 1985a).

The primary forms of medical treatment are surgery, radiation and chemotherapy. Their use depends on both stage and site of the cancer. Tumors are surgically removed whenever possible if the cancer is localized or spread only regionally (Stages 0-III). In addition to the usual trauma of surgery, such surgery may lead to permanent disfigurement or disability. The loss of a breast to cancer, or the need for a colostomy for patients with colon cancer, often damages self-image and sexual functioning as well as physical capacities. Fortunately, earlier detection and newer, more conservative treatments have reduced the incidence of mutilating surgical procedures. However, surgery itself is inevitably feared, and brings about at least short-term changes in patients' abilities to work, perform family and home responsibilities, function sexually, and feel competent and independent (Burish & Lyles, 1983; Kerson, 1985a).

Over 50% of patients receive radiation therapy, often in conjunction with surgery. Radiation is used most for localized cancers. In addition to the more common external beam radiation used for site specific cancer, radioactive implants can be used for more widely

TABLE 3.1 Incidence, Death and Survival Rates by Cancer Site

Site	Incidence	Annual Deaths	Percent Surviving 5 Years
Lung	150,000	136,000	13%
Colon-Rectum	145,000	60,000	52%
Breast	130,000	41,300	74%
Prostate	96,000	27,000	70%
Uterine	48,000	6,800	66% (Cervical) 83% (Endometrial)
Bladder	45,000	10,600	75%
Oral	30,000	9,400	51%
Leukemia	26,400	17,800	33%
Pancreatic	26,000	24,300	3%
Ovarian	19,000	11,700	38%
ALL SITES	965,000	483,000	40% 49% age adjusted

SOURCE: Adapted from *Cancer Facts and Figures – 1987,* American Cancer Society

spread cancers. Short-term reactions to radiation include skin sensitivity, nausea, and fatigue. Finally, chemotherapy is frequently used as an adjunct to surgery for Stage III soft tissue cancer, and may be used alone to slow the advance of some Stage IV cancers. Chemotherapy often causes a variety of temporary, but intrusive, reactions, including hair loss, nausea, vomiting, diarrhea, and appetite loss. More serious problems include the destruction of white blood cells and platelets, making patients more vulnerable to infections, as well as possible damage to the heart, nerve tissue, or bone marrow (Burish & Lyles, 1983; Kerson, 1985a).

Some combination of the above interventions may either eradicate the cancer, slow or reverse its growth, or be ineffective. Often the course of the disease stretches over years, with varied and unpredictable patterns. As we will see below, patients may experience a grueling series of medical interventions (and their often debilitating aftermaths) remissions, and recurrences. Both patients and their families share the emotional upheavals on this medical odyssey.

For the majority of cancers that eventuate in death, the last stages of the disease involve palliative care for the patient to provide symptom relief and pain control when necessary. Although most people view cancer as a painful disease, Morra and Potts (1980) remind us that pain is not commonly experienced by patients in most stages of the disease. In fact, less than half of patients experience pain even in the most advanced stages.

The main challenges to patients coping with cancer involve the initial experience of fear and hopelessness, the possible disfigurement produced by surgery for some cancers, the aversive side effects accompanying all current treatments, the social stigma that still attaches to this illness, and the long uncertainty regarding outcome. Cantor (1978) sees patients' lack of control as a key element of their reaction. The pervasive, continuing uncertainty regarding one's fate invariably forces patients and families to confront fears of death and helplessness throughout their continued struggle with this illness.

PSYCHOSOCIAL REACTIONS
OF CANCER PATIENTS

The patterns and variations in the disease of cancer described above contribute to the common psychosocial reactions and problems of cancer patients and their families (Cohen, Cullen, & Martin, 1982). Most of the research discussing the psychosocial reactions of patients or families focuses on either the first or last phases of cancer. For example, Weisman and Worden (1976-1977) provide data from 120 newly diagnosed cancer patients showing that the first three months of the illness produce heightened concern regarding patients' continued existence, which the authors label the "existential plight." Their subsequent work (Weisman, 1984) identifies three psychosocial stages that occur in terminal stages of the illness. Very little is known, however, about the often extensive period of survival that follows the initial medical intervention (Mages & Mendelsohn, 1979). There is also a substantial group of studies examining the psychosocial impact of mastectomy, but other patient categories have been followed up only infrequently (Friedenbergs et al., 1981-1982). As we shall see, this gap in knowledge also extends to caregivers.

Burish and Lyles (1983) suggest that adjustment problems may emerge either from individuals' reactions to the disease itself or to its treatment. Although some of these problems are common to all people undergoing life stresses due to illness, many of the reactions experienced by cancer patients and their families relate closely to cancer's extended and unpredictable disease course, as well as to patients' more general life status. Martin (1982), for instance, viewed both age of patients and their available support system as key determinants of psychosocial reactions. Mages and Mendelsohn (1979) agreed that life stage is a central personal factor affecting patient reactions. They also found gender differences in reactions, with men showing more negative effects. Weisman and Worden (1976-1977) found that more distressed patients had more life problems prior to diagnosis, were not married, and expected less support from others. In a later study, Worden and Sobel (1978) found that cancer patients scoring higher in ego strength adapted better over time to their diagnoses.

It is noteworthy that interest in the psychosocial impact of cancer on patients has emerged over the last two decades, and only within the last decade has there been sufficient empirical work to be synthesized (Friedenbergs et al., 1981-1982; Lewis & Bloom, 1978-1979; Meyerowitz, 1980). Meyerowitz's (1980) review of studies of breast cancer patients identified many patient variables found to affect patient adaptation to surgery, including the centrality of physical appearance to self-image, age (older women were less upset), and preoperative expectations regarding surgery. Postoperatively, several studies found that the psychological defense of denial was common for many women with cancer. Furthermore, in contrast to the general view of denial as negative, many writers believe that it may facilitate patient adaptation.

Many writers, including Abrams (1974), Mages and Mendelsohn (1979), Northouse (1984), Thomas (1978), and Weisman (1984), have suggested that the stage of the illness is a crucial factor in understanding the patterns of communication and responses of patients, their physicians, and families. Friedenbergs et al. (1981-1982) reviewed a number of studies supporting this position. M. Cohen (1982b), however, reminds us that patients' emotional states are often labile and nonlinear, with dramatic fluctuations in mood throughout the disease course. Since most observations of cancer patients identify psychosocial issues that emerge at different stages of the illness, we will discuss them within this context. Mages and Mendelsohn (1979), for example, identify the adaptive tasks with which patients must deal at different stages of the

disease as including (a) discovery and diagnosis of cancer, (b) treatment, (c) permanent damage stemming from the disease or its treatment,
(d) maintaining continuity with one's normal life, (e) dealing with the
possibility of recurrence or progression of the disease, (f) further spread
of cancer, and (g) terminal illness. Thomas (1978) isolates ten critical
event periods in the experience of breast cancer patients and their
families that evoke distinct emotional reactions. In this chapter, we will
use a stage perspective to examine research relating to the psychosocial
reactions of patients and their families, beginning with the initial
diagnosis.

Initial Diagnosis

The decision to seek medical help often comes after the detection of
troubling symptoms. Because of fear or denial, some will delay their
first medical contact (Abrams, 1974). The diagnosis of cancer usually
evokes the turbulent feelings of shock, fear, anger, and denial that
accompany all life-threatening trauma. This is a time of severe stress
for patients (Northouse, 1984). Patients are also concerned with the
impact of their disease and treatment on their ability to perform work
and family roles. J. Cohen (1982) points out that additional clinical
reactions, more specific to cancer, are frequently observed. A diagnosis
of cancer is often viewed as a sentence of death. Despite a physician's
optimistic prognosis, the morbid aura surrounding this illness can ex-
acerbate patients' psychosocial reactions. Furthermore, since the etiology of most cancer remains unknown, individuals often project their
own causal beliefs onto the disease, including their own culpability for
its emergence. Although such beliefs impose added burdens of self-
blame, they can also exert more positive influence by mobilizing patients' efforts to participate in medical efforts toward recovery. Some
patients also fear exposing others to their disease, believing it could be
possibly contagious (Abrams, 1974; Kerson, 1985a; Schnaper, Legg-
McNamara, Dutcher, & Kellner, 1983).

In view of these reactions, it is not surprising that Jamison, Wellisch,
and Pasnau (1978) found that almost half (42%) of the mastectomy
patients in their study reported the preoperative period as the most
emotionally problematic. They suggest the need for counseling during
this early period. Early and continuing social support by professionals,
family, and other patients has repeatedly been emphasized by other

writers focusing on psychosocial adjustment (Lewis & Bloom, 1978-1979; Meyerowitz, 1980).

Treatment Phase

Despite trepidation regarding treatment and its side effects, most patients want to rely on their doctors and believe in the efficacy of the planned intervention. Surgery, radiation, and chemotherapy will each, as Mages and Mendelsohn (1979) state, hold their own terrors for patients and families. Unlike most illnesses where medical intervention is looked to for symptom relief and recovery of functioning, cancer patients often feel quite healthy before treatment. Consequently, treatment constitutes a major medical assault on their apparently healthy bodies. Anxiety and depression may alternate with hopefulness during this period. Fears are common during the period preceding each medical treatment, and the aftermath is usually accompanied by varying aversive physiological and psychological side effects.

Patients are frequently self-absorbed and emotionally labile during this period. The forced dependency and inactivity that accompany treatment also create problems for patients. They may worry about the burden they are creating for their families with their illness, and may resent losing control of their normal life and being plunged into an alien world for which they feel unprepared and helpless.

For some patients, surgery may leave permanent impairments that require new adaptations. They may need to mourn the loss of their bodily integrity while they learn to cope with permanent disability. Efforts at rehabilitation may start in the hospital, but often require continued follow-up efforts. The prescribed postsurgical regimen of radiation and chemotherapy also cause intermittent cycles of disruption (Abrams, 1974).

Posttreatment Reactions

Longer term effects of cancer and its treatment vary greatly, largely according to the specifics of the disease and treatment. However, despite the extended posttreatment time span, much less is known about this period (Mages & Mendelsohn, 1979). Perhaps the limited contact with the treatment system at this point inhibits both direct observation and research efforts on the aftermath of cancer treatment. Further, adjustment struggles may be less visible and dramatic as patients and families react to intrapsychic and interpersonal stressors.

If surgery is not permanently disabling, and if the prognosis is positive, patients may return to previous levels of functioning with few obstacles. Even here, however, the fear of cancer and its recurrence exert a powerful force on both patients and those with whom they interact (Northouse, 1981). Life may seem both more precious and more precarious during the long period before the cancer may be judged as eradicated. In Morris, Greer, and White's (1977) study, 46% of patients were reporting stress three months after surgery. Readjustment was attained by most within the first year, although one quarter could still be considered at risk.

A survey by Meyerowitz, Heinrich and Schag (1983) found that 86% of patients reported some difficulties in communicating with family and friends. Many (55%) of these significant others tried to reassure patients by saying that they looked good, when the patients knew they didn't, and 51% avoided any reference to the disease. Meyerowitz et al. also found that 72% of patients had problems communicating with medical staff, including asking relevant questions, expressing feelings, or understanding key medical information.

For patients with permanent impairments there are additional challenges. They may need to adjust their self-image to incorporate the disability; for example, women may see themselves as less attractive and feminine after mastectomies (Burish & Lyles, 1983). Worden and Weisman (1977), however, found no greater symptoms of depression in postmastectomy patients as compared to those with other forms of cancer. Meyerowitz's extensive 1980 literature review of studies of the psychosocial impact of breast cancer found that most patients returned to preoperative levels of stress and living patterns.

Women with genital cancers may have chronic sexual dysfunction after treatment, and other patients may have sexual difficulties as well (Goldberg & Tull, 1983). These sexual problems can result in disturbed marital relationships, which are also found in some mastectomy patients (Burish & Lyles, 1983). Generally, however, couples who have had good marriages prior to diagnosis deal well with the interpersonal demands of the illness.

Patients may also need to renegotiate their prior role responsibilities. Some may no longer have the capacity to perform their former work roles. Feldman (1982) found that 69% of patients desired a job change of some kind after treatment, though many could not act on this wish.

More generally, Feldman's study revealed that 84% of cancer patients reported some work problems linked to their illness, including demotion, loss of work benefits or promotion, and negative co-worker behaviors. The stigma of cancer may leave patients feeling isolated and abandoned as others withdraw from contact (Goldberg & Tull, 1983).

Relapse

New tumors, which signal the spread of the cancer to other sites, create new disruption and despair. It is at this point that patients and families often recognize that their cancer may not be controllable by medical interventions or by their own efforts (Goldberg & Tull, 1983). These feelings of personal helplessness may change patients' subsequent interactions with the medical establishment. Doctors may be looked to more desperately for security and salvation as patients become more compliant and passive. Communication between patients, families, and doctors may become more guarded as the disease progresses and optimism recedes. Fewer questions may be asked and briefer answers given in such exchanges. Patients may also begin to withdraw from those closest to them as they confront the increasing reality of their mortality. Depression and denial are present and often alternate, causing unpredictable mood swings (Abrams, 1974; Cohen, 1982). However, Weisman and Worden (1985-1986) found that patient reactions to reoccurrence were not more extreme than they were to the initial diagnoses.

Terminal Phase

Such withdrawal may increase as the disease advances, and an often extended period of waiting begins. Patients may need to conserve their resources for their final battle with the disease. The patients' worsening conditions will lead to diminishing ability to perform normal roles, and an increased dependence on others. Personal humiliation may accompany the need to rely on others for formerly independent self-care functions (Abrams, 1974; Kerson, 1985a).

As death approaches, pain and medication may also contribute to this withdrawal. Although some patients may wish to talk to families during this period, many become increasingly remote. Unfortunately, this apparent rejection of loved ones becomes an additional burden for families.

FAMILY REACTIONS TO CANCER

In a recent study of cancer patients and their spouses, Oberst and James (1985) concluded that " learning to live with cancer is clearly no easy task. Learning to live with someone else's cancer may be even more difficult precisely because no one recognizes just how hard it really is" (p.56).

It should be clear from the above discussion that cancer represents, among other things, an interpersonal crisis for patients and those who love them. It disrupts normal family equilibrium and necessitates the renegotiation of well-entrenched patterns of nurturance, dependency, initiative, and power. Roles of both spouse and children require continuing realignments as the crisis continues (J. Cohen, 1982; Vettese, 1981).

Research that examines family adjustment to cancer begins with the premise that a diagnosis of cancer triggers a broad array of reactions. Frequently operating from a family systems perspective, such studies recognize that this diagnosis constitutes a family crisis that induces both stress and coping responses in all family members (Chekryn, 1984; Giacquinta, 1977; Lewis & Bloom, 1978-1979; Quinn & Herndon, 1986). Predictable crisis reactions such as denial, anger, depression, and fear, accompanied by anticipatory grieving over possible death and loss, are common to both patients and families. Further, central beliefs regarding life's priorities and meanings are challenged and often clarified by this existential crisis (Grandstaff, 1976; Weisman, 1979). These reactions of patients and family members are compounded by communication problems among family members who have differing needs for information and affective sharing, and between families and professional caregivers (Northouse & Northouse, 1988).

CURRENT STATUS OF RESEARCH
ON CANCER CAREGIVING

Even though there has been much greater acknowledgment of family stresses in recent years, we still have limited empirical data on the difficulties experienced by those who care for cancer patients. Early research shifted the focus to families only when patients could no longer be helped and were nearing death. In the past decade, however, we have begun to study the impact of cancer on family members. The first studies examining this issue systematically appeared in the late 1970s, focusing primarily on the husbands of postmastectomy women. Since then, there has been a steadily increasing body of literature through the 1980s, much of it published in nursing journals.

Research on the psychosocial impact of cancer on families generally falls into disease stage categories identified in the more general literature on cancer patient reaction. Although many studies of cancer patients have focused on those in early stages of the illness, there is little literature on family reactions during these periods. Most research on families focuses on the stresses of the terminal phase (Freidenbergs et al., 1981-1982). In fact, the burgeoning academic interest in issues of death spawned many studies that spotlighted the families of terminal cancer patients, who constitute the majority of subjects for research on loss and bereavement. In contrast, the families of cancer survivors have often eluded research scrutiny once patients complete their treatments (Oberst & James, 1985). Thus, as with patients, we know least about caregiver strains during the period of survival between initial treatment and the final stage, although it is commonly the most extensive time span.

Because of the recency of emphasis on family reactions to cancer, available research is limited in quality as well as quantity. Methodologically, most studies currently available have been based on small sample sizes and ad hoc groups, usually recruited in hospitals during inpatient or follow-up care visits. Although research on the earlier stages of the illness frequently has focused on specific groups of cancer patients (women who have had mastectomies have been studied most extensively), the more limited studies of later stage patients have often included patients across sex, age, cancer type, and disease phase. Because many of these variables interrelate, the inability to control for other factors creates problems in interpreting associations found between them and caregiver distress. Unfortunately, the small sample sizes of most current studies do not permit subgroup comparisons that may help to clarify the separate impact of each variable on family adjustment (Freidenbergs et al., 1981-1982). Without such subgroup analyses it is impossible to isolate the contribution of any one factor.

As mentioned above, data on families who are in intermediate stages of illness are relatively scarce, particularly if patients are not receiving medical services. In almost all cases, spouses of patients have been the designated caregiving respondents. Rarely have children or other family members been examined. Even when studies have included a variety of family caregivers, only one family member typically has been the key informant on family reactions. Thus, although many writers discuss family reactions from a systems perspective, comprehensive data on all family members, which would be the logical base for analyses stemming from this theory, have not been collected.

Study designs have been generally weak. Most studies have been cross-sectional, although a few have used panel designs involving at least one follow-up data collection effort (Vachon et al., 1977). The absence of longitudinal designs makes it difficult to infer that psychological distress of caregivers is, in fact, a consequence of the illness rather than preexisting.

Furthermore, comparison groups, either with other patient groups or with well populations, have been almost nonexistent. Such comparisons could help to clarify baseline levels of distress expected from non-caregiving counterparts, as well as the amount of distress found in caregivers of other illnesses. Measures of psychosocial problems rarely have been psychometrically sophisticated, commonly relying on simple self-reported difficulties. However, there does appear to be an encouraging trend, in more recent work, toward improved measures as well as overall enhancement of methodological rigor. Further improvements in these areas, as well as the development of theoretically grounded studies that develop predictive models of psychosocial impact on families, are still central to future research in this area (Lewis, 1986). Most of the current research, for instance, measures overall caregiver stress without identifying the aspects of caregiving that may be causing difficulty. Therefore, we cannot clearly identify whether such stresses emerge out of specific caregiving demands related to cancer, or out of the more general stresses attending any family illness. Although we will try to identify the likely demands for caregiving at each point in the disease course, the literature currently available does not delineate aspects of caregiving causing distress for families during the intermediate illness stage.

CAREGIVING STRAINS IN CANCER

There appear to be some common issues experienced by families of cancer patients at varying stages of the disease. Cantor (1978) suggests that families experience many of the same feelings as patients as the crisis disrupts the continuity of their lives and their hopes for the future. The challenge for caregivers is to maintain a balance between their own needs and the caregiving responsibilities generated by the illness.

Lewis (1986) reviewed eight years of research articles focusing on family impact. She identified 11 central themes in the 15 studies she examined. These themes appear to cluster around three distinct realms of caregiver reactions: (a) affective and emotional responses, (b) behavioral demands, and (c) reactions to the service system. The emotional responses commonly felt by spouses were:

(1) fear of the patient dying;
(2) emotional strains such as anxiety, fears, and helplessness;
(3) existential concerns regarding life's meaning; and
(4) continued uncertainty regarding the patients' health status.

In addition, spouses must cope with added behavioral demands, such as:

(5) alterations in household roles and lifestyle,
(6) changes in sexual needs and behaviors,
(7) the need to comfort and support the patient,
(8) increasing demands for direct patient care at later stages of the illness, and
(9) to a lesser degree, financial concerns and obligations.

Compounding these physical and emotional burdens were two additional factors related to the service system:

(10) the needs of spouses may not converge with those of patients (with the spouses' needs often being neglected), and
(11) supportive services are often viewed as inadequate, leaving families to cope on their own.

Beyond these general family reactions, the cancer literature has consistently highlighted the centrality of disease stage on family reactions. Recent studies by Oberst and James (1985) and Stetz (1987) support this stage model for caregivers. Therefore we will, following Northouse (1984), examine family issues at three phases of the disease: (a) The initial diagnostic and hospital stage, (b) the outpatient period,

during which some patients may be receiving adjuvant therapies, and
(c) the terminal phase and its aftermath for families. For each phase we
will first review the major issues identified in the general literature
on family impact, and then turn to the more limited research literature currently available. In many cases there are limited empirical
data confirming the speculative literature, and sometimes there appear
to be direct contradictions. These discrepancies will be noted when
encountered.

Initial Phase

The reactions of families parallel those of patients on first hearing
the diagnosis. Anxiety, anger, helplessness, and guilt often alternate
once the initial numbness of the acute trauma recedes (Abrams, 1974;
Kerson, 1985a). The initial phase is one of the most stressful for families
as well as patients, and fears and uncertainties dominate (Northouse,
1984). For families, the feeling that they cannot protect patients from
the required treatment adds to their feelings of impotence. They often
experience conflict between their own fears and the need to support and
reassure patients. Perhaps as a consequence of these strong competing
emotions, families often direct their anger at the diagnosing physician
for having generated their plight (Schnaper et al., 1983). However, if
the prognosis is positive, families commonly regain their equilibrium
and approach medical treatment with some optimism.

The initiation of medical intervention often brings new sources of
difficulty. Families may feel ignored by medical staff who reserve their
concern and attention for patients. Although families are sometimes
expected to provide tangible assistance to patients, including transportation for treatments, they are left to cope on their own. Yet, as Burish
and Lyles (1983) note, cancer treatment creates multiple problems for
caregivers as they help patients cope with the physical and emotional
traumas of surgery, radiation, chemotherapy, and their aftermaths.

Caregivers may not only find themselves in the position of providing
tangible and emotional support for patients during this period, but also
may need to become mediators and advocates in patients' contacts with
the medical system. Information-seeking often combines with more
assertive efforts to insure the best care for patients (Goldberg & Tull,
1983).

Research on Caregiver Strains During Diagnostic and Hospital Stages

Despite the suggestions of the above writers that the emotional demands on families during this highly charged initial period are considerable, very little is known about the psychosocial adjustment problems of family members during the initial stages of cancer. Although our earlier discussion suggested the emotional shock waves triggered in patients by a diagnosis of cancer, research tracking family reverberations is not readily available. Perhaps the absence of tangible caregiving demands during this period contributes to this omission, because stresses on caregivers have received most attention when patients are most dependent on caregivers for specific tasks. Yet, patients may need substantial emotional support from others at this time. Family members experience the same shock reactions as patients to a diagnosis of cancer, and often share the common belief that the diagnosis is a death sentence. Thus we can speculate that they might first be confronting anticipatory loss during this period. Family members, as well as patients, must be fearful of the debilitating effects of medical interventions, with particular awareness by caregivers of the physical and emotional demands on them precipitated by the illness.

An early study by Wellisch, Jamison, and Pasnau (1978) found that husbands participated actively in decisions regarding their wives' treatments. In this study, husbands of 31 mastectomy patients reported retrospectively that they were very much part of their wives' initial decision making regarding the type of surgery the women would request.

Gotay's (1984) comparison of 19 mates of early stage cervical cancer patients with 20 men who were mates of advanced stage gynecological and breast cancer patients found the men had many concerns that endured throughout the women's illness. The men also had great difficulty dealing with the women's emotional distress. Gotay found that many men attempted to cope during this early period by seeking direction and information from those in authority. Thus the men seemed to deal with their emotional distress by making efforts to seek cognitive information.

Cooper's (1984) study of 15 lung cancer patients and their spouses, interviewed within 2 to 9 months of diagnosis, presents some qualitative data on this early stage. Acute stress reactions of shock, denial, fear, and depression were at the forefront for spouses during this time although spouses appeared to suppress their feelings more than patients did. In support of this observation, Cooper reported that 9 of the 15 spouses reported that they felt emotionally isolated after diagnosis; only 2 of the patients expressed this feeling. Overall, spouses reported twice as many stress symptoms as patients did—most commonly experiencing sleeplessnesss (9 spouses) or nervousness (8 spouses). (Male spouses seemed particularly reticent in emotional expression.)

Cooper suggested four factors that may account for the greater stress symptoms of spouses: (1) Health care providers may be meeting the needs of patients but not their spouses, (2) others in the support system may also focus primarily on patients' needs, (3) spouses may withhold feelings from their ill partners, cutting off their primary context for expressiveness, and (4) spouses may be confronting their feelings of anticipatory loss, a facet of the crisis not shared by patients.

Once patients are hospitalized for surgery, we know a little more about family reactions. Grandstaff's (1976) study of mastectomy patients and their spouses found that waiting for the results of surgery was one of the most difficult times for spouses. After surgery, the spouses' main responsibilities were twofold, (1) maintaining household tasks formerly performed by patients, and (2) hospital-related activities, including insuring the comfort and care of patients and mediating with the medical staff regarding patients needs. Wellisch et al.'s (1978) study found that most husbands reported that they had visited their wives daily, and 40% reported sleep disturbances. More recently, Oberst and James's (1985) study of 40 spouses of bowel or genito-urinary cancer patients also found spouses to express strong feelings of fatigue during patients' hospitalization, as well as problems with eating. Looking at overall emotional state, Northouse and Swain (1987) found that the 50 husbands of mastectomy patients in their sample were significantly more distressed than a comparison group soon after their wives' surgery. In fact, at this point their stress levels were comparable to those of their wives. Northouse and Swain conclude that spouses, as well as patients, need support during this early period.

Even more dramatically, Oberst and James (1985) found that spouses were more anxious than the patients themselves during the hospital period. They attributed this to greater fatigue and responsibility felt by caregivers while their spouses were hospitalized, which drained their emotional reserves. Oberst and James's data also revealed that during this early period spouses as well as patients were centrally concerned with the patients' situation. These data, it may be recalled, echo Cooper's (1984) findings from a nonsurgical population of lung cancer patients, and further suggest that spouses may have a high need for support during this early period.

Adaptation Phase

The descriptive literature on this phase suggests several new demands on family members when patients leave the hospital. Although surgery and its follow-up represent acute crises for families, they may be reacted to as short term challenges to be overcome. It is the day-to-day challenges of living with cancer that often erode caregiver energy and morale. At best, if there is no permanent debilitation or disfigurement and if the prognosis is positive, family functioning may recover much of its normalcy. Even then, however, the need to live with long-term uncertainty regarding cure may create new tentativeness for plans about the future. Families may also need to decide who will be told about the disease, because stigma and rejection are always possible.

If patients have permanent limitations, more comprehensive changes in life-style may be required. Role shifts or reversals may occur as patients' dependencies require greater responsibility and initiative from spouses or children (M. Cohen, 1982b; Kerson, 1985a; Northouse, 1984; Vettese, 1981). Caregivers may experience conflicts in efforts to maintain other family and work roles while assuming the added tasks involved in caring for patients. It is not uncommon that resentment or anger accompany these changes, along with guilt for having such unacceptable feelings (Thomas, 1978; Vettese, 1981). The financial costs of treatment and the need to assume more of the economic burden for family maintenance may be added burdens for family members (Goldberg & Tull, 1983).

Another factor that complicates the emotional life of caregivers is the possibility of strains in their relationship with patients. This often occurs in marriages where spouses feel cut off from the emotional support of their ill partners while needing to deal with their own stresses (Burish & Lyles, 1983). Marital strain can also result from the sexual withdrawal that often accompanies surgery. It has been suggested that this loss of both emotional and sexual intimacy may create added burdens for each partner (Goldberg & Tull, 1983; Thomas, 1978).

Family members may be less supportive and more distanced as they grapple with reestablishing their own equilibrium (Thomas, 1978).

If cancer recurs, new disequilibrium is created. If the family is alerted to the invasive spread of the disease, members many reexperience the acute emotional reactions of previous stages (Abrams, 1974). Although fears of death and loss could be denied at earlier points, they must now be confronted. Whereas earlier stresses were tempered by a belief in the possible helpfulness of the treatment interventions, optimistic faith in the medical establishment is now eroded.

Research on Caregiver Strains During the Adaptation Phase

The current research literature documents the overall level of caregiver stress during the posthospital period, as well as its consequences for the couple's marital relationship. It also provides us with some data regarding the continued caregiving needs of patients. Despite the large and growing number of patients in remission, however, we have very few studies of families once patients have completed treatment.

The sources of family stress appear to shift somewhat during the postdischarge period. Once the direct caregiving tasks of convalescence subside, caregivers appear to be able to focus more on their own feelings. One month after patients returned home, Oberst and James (1985) found spouses to be more self-concerned than they had been during the patients' hospitalization. Spouses often experienced a variety of somatic symptoms, and were able to focus more on their own problems. Not surprisingly, spouses continued to conceal their own difficulties from their ill partners, who showed no awareness of these problems. Such concealment efforts may add to the burdens of spouses, which appeared to peak at around two months posthospitalization. Oberst and James suggest that the continued efforts of spouses to function eventually give way to exhaustion and depression. Furthermore, spouses may often begin to harbor resentment of their status as they continue to feel little support or understanding from others, including patients. Throughout their period of observation, which extended to 2-, 3-, and 6-month follow-ups, Oberst and James found that spouses continued to show greater emotional problems than did patients. These problems peaked at 60 days, but were found throughout the 6 month period of follow-up.

Similarly, Baider and DeNour's (1984) study of 20 Israeli mastectomy patients and their husbands 4 to 34 months postmastectomy found that the husbands' adjustment problems increased over time while the wives' subsided, indicating the effects of accumulated stress on family caregivers over time and treatment.

In contrast, Northouse and Swain's (1987) follow-up of husbands one month after patient discharge found a somewhat different pattern. Although patients and their husbands had similar levels of distress and moodiness at this time, husbands were experiencing fewer role adjustment problems than were patients. And Cassileth, Lusk, Brown, and Cross (1985a) found caregivers to have lower mood disturbance than patients in both active treatment and posthospital periods. Thus, while it is clear that spouses are still distressed after hospital discharge, studies differ on the level of caregiver distress relative to patient distress. There is agreement, however, that stress levels of patients and caregivers are mostly within normal ranges.

The reactions of caregivers subside over time as patients' posthospitalization direct care needs diminish and their capacities return. Contrary to much of the speculative literature cited earlier, current research suggests that spouses readily seem to recapture prior levels of satisfaction with their relationships after convalescence. Generally, cancer patients appear quite satisfied with the care they received from their partners during their illness (Meyerowitz, 1980). For example, Wellisch et al.'s (1978) study of 30 husbands of mastectomy patients found little change in couples' sexual relations after surgery. Although the men reported a decline in frequency, the quality of lovemaking was unchanged, and the women's capacity to achieve orgasm was undiminished for 84% of the couples. Wellisch et al. concluded that most men coped well with the crisis.

Grandstaff's (1976) study of mastectomy patients and their spouses suggested that the husbands' initial reactions to viewing their wives' surgical scar was crucial to the longer term intimacy in their relationship. Although husbands wanted to show support and acceptance, they were often fearful of viewing their wives' disfigurement. Grandstaff also emphasized that couples who coped well often found new levels of intimacy and humanistic values in their lives together as a result of this crisis.

The preceding studies reported caregiver reactions during the immediate period following initial patient treatment. There are also a number of studies that have focused on family adaptation of broader cross sections of cancer patients who were receiving longer term follow-up care. Cassileth et al.'s ongoing study (1985a, 1985b) found that outpatients and their relatives shared similar moods and feelings at all stages of the illness. These reactions were generally within normal mental health ranges, indicating the overall resilience and adaptability of families in coping with the continuing stresses of cancer. Cassileth et al. also found that both partners showed increased mood disturbance during active treatment periods (including chemotherapy and radiation), and a return to lower levels at other points. These fluctuations continued until the terminal phase of palliative care, when steep increases in relatives' mood disturbance for the first time exceeded the mood disturbance of the patients themselves.

Hinds (1985), in a study of 33 families caring for patients at home, found that their most frequent problems related to patients' treatments (70%), followed by specific problems of nausea, vomiting, and pain. Families generally expressed a need for more information and skills regarding patient care. Although 79% had someone they could call on to stay with patients if they needed to be out of the house, 21% had no such resource. Only 8% of the families used any community support services, most commonly nursing or homemakers. Thus most families coped with the problems of this period alone, relying on occasional support from others in their families (44%), friends (22%), or neighbors (16%). Hinds concluded that 31% of the families in her study were coping poorly with patient physical care needs, and could benefit from a variety of support services.

Despite the fact that both Wellisch et al.'s (1978) and Hinds's studies suggested that treatment-induced patient problems, including nausea and vomiting, were distressing for caregivers, there is limited research on caregivers' reactions to posthospital adjuvant treatments. It is probable that such treatment would involve additional time and transportation demands on caregivers. Furthermore, the physical and emotional tolls of chemotherapy would necessarily increase burdens for caregivers as well as create new needs for mediation with medical staff concerning patient treatment issues. A recent study by Hart (1986) of 25 chemotherapy patients and their significant others found the side effects of chemotherapy to be less stressful for caregivers than the cancer diagnosis itself. This overarching concern with patients' conditions was followed by concern with treatment-related stressors. Much less concern was expressed about changes in relationships and tasks brought on by the illness.

An earlier study by Lieber, Plumb, Gerstenzang, and Holland (1976) support the stability of relationship factors during chemotherapy. Their study of 37 long-term married couples only included patients with advanced cancer who were 3 to 4 years beyond their initial cancer diagnosis. They observed increases in positive feelings and physical closeness during chemotherapy. Couples were generally functioning well, and had either grown closer or maintained prior patterns of relationship, rather than withdrawing from each other. More recently, Lichtman, Taylor, and Wood's (1987) study of 78 breast cancer patients confirmed that patients with more support from spouses showed better later adjustment. In fact, three quarters rated the support they received very highly. Even in these strong marriages, however, communication barriers existed as each spouse contained personal concerns rather than risk upsetting the other, whom they saw as having had the more difficult time. Lichtman et al. conclude that "in the face of role shifts, fears of recurrence and death, and often debilitating treatments, most couples said that their marriages had stayed the same or improved" (p. 70).

The foregoing literature suggests that caregivers of cancer patients generally coped well with the stresses of diagnosis and treatment, and appeared to return to normal adjustment levels once immediate caregiving needs subsided. This equilibrium is maintained throughout the posthospital period, despite the added stresses of chemotherapy. Unfortunately, very little is known about another key event that all too many families must cope with—the eventual discovery of new signs of cancer. Despite extensive acknowledgment that fear of cancer recurrence is almost universal, the impact of recurrence on families has hardly been examined. Chekryn's (1984) study of 12 wives experiencing a recurrence of gynecological cancer is among the few that examine the impact of this new crisis on couples. She identifies four domains of concerns for husbands, (1) impact on the family, (2) existential concerns, (3) concern for patient's illness, and (4) impact on work and finances. The levels of distress between spouses were, as in other studies, highly correlated and well within normal ranges of functioning. Thus couples appeared to weather new crises with the same resilience shown at earlier stages.

More recently, Weisman and Worden (1985-1986) studied 102 patients from their earlier research who had a cancer recurrence. Contrary to expectations, they found no greater distress for patients than was present at the time of initial diagnosis. Most patients were not surprised by the recurrence, because they had recognized this possibility from the outset. Those who had not expected a recurrence were highest in distress. Patients generally reported fewer problems than they had initially, and viewed their marriages as stronger than most. Weisman and Worden suggest that marriages surviving the challenges of the initial cancer experience were strong enough to mobilize for the new onslaught of its recurrence. In fact, the initial experience may have created a stronger bond and greater ability to deal with further life crises.

Terminal Phase

The descriptive literature suggests that as patients' diseases progress further, normal roles become permanently disrupted. Patients withdraw into passive dependency on focal caregivers, often spouses or children, whose burdens at this point may mount and expand as the illness continues. Primary caregivers become patients' protectors, monitoring contacts between patients and others, as well as playing the role of emotional counselor. Further, they may need to be nurse's aides as patients weaken and the disease interferes more with normal physical functioning. Families as well as patients may need to rely more heavily on medical personnel as the illness proceeds. At the same time, caregivers often need to take over additional domestic responsibilities that were formerly performed by patients (Abrams, 1974; Goldberg & Tull, 1983; Vettese, 1981).

Northouse (1984) identifies the central family issues during this period as being (a) the need to provide care and support for the dying, (b) the need for family members to communicate with one another about the approaching death, and (c) the need to deal with feelings of separation and loss.

It is ironic that those who have the most to do must also be the ones with the most to lose. Fears of abandonment and anticipated loss are difficult to quell despite the caregiving demands. The patients' withdrawal and silence presage the end and may be harder for families to deal with than the patients' death (Abrams, 1974). Caregivers' isolation and loneliness at this time are at a peak. It is not surprising that caregivers may become a focus of concern during this period. The support they receive through this difficult time may contribute to their longer term recovery from loss, while patient care during this terminal period is, of necessity, considered palliative and time-limited.

Research on Caregiver Strains
During the Terminal Phase

Research data document the peaking of caregiver distress during the period of increasing demands accompanying advanced cancer. Although Gotay (1984) found many similar concerns during early and advanced cancer for husbands of breast and gynecological cancer patients, husbands of the advanced cancer patients were "much more likely to be disturbed by thoughts of the patient's dying" (p. 611). They also found it difficult to deal with seeing their wives in emotional distress and focused on assistance tasks, such as physical care, emotional support, and prayer, during this later period.

A number of studies have examined the needs of caregivers during the period of home care preceding death. Most found that caregivers often felt that they lacked the skills and emotional resources required during this difficult time. Welch's (1981) study of 41 family members of cancer patients requiring home nursing care found that 63% expressed some difficulty with their role. Even so, most felt the desire for services related to patient care rather than their to own concerns. Skorupa and Bohnet's (1982) study of caregivers of terminally ill cancer patients makes a similar point—that caregivers are most concerned with assuring that patients are well cared for, and seek information and skills that may enhance patient comfort.

Like Welch's study, Grobe, Ilstrup, and Ahmann's (1981) study of 28 families of advanced cancer patients and 29 family members of deceased patients who had received home hospice services found that many families (65%) felt a need to learn some additional skills. These skill needs mounted as patients declined, and were most commonly dealt with by caregiver trial and error learning rather than by direct instruction from home health care providers.

Welch (1981) suggested that good quality nursing care for patients can give families greater peace of mind, and may relieve them of the need to stand constant vigil. The presence of a nurse also can alleviate the fear (expressed by 34% of family members) of leaving patients unattended.

A pilot study of the needs of 15 patients and their families by Googe and Varricchio (1981) found that 80% needed household help, and 73% needed help with shopping and with their added expenses; 67% were not getting adequate sleep. Despite these high levels of need, most families (73%) felt that they were managing very well and the remaining 27% believed they were managing fairly well during this time.

Stetz's more recent interview study (1987) of 65 spouses of advanced cancer patients receiving home health care further confirmed and extended these earlier findings. Once more, caregivers' dominant concerns were with the physical care of the patients: 69% reported concerns relating to the physical care needs of patients, and 39% reported concerns about managing finances and the need to be on hand for patients. Overall, patient care needs appeared to dominate the caregivers' days. On average, spouses reported spending an average of 23.2 hours daily at home with their bedridden patients. In fact, 75% reported that they typically never left the house at all.

The needs of this final illness period also appear to impact on other role sectors. A recent study by Muurinen (1986), using data from the National Hospice Study, examined the impact of family home care on caregiver employment. He found that family caregivers of home hospice patients spent an average of 10.2 hours a day in patient care, twice the number of hours needed by families whose patients were in institutional settings. Caregivers with lower labor market involvement were more likely to keep patients at home during this terminal phase, and also more likely to spend more time at home with home hospice patients. In fact, 33% of home hospice caregivers stopped working totally during this period. Of those who maintained employment, mostly younger and male, 69% reported lost work hours and 60% reported lost income. Muurinen concluded that these employment consequences were unacknowledged caregiver costs in providing home care. He reminds us that such "high informal care costs can reduce the caregiver's ability to supply care" (p. 1016). It should be noted that this cost-benefit analysis could not deal with the types of costs incurred by unemployed primary caregivers, who make up the majority of those who choose home hospice. They frequently cut back on rest, recreation, and other activities that contribute to their mental health. Such nonmonetary costs cannot be quantified and may consequently be neglected in our consideration of the costs of caregiving.

Finally, Vachon et al.'s (1977) early longitudinal study of 73 widows of cancer patients emphasized the stresses and isolation felt by these women during the final phases of their husbands' illness. The spouses of terminally ill patients are commonly overlooked in research studies, yet they may be among the most burdened of groups. Vachon et al. identify the "social death" felt by these women as family and friends drifted away during the long period of their husbands' decline. Further, their own physical and emotional health often deteriorated as they negotiated the patients' care and other family responsibilities at the expense of their own needs. In contrast to wives of cardiovascular patients, wives of cancer patients reported feeling more stress, anger, guilt, and helplessness during the final period preceding their husbands' death.

Not surprisingly, the widows of cancer patients continued to have greater emotional reactions than did widows of heart attack victims after their husbands' deaths. More reported symptoms of poor emotional or physical health and had nightmares. In addition, cancer widows revealed much greater anger at the medical care given their husbands, identifying three areas of complaint: (a) the poor quality of nursing care provided their hospitalized husbands, often perceived as neglect; (b) their limited access to doctors; and (c) the lack of accurate information on their husbands' condition. Vachon et al. (1977) concluded by wondering whether the hospital system exacerbated the suffering of families dealing with terminal cancer. They suggested that for their sample of cancer widows "the shadow of a terminal illness was far worse than the stress of widowhood" (p. 1191).

In summary, the studies currently available document the peaking of caregiver physical and emotional stress during this period, and testify to the perceived emotional tolls on caregiving families. They provide us with little evidence, however, concerning the longer term consequences of these burdens on caregivers. We know that caregivers often lose sleep, lose income, and draw extensively on emotional reserves during the acute and terminal phases of cancer yet the enduring costs of the illness are undocumented. While it is possible that family caregivers return to prior levels of functioning after the patients' illness, some effects may persist. Vachon et al. (1977), for instance, found that cancer widows still viewed the final illness of their husbands as worse than widowhood two years after their husbands' death.

At present, the absence of other longitudinal studies of cancer caregivers makes it impossible to assess the long range impact of the disease, especially for families of nonterminal patients. Furthermore, the soft measures of stress used in most studies, consisting mainly of global self-reported stress, make it hard to assess any clinically abnormal levels of distress found in cancer caregivers. At this point we must conclude that caregivers of cancer patients are subject to severe and varied stresses during the illness, and that such stresses mount during active interventions and peak during the terminal phase. It should be recalled that these are the best documented phases because families are most in contact with medical services during these periods. Thus even this conclusion is offered tentatively.

SERVICES AVAILABLE
FOR PATIENTS AND FAMILIES

Psychosocial interventions for adult cancer patients and their families are a relatively new phenomenon compared to the much longer availability of such services for families of children with cancer (Goldberg & Tull, 1983). Nonetheless, many patient social services have now become standard components of medical care. In addition to the typical information and medical support given by the medical system regarding cancer treatments and their aftermath, other common services derive from patient self-help efforts. These efforts occur both during hospitalization and afterwards, and are frequently differentiated according to cancer site. Many are sponsored by the American Cancer Society, although they often emerged from patient initiated activities. There are also a number of supportive services offered through voluntary agencies in the community.

Supportive services to caregivers of adult cancer patients are very limited until the terminal phase of the illness. Goldberg and Tull (1983) believe that the treatment team providing care for the cancer patient also needs to recognize that caregivers need support, and that the provision of such support should become a service priority throughout all phases of treatment of the disease. They state that medical professionals can help family caregivers assume five critical tasks as follows: to help maintain the social support system of patients, to promote the patients' sense of autonomy, to be an advocate for patients when necessary, to encourage communication between patients and family and friends, and to facilitate the expression of feeling. The assumption of these tasks by caregivers can assist patients to cope better with their disease and can also help address issues of caregiver distress. By assisting caregivers to perform these tasks, the treatment team must recognize that there are a number of potential obstacles, such as grief, stress, the need for role changes, and fear, which may make it difficult for caregivers to give and receive support. Health care professionals need to be sensitive to these issues and help caregivers to address them.

During initial hospitalization, new patients can be visited by patients recovering from cancer. The Reach to Recovery program of the American Cancer Society consists of women treated for breast cancer who have received training to assist other women undergoing similar treatment. Program volunteers are available to visit women while they are still in the hospital. The CanSurMount program, designed to help people cope with cancer on a broad basis, is a short-term effort to help families in the initial acute stage of their experience with the disease. During the visit, patients and their families can tap the visitor's experiences to reduce the mystery and fear surrounding diagnosis and treatment. Videotapes are another technique utilized by hospitals to provide information about specific kinds of cancer and the issues faced by patients who undergo specific surgical procedures.

A number of self-help and agency-based programs are also available after treatment. I Can Cope, a program of the American Cancer Society, is designed to increase understanding of the problems of cancer through education for all cancer patients and their families. Make Today Count is a national organization of patients, families, and friends affected by cancer (Williams & Williams, 1986). In addition, Reach to Recovery provides support for mastectomy patients, the Lost Chord Club is for those whose larynx was removed, and the Ostomy Association provides support and information for those with colon excisions. As with any self-help group, there are some individuals who are not comfortable participating in groups, either patients who don't wish to interact with other patients, or caregivers who feel uncomfortable in group situations. Professionals must be aware of this and assist such patients and families to obtain support in less threatening ways (Goldberg & Tull, 1983). In addition to self-help organizations, community agencies, such as the Salvation Army, the YMCA and YWCA, American Red Cross, and numerous other voluntary organizations, offer a large variety of supportive services for cancer patients and their families (Williams & Williams, 1986).

Some professional programs are available for patients with specific postoperative problems. General counseling services may help families deal with many of the psychosocial problems mentioned above. Sex therapy may help couples who are experiencing difficulties in resuming sexual activity. Training programs that provide skills for managing postoperative symptoms or pain are sometimes recommended for patients. These may include relaxation training, biofeedback, hypnosis, or behavioral techniques.

Tangible posthospital supports are also available for patients who require continued physical assistance. Home health care workers and transportation services are standard resources during this time. And, as terminally ill patients reach the final stage, hospice programs provide a number of services including information, support, pain control, and preparation for dying. It should be noted that, until the terminal phase, families are considered ancillary to patients, who are the primary recipients of most existing programs. It is hypothesized that prebereavement interventions for caregivers of cancer patients may have an effect on their postbereavement adjustment process, but to date there has been little empirical investigation of this issue.

FACTORS AFFECTING STRESS
IN CANCER CAREGIVERS

The previous section reviewed the research literature documenting the levels and types of caregiver stress experienced at different phases of illness. In this section we will use the theoretical model developed in Chapter 2 to organize the factors that thus far have been found to relate to caregiver burdens. It should be noted that the literature on variables predicting caregiver stress in cancer is relatively recent. It emerged slowly in the mid-1970s and has only shown rapid growth in recent years. Our review is thus limited by the methodological problems discussed earlier, as well as (1) the absence of samples large enough to permit researchers, through multivariate analysis, to isolate the independent effect of each predictor while other factors are controlled; (2) the lack of parallel variables across studies, which frequently forces us to rely on a pattern found in one isolated research effort; and (3) in cases where similar predictors have been studied across studies, findings have sometimes been hard to interpret because of other study differences, such as variability in disease types or disease stages, or differences in the stress measures used in assessing caregiver impact. These generic problems should be kept in mind during the following discussion.

Despite these inferential barriers, we will attempt to examine what is currently known about both the objective stressors and the contextual variables relating to caregiver reactions to cancer. Most of the following studies employ some subjective measure of perceived stress as their dependent variable, although role readjustments in family relationships (Vess, Moreland, & Schwebel, 1985a, 1985b) and in work involvements (Muurinen, 1986) have been examined in more recent studies of caregiver effects.

Objective Stressors

The literature on the direct impact of cancer-related variables on caregivers suggests a number of illness factors that appear to affect caregiver adjustment. We will review these variables below, after identifying one pervasive problem in the current literature. The illness-related variables examined are heavily interrelated. Thus certain forms of cancer that have poorer prognoses will also have more patients in advanced cancer stages where patient psychosocial problems, as well as caregiving demands, reach their peak. The empirical confounding of this network of objective stressors has not been controlled in most current studies. We are, therefore, still far from understanding which of these objective stressors may be central to caregiver reaction. With this caveat in mind, we turn to the illness-related variables that affect caregivers.

Illness Stage and Prognosis

Because stage of illness is a central organizing variable in many discussions about the psychosocial impact of cancer, it follows that illness stage has been consistently found to relate to caregiver distress. In the current literature, illness stage is so tightly bound up with prognosis that they cannot be examined as separate variables. The current discussion will therefore view them as isomorphic. Wellisch, Fawzy, Landsverk, Pasnau, and Wolcott's (1983) study of home health agency records of 447 married cancer patients found families had significantly greater psychosocial problems if the cancer had metastasized. Compared to the nonmetastatic group, such families had more impaired family relationships, felt more overwhelmed, and showed more mood disturbance. Further supporting this pattern, Wellisch et al. also found families of patients with poorer prognoses, especially those who were terminal, to feel significantly more overwhelmed than those with fair or good prognoses.

Other studies have documented the peak psychosocial stresses during the final stage of cancer. Cassileth et al. (1985a, 1985b) found in their ongoing study of hospital outpatients and their relatives (N = 201 [1985b], N = 374 [1985a]) that mood disturbance, anxiety, and mental health problems were significantly higher during the period of palliative care that precedes death. Although earlier periods of active treatment led to some increases in anxiety and mood disturbance for relatives when compared to noninterventive follow-up care, the approach of death signified by palliative treatment evoked the most pronounced psychosocial problems. Nonetheless, patients and relatives generally revealed high emotional stability, with their scores on each of three psychosocial indicators comparable to general population norms.

In addition to explicit measures of illness stage, two other variables that seem closely connected to illness stage have been found to predict caregiver strain. These stage-related variables, caregiving demands and illness duration, will be discussed next.

Caregiving Demands

The level of patient care needs has also been found to relate to caregiver distress. Like Cassileth et al. (1985a, 1985b), Baider and DeNour (1984) found that the 20 spouses of their mastectomy study patients were more distressed during periods of adjuvant treatment. Cassileth et al.'s (1985b) study of cancer outpatients also found that mood disturbance peaked when patients were bedridden. Mor, Guadagnoli, and Wool's (1987) study of 217 cancer patients and their families found that caregiver perceived burdens were strongly related to the amount of physical care needed by patients. Oberst, Thomas, Gass, and Ward (1989) found a similar relationship between patient dependency and caregiver burden. Muurinen's (1986) study, it may be recalled, showed that the 695 families caring for terminal cancer patients at home, compared to other hospital based alternatives, had greater work disruption, suggesting another arena of consequence during this final period of peak caregiving demands.

Such studies, although revealing the terminal period to be most demanding of caregivers, do not isolate the critical factors in this relationship. Patients clearly demand most care at this time. Other role demands often are disrupted. Furthermore, patients are often withdrawing from interactions, possibly providing less support for caregivers. This period is also distinctive in confronting caregivers with the reality of approaching death and the need to begin coming to terms with the loss of their loved ones. Thus caregiver distress could also reflect anticipatory grief. At present, it is impossible to identify whether the psychosocial problems of family members, mostly spouses, are related to their caregiving responsibilities during the terminal period or to the imminent loss of their partners.

Illness Duration

An additional component of the terminal period is that it represents the outer limits of illness duration. The literature is not clear, however, about whether the duration of illness is itself a crucial element in the above studies. Studies examining the relationship between illness duration and caregiver stress have frequently not found a significant association (Cassileth et al., 1985b; Hart, 1986-1987). In contrast, some studies have found duration associated with increasing strain. The small exploratory study by Baider and DeNour (1984) of 20 breast cancer patients did find that the husbands' adjustment declined over time since the wives' mastectomies. Cone's (1985) study of 75 women outpatients and their husbands also found the men's adjustment to decline over time. More recently, Oberst, Thomas, Gass, and Ward (1989) found a significant positive relationship between length of time in treatment and caregiver load for 41 radiotherapy patients. Vachon et al.'s (1982) study of 73 widows of cancer patients found that women whose husbands had a longer, lingering final illness showed significantly greater physical and emotional distress after their husbands' deaths than did women whose husbands had a shorter final illness. The length of the terminal period itself, rather than the entire length of time since diagnosis, may be the key element of the widows' reactions in Vachon et al.'s (1982) study.

Cancer Site

In addition to illness stage stressors, at least one other illness-related variable appears to affect caregiver strain. Two studies that included patients with diverse forms of cancer found the disease site to be related to family adjustment. Wellisch et al. (1983) found that, compared to other cancer groups, families of lung cancer patients exhibited greater mood disturbance and more feelings of being overwhelmed, and families of cervical cancer patients had more impaired family relationships. Cassileth et al. (1985b) also found psychosocial effects of relatives to vary by type of cancer, with brain cancer producing the most severe family reactions. Unfortunately, neither study suggested reasons for these sites being more problematic.

Patient Distress

One additional patient variable affects caregiver response. Patients' own reactions to illness appear to reverberate in the caregivers. Several studies have found that patient problems relate closely to caregiver stress. When patient adjustment was good, spouses and relatives showed less psychosocial disturbance. Families of patients with greater distress, however, showed more adjustment problems (Baider & De-Nour,1984; Cassileth et al., 1985; Mor, Guadagnoli, & Wool, 1987; Wellisch, Wolcott, Pasnau, Fawzy, & Landsverk, 1989). It is likely that Vachon et al.'s (1977) findings were also, at least in part, based on the emotional difficulties felt by wives in witnessing the distress and suffering of their ill husbands during an extended final illness stage. It should be noted that Northouse (1984), while acknowledging this consistent pattern in her review of relevant literature, suggested that the relationship between patient adjustment and family adjustment may not be direct, but mediated by other factors in relational, personality, or illness domains. Regardless of its source, it seems very clear that patient adjustment is a significant factor contributing to caregiver reactions. In fact, Wellisch et al. (1989) suggest that it may be a central determinant of family adaptation.

Overall, current research shows that the impact of cancer peaks during the terminal phase, especially if it is extended and requires high levels of care. Viewing their data, Mor et al. (1987) conclude that cancer

wreaked havoc on the lives of both patients and caregivers. The burden of caretaking in the context of extended illness, advanced stage of cancer, and poor prognosis not infrequently leads to emotional conflict, strain, or guilt. This burden is most stressful for caretakers who have other familial and personal complications and those who care for the most impaired patients. (p. 15)

Yet despite the objective stressors identified above, most family members endured the demands made upon them without evidence of pathology either during the patients' illness or beyond. It should be noted, however, that few studies have followed caregivers' reactions longitudinally to track such long-range impact.

Contextual Variables

Studies of caregiver distress have frequently examined the characteristics of caregivers that affect their reactions. Demographic characteristics of caregivers have been most commonly examined, yielding a wide (and occasionally conflicting) array of predictors associated with caregiver distress. Personality, relational, or support variables have been the focus of attention less frequently. In this section we will first discuss those caregiver characteristics affecting adjustment, and then turn our attention to relational factors impacting on caregiver outcomes. In contrast to the theoretical model presented in Chapter 2, such studies have simply examined the main effects of contextual factors on perceived distress, rather than viewing them in interaction with the objective stressors delineated above. It should be noted that many of these studies studied patient groups that were homogeneous in illness stage and site, thereby not allowing much variability in objective stressors.

Caregiver Characteristics

Age of Caregiver. A number of studies have found that younger caregivers showed greater emotional distress than did those who were older. Studies of bereaved spouses by Goldberg and Tull (1983) and Vachon et al. (1982) found that younger spouses had more adjustment problems at both immediate and subsequent follow-up periods. At earlier stages of illness, Wellisch et al. (1983) found that husbands of postmastectomy patients who were under age 50 revealed greater role difficulties and relationship impairment than did older spouses, while Mor et al.'s (1987) more recent study of 217 cancer patients and their families found younger caregivers had more financial problems. Both Wellisch et al. (1978) and Northouse and Swain (1987) found a direct relationship between age and patients' postmastectomy adjustment. Because patient adjustment relates so closely to spouse adjustment (Northouse & Swain, 1987), one can view this as further evidence for the impact of age on spouse distress. It should be noted, however, that Cassileth et al.'s (1985a, 1985b) continuing research on home health care patients and their families found no such age effects.

Although the evidence indicates that younger spouses react more emotionally than older partners to their spouses' illness, the work of Wellisch et al. (1983) and Mor et al. (1987) suggests that aging couples may have different forms of difficulty. These studies indicate that older spouses found it harder to deal with caretaking tasks than did younger spouses. In addition, Muurinen (1987) found that older caregivers of home hospice patients were more likely to withdraw from the labor market to care for patients. Thus it appears that aging caregivers may have more trouble dealing with the tasks and physical demands of their spouses' illness, while younger caregivers have their greatest difficulties in affective domains. Wellisch et al. (1983) suggest this conclusion when they state: "It seems that although the younger couples were likely to resent the situation and feel frustrated and angry, they did not feel overwhelmed and depressed, as did the older couples in the study" (p. 14).

Gender. A number of studies have found gender effects in caregiver adjustment. These usually document the greater distress of female caregivers, although a few have found no gender differences in family reactions (Cassileth et al., 1985a, 1985b). It should be noted, however, that many other studies have used single sex samples, most commonly mastectomy patients, and, as a consequence, have not been able to explore this issue.

An early study of 38 patients receiving chemotherapy and their spouses (Lieber et al., 1976) examined the emotional needs of couples during this stressful treatment period. In addition to noting an overall increase in the desire for physical closeness in all partners as well as a decrease in sexual desire, their data revealed gender differences in spouse adjustment. Wives of male patients showed significantly more depressive symptoms than did the husbands of female patients. Lieber et al. (1976) suggested that couples in which the woman is the patient had greater synchrony in affectional needs, leading to less marital tension. In these marriages, the wife could vent her feelings while the husband remained stoic, in keeping with traditional gender roles. However, wives of male patients showed more affectional discrepancies with their husbands. They had greater needs and depressive symptoms than did their patients, despite the fact that their ill husbands were having fewer problems than were the female patients. Lieber et al. suggested that male patients and their spouses may need help with marital tensions. More surprisingly, they concluded that husbands of female cancer patients may also need help because they were not getting their affectional needs met, despite not revealing emotional distress. In general, however, the couples were functioning well, showing depression scores well within normal ranges and revealing marital closeness, rather than withdrawal, as their coping mode. Noting this pattern, Lieber et al. point out that the couples agreeing to participate in their study may have been functioning unusually well.

Other studies have also suggested that wives of male patients may be more distressed. Families of male patients were more overwhelmed by home care (Wellisch et al., 1983), and were more likely to give up their jobs to care for their home hospice patients (Muurinen, 1986). These efforts by female caregivers appear to result in better patient care. Mor et al. (1987) found that patients with female caregivers had more of their needs met than did those with male caregivers. Concerns with meeting patient needs may also increase the emotional burden of female caregivers. Both Hart (1986) and Cassileth et al. (1985) found that female relatives of cancer patients showed more evidence of stress and mood disturbance than male relatives did.

A recent study by Stetz (1987) further detailed the gender differences in types of perceived role demands of male and female caregivers. Women perceived more caregiving demands on them than did men, and expressed more feelings of needing to stand by for their husbands, although they also found it more difficult to watch their husbands' physical decline. In contrast, male caregivers, although perceiving fewer overall demands, were more concerned than female caregivers with finances and household management needs. Thus women caregivers may orient more to helping their husbands deal with their illness, while male caregivers appear to focus on more general household management concerns. It seems possible that women's focus on their husbands' physical and emotional needs exerts higher psychosocial costs than does men's more general concerns, thereby accounting for women's higher distress. On the other hand, women may simply feel more comfort in expressing their emotional reactions.

Socioeconomic Status. Indicators of lower socioeconomic status also have been found to relate to caregiver reactions. Unemployed wives revealed more problems during their husbands' final illness than did those who worked (Vachon et al., 1982), and caregivers with lower incomes and education were more likely to leave the labor market when caring for home hospice patients (Muurinen, 1986). More recently, Oberst et al. (1989) found that caregivers from lower socioeconomic statuses (SES), and those with less education, felt more threatened by the patients' illness.

Other Demographic Factors. Additional demographic factors found to relate to greater caregiver distress are being white (Cassileth et al., 1985a), being Jewish (Vachon et al., 1982; Wellisch et al., 1983), and receiving less comfort from religion (Vachon et al., 1982).

Other Life Stressors. A number of other background variables found to relate to caregiver distress may be viewed as indicators of other life stresses. One such factor is the caregivers' own health status. For example, Vachon et al. (1982) found that wives in poorer health expressed more physical needs during their husbands' final illness and showed more distress, both short-term and long-term, after widowhood. Caregivers in poorer health were also more likely to give up their jobs when caring for home hospice patients (Muurinen, 1986) and also felt more threatened by the illness (Oberst et al., 1989).

In addition to health, Grandstaff's (1976) early observations suggested that recent stress events increased family reactions to cancer. Vachon et al.'s (1982) study of widows confirmed that women with other life problems and stressors were more prone to psychosocial problems, and that those with multiple stressors were at greatest health risk.

It would thus appear that the data converge on the inference that those who already have more stresses in their lives may be more vulnerable to the demands of caregiving, and are at greater risk of negative psychosocial consequences.

Prior Experience with Cancer. At least two studies have examined whether earlier experiences with cancer affected caregiver and patient reactions in similar ways (Mages & Mendelsohn, 1979), but the data were inconclusive. Grandstaff (1976) suggested that prior experience had an impact, but Hart's (1986) more recent study found no relationship between prior experience and family stress.

Overall, the general literature on caregiver characteristics that affect psychosocial adjustment suggest that female caregivers with other life stressors may be most vulnerable. Age also impacts on caregiver reactions: young caregivers may feel more emotional distress, and older caregivers may be less able to cope with the physical tasks of caregiving.

Relational Variables

Several researchers have examined the impact of a variety of relational variables on caregiver reactions to cancer. Although these variables may be viewed as another subcategory of the contextual factors discussed above, their focus on interpersonal aspects of caregiver response seems to merit separate consideration. Therefore, we now consider those studies that focused on the impact of the general quality of the marital relationship (Muurinen, 1986; Vachon et al., 1982; Wellisch et al., 1978), the specific nature of communication between the spouses (Chekryn, 1984; Northouse, 1984; Vachon et al., 1977), the family life stage (Grandstaff, 1976; Vess et al., 1985a, 1985b), and the general informal social support systems available to caregivers (Northouse, 1988).

Quality of Marriage. The studies that focus on the impact of marriage quality on caregiver reactions reveal a mixed picture. Couples in better marriages show better adjustment during most stages of illness, but spouses in close relationships may suffer more during the terminal period and its aftermath. Both Grandstaff (1976) and Wellisch et al. (1978) found that couples with a stronger preexisting marriage were able to weather the stresses of mastectomy more easily. In the Wellisch et al. study, husbands in better marriages were more involved in their wives' decision making regarding surgery, as well as perceiving less psychosocial adjustment difficulties after surgery. These studies both suggest that caregivers in stronger marriages are more able to cope with the initial stresses of surgery and its aftermath.

A longitudinal study by Vess et al. (1985a, 1985b) included several measures of marital interaction. Their sample of 54 couples, initially interviewed after at least a period of hospitalization, revealed that families that were more adaptable in role assignments, rather than adhering to traditional gender role assignments, showed greater cohesiveness and competence in new illness-induced role demands. In addition, their five month T2 follow-up data indicated that these couples showed greater improvement in role relationships over time than others did. Vess et al. also found that most couples in their sample generally improved the quality of their interactions over time, showing lower role conflict, role strain, and family conflicts, while revealing increased family communication and cohesion at T2. These trends in the Vess et al. study lend support to conclusions reached by Mages and Mendelsohn (1979), based on their earlier research findings, that "for those couples and families who are able to master the stresses of cancer, the experience of surmounting crises together and perhaps communicating in ways in which they never have before may lead to a satisfying growth and deepening of relationships" (p. 278).

Although stronger marriages may facilitate coping at earlier stages of cancer, caregivers in closer marriages may feel more strain at terminal stages of the disease. Muurinen (1986) found that caregivers with closer relationships to patients in home hospice were more likely to withdraw from the labor market during patients' final illness. Most tellingly, Vachon et al. (1982) found that wives who felt closer to their husbands, and perceived their marriages were better, felt more distress and physical health problems both during their husbands' final illness and after their deaths. They suggest that grief reactions are stronger and exact a higher toll for widows in such close marriages.

One aspect of good marriages, the level of communication between spouses, has been singled out for separate investigation. There is some evidence that the general quality of marital communication facilitates adjustment. Although Chekryn (1984) found no association between communication and adjustment in couples dealing with wives' cancer recurrence, Cohen, Dizenhuz, and Winget (1977) found that better family communication predicted better adjustment to bereavement. And Vess et al. (1985) found that couples with better communication were more able to deal with role demands, were more cohesive, and showed less role conflicts, role strain, and family conflicts than did other couples. Furthermore, T1 communication was significantly related to couples' later role functioning.

In additional to general marital communication level, the ability to talk explicitly about approaching death appeared to help couples achieve greater closeness in the terminal stages of cancer (Hinton, 1981), and resulted in an easier bereavement for widows (Vachon et al., 1977). In support of these findings, Northouse's (1984) literature review reported that couples who discussed death achieved greater closeness, and that greater family communication prior to death was related to better postbereavement adjustment. Overall, the data currently available suggest a link between communication and caregiver adjustment in the terminal stages of cancer. However, this suggested relationship must be viewed with caution. Not only are these data derived exclusively from terminal cancer patients, but they are also limited by self selection factors, such as general coping, that could promote both more communication and better adjustment.

One provocative finding from the Vess et al. (1985) study merits special note. As one of the rare studies following families longitudinally, it was able to examine the impact of family relational characteristics on patient mortality. It found that patients in marriages that showed better communication, greater cohesion, and lower family conflict at T1 interviews were more likely to be alive five months later, at T2, than were patients in more troubled marriages. Although this study suggests that family dynamics may impact on patient mortality, it only indirectly relates to caregiver stress, which will obviously peak when the partner dies. Furthermore, its small sample of nonsurvivors, numbering only 9 of the initial 54 patients, urges caution in generalization.

Family Life Stage. A number of authors (Gray-Price & Szczesny, 1985; Mages & Mendelsohn, 1979) have suggested that the life stages of patients and caregivers may be central to their psychosocial adjustment problems. Young couples may be disturbed by the pressures placed on their still evolving intimacy, mid-life couples may already be fully involved in work and parenting, and older couples may show premature dependency in response to this crisis. The concept of family life stage summarizes an array of factors related to role involvements and demands, family dynamics, and life course developmental tasks, as well as actual age, that exert strong impact on couples' reaction to cancer.

While this variable has been rarely studied, Vess et al.'s (1985a, 1985b) longitudinal studies of 54 couples tested five hypotheses explicitly derived from family life stage concepts. Dividing their sample into three life substages, they found that families at different developmental stages showed different role problems and role adaptations. Specifically, couples with young children had greater role conflicts, lower cohesiveness, and relied more on outside help than did more mature families. Couples with school-age children experienced fewer role problems and felt less need of external services, but experienced greatest family conflicts. Older couples, in contrast, appeared to show least disruption on all family indicators used.

As predicted from the writings of family life stage theorists, the Vess et al. study provides suggestive evidence that family stage may affect the types of strains felt by caregivers. The theoretical literature also argues, however, that age of children is an additional key factor in family adjustment. Grandstaff's (1976) qualitative observations suggested that different family members may have unique concerns. Teenage and older daughters may be very supportive of mothers with breast cancer, although sons may have difficulty with this form of cancer. Cooper (1984), in one of the few studies to include data on children, found that adolescents reported more maladaptive reactions to their parents' cancer than did younger children. We have little understanding of the degree to which children, prior to adulthood, are involved in caregiving tasks. Adult children are sometimes (though not commonly) included in samples of caregivers, but they have rarely been examined as a separate subgroup. Consequently, we have little knowledge relating to caregiver role relationship to patient as an additional predictor of caregiver stress.

Social Support. Several studies have found social support to be a significant factor in the psychosocial adjustment of cancer patients (Cone, 1985; Dunkel-Schetter, 1984; Jamison et al., 1978; Mishel & Braden, 1987; Northouse, 1981; Worden & Weisman, 1977), although a few have identified some social support problems induced by a diagnosis of cancer (Dunkel-Schetter & Wortman, 1982; Revenson et al., 1983; Tilden & Galyen, 1987; Wortman, 1984). In many studies, family members, mainly spouses, are viewed as a central social support source for patients. Despite the growing emphasis on social support as a factor affecting patient adjustment, caregiver social support has rarely been studied as a predictor of caregiver outcome. At least one study (Cone, 1985) supports the suggestion in many discussions that caregiver support needs are often neglected by medical personnel, friends, and others, who focus on meeting patient support needs. Cone found that husbands of cancer patients were less likely than their wives to seek support as a method of coping with the illness. More recently, Northouse (1988) found that although mastectomy patients and their husbands perceived similar levels of support from each other and from other family members, husbands felt significantly less support from friends, nurses, and doctors. Overall, the husbands in Northouse's study perceived significantly less social support than did their wives. There is thus some evidence suggesting that caregivers may receive less social support than patients. In order to move beyond this descriptive pattern, however, we need to understand whether social support impacts caregivers' adjustment the same way it appears to impact on patients.

The Northouse (1988) study discussed above recognizes this gap in the preexisting literature, and provides groundbreaking data on the impact of social support on the initial postmastectomy adjustment of 50 husbands of breast cancer patients. Her study found greater perceived support to be the only significant correlate of husband adjustment (R = .20). Further, her one month follow-up of husbands found that continuing support was more important than initial support in affecting husbands' later adjustment. She concludes by suggesting that social support may be as important for husbands as for wives in the immediate postsurgical period and its aftermath.

In summary, there appears to be a variety of evidence suggesting that relational factors such as marriage quality, communication between spouses, family life stage, and social support may affect the psychosocial adjustment of caregivers. It is less clear how these factors may interact with other contextual factors, and how they may relate to objective illness-related stressors. For example, spouses in closer marriages may be more likely to perform their caregiving tasks more willingly during the terminal period, yet they would also be the caregivers most affected by their partners' pain, withdrawal, and approaching death. They may also put more pressure on themselves to be at their spouses' side, even at the cost of their own health and of their other roles.

In conclusion, the emerging literature examining the predictors to caregiver distress suggests a number of illness-related variables, caregiver characteristics, and relational qualities that appear to impact on caregiver distress. This research does not focus exclusively on caregiving issues, however, but looks more generally at family stresses in reaction to patients' illness. These studies rarely measure the range of actual tasks performed by the family members studied. Thus we cannot assess how much of the caregivers' psychosocial difficulties relate to the direct activities of caregiving, and how much may be due to the presence in the family of a spouse with cancer.

It is reassuring to observe that both partners and patients hold up remarkably well to the strains of this disease, but we also know from the above studies that some caregivers experience great difficulty. This subgroup of family members could very well benefit from intervention. The current literature suggests some of the factors that might signal the need for caregiver assistance, but does little to suggest the specific sources of caregiver distress. It remains unclear to what extent the caregiving role itself, as contrasted to the more general strains emerging from living with someone with cancer, has contributed to the psychosocial effects found in the current research.

4

Caregiving in Heart Disease

INTRODUCTION

Cardiovascular disease is currently the cause of almost half of all deaths in the United States (Kerson, 1985b). In 1985 nearly one million Americans were killed by heart and blood vessel diseases: 47.6% of all deaths that year. Cancer, the next most frequent cause of death, was responsible for only half that number of deaths during the same time period. Heart disease must be seen as by far the most serious killer of Americans in recent years (American Heart Association, 1988).

Unlike many other causes of death, heart attacks have reached this rate of incidence only in the twentieth century. Since the beginning of this century there has been a steady increase in heart attacks, peaking in the mid-1960s. Despite a substantial 30% decline in the death rate from heart attacks in the two decades following 1965 (Kerson, 1985b), the United States continues to have the highest heart attack death rate, followed by other developed, westernized societies. In contrast, Japan has the lowest incidence of heart attacks (Passamani, Frommer, & Levy, 1984). This dramatic increase in the United States and other countries led the World Health Organization in 1961 to label heart disease an international epidemic (Finlayson & McEwen, 1977).

These major variations in incidence of heart disease over time and space indicate the extent to which living patterns can affect cardiovascular disease. Three major risk factors that can be controlled are (1) cigarette smoking, which doubles the risk of heart attack; (2) high blood pressure; and (3) blood cholesterol level. Other important controllable factors also known to contribute to risk are obesity, physical inactivity, stress, and diabetes (American Heart Association, 1988). A cluster of personality characteristics, including high competitiveness, work overcommitment, time urgency, and impatience form a syndrome

105

known as Type A behavior, which also has been found to correlate with heart disease (Kerson, 1985b; Razin, 1984).

Because symptoms of heart disease, including heart attacks, occur only when the disease is already well advanced, many scientists view multifaceted preventive efforts to reduce the risk factors as the most effective way to reduce future incidence of the disease (Kannel,1984). This strategy gains support from the fact that past efforts to control hypertension, improve diet, and reduce smoking have been credited with the 30% drop in cardiovascular deaths in the past 20 years (Kerson, 1985b).

In addition to heredity as a nonchangeable risk factor, a cluster of demographic characteristics, most notably age and gender, also affect risk. The majority (55%) of all heart attack victims are at least age 65 (American Heart Association, 1988), and men are at much greater risk of heart disease than women. It is, in fact, the leading cause of death in men from age 40 onward. Because the disease likelihood increases for men after age 45, one in five men will develop coronary heart disease before reaching age 60. While women's risk increases markedly in their 50s, after menopause, their risk lags 20 years behind men's until old age. It is only past age 60 that heart disease becomes the leading cause of death in women. Viewed from a slightly different perspective, 55% of men's attacks occur before they reach age 65, but only 27% of women victims experience attacks before this age (Kannel, 1984; Kerson, 1985b; Passamani et al., 1984). One consequence of this imbalance is that most of the research literature on coronary patients focuses on male patients and their caregiving wives.

Patterns of heart disease also differ by race. Hypertension is significantly higher in blacks than in whites. The differences in hypertension by race are particularly dramatic for women, only 25% of white women having high blood pressure in contrast to 39% of black women. White males, with a 33% rate, are much closer to the 38% hypertension rate of black males. As a consequence of these generally higher rates, blacks are much more likely than whites to die of strokes, although whites have more heart attacks (American Heart Association, 1988; Kerson, 1985b).

In addition to these demographic characteristics, Lynch (1977) found that married people had lower coronary disease rates than their single counterparts. This relationship held for both sexes and for both blacks and whites. Lynch attributes the higher rates for singles to loneliness. In further exploration of this hypothesis, he found that those experiencing marital difficulties had a higher incidence of heart disease than those in happier marriages.

TYPES OF CARDIOVASCULAR DISEASE

Thus far, we have discussed heart disease as any problem of the heart or blood circulation. These problems usually stem from atherosclerosis, a natural process of thickening and hardening of the arteries with advancing age. Atherosclerosis can cause a variety of cardiovascular diseases (Kerson, l985b). The three most common are (1) heart attacks (myocardial infarctions), in which part of the heart muscle dies as a consequence of inadequate blood flow; (2) angina, or chest pains, caused by lack of blood and oxygen to the heart muscle (known as ischemia); and (3) stroke, in which brain tissue is destroyed by a blockage of blood and oxygen flow. (Because this consequence of cardiovascular disease has such a different disease course, treatment, and caregiver problems, it will be discussed in Chapter 5 as a separate chronic illness.)

Overall, nearly 65 million Americans, one in four, have some form of cardiovascular disease, most commonly hypertension (59 million). Each year, 1.5 million Americans become new victims of coronary vascular disease. Coronary heart disease, indicating past experience of heart attack or angina, affects almost 5 million.

The 20% to 30% of coronary patients that suffer from angina have more pain, need more medication, and have more physical limitations and psychosocial problems than the more studied victims of heart attacks. Currently, an increasing number of angina patients are receiving elective bypass surgery every year (Naughton, 1984). Interest in the effectiveness of bypass surgery has produced research on the subpopulation of angina patients, but their psychosocial problems remain unknown. Consequently, most of the information reported in subsequent sections derives from research on victims of heart attacks.

Of the 1.5 million heart attacks every year, one third result in death. Approximately half of these deaths are sudden. In fact, for 20% of heart attack victims, death is the first symptom of cardiovascular problems. Most heart attack deaths (60%) occur outside of hospitals and frequently involve the majority of victims who have waited more than two hours before seeking medical help (American Heart Association, 1988;

Kannel, 1984; Passamani et al., 1984). Many of these patients had experienced some symptoms for months prior to their attacks, which they refused to acknowledge (Finlayson & McEwen, 1977).

Treatment of heart problems varies by type and severity of problem. Quick identification of heart attack symptoms allows patients to seek emergency help with little delay. Immediate emergency cardiac care not only improves chances of survival but can also decrease the amount of permanent damage to the heart. In addition to continued heart monitoring and possible resuscitation, drugs may be used to dissolve blood clots, or arteries may be expanded with arterial balloons inflated at the point of blockage, a procedure known as angioplasty. After such emergency procedures stabilize patients, transfer to a coronary care unit permits intensive observation for the days following the attack. In the following weeks, doctors may decide to perform coronary bypass surgery, replace heart valves, insert pacemakers, or perform angioplasties to improve heart functioning and blood circulation (American Heart Association, 1988; Kerson, 1985b). Heart transplants have recently become a final option for extreme cases. Most patients leave the hospital within one to two weeks, and fewer than 15% of patients die during their hospitalization (Kerson, 1985b; Naughton, 1984).

Beyond the medical interventions outlined above, patients are invariably advised to reduce their future risk by modifying their life-styles. They are cautioned to stop smoking, reduce cholesterol, reduce weight, increase exercise, and reduce stress. Drugs may be prescribed to lower blood pressure or dilate narrowed arteries to increase oxygen supply (Kerson, 1985b). Following such treatment regimens, 80% of patients are able to return to work within three months of their attacks (American Heart Association, 1988).

In recent years, medical treatment has been modified to improve functioning and reduce disability of hospitalized coronary patients. Patients are now encouraged to move around early in the recovery process, they are routinely screened for the relatively new procedures of coronary bypass surgery and angioplasty, they receive sophisticated exercise testing and training, they and their families are given more information and education regarding recommended life-style changes, and they are discharged more quickly from hospitals. These measures are designed to permit patients to function more fully upon return to their families (Wenger & Hellerstein, 1984).

Despite such efforts, life continues to hold problems for the 70% who survive their first heart attack. The location and extent of destroyed heart tissue affects the patient's chances of survival and his or her functioning limitations, as well as the additional medical interventions that may be needed. One third will experience angina symptoms for the first time after their attack. Because of their well advanced atherosclerosis many may feel pain and shortness of breath and be at risk during strenuous activities that require normal blood flow. They also must live with the continued threat of sudden death. Croog and Levine (1982), for example, found that after one year, 5% of their sample of first heart attack patients had died and 20% had been rehospitalized. After eight years 27% had died and 23% had been rehospitalized at least once for additional heart problems. Including those who were hospitalized for other illnesses, only 30% survived eight years without further hospitalization. Other studies, with more seriously ill patients, have found a 50% mortality rate within five years of an attack. The well advanced problems that predate heart attacks ordain that most victims will continue to suffer progressive deterioration and further threats in their future experience with this chronic disease.

Despite these continued threats, most patients and their families adapt to the illness without undue stress. One factor that may minimize adjustment difficulties is the potentially high degree of control that heart patients have over the course of their illness. Unlike many other chronic illnesses, patients with cardiovascular problems are given many behavioral opportunities to impact on their future outcomes. Although they and their families may struggle with some of the recommended life-style changes indicated above, they also are empowered by such control opportunities.

PSYCHOSOCIAL REACTIONS
OF CARDIAC PATIENTS

The research literature on coronary heart disease, apart from focusing on etiological variables, has had a long-standing interest in the recovery process. A 1968 review of literature on factors predicting recovery, however, revealed a dearth of studies focusing on psychosocial variables (Croog, Levine, & Lurie, 1968). A decade later, Doehrman's (1977) update of this literature showed increasing attention to a variety of psychosocial factors affecting patient recovery. Drawing on this literature we will examine heart attack patients' experiences from the time of admission to coronary care units through transfer to less intensive hospital care, and then review what is known about their adjustment difficulties upon return home. It should be noted that most of the current research involves only victims of heart attacks, primarily male, rather than patients with other forms of coronary disease.

During Hospitalization

After hospitalization for a heart attack, most patients experience a short initial period of heightened anxiety. The coronary care unit (CCU), however, with its extensive monitoring and resuscitation equipment and specialized personnel, represents a safe haven for the majority of newly admitted patients (Hackett & Cassem, 1984). The literature reviewed by Doehrman (1977) found that most patients felt secure and protected during this early hospital period, despite the alien atmosphere. The structure of this unit at this early stage of recovery may insulate patients from emotional response and encourage passivity (Kerson, 1985b).

After transfer to a medical floor, patients begin to process their experience and often feel anxiety and depression. Anxiety peaks and then begins to subside within five or six days following a heart attack (Doehrman, 1977). The threat of death, as well as symptoms such as angina and shortness of breath, may be at the forefront of consciousness during this period. In contrast, depression does not usually emerge until patients leave the CCU, then lingers throughout the hospital and post-hospital periods of convalescence until normal roles can be resumed (Kerson, 1985b). As many as half of all coronary patients show serious depressive symptoms while in the hospital (Stern, 1984). Both anxiety and depression are considered to be normal reactions to heart attacks (Hackett & Cassem, 1979), but they are unrelated to severity of the attack (Stern, 1984).

Many patients attempt to manage their emotional reactions to their heart attacks by denying the seriousness of their coronary problems (Doehrman, 1977; Kerson, 1985b). Mayou, Williamson, and Foster (1978) found, for example, that 22% expressed no concern about their condition, 67% showed only mild distress, and the remaining 11% showed moderate distress. None were classified as severely distressed. Spouses had stress levels that were somewhat, but not much, higher. Stern (1984) suggests that approximately 25% of patients are "major deniers." Such denial may have the positive effects of reducing patient anxiety and facilitating return to prior roles. On the other hand, it may limit patients' willingness to modify their life-styles and adhere to recommended medical drug, diet, and exercise regimens. Hackett and Cassem (1984) state that denial leads to greater survival and speedier return to sexual and occupational functioning. This connection is still under investigation, however, because other studies do not invariably confirm this finding (Doehrman, 1977: Krantz & Deckel, 1983).

The above problems are exacerbated when surgery is required. The fear and physical effects of surgery further complicate the recovery process. Particularly with open heart surgery, which has become more common due to the increasing popularity of coronary bypass procedures, recovery is slow, painful, and often accompanied by depression (Kerson, 1985b). The large scar may be seen as mutilating. As with all illnesses, there is some interaction between the severity of the problem and the procedures implemented, making it difficult to tease out the separate impacts of each.

Length of hospitalization is largely dependent upon both of the above variables, as they combine with quickness of recovery. Currently, patients are generally encouraged toward ambulation and activity earlier in their hospital recovery. They are also trained in an exercise regime that will be increased and maintained beyond their hospital stay. Physical conditioning is thought to counteract depression as well as improve patient strength and endurance (Hackett & Cassem, 1984). Furthermore, both patients and their families are educated about the recommended life-style changes of diet, smoking, stress, and activity that may prevent further coronary problems. Finlayson and McEwen (1977) found both patients and families to be optimistic as discharge approached. Although better prepared than previously, patients are usually released from hospitals earlier, commonly within one to two weeks, requiring more extensive posthospital convalescence (Kerson, 1985b). They often still feel weak and debilitated, and many will experience angina pains. Only one quarter will be symptom free three months after the attack (Finlayson & McEwen, 1977).

Posthospital Convalescence

Two stages are distinguished for released coronary patients, (1) the convalescent period, typically lasting two to four weeks; and (2) the longer term recovery period, during which normal roles can be resumed.

This section will review what is known about patients' initial psychosocial reactions during the convalescent period and the changes that subsequently occur during the longer process of recovery.

Coronary patients commonly experience continuing anxiety and depression after their return home. For many patients, the euphoria of homecoming is quickly followed by a confrontation with their weakness and fatigue. These feelings combine to produce what Hackett and Cassem (1984) call "homecoming depression," which may last several months following hospitalization. Hackett and Cassem (1979) believe that depression is a common corollary of an infarction, usually triggered by loss of autonomy and its negative consequence for self-worth. The perpetual threat of sudden death combines with fear of incapacitation to produce serious adjustment difficulties (Krantz & Deckel, 1983). Although the actual figures vary from study to study, around half show feelings of depression, and 60% to 70% feel anxious (Block, Boyer, & Imes, 1984). For most, the levels of distress are mild, although still exceeding those expressed during hospitalization (Mayou, Williamson, & Foster, 1978). Interestingly, wives perceive their husbands to have higher distress than husbands themselves reveal.

For about half the patients, anxiety and depression subside within two weeks. Only 15% to 20% were still depressed six weeks after homecoming (Stern, 1984). The reactions of this subgroup of patients can continue for considerable lengths of time, and may be of sufficient severity to require medication. Continuing depression appears to correlate negatively with long-range patient adjustment and functioning (Krantz & Deckel, 1983). Neither anxiety nor depression seem to be related simply to the severity of the heart attack, and may impede recovery if untreated (Gulledge, 1979). Depressed patients have significantly lower rates of return to work and sexual functioning, as well as significantly higher rates of rehospitalization (Stern, 1984).

Recovery Period

As their strength improves, patients' anxieties center around two areas—their ability to resume their work roles and their sexual functioning (Krantz & Deckel, 1983). Initially, 90% of patients report diminished activities one month after returning home (Mayou, Williamson, & Foster, 1978). Although the majority of previously employed patients return to work—75% within 6 months and 85% within a year—they often have more restricted work patterns (Block et al.,

1984). Mayou, Foster and Williamson (1978b) found two thirds of workers had changed their physical activities at work. Younger and more professional workers have better work outcomes (Doehrman, 1977), while less educated, blue collar workers are less likely to reenter the labor market (Kerson, 1985b; Krantz & Deckel, 1983). Croog and Levine (1982), however, found that many professionals believed, eight years later, that their illness had impeded their career advancement. Further, most employed men (75%) continued to believe that the demands of their jobs had contributed to their heart attacks.

Most researchers report a significant decline in sexual activity following a heart attack (Block et al., 1984; Kerson, 1985b; Stern, 1984). Mayou, Foster, and Williamson (1978a) found a reduction of sexual activity in half the marriages one year later. This decline was related less to physical factors than to the fears of both partners of a recurrence or because of patient depression, although prescribed medications can also limit sexual response (American Heart Association, 1988; Gulledge, 1979). People are capable of resuming sexual relations within three to four weeks after a heart attack but many never do, or do so with diminished frequency and enjoyment (Stern, 1984).

Another role arena that may be affected is the patients' home responsibilities. Although Croog and Levine (1982) found that most men felt they were able to maintain their prior home roles, other family members often took on some of their tasks. Where such role shifts occurred, they seemed to be less related to illness severity than to the preexisting power dynamics in the marital relationship. Some patients may respond to their families' protective efforts by developing a pattern of passivity and dependency known as "cardiac invalidism." This common reaction leads patients toward overall restrictions in activity that are not required for health reasons (Gulledge, 1979; Hackett & Cassem, 1984; Krantz & Deckel, 1983).

In addition to the impact of the heart attack on work, sex, and family roles, many patients show decreases in overall levels of physical and social activities (Croog & Levine, 1982: Finlayson & McEwen, 1977). Even after four years, over half the men in Finlayson and McEwen's sample had more restricted leisure activities. They also expressed loss of self-confidence and self-esteem, and overall difficulties in adapting. Many felt humiliation at having family and others oversee or attempt to constrain their behavior. They conclude that "the male role as a strong, independent, virile husband and father, responsible as chief breadwinner in the family and capable of solving his own problems, appeared to be called into question to a greater extent than is the case in most other illness" (p. 171).

Many patients also find it difficult to make recommended life-style changes. They often do not take prescribed medication, nor maintain exercise programs (Block et al., 1984: Gulledge, 1979), and resent the deprivations required by cessation of smoking, diet restrictions, and activity limitations. Deniers and Type A patients may have greater problems with these restrictions (Kerson, 1985b). In Croog and Levine's (1982) sample, over one half indicated areas of noncompliance. Highest compliance was found for taking medications, but smoking cessation caused difficulties for many. Whereas most patients eliminated cigarettes while in the hospital, only one third were still non-smokers six months later (Finlayson & McEwen, 1977).

Croog and Levine (1982) suggest that the degree of patient compliance may vary directly with the specificity and clarity of recommended changes. Unfortunately, Mayou et al. (1978) found that 55% of their sample received vague advice from doctors, and expressed displeasure with its unhelpfulness. Finlayson and McEwen (1977) suggest that an additional problem for heart patients resides in the "double bind" created for them by the medical establishment, which communicates the expectation that their lives return to normal while also cautioning patients to avoid the many prior aspects of their lives that were harmful.

Longer Range Consequences

Overall, heart disease is not incapacitating or psychologically devastating for most patients. Most adjust quite well in the months following hospitalization (Stern, 1984). Finlayson and McEwen (1977) found that most of the patients and spouses in their study judged the illness to be over a year after the heart attack. By then 80% had returned to work, although some later withdrew again (Naughton,1984). Stern (1984) found that one year later, over 75% showed no abnormal anxiety or depression. Furthermore, a significant number, as many as 75% in Stern's study, viewed their heart attacks as having enhanced their perspectives and given them new appreciation of their lives (Finlayson & McEwen, 1977; Stern, 1984).

Nonetheless, current research suggests that some coronary patients suffer continued psychosocial problems in the months following their attacks. Finlayson and McEwen (1977), for example, found that normalcy was never restored for some of the patients in their study. They continued to struggle with recommended life changes, and often resented the perceived restrictions on their lives. They and their families lived in fear of sudden death. Many continued to experience pain and debilitation that impaired their ability to perform fully. Even after one year, two thirds of heart attack patients in Croog and Levine's (1977) sample had at least one physical symptom, and two out of three men in Finlayson and McEwen's (1977) study were experiencing chest pains four years later. These symptoms were frequently not reported to physicians, though, because patients continued to minimize their problems. With this tendency, it is not surprising that few avail themselves of any additional social services after leaving the hospital.

When we look at the predictors of longer term recovery we find few demographic, social, or psychological factors that consistently predict health outcome. The strongest predictor is severity of initial coronary problems. In addition, patients with lower occupational status and with greater depressive symptoms have worse health outcomes (Croog & Levine, 1982). Deniers may enjoy more rapid recovery, particularly in return to work, despite their greater likelihood of noncompliance with medical regimens (Naughton, 1984).

Interestingly, although men are more frequent victims, more women have further medical problems after their attacks. Stern's (1984) study, which included patients of both sexes, found that most women patients (nearly 80%) were rehospitalized within a year, in contrast to less than 10% of male patients. Further, within the first year, 45% of women died as compared to 20% of male victims (American Heart Association, 1988; Kannel, 1984; Passamani et al., 1984).

It is important to note that coronary patients' postinfarct adjustment is best predicted by prior levels of psychosocial adjustment rather than by health status (Block et al., 1984). There is some evidence that bypass surgery may be related to lower return to work and sexual functioning, although there may be less anxiety and depression because patients are prepared in advance for this elective surgery that could eliminate their persistent angina pains (Hackett & Cassem, 1984; Stern, 1984). In addition, patients who have better social support systems appear to adjust better upon return home (Croog & Levine, 1982). Lower class patients may also show worse psychosocial adjustment (Stern, 1984). Further, Stern also found that women patients showed significantly worse adjustment than did men. Most (80%) were depressed or anxious, and only a minority had returned to work or resumed sexual functioning within a year after their attacks.

PSYCHOSOCIAL REACTIONS
OF THE FAMILY

Until the late 1960s, research on heart disease did not examine the impact on family members. Clinical literature emphasized the need to involve the family in informational and therapeutic efforts, but little empirical information was provided to support this judgment (Croog et al., 1968). More recent, examination of family reactions has focused primarily on the ramifications for patients. As with family caregivers of the mentally ill, recommendations for family interventions have been justified from the perspective of improving patient outcomes rather than helping family members deal with their own difficulties. Stern (1984) concluded, "the spouse is frequently forgotten in a medical environment devoted to the patient" (p. 464). In view of this neglect, it should not be surprising that few studies have examined stresses of family members. Stern's (1984) review of existing literature suggested that 25% of spouses may experience anxiety and depression. Among the few longitudinal studies that included spouse interviews, Finlayson and McEwen (1977) found that family reactions, as well as patients', changed over time. During hospitalization, once the initial crisis abated, families were grateful for the medical care patients received as well as for their survival. They, like the patients, were optimistic and euphoric as patients neared discharge.

Once the patients returned home, optimism often faded as longer term implications were considered. As we have seen, the convalescent period requires family members to assume some of the role responsibilities previously held by patients. Sometimes spouses become oversolicitous in their efforts to relieve patients of domestic tasks and patients may feel useless and resent their dependence on others. Spouses often police patients' compliance with recommended regimens, becoming over-protective monitors of their well-being. These family responses may be particularly difficult for Type A patients, who often resist efforts to constrain their behavior.

Family members also may try to insulate patients from stress by concealing both problems and feelings. They may, in fact, feel that they contributed to the original attack by upsetting the patients (Gulledge, 1979; Kerson, 1985b). Twenty-two percent of the wives in Croog and Levine's (1982) sample believed that they had contributed to their husbands' attacks, and 26% of those with children believed that problems regarding their children had an impact. These attempts to avoid stress and family conflict may cause distance among family members.

Despite these strains, neither the physical nor emotional long-term demands on families of coronary patients seem excessive. Families seem to reintegrate the returning patients into their lives, and make necessary adjustments in life-style without undue stress. The literature conveys the impression that caretaking demands are short-term, focused primarily around the convalescent period, and involve minimal disruption for other family members. Caregiving stresses appear to focus around clashes involving patient adherence to recommended life-style changes, rather than around the physical demands of care.

AVAILABLE SERVICES
FOR PATIENTS AND FAMILIES

Most services for coronary patients begin during hospitalization. In addition to medically oriented interventions, such as physical therapy, relaxation training to lower stress, and diet instruction, patients and their families are now routinely offered the chance for individual and group social service interventions. More hospitals now involve spouses in educational aspects of their work with patients. Caregivers thus receive the same instructions regarding life-style changes that are offered to patients. Further, discussions about sexual issues are now likely to be initiated during the hospital stay. These individual efforts are commonly supplemented by a series of group meetings for patients and families, staffed by medical professionals. These group meetings, starting during hospitalization and extending for several months after homecoming, allow families to obtain information and to share experiences and problems in the recovery process. The groups, often called coronary clubs or cardiac clubs, have become a major mechanism for facilitating psychosocial adjustment. Patients who have had open-heart surgery have specialized groups, including "Mended Hearts" and so-called "Zipper Clubs," to deal with surgical sequelae.

Less commonly, patients are offered vocational services upon release, to better prepare them to reenter the work world. For those experiencing adjustment difficulties, individual, family, or group psychotherapy is available.

Despite greater recognition by the medical establishment that support services may facilitate patient recovery, very few patients receive more than routine medical follow-ups. As recently as 1984, Naughton observed that only 7.4% of recovered coronary patients had received any supportive services to facilitate rehabilitation.

RESEARCH ON CAREGIVER STRAINS
IN HEART DISEASE

As mentioned above, there have been only a handful of research studies that examine the stresses for caregivers of coronary patients. These studies first emerged in England during the early 1970s, and British samples still predominate in the data currently available. The population groups examined thus far are quite circumscribed. All of the five studies reviewed here focus their attention exclusively on heart attack victims who had been hospitalized after their first myocardial infarction. Furthermore, most of the studies limit their samples to middle-aged, married, male patients. A few have included patients over age 60 (Mayou et al., 1978; Skelton & Dominian, 1973), female patients (Dhooper, 1983; Mayou et al., 1978), those without spouses (Mayou et al., 1978), or the children of patients (Dhooper, 1983), but these subgroups remain in the minority.

The limited research currently available provides data that mainly document the scope and duration of caregiver strains. A few studies examine the links between such caregiver strains and patient adjustment. Only one study has focused on identifying the variables predicting differential strain among coronary caregivers. Thus, although we will highlight the few findings that examine such predictors, they will almost invariably be based on isolated studies. Only a limited number of predictors have thus far been examined by any studies, and few studies have included the same potential predictors. Even simple demographic comparisons are lacking. The few studies that have included varied demographic groups, such as male and female patients and their spouses, have not compared their differential reactions. Consequently, we do not know whether these subgroups respond in unique ways to heart attacks. Current findings regarding factors affecting caregiver stress should therefore be viewed as partial and suggestive rather than definitive.

Notwithstanding these considerable limitations, the current empirical literature provides us with reasonable data on the types of strain typically experienced by caregivers of heart attack patients. It also documents the duration of these strains, as well as their shifts over time, by longitudinal follow-ups of both patients and their spouses after hospital release. Because the studies reviewed here all sample general populations of first heart attack patients, rather than those seeking clinical help for adjustment problems, we can regard them as representative of typical patients. We will begin this section by examining the current findings regarding caregiver strains during the hospital and recovery periods, and then consider the more limited research on predictors of such strains.

Caregiver Reactions During Patient Hospitalization

The first study to investigate the psychological stresses of family members after a heart attack was published in 1973. Skelton and Dominian (1973) studied 65 wives of British patients who were interviewed during their husbands' hospitalizations and then at 3, 6 and 12 month follow-ups. This early work set the stage for subsequent studies in documenting that "a myocardial infarction can result in appreciable psychological difficulties for the wife" (p. 103). Skelton and Dominian observed that the wives' initial crisis reactions of numbness and a sense of unreality were quickly followed by feelings of guilt and self-blame as the women attempted to account for their husbands' attacks. Most showed early symptoms of depression and anxiety, nearly half ($N = 28$) in the severe range. Many also experienced psychosomatic symptoms during this time, ranging from headaches to stomach and chest pains.

Other studies, both in the United States and Great Britain, have confirmed these acute reactions of spouses. Mayou, Foster, and Williamson (1978b), studying a sample of 100 British admissions, observed that spouses often exhibited more initial distress than did the patients themselves, although the types of reactions, anxiety and depression, were similar. More recently, Dhooper's (1983) sample of 40 American families and patients revealed that strain and disruption of routines were almost universal among family members in the immediate aftermath of a heart attack. Nearly one quarter of these families were judged to have poor adjustment at this time.

Finlayson and McEwen's (1977) study of 76 British male patients suggests one of the factors that may be generating distress for spouses. Even at this early point, three quarters of the wives were already anticipating the difficulties they would have in dealing with their husbands during their convalescence. Interestingly, the women's greatest concern was that their husbands would be unwilling to change their behavior.

Caregiver Reactions During Patient Convalescence

Dhooper (1983) found that almost half the spouses had reestablished their normal role activities one month after hospitalization, although most (90%) were still experiencing some anxiety symptoms. By this time 30% were worrying about financial strains, which had not been of earlier concern. In contrast, their children's lives had pretty much returned to normal. All in all, adjustment problems had declined somewhat, although almost one quarter of the families were still experiencing serious emotional problems.

At two months, spouses in Mayou et al.'s (1978) sample expected that the patients' illness would have little residual impact on their lives. Most spouses (86%) had continued to work, and three fourths of those who smoked did not intend to quit, although they recognized the need for patients to stop smoking. More than one fourth, 27%, expected to continue to have increased role responsibilities. Overall, 25% of spouses were classified as showing severe stress at this point, somewhat belying the minimal behavioral changes perceived.

Dhooper (1983) observed that most of the families in his study had normalized their functioning after three months; although three quarters still expressed some anxiety, overall adjustment levels had improved noticeably. In contrast, Skelton and Dominian (1973) still found considerable anxiety and depression in 25 of 65 spouses three months later, which manifested itself in sleep disturbances and fear of reoccurrence, and seemed linked to husbands' reactions to their illness.

Longer Term Impact

One year after the heart attack, according to Skelton and Dominian (1973), 16 of the 65 caregivers continued to show poor adjustment, with continued depression, anxiety, and sleep disturbances. Although Mayou et al. (1978a) also found continued major psychosocial symptomatology in a substantial number of couples (approximately one third), they were also struck by the number of couples reporting positive marital impact. Despite the fact that frequency of sexual intercourse had declined in half of the marriages, one quarter of the couples reported that their marriages had improved following the heart attack, and another 56% indicated no change. Furthermore, the authors were able to classify 66% of the families as having a good marital outcome. Mayou et al. (1978a) interpret this finding as demonstrating that couples may have begun to appreciate each other more, and no longer take their partners for granted after this life-threatening experience. Finlayson and McEwen (1977) also found some wives reporting that their husbands had become more considerate or better tempered upon return home. In further support, 40% of the families in Dhooper's (1983) study reported improvements in family functioning that could be attributed to the crisis.

A number of the above studies suggest that outcome indicators measuring the amount of role change show more caregiver impact than do indicators measuring adjustment. For example, even after a year, families in Mayou et al.'s (1978a) study reported that over half the patients had decreased their participation in household tasks, with another 11% of families indicating a considerable decrease. A great deal of protectiveness was still manifest, with 35% of spouses constantly expressing concern over patient actions, and another 29% showing occasional protectiveness. As we have seen, most families did not show long-term distress, however, and often saw improvements in family relationships. This suggests that families had modified their task allocations and interpersonal dynamics without undue difficulty.

Finlayson and McEwen's (1977) more intensive examination of 76 British wives' adaptation confirmed the above patterns, revealing that half the wives still felt increased role responsibilities one year later. Although some wives showed increasing health problems themselves, most accommodated to such changes with little perception of difficulty. Finlayson and McEwen suggest that the wives saw their adaptations as part of their normal family role, rather than as a new burden. They managed to adjust to the required changes with little change in other roles, especially work. Perhaps the wives' early anticipation of changes during the hospital period, mentioned above, facilitated their longer term adjustment.

Along with other researchers, Finlayson and McEwen also found that wives' work roles were not impeded beyond the initial crisis period surrounding hospitalization. Work involvement, in fact, was viewed as both a source of financial security and a welcome distraction from worry by most working wives in their sample.

Croog and Levine's (1982) ambitious longitudinal study of 345 married male patients supported the pattern found by Finlayson and McEwen. The patients in their sample also perceived little change in their roles or life-style after either the one year or the eight year follow-up. Most patients, however, did perceive changes in their wives' behavior. After eight years, patients reported that 63% of wives still showed psychosocial effects, with 38% manifesting anxiety and 21% displaying overprotectiveness. Even among those not classified as over-protective, Croog and Levine found that 81% of husbands felt that their wives were still trying to restrict their activities. Interestingly, these restrictive efforts were uncorrelated with the severity of the patients' illness. An early study by New, Ruscio, Priest, Petritsi, and George (1968) suggests one possible reason for this discrepancy: family perceptions of patients' functioning level is frequently inaccurate. New et al.'s data revealed that only 2 of 18 heart and stroke patients and their families were in agreement regarding patient functional capacity. Spouses were equally likely to err on either side of reality, but children were more likely to perceive their parents as more dependent than the parents judged themselves. These data suggest that family perceptions of illness severity are not closely related to the reality of patients' conditions. Such perceptions may, in fact, be better predictors of family reactions than patients' actual physical conditions. No study has yet included this variable in its investigation.

Overall, family reactions to the crisis of a heart attack appear to show appropriate behavioral adaptations to patients' illness, with only limited interference with other life roles. Actual care demands do not appear to be extensive. The major caregiving burdens are psychological, involving the continued fears of sudden death and the related desire to protect patients from life-threatening activities, stresses, or exertions. A significant minority of spouses, ranging from one quarter to one third, show long-term, continuing psychosocial distress. As Crawshaw stated:

> It has been said that the patient may recover from his coronary but that his wife may not. She has often seen her husband when he looked near to death, she may have been warned that he could die. . . . She has the same fears,

lack of knowledge, and misconceptions as her husband. . . . Months after the infarct many wives report that they lie awake listening to their husbands' breathing to make sure that he is still alive. . . . Alternatively, wives may take over decision-making and bread-winning roles and become highly overprotective; this may increase the patient's feelings of helplessness and despondency. (Gulledge, 1979, pp. 116-117)

RESEARCH ON FACTORS AFFECTING CAREGIVER STRESS

Although the five studies reviewed above measure and document the degree, type, and duration of stresses for caregivers, only Dhooper (1983) focused on isolating the factors affecting caregiver adjustment. Although his study is limited by both sample size and variables included, it does represent an initial effort to identify variables important to both spouses' and children's adjustment at different points in the recovery process. Therefore, the following discussion of the research literature, dealing with factors identified in Chapter 2 as relevant to caregiver reaction, will draw primarily from Dhooper's analysis, but will also incorporate the more fragmentary findings relevant to this issue that were part of the four earlier studies.

Objective Stressors

Severity of Illness

Illness severity is a key factor in family reaction, both during the initial period of hospitalization and in its aftermath. In the immediate hospital period, Dhooper found that family adjustment could be partially explained by the objective circumstances of the severity of the illness. Interestingly, severity of illness became a more important predictor in Dhooper's one month and three month follow-ups, when it emerged as the most influential variable in the family's psychosocial adjustment.

Earlier studies had previously suggested the centrality of the illness severity variable identified by Dhooper. For example, Skelton and Dominian (1973) found that wives' long-range adjustment was better when their husbands had returned to work within the first year, indicating a better overall recovery. Croog and Levine's (1977) long-term follow-up studies emphasized the salience of illness severity as a key factor in both patient and family adjustment (as reported by the patient). Thus severity of illness seems to be a replicated predictor to family adjustment. In fact, this variable emerges as the strongest and most consistent predictor of family response of any studied so far.

Patient Reaction

Beyond Dhooper's study showing the longitudinal impact of illness severity on family adjustment, little else can be found that focuses on objective variables affecting adjustment. There is, however, some suggestion in Skelton and Dominian's (1973) study that husbands' reactions to their illness may impact on their wives' adaptation. Specifically, Skelton and Dominian suggested that when husbands showed continued dependency and irritability, wives had more adjustment difficulties. This finding seems reasonable, because such patient behaviors would increase the task demands on spouses.

In apparent contradiction to Skelton and Dominian's findings regarding dependency, Mayou et al. (1978) found that wives of the 25% of patients who had returned to work within two months showed more strain than wives whose husbands were still at home. These patients may have returned to their jobs before they should have, and may have been generally more difficult for their wives to deal with concerning general issues of compliance. Perhaps these two contrasting findings may be reconciled if we view both premature and delayed return to prior activities as problematic for caregivers. Either of these extreme patient reactions may create problems for caregivers.

In summary, severity of illness is the main factor found to predict to family adjustment. Beyond this variable, there is some indication that patients who resume their normal roles either very early or very late may create additional caregiver strains.

Contextual Variables

Despite the ease with which demographic variables can be incorporated into most research studies, very few of the studies reviewed above chose to examine caregiver background factors that affect strain. This omission appears to be a consequence of homogeneity in the samples studied. Thus studies that focus on the wives of middle-aged, middle-class men have already controlled for most central demographic factors. In this section, we will review first the limited findings in caregiver characteristics that affect their strain, and then proceed to the more extensive arena of relational variables impacting on caregiver reaction.

Caregiver Characteristics

There is some evidence that caregiver reactions at any point in the recovery process are best predicted from prior psychosocial status. An early finding of Skelton and Dominian (1973) was that wives with greater prior psychosocial problems were more vulnerable to the impact of their husbands' heart attacks. Longitudinal studies have generally found consistency between early and later psychosocial stresses for caregivers following the heart attack. Dhooper (1983) found that lower class families revealed fewer adjustment difficulties than their middle-class counterparts, and Skelton and Dominian (1973) found early evidence that younger wives exhibited greater distress than their older counterparts.

More recently, Young and Kahana (1987) have provided much more detailed data on the impact of gender and relationship on caregivers' reactions. With regard to gender, women caregivers showed more negative impacts than did men on a number of outcome indicators. Female caregivers reported both more physical and mental health symptoms as well as great social impact on other aspects of their lives. They also reported being more upset by patients' moods. Overall, they felt significantly more burdened by their caregiving role than did men (which corresponded, probably not by chance, to the objective fact that they also provided more hours of assistance).

In addition to gender, Young and Kahana also found differences based on caregiver relationship to patient. Spouses, who constituted the majority of caregivers, were in poorer health than nonspouse helpers (mainly daughters). Despite the findings that spouses were older, in worse health, and gave more hours of care than did nonspouse caregivers, Young and Kahana also found that spouses felt less burdened by their caregiving role than did nonspouses. They suggest that the marital role may include the expectation of such caregiving needs in later years, which facilitates spouse adjustment.

Based on these data, women had greater difficulty than men with the caregiving role, although wives expressed fewer problems than did daughters. These gender differences parallel those found in other caregiving populations, as did the suggestion that earlier adjustment difficulties may affect later reactions of caregiving.

Relational Variables

As stated above, relational factors affecting caregiver adjustment have received research attention over the past decade. A few studies have examined the relationships among family members; more have focused on the factor of social support in caregiver adjustment.

Family Relationships

The early Skelton and Dominian study (1973) first suggested that the general quality of the marital relationship prior to the crisis may affect wives' adjustment. In support of this variable, Finlayson and McEwen (1977) found that families in their research that had less communication and expressiveness also had less adequate adjustment. They suggested that, for wives in such circumstances, the presence of other supports could provide a buffer against psychosocial problems. In further support for the impact of family functioning, Dhooper's more recent research (1983) found that the families' internal cohesion was significant for adjustment both during patients' hospitalization and during the one- and three-month follow-ups. Thus the evidence currently available suggests that caregivers in closer relationships with patients adapt better to their role.

Social Support

Many of the earlier studies dealing with caregiver impact emerged out of a social networks orientation, providing much data on the variable of social support. The following discussion reports data on the social support patterns found, as well as the relationship between support and caregiver outcome.

Croog and Levine's (1977) groundbreaking longitudinal study in the United States on psychosocial factors in recovery established the centrality of social support for patients at different points in their experience—during hospitalization, after one year, and eight years after the heart attack. Their work provided evidence that social support is a key factor in patient adjustment, and they identified the family as the key element in patient support, with the contributions of adult children increasing over time. Croog and Levine (1977) also found that close kin, such as parents and siblings, were also of continuing support. Their work emphasized the equivalent contributions of friends and neighbors, who became "quasi-family" in helping patients deal with the aftermath of their heart attack. It is worth noting that even eight years later, 97% of the patients in Croog and Levine's study were still receiving some help from others. As Croog and Levine noted, however, patients rarely made use of formal agency services.

During the same time period, Finlayson and McEwen (1977) were also studying the impact of social networks on a sample of British heart patients in England. Their study is especially valuable because it was the first to ask patients' wives about their own social supports. Most of the wives received high levels of support from many people during the initial hospitalization. Children were a source of help in 60% of the families, and half received some assistance from close kin, usually mothers or sisters. Comparable to the patients' reports in Croog and Levine's study, after one year the level of support from kin had declined greatly, although children's help continued. Finlayson and McEwen also found some class differences in the patterns of help received. Wives of manual workers tended to rely more on children, but wives of higher level patients sought more support from their husbands and nonkin. Finlayson and McEwen observed more help from the husbands' work associates in middle-class families.

Finlayson and McEwen found that wives who received more support during the initial crisis appeared to show better psychosocial outcomes. They also found, as did Croog and Levine, that this support is predictive of a better recovery for husbands. Thus social support for the wife, as well as for the patient, seems an important factor in later adjustment.

More recently, Dhooper (1983) found that families' social integration and support during hospitalization was crucial to their initial psychosocial adjustment. After one month the amount of help received from others was a much weaker predictor, suggesting that such assistance may recede rapidly in the wake of the crisis. Other social factors retained their importance at later points. Specifically, family cohesion and social integration were still important correlates of family adjustment. In Dhooper's view, this continued salience of social integration argues for the importance of social network links in family adaptation to a coronary crisis.

In a later study, Dhooper (1984) studied characteristics that predicted to social support. His data suggested the central place of adult children in support-giving. Siblings, friends, and neighbors were other important sources of support. Dhooper also found social class differences in support, with those in higher social classes receiving more informal social support.

Mayou et al. (1978a) found patterns of support that paralleled those reported by Dhooper. They also noted the centrality of adult children in the helping process, particularly after return to the home. At this point, children took on many of the household tasks, as well as helping with patient care during convalescence, and their help was still in evidence after a year. Mayou et al. (1978a) also found, again in agreement with other studies, that friends and neighbors were very supportive during the early hospital period, but were not as available at later points. Finally, they were struck by the dearth of professional assistance received by the families in their study. Only 7 of the 40 families had any formal intervention, all from social service departments during husbands' hospitalization. They noted the lack of such services for the other 33 families, and the total absence of any services after hospital release, when financial concerns begin to emerge for many families.

The above examination of informal social supports for coronary patients provides us with some evidence that such support does influence both patients and families in their later adjustment. It also suggests the consistently central role of adult children in helping their parents weather this crisis. Their efforts are supplemented by those of close kin, mainly mothers and sisters, during the early period of hospitalization. For many, friends and neighbors often provide as much help as kin during this time. And for many families, especially those of higher social class, work associates serve as an additional aid source.

In conclusion, the current literature reviewed above only begins to examine the range of possible variables relevant to caregiver adjustment. There appears to be strong evidence that illness severity is a critical factor in adjustment, that women react more strongly than men do, and that social support facilitates family adaptation. More tentatively, we can view these findings as also suggesting that older, lower-class spouses, who are psychologically healthy and have good marital relationships, as well as good support systems, adapt better, especially if their husbands' heart attacks resulted in fewer adjustment problems for the husbands. It should be kept in mind that these isolated associations emerge from studies of small samples of British patients that may not typify the coronary population elsewhere.

5

Caregiving in Stroke

Coauthored with Marie T. Rau

Stroke is a syndrome involving neurologic deficit of relatively rapid onset produced by one of several conditions that impairs circulation of blood to the brain or spinal cord. There are many causes of stroke, including infarction resulting from thrombotic or embolic occlusion of a cerebral artery, or spontaneous rupture of a vessel resulting in intracerebral or subarachnoid hemorrhage. Occlusions or ruptures due to traumatic, neoplastic, or infectious processes that produce vascular pathology are not included as part of this syndrome.

There can be a wide variation of symptoms of stroke affecting motor, sensory, cognitive, language, and other functions depending on the areas of the brain involved. The majority of strokes (approximately 80%) involve infarcts, or the blockage of blood flow to the cerebral hemispheres.

Stroke is one of the most frequently occurring acute health crisis events afflicting older persons. Estimates of the annual incidence of all types of strokes in the United States range from approximately 600,000 (Robins & Baum, 1981) to 750,000 (Rubenstein & Federman, 1982). The annual incidence of initial strokes is 300,000 (Robins & Baum, 1981). Prevalence studies indicate that approximately 2.7 million Americans age 20 and over have had at least one stroke when both hospitalized and nonhospitalized persons are included. The national prevalence rate is about 1.6 million if only persons who were hospitalized for the stroke are included (Baum, 1982; Kuller, 1978).

NOTE: Marie T. Rau, Ph.D., Audiology & Speech Pathology Service, Veterans Administration Medical Center, Portland, Oregon.

Stroke is largely a disease of older persons; 57% or 1.5 million stroke survivors are age 65 and older. Of the new strokes that occur in this country each year, 80% affect persons over age 65 (Freese, 1980; Stallones, Dyken, Fang, Heyman, Seltser, & Stamler, 1972). The incidence of strokes of all types, including brain infarction and cerebral hemorrhage, increases sharply with increasing age (Freese, 1980; Robins & Baum, 1981). The median age for first strokes in men in the United States is 71 years, and for women is 74 years (Weinfeld, 1981).

Stroke is the third leading cause of not only mortality in older persons, but also of chronic long-term disability. About 60% of stroke victims survive the acute event, and 40% of the survivors require some type of special services or assistance (Freese, 1980). In his analysis of the results of a community survey of a national stroke sample, Baum (1982) estimated that 70% of stroke victims were somewhat limited in their activities, and more than two thirds were limited in their major activities. Results from the Framingham Study of stroke survivors indicated that 31% were dependent in self care, 20% were dependent in mobility, 71% had decreased vocational function, 62% reported decreased socialization outside the home, and 16% were institutionalized when evaluated a minimum of six months after the onset of a stroke (Gresham, Fitzpatrick, Wolf, McNamara, Kannel, & Dawber, 1975).

Although the annual incidence of stroke has been declining steadily in recent years in the United States as well as in other industrialized nations (Garraway, Whisnant, & Drury, 1983: Soltero, Liu, Cooper, Stamler, & Garside 1978), survival rates have been increasing (Garraway, Whisnant, Kurland, & O'Fallon, 1979). This suggests that the decline in stroke incidence has not resulted in a comparable decline in the number of disabled stroke survivors and their families requiring support and assistance. In fact, the prevalence of stroke in the population has remained constant over the past several decades because of major improvement in long-term survival following cerebral infarction (Garraway, 1985). In the Framingham stroke study, women had a five-year survival rate of 60%, and men had a five-year survival rate of 52%. The ten-year survival rate in this study overall was 35% (Sacco, Wolf, Kannel, & McNamara, 1982). In recent long-term follow-up studies of stroke patients who had participated in rehabilitation, the mean survival time exceeded seven years (Anderson, Anderson, & Kottke, 1977; Anderson & Kottke, 1978). Thus while a substantial percentage of stroke sufferers (approximately 30%) do not survive the first 30 days, a large number of stroke patients will survive many years with chronic physical and psychosocial disabilities. Furthermore, a very high percentage of these people will be cared for at home or in the community, primarily by spouses and other relatives (Ahlsio, Britton, Murray, & Theorell, 1984; DeJong & Branch, 1982; Holbrook, 1982).

IMPACTS OF STROKE
ON PATIENTS AND CAREGIVERS

In addition to its acute, life-threatening aspects, the occurrence of a stroke is often followed by significant negative life changes for the victim, including role loss, relocation to sheltered care settings, and increased dependency on others because of physical and cognitive disabilities. Furthermore, a cerebrovascular accident frequently disturbs an individual's ability to communicate and to interact socially in other ways with family and friends. Equally as important are the impacts of the stroke on the primary caregiver and other members of the family. Buck (1968) has correctly characterized stroke as a "family disease."

The available literature on the impacts of stroke on the patient and family is largely descriptive, not often data-based, and almost always lacking in comparison or control groups. Nevertheless, the existing reports and studies do suggest a strong relationship between stroke outcome (as measured by adaptation, physical and psychological well-being, and functional independence) and a variety of family interactional and psychosocial variables. This points to the importance of exploring the impacts of this chronic, disabling illness on both victim and family members.

Clinical Impact on Patient

Clinical reports and review articles on the sequelae of brain damage describe cognitive, behavioral, and personality changes which may accompany stroke (Binder, 1983; Gordon & Diller, 1983; Horenstein, 1970; Lezak, 1978a, 1978b; Stein, Hier, & Caplan, 1985). Common emotional problems seen in stroke patients include emotional distress, especially anxiety; frustration; and depression (Binder, 1983). Estimates of the prevalence of clinically significant levels of depression after stroke range from 26% to 60% (Feibel & Springer, 1982; Robinson & Szetela, 1981). Robinson and his colleagues (Robinson, Bolduc, Kubos, Starr, & Price, 1985), who evaluated 50 stroke patients in the hospital and at six months after discharge, found that in-hospital depression as well as physical and intellectual impairments predicted social functioning at six months' follow-up.

Other common problems observed in stroke survivors include: overdependence on others, inflexible and rigid thinking, impatience, irritability, impulsivity, denial and lack of awareness of problems, insensitivity, poor social perception, perplexity, distractibility, and fatigue (Binder, 1983; Lezak, 1978b; Stein et al., 1985). Lezak (1978a) cites five broad and somewhat overlapping categories of characterological alterations secondary to brain injury that are most likely to create adjustment problems for families: (1) impaired capacity for social perceptiveness manifested as self-centeredness, and diminished empathy and self-reflective or self-critical attitudes; (2) impaired capacity for control and self-regulation, resulting in impulsivity, random restlessness, impatience, and conceptual and behavioral rigidity; (3) stimulus-bound behavior, reflected as social dependency, difficulty in planning and organizing activities or projects, decreased or absent behavioral initiative, and rigidity; (4) emotional alterations manifested as apathy, silliness, lability, irritability, and changes in the sex drive; and (5) inability to profit from experience, leading to lessened capacity for social learning. Even mildly impaired stroke patients will complain of what Lezak (1978b) has called "subtle sequelae of brain damage": perplexity, distractibility, and fatigue. Although not all persons who suffer a stroke, and their families, will have to deal with all of these behavioral and cognitive changes, it is readily apparent that most of this list has the potential to cause serious disruption in social interaction between the stroke victim and significant others.

While some behavioral and cognitive changes may be characteristic of brain damage per se, other changes are related to the site of the lesion, specifically to whether the stroke affects the right or left cerebral hemisphere. Right hemisphere brain damage has been associated with lack of concern and awareness of stroke-related deficits, reduced perception of recognition of the affective and emotional aspects of communication, less spontaneity, increased latency of action, and difficulty in persevering with a task, in addition to visual-spatial and constructional deficits (Stein et al., 1985). Patients with left hemisphere damage, on the other hand, are more likely to experience significant speech and language deficits because the left cerebral hemisphere plays a crucial role in verbal and written communication. Although the effects of a left hemisphere stroke on interactions with family and friends may appear to be more critical, some persons with relatively small right hemisphere lesions do not make the expected social, family, and work-related adaptations following a stroke.

Data-based studies have tended to confirm the clinical reports and reviews of the impacts of stroke. Some studies have focused only on the stroke victims, others only on the principal caregivers, while others have studied the impacts of stroke on both. Taken as a whole, these studies suggest that, while the problems related to physical disability and physical changes may be considerable, disruptions in the social lives of stroke families cannot be explained on the basis of the severity of the stroke or of the physical disability alone.

Psychosocial Reaction of Stroke Patients

Labi, Phillips, and Gresham (1980), who studied long-term survivors of stroke in the Framingham Study, found that a significant proportion of the stroke survivors manifested psychosocial disability despite complete or near complete physical recovery. Specifically, three parameters of social function were analyzed to determine the degree of social reintegration of these long-term survivors of stroke: socialization in the home, socialization outside of the home, and hobbies and interests. Labi and her colleagues found that in a group of those who could ambulate independently, or who had not experienced any change in their mode of transportation nor taken any falls, about half decreased their socialization outside the home after the stroke. Further, there was no significant difference found in social activities between those who had fallen during the previous year and those who had not. About one third of the subjects who had resumed most or all of their household responsibilities did not resume their prestroke social activities. Of those with no residual neurologic deficits (hemiparesis, hemisensory defect, hemianopsia, dysarthria, aphasia), 40% had decreased their socialization outside the home, 32% had decreased their participation in hobbies and interests. The authors concluded that "much of this social disability cannot be accounted for by age, physical impairment, or specific neurologic deficits" (Labi et al., 1980, p. 561). A strength of this investigation was the use of an age-matched control group of nonstroke victim study participants.

A possible explanation for the results of the Framingham Study is what Hyman has called the "stigma of stroke" (Hyman, 1971). In studying the rehabilitation motivation and the amount of functional improvement in a sample of 110 stroke patients with hemiplegia, Hyman hypothesized "that feelings of stigma may render the prospect of social interaction unrewarding to the patient. He would therefore become conditioned to minimizing his social contact" (Hyman, 1971, p. 133). Hyman operationally defined feelings of stigma in patients as the belief "that others think less of them, avoid them, or feel uneasy with them because of their illness or disability" (Hyman, 1971, p. 132). He further speculated that patients who reported feelings of stigma at the beginning of a rehabilitation program would be rated by their physical therapist and physician as less motivated after one month of therapy. Hyman found that feelings of stigma manifested at the start of the program adversely affected motivation at one month as well as functional status at discharge, despite the fact that both the stigmatized and nonstigmatized patients had been comparable on levels of functional ability and on other medical variables at the beginning of the program. Patients who felt stigmatized at the start of rehabilitation were less likely to resume household tasks performed prior to discharge. He also found that of the patients without feelings of being stigmatized, 73% resumed all premorbid leisure activities, and of the stigmatized patients, only 45% had resumed all premorbid leisure activities. Interestingly, these negative relationships between degree of stigma and level of motivation and ADL independence were limited to those patients who premorbidly were more socially active.

Hyman also, and perhaps more importantly, found a nonsignificant but suggestive association between the patients' feelings of stigma and their relatives' perception of them as stigmatized. This study suggests important connections between individual reactions to chronic impairment and the social network's reactions to the individual.

Other recent descriptive studies of stroke outcome have tended to confirm that psychosocial impairments and distress in stroke survivors cannot be explained by the level of physical disability alone. Isaacs and his colleagues (Isaacs, Neville, & Rushford, 1976; Isaacs, 1982) followed for three years, or until they died, a group of 29 stroke survivors who were discharged home. Of the 18 who were still living after three years, none had returned to employment, and few engaged in any activities outside the home.

A Swedish study (Ahlsio et al., 1984) followed 96 recent stroke patients for two years, completing interviews with 50 of the subjects at all four interview times (at discharge, and at one month, six months, and two years postdischarge). Of the survivors at two years, 76% were independent in activities of daily living (ADLs) and lived at home. The researchers had subjects rate their quality of life before and after the stroke using a visual analogue scale. Results indicated that most stroke victims had experienced a decrease in their subjective quality of life, and that no improvement in this aspect of their lives was observed over the two-year period. Although ADL function improved during follow-up, quality of life did not. Depression and anxiety were found to be equally as important as ADL status in predicting quality of life. Furthermore, depression or anxiety in the acute phase of the illness was predictive of greater decrease in quality of life at two years.

Lawrence and Christie (1979) found evidence of poor adaptation to their poststroke situation in 45 persons who had suffered a stroke three years previously. They classified subjects as having "minimal" or "moderate" levels of physical disability, having no survivors in their sample with severe residual physical disability. They classified reactions to disability and to the stroke victim's situation as appropriate or inappropriate. An appropriate response was defined as either minimal disruption in the person's prestroke life situation, or realistic response to disability and life-style changes. Inappropriate responses were categorized as those reflecting denial or exaggeration of problems, little adaptation to stroke-related changes, or frank behavioral disturbance. Over one half of these stroke survivors were judged to have an inappropriate response to their situation, including 44% of those with minimal impairment. Twenty-two of the subjects exhibited either denial or exaggeration of their problems, with little or no constructive effort been made to adapt to difficulties, while two were felt to show gross behavioral disturbance with "little grasp of reality." These researchers found no significant relationship between the degree of disability and the appropriateness of the adaptive response. Though they did find a significant association between level of disability and degree of optimism about the future, over half of the subjects with minimal disability were uncertain or pessimistic regarding the future. Other negative changes experienced by these stroke survivors in the three-year period included a marked change in occupational status, significant decreases in active leisure activities, and deterioration of interpersonal relationships within the household in one third of those with minimal disability and two thirds of those with moderate physical impairment.

In another study that examined quality of life issues, Trudel, Fabia, and Bouchard (1984) interviewed 50 persons who had undergone carotid endarterectomy from 81 to 105 months prior to the investigation. Some of these persons had experienced completed strokes, that is, stroke-related neurological symptoms which persisted for longer than 24 hours; however, all subjects were described as having minimal dysfunction in ADLs and cognition. Subjects were retrospectively classified into low or medium preoperative risk groups based on other medical problems and severity of cerebrovascular disease as determined by angiography. Those in the medium-risk group were found to have marked dysfunction in home and outside activities and social interaction, and half of those previously working had taken early retirement. Quality of life, the authors concluded, appeared to be more affected by cardiovascular problems in the medium-risk group, and by neurologic problems in the low-risk patients. Overall, only 10 of the 50 subjects were found to have a normal functional level. We thus see that even in a population with minimal impairment, and who underwent carotid artery surgery to prevent the occurrence of a debilitating stroke, psychosocial outcomes were, on the whole, poor.

In summary, the studies of the impacts of stroke on patients lead to the conclusion that psychological and social factors, including interpretation of the stroke event and social support, may be just as important as physical status or initial level of disability in determining outcomes such as quality of life and return to prestroke levels of social and work-related activities. This conclusion should be qualified by two observations. First, self-report data regarding subjective well-being and quality of life is limited to patients with relatively low levels of impairment since the severely cognitively impaired would have difficulty communicating with researchers. Second, we must be cautious in interpreting stroke patient self-reports since it is difficult to know whether evaluative or affect-laden reports are the direct consequence of neurological damage or the indirect consequences of being aware of having had a stroke and/or being disabled.

SUPPORT SERVICES
FOR PATIENTS AND CAREGIVERS

A stroke episode typically begins with an acute event that causes the patient to be hospitalized. In the hospital a variety of imaging methods are used to identify the location and extent of brain damage resulting from the stroke. At the same time, behavioral and cognitive function tests are used to assess the magnitude of functional disabilities resulting from the stroke. Recovery from disabilities depends on a number of factors including the amount of brain damaged, the age of the patient, and the magnitude of the rehabilitation effort. Depending upon the types of functional disabilities exhibited by the patient, rehabilitation may consist of physical, occupational, and speech therapy. Counseling or formal psychological support services aimed at helping the patient cope with sequelae of stroke are rarely provided. However, many hospitals provide informal support services to both patients and family members to help them cope with stroke. Most often these services are provided through support groups that meet on a regular basis. These groups may be composed exclusively of patients or caregivers, and in some cases of both. Although there are both theoretical and practical reasons for believing that support groups provide a valuable service to patients and caregivers, no data are available to substantiate this.

IMPACT OF STROKE
ON CAREGIVERS AND FAMILIES

Studies examining the impact of stroke on caregivers fall into two general categories. The majority focus exclusively on assessing impact on the caregiver or primary support person; the remainder attempt to simultaneously appraise the reactions of both the patient and the caregiver. In the discussion that follows, we consider first those studies that assess both patient and caregiver outcomes.

Belcher, Clowers, and Cabanayan (1978) interviewed 73 poststroke individuals with a mean age of 60 years. Forty-two were married, and 31 single. The spouses of the married stroke victims were also interviewed. The focus of this study was on the current rehabilitation needs of this population. While vocational needs were more important to the single stroke survivors, social psychological needs were found to be more important to the married stroke victims and their spouses. The authors concluded that while many postdischarge stroke patients express the need for more physical rehabilitation, a more predominant concern is psychosocial rehabilitation. Neither levels of distress nor other symptoms of psychological dysfunction were measured in this study.

In a three-year follow-up study of 32 stroke families, Cohen (1978) found that two thirds of the 21 survivors were ambulatory and continent at the end of the three-year period. All 32 had been discharged to live in the community—half home to their own immediate family, 4 to live with children, and 12 to live alone in the community with some assistance. These relatively independent stroke survivors were found at three years to be gloomy, reserved, and withdrawn, with little effort shown to maintain social contacts. Significant personality changes were observed, which the author attributed to the effects of brain damage and to changes in patterns of living imposed by restricted opportunities for socializing. Families reported such problems as irritable, combative, and uncooperative behavior; marked depression; incontinence; and loss of appetite. Before their CVAs 18 of 32 had been employed full-time and 7 were performing housekeeping activities with no problem. After the stroke, none returned to gainful employment, and only 3 were able to resume some housekeeping activities. More than half suffered a substantial decrease in their economic well-being. About half of those who survived the first year did not leave the house, and others got out only occasionally.

Holbrook (1982) reported data from two follow-up studies of a total of 180 stroke patients and families interviewed two to five years after the stroke. She found that stroke patients and their caregivers reported different concerns and different negative impacts of the stroke. Stroke survivors reported that the stroke had adversely affected their relationship with the family, their relationship with their spouse, and their sex life. Specific concerns centered around mobility, health, and finances. For the caregivers, adverse effects of the stroke were related to finances, social mobility and social life, interpersonal relationships, sex life, working life, and physical health. One third of both stroke victims and caregivers described themselves as "not adjusted" to the stroke two to five years afterward. The investigators noted that adjustment did not necessarily occur if the residual physical disability was slight, and that stroke victim adjustment did not necessarily predict caregiver adjustment.

A younger sample of stroke survivors and their spouses was studied by Coughlan and Humphrey (1982). They interviewed, by means of a mail questionnaire, 170 spouses of stroke patients who had received rehabilitation up to eight years earlier. Information was obtained from these spouses about both the stroke victim's status and their own experience regarding the stroke. All stroke victims were less than 65 years old at the time of the CVA, and 40% were under 50. At three to eight years after the stroke, two thirds of the stroke survivors were described as having some problems with self-care while almost half had restricted mobility. Of the total group, one fourth had marked personality change, and two thirds had some personality change, although this did not correlate with either side of lesion or the presence of hemiplegia. One fourth of these stroke victims had experienced communication loss, and one third had reported memory loss. Of the male stroke victims who were under 65 years of age at the time of follow-up, 30% were in paid employment, and five others had worked at some time following the stroke. Of the female stroke victims, 17% of those under 60 were gainfully employed, compared to 58% of those under 60 at the time of the stroke who were employed. Personality changes in stroke victims reported by their spouses included irritability, loss of self-control, impatience, decreased frustration tolerance, emotional lability, self-centeredness, and decreased initiative. Spouses of stroke victims rated the stroke survivors' enjoyment of life since the stroke as "much less" in 41% of cases, compared to enjoyment of life before the stroke. They attributed their spouses' loss of enjoyment to residual disabilities, loss of independence, and lack of occupational interests. For the caregivers, occupational changes and decreased life satisfaction had also been experienced. Five male and 18 female caregivers reported not working since their spouse's stroke. Of the caregiver spouses, 32% reported that their enjoyment of life was "much less." Although the spouses of hemiplegic stroke victims were more likely to report decreased enjoyment of life regardless of side of hemiplegia, they were significantly more likely to report of loss of enjoyment of life if the stroke victim had suffered a right hemisphere stroke with left hemiplegia than if the stroke victim was nonhemiplegic. Spouses attributed their decreased enjoyment of life since the stroke to loss of companionship, increased domestic responsibilities, and interference with leisure and social activities.

To summarize, studies that have considered the outcome of stroke for patients and caregivers together indicate some differential impacts of the stroke depending on whether one is the patient or caregiver. They also point to the possible interactive effects of characteristics of the stroke, patient personality changes, and caregiver well-being.

Studies Focused on Primary Caregivers

Several studies reviewed focused only on the adjustment of well-being of the primary caregivers of stroke survivors. Some of these investigations were concerned with strokes in general, some focused on the caregivers of stroke victims with significant communication deficits, and others compared the outcomes for spouses of patients with and without the language deficit of aphasia. These studies are briefly summarized below.

Mackay and Nias (1979) interviewed the caregivers of 28 younger (under age 65 at the time of the stroke) incapacitated stroke victims who required substantial home care six months after the patients' discharge from the hospital. Focus of the interview was on the caregivers' own social, economic, and emotional problems related to the stroke. Eight of 12 who had been working prior to the stroke had had to give up their jobs, 8 caregivers considered themselves worse off financially since the stroke, 25 of 28 had to now spend most or all of their time at home, and 8 had taken tranquilizing medication since the CVA. Yet 20 of 28 caregivers were judged by the interviewer to be "moderately happy and confident." The remaining 8 of the 28 caregivers reported feeling "very depressed" and were described as struggling to cope. Only a small number reported feeling that their relationship with the stroke victim had deteriorated (3 of 28). Unks (1983), who interviewed 50 elderly wives of chronic stroke patients, also found relatively high levels of morale in these caregivers. He utilized the Philadelphia Geriatric Center Morale Scale as the outcome measure. These wives had morale scores which were comparable to or only slightly below those of the general elderly population.

Brocklehurst and his colleagues (Brocklehurst, Morris, Andrews, Richards, & Laycock, 1981) interviewed the primary caregivers of 97 new stroke patients between four and six weeks after the stroke and at "regular intervals" for one year. Reported deterioration in the caregiving person's self-reported health was common during the first year, tripling from the first interview to the one year poststroke interview. Over 25% of the caregivers had responsibility for other persons in addition to the stroke victim. Major problems cited by the caregivers were related to the behavior of the stroke victim, the need for constant supervision, and loss of sleep. Although there had been a large amount of assistance offered to the caregiver by relatives, friends, and neighbors during the early poststroke period, little assistance was being received by the primary caring person at the end of a year. Of this caregiver sample, 14% had given up their jobs because of the stroke. It should be noted that this was quite a dependent stroke sample—55% were dependent for everything but personal care, and 25% were totally dependent.

Silliman (1984) interviewed 89 caregivers of elderly stroke patients, 82% of whom returned home following hospitalization. Silliman compared the changes experienced by those persons who were caring for their family member at home with those whose relative had been discharged to a nursing home (potential caregivers). She found that caregivers reported both good and bad effects of the stroke on their lives. Most home caregivers (84%) said that they felt better about themselves because they had learned to manage their relative's illness, and 69% reported closer relationships with the patients because of the illness and caregiving experience. On the other hand, 75% worried about the consequences of caregiving on their own health, 40% to 45% attended church less often, had less time for other members of their families, noted more financial burdens, and had less time for themselves. In addition, 40% scored high on the General Health Questionnaire, an instrument designed to screen for symptoms of emotional ill health. This is twice the prevalence reported in community surveys. Unexpectedly, Silliman found no differences on the measures of emotional health and adjustment between those actually caring for stroke-victim relatives and those whose relatives were in nursing homes.

Three studies compared the impacts on the caregiver of stroke resulting in left hemisphere brain damage and aphasia with stroke without the presence of aphasia (Artes & Hoops, 1976; Fengler & Goodrich, 1979; Kinsella & Duffy, 1979). Artes administered a 263-item questionnaire to 65 wives of stroke victims whose husbands were residing at home. Thirty-five of the stroke victims were aphasic, while 30 were noted to have no communication impairment. The wives of the aphasic individuals rated all problem areas explored (health and physical care, economic changes, communication behavior, and psychosocial aspects of behavior) as of more concern to them than did the nonaphasic victims' spouses. Interestingly, however, less than half of the wives of aphasic persons considered the communication impairment itself to be the major problem with which they were faced. They reported less opportunity for social activity (43%), visitors calling once a week or less often (49%), and that the aphasic spouse was "hard to get along with" poststroke (46%). In contrast, only 17% of the nonaphasics' spouses reported less opportunity for social activity, although 33% reported that their stroke-victim spouses were difficult to get along with since the stroke. Almost 30% of the wives of aphasic victims reported that they never got away from the house by themselves compared to 13% of the nonaphasic group's spouses. Forty-four percent of the wives of the nonaphasic stroke victims reported a 10% or less curtailment of their social activities, but only 12% of the aphasic individuals' wives experienced that low a level of diminished social activity.

Kinsella and Duffy (1979) also found more severe poststroke adjustment problems in the spouses (70% female) of aphasic persons compared to the partners of nonaphasic stroke survivors. Spouses of aphasic, hemiplegic persons were found to have significantly poorer overall adjustment, to be significantly more lonely and bored, and to be more maladjusted in their marital relationships. These investigators found that spouse adjustment was *not* significantly related to the stroke victim's dependency, severity of hemiplegia, or severity of the victim's aphasic impairment. More disturbing, the greater the time between the onset of the stroke and time of interview, the significantly worse the adjustment score. This was a cross-sectional study, however. Similar results comparing the interpersonal situations of spouses of aphasic and nonaphasic stroke survivors were found by Fengler and Goodrich (1979).

Common themes characterize descriptive reports of the stresses and concerns of families of aphasic stroke survivors. These anecdotal accounts have documented the disruptions that occur in interpersonal interactions when a family member suffers from aphasia. Webster (1980; Webster & Newhoff, 1981) described the most commonly reported problems of wives of aphasic stroke victims: problems relating to the assumption of many of the duties formerly performed by the spouse; lack of time for themselves; lack of companionship; lack of people with whom to talk. These women reported that they could not discuss their feelings of isolation with their families or neighbors for "fear of stirring guilt in family members, or appearing to neighbors as bad wives" (Webster, 1980, p. 351). Malone (1969) interviewed 25 persons representing the families of 20 aphasic adults, including spouses, children, and other relatives. He found that in every case, families reported that the family as a closely knit unit no longer existed. Role changes were one of the most frequently mentioned problems. Nearly all families stated that their friends gradually stopped coming to visit. Several of the families reported health problems in the non-aphasic family members since the stroke, which left them less able to cope. Malone also found that spouses frequently mentioned the negative effects of having an aphasic family member on the social development of the children.

In the only published study found dealing especially with the impacts of aphasia on the lives of children of aphasic individuals, Chwat, Chapey, Gurland, and Pieras (1980) administered a 50-item questionnaire to 16 children of 16 aphasic adults. The children ranged in age from 16 to 41 years, with a mean age of 26 years, and all were reported to be in face-to-face contact with their parent at least three times weekly. Almost 70% of the respondents reported playing the role of parent, bearing a greater share of the responsibility for household tasks and other necessary chores than siblings, at least part of the time. Half reported that they lost patience with their aphasic parent and felt irritable after spending time with them, while more than one third indicated that making visits to their parent was anxiety provoking. Two thirds of the children felt that they interacted with their communicatively impaired parent an inappropriate amount of time (either too much, or too little, about equally divided). Almost 40% of the respondents felt that their social lives had changed considerably since the stroke and that care of their parent frequently took time away from their own social activities.

In summary, what can be said about these descriptive and correlational accounts of the impacts of stroke? There are many problems with these studies as a group. Small sample sizes, questionable validity of some of the outcome measures, and absence of control groups limits their interpretation and generalizability. In addition, studies are rarely designed to test multivariate models of the type described in Chapter 2, and longitudinal studies of caregivers are rare. However, several recently completed studies designed to identify factors affecting caregiver stress address some of these shortcomings.

RESEARCH ON FACTORS
AFFECTING CAREGIVER STRESS

A recently completed study by Schulz and his colleagues (Schulz et al., 1988; Tompkins et al., 1988) was designed to test the multivariate stress-coping model described in Chapter 2. In this study, 162 individuals who had suffered a first stroke and their primary support person participated in three waves of data collection, carried out at six-month intervals beginning seven weeks after the stroke. The caregiver data were collected via a structured interview carried out in caregivers' homes. Four categories of data were collected representing the four major components of the model described in Chapter 2: objective stressors, perceived stress or burden, enduring outcomes including depression and psychological well-being, and conditioning variables. Multivariate hierarchical regression analyses were used to identify predictors both cross-sectionally and longitudinally, and discriminant function analyses were used to identify factors associated with being at risk for clinical depression 8 months and 14 months poststroke. Major findings of this study are presented below.

Objective Stressors

As expected, the severity of the stroke was significantly related to both burden and depression at all three measurement points. This finding did not change even after controlling for relevant covariates of burden and depression such as age, relationship to the patient, income, and the health of the caregiver. A similar finding was obtained for a measure assessing the impact of changes in personality characteristics of the patient. Caregivers felt more burdened and depressed when patients exhibited a decrease in positive personality characteristics (e.g., thoughtful, patient) or an increase in negative characteristics (e.g., irritable, self-centered).

These findings were replicated by Thompson et al., (1989) who showed that the physical impairment of the patient was an important independent predictor of depression among caregivers.

Contextual Variables

A large number of potential conditioning variables were investigated in the study by Schulz, et al. (1988) including age, income, and social support available to the caregiver. The role of these variables in predict-ing caregiver depression changed dramatically from the acute to the chronic phase of the patient's illness. In the acute adjustment phase, socio-demographic factors such as age and income were not related to level of depression; however, approximately eight months poststroke these variables were significantly related to depression. Individuals who had higher incomes, good health, and who were older were least depressed. The picture that emerges from these data is that psycholog-ical well-being in the acute adjustment phase is highly related to aspects of the stroke, and that demographic factors such as age and income do not appear to attenuate these relationships. Over time stroke-related variables become less important as traditional socio-demographic vari-ables emerge as predictors of caregiver well-being.

Social relationship variables also played a role in determining care-giver depression. Caregivers who were married to the patient reported higher levels of depression and caregivers who experienced a reduction in confiding relationships reported an increase in level of depression. These data suggest that having the opportunity to engage in reciprocal opinion exchange and confiding has important implications for the mental health of caregivers.

Perceived Burden and Depression

Since comparative data on burden were not available in the Schulz et al. (1988) study, it is difficult to interpret the levels of burden reported by caregivers. Reported levels of depression can, however, be compared with age and gender matched population norms. CES-D scores for the stroke patient caregivers revealed depressive symptom-atology rates that were two-and-one-half to three times higher than rates found among noncaregiving samples. Moreover, individuals who ex-hibited high levels of depression during the acute adjustment phase were also more likely to report high levels of depression a year after the stroke, despite significant improvement in patient functioning.

In conclusion, the data from our study, as well as earlier research on the impact of stroke on caregivers, yield a number of consistent find-ings. First, caregivers report high levels of stress and burden and significant levels of clinical depression. Second, patient characteristics such as the level of physical disability and altered personality attributes are highly related to caregiver outcomes. Finally, a number of intervening variables contribute importantly to caregiver well-being: being married to the patient, being a female, and experiencing declines in standard of living or in confiding relationships are related to higher levels of caregiver depression.

Although the literature on support-person adjustment to stroke is extensive, existing research needs to be replicated and extended. For example, the stroke patient sample in the Schulz et al. study was limited to first-occurrence stroke patients with relatively mild physical disabilities; the interaction among factors predicting psychosocial outcome may be different for the support persons of patients with more extensive and more long-lasting functional impairments. In addition, a more detailed assessment of cognitive and behavioral change should be used to evaluate the impact of stroke severity on support-person outcomes. Finally, research should be initiated to examine the type and timing of interventions most appropriate for the large proportion of support persons who are likely to face psychosocial adjustment problems after stroke. Preliminary evidence suggests that both counseling and educational interventions can be beneficial to family members caring for a stroke patient (Evans, Matlack, Bishop, Stranahan, & Pederson, 1988).

6

Caregiving in Alzheimer's Disease

The terms dementing illness or dementia are used to refer to diseases that lead initially to the loss of cognitive functioning and in later stages to the loss of motor and physical functioning. Formal definitions of dementia include: (a) loss of intellectual abilities sufficiently severe to interfere with social and occupational functioning; (b) memory impairment; (c) problems with abstract thinking, impaired judgment, personality change, and/or other disturbances of brain function such as aphasia (language problem due to brain damage), apraxia (inability to carry out a requested action despite good comprehension and physical ability to perform the action), agnosia (failure to recognize or identify objects despite good vision and sense of touch), or constructional difficulty (inability to do such tasks as copying three dimensional figures, or assembling blocks or sticks in specific designs although there is no paralysis or visual problem); and (d) state of consciousness is not clouded (i.e., does not meet the criteria for delirium or intoxication). Since many diseases can cause dementia symptoms, a good clinical diagnosis requires that the patient's history, physical examination, or medical laboratory tests give evidence of a specific organic factor judged to contribute to the disturbance, or that an organic factor can be presumed because other conditions have been ruled out.

Although there are more than 70 different conditions that can cause dementia, the two most common causes in elderly persons are Alzheimer's disease and multi-infarct dementia (see Chapter 5, stroke). A clinical diagnosis of Alzheimer's disease is based on the presence of dementia symptoms, an insidious onset followed by a progressive deteriorating course, and the exclusion of all other specific causes of dementia and dementia-like symptoms by history, physical examination, laboratory tests, and psychometric and other studies. Alzheimer's disease is also associated with various physiological changes in the brain, including loss of neurons, widened fissures, narrower and flatter ridges, senile plaques scattered throughout the cortex, and the replacement of normal nerve cells in the basal ganglia with tangled threadlike structures.

The age of onset for Alzheimer's disease can be either early (ages 40 to 65) or late (ages 66 and over). It is estimated that the prevalence of mild dementia is 11% to 12% among those aged 65 and over and that the prevalence of moderate to severe dementia is about 6% (Mortimer, 1988). In studies that exclude institutionalized persons, the prevalence rate of moderate or severe dementia is somewhat lower, about 4%. The 2% difference between the two types of studies is explained if we assume that about half of the institutionalized population in developed countries have moderate or severe dementia. A recently completed study suggests that the prevalence of Alzheimer's disease may be much higher than first estimated. Evans, Funkenstein, Albert (1989) found that 10.3% of those over the age of 65 had probable Alzheimer's disease and that prevalence increased dramatically with age. Of those over the age of 85, they found that 47.2% had probable Alzheimer's disease.

Converting these percentages to cases yields approximately 1 million cases of severe dementia and 3 million mild to moderate cases of dementia in the United States. Moreover, of the 1.5 million Americans who are cared for in nursing homes, it is estimated that about 63% suffer from some form of cognitive impairment. The number of severe dementia cases is expected to increase to approximately 4.5 million by the year 2040. Currently, dementia is estimated to account for 100,000 to 120,000 deaths annually, making it the fourth leading cause of death in the United States.

Incidence rates for dementia of the Alzheimer's type have been difficult to obtain because of the difficulty in diagnosing the illness and because few large scale population based studies have been carried out. Data obtained from the Baltimore Longitudinal Study (Sayetta, 1986) indicate incidence rates of .083% at age 60, .333% at age 70, 1.337% at age 80, and 5.371% at age 90. The pattern of increasing rates with increasing age has been replicated in other studies (e.g., Akesson, 1969; Hagnell, 1970), although there is wide variability in rates reported by different investigators. Efforts are currently underway to obtain more accurate incidence and prevalence data in a number of cohorts located throughout the United States.

The onset of Alzheimer's disease is deceptively mild, and its course is one of steady deterioration. In Stage One, patients may exhibit minor symptoms and mood changes. They may also have less energy, less drive, be less spontaneous, be slower to learn or react, and forget some words. Patients may also lose their temper more easily than they did before. Frequently, these symptoms go undetected or are attributed to temporary changes in the environment or the individual.

In Stage Two, patients may still be able to perform familiar activities, but are likely to need help with complicated tasks. The ability to speak and understand are noticeably impaired, and they may be insensitive to the feelings of others.

Stage Three is characterized by profound memory deficits, particularly of the recent past. Patients may forget where they are, the date, time, and season, and may fail to recognize familiar people. Behavioral problems may become prominent and psychotic symptoms such as delusions, hallucinations, paranoid ideation, and severe agitation may become manifest.

Memory continues to deteriorate in Stage Four, and patients are likely to need help with all activities. They are often completely disoriented, unable to recognize close friends and family members, and often lose control of bowels and bladder. Finally, patients may become completely mute and inattentive, and be totally incapable of caring for themselves. The process of deterioration ultimately leads to the final stage, death, although this may take anywhere from one to ten years.

Dementia of the Alzheimer's type cannot be prevented now, nor can its course be slowed or reversed. In many cases, however, the severity of its impact on individuals or family may be reduced through early detection and appropriate treatment of associated problems.

IMPACT ON THE PATIENT

In some ways dealing with Alzheimer's disease is the reverse of dealing with cancer. Alzheimer's disease leaves bone and flesh intact while erasing judgment, memory, and the sense of self. Most types of cancer destroy the physical being while leaving cognitive abilities intact. Both present profound, life shattering challenges to the individual, and in that respect they have many things in common.

Receiving a diagnosis of Alzheimer's disease has been likened to receiving a death sentence. Patients respond with variety of strong emotions including shock, anger, disbelief, fear, and despair. A minority of patients may deny or refuse to acknowledge their condition altogether.

The themes of death and loss are prominent in patients' response to a diagnosis of Alzheimer's disease, in large part because the illness conveys an image of profound loss and is perceived as incurable and life-shortening. In the early stages of the disease, Cohen and Eisdorfer (1988) report that many patients are desperate to talk about what it means for their future and for their family. Patients want to remain as active as possible for as long as possible to be included in family decisions and in making plans regarding their future. Another feature of patients in this stage of the disease is a fear and sadness brought about by knowing that as the dementia progresses they will be unable to relate to family members with dignity and respect.

Perhaps the most distressing part of knowing that one has Alzheimer's disease is existing in a transitional limbo, being aware of having profound cognitive deficits that will only get worse. Observing the unraveling of a self-identity that one has spent a lifetime creating is a load that virtually no one can bear with equanimity.

These observations are derived primarily from case studies of Alzheimer's patients (Cohen & Eisdorfer, 1988). Systematic studies based on representative samples of Alzheimer's patients and their response to the diagnosis and subsequent decline are nonexistent. The lack of studies on this topic can be attributed to a number of reasons. First, an Alzheimer's diagnosis typically evolves gradually over an extended period of time. As a result, it is difficult to pinpoint when patients become aware of this diagnosis and the extent to which patient response is influenced by the events and experiences that preceded the diagnosis. Ideally, one would want to begin studying patients when they first suspect dementia problems and follow them through the diagnostic process. Second, data regarding patient response to illness is usually based on self-report. This makes studying Alzheimer's disease difficult because the disease itself may interfere with patients' ability to provide useful self-report data. Nevertheless, it would be useful to collect such data in the early to middle stages of the disease. Finally, there might be objections to collecting such data because it may be too stressful to the patient to dwell on feelings related to their own impending decline and death. This argument certainly applies to some patients, but it could also be contended that some patients would benefit from the opportunity to discuss their feelings. On the whole, researchers primarily have been concerned with assessing the cognitive and functional status of patients and have paid little attention to how patients feel about what is happening to them.

SERVICES FOR
PATIENTS AND FAMILIES

Just as the number of individuals suffering from Alzheimer's disease has increased so have the number and diversity of services available to patients and caregivers. Existing patient services include diagnostic and treatment centers located at major universities throughout the United States, patient support groups, day-care centers, and specialized units designed for Alzheimer's patients in long-term care facilities.

University Alzheimer's centers play a major role in providing diagnostic services to the community, offering experimental treatments as they become available, and in carrying out research aimed at better diagnosis and treatment. Patient support groups can provide valued emotional support to patients in the early stages of the disease, and adult day-care centers provide a safe and caring environment for patients in the middle stages of the disease. Alzheimer's disease patients often participate in general day-care programs, but there is a growing trend toward the establishment of specialized day-care programs for Alzheimer's patients. In the later stages of the disease the majority of patients require institutionalization, and a number of institutions have responded to this need by creating special low stimulus environments for Alzheimer's patients.

In response to extreme challenges associated with caring for Alzheimer's patients at home, a number of national organizations have focused their energy and resources in providing services for the family. Foremost among these is the Alzheimer's Disease and Related Disorders Association (ADRDA). The ADRDA coordinates a national network of support groups for caregivers of Alzheimer's patients, provides information and referral services, supports research on Alzheimer's disease, and plays an active role in the development of new programs and services for Alzheimer's patients and their families.

Pfeiffer et al. (1989) note that three different types of support groups for family caregivers of Alzheimer's disease patients have been developed. These include: professionally led groups that are assisted by lay leaders; lay led groups that have limited or no professional involvement, such as those groups affiliated with ADRDA; and groups affiliated with or sponsored by community-based organizations that represent a combination of lay and professionally led groups.

State units on aging have also been active in developing and promoting services for caregivers of Alzheimer's patients. Available services range from financial incentives such as tax credits designed to ease the burden of caring for the patient at home to the development of respite programs that afford the caregiver the opportunity of obtaining temporary relief from the burden of caregiving. Respite services are both in-home and institutionally based. In-home respite services include companion/homemaker, generally utilized two to four hours per day, one to three days a week, and homemaker/health aide services, commonly offered for 8 to 24 hours per day for a two week period. Institutional respite services are offered by hospitals and nursing homes, usually for a several day to two-week period. They provide respite to caregivers of Alzheimer's patients who are in the middle or late stages of the disease (Pfeiffer et al., 1989). Although formal evaluations of programs such as these are rarely carried out, the fact that people use them can be construed as evidence of their value.

IMPACT ON FAMILY MEMBERS

Research on the impact of Alzheimer's disease on caregivers is extensive and continues to grow at a rapid rate. Data are now available on virtually all variables of the model described in Chapter 2.

Objective Stressors

On the whole, the existing literature on relationship between patient status or symptomatology and caregiver outcomes suggest that the two are moderately related. The one frequently cited exception to this generalization is the study by Zarit et al. (1980) in which they found no relationship between reported burden and patient characteristics such as frequency of memory and behavior problems, or the extent of function and cognitive impairment in a sample of 29 caregivers of Alzheimer's patients. The majority of subsequent studies of caregivers of Alzheimer's patients (e.g., Schulz, Biegel, Morycz, & Visintainer, 1989) and caregivers of heterogeneous disabled elderly (e.g., George & Gwyther, 1986; Poulshock & Deimling, 1984) report moderate to strong relationships between level of dysfunction and caregiver outcomes. For example, Schulz, Williamson, Morycz, and Biegel (in press) found strong correlations between ADL/IADL functioning and caregiver burden and depression. Moreover, as function declined, depression increased. When asked to identify which aspect of patient disability they found most distressing, the majority reported patient memory and communication problems, followed by personality changes. Because the patient sample in this study was composed primarily of mildly demented Alzheimer's patients, the stressors identified are representative of early stages of the disease. It is likely that problems such as disorientation, eating, and incontinence emerge as the dominant concerns of caregivers in the later stages of the disease.

Contextual Variables

Demographic variables such as age, gender, and relationship to patients (spouse, daughter, or son) have been examined in the large majority of Alzheimer's caregiving studies. Unfortunately, it has been difficult to assess independently the importance of each of these factors because they tend to covary with each other and study samples are typically too small. For example, wife caregivers are consistently older than daughter caregivers; as a result, it is difficult to separate the role of age from type of relationship without an extremely large sample available that has a wide distribution of ages for both wives and daughters. Nevertheless, a number of consistant findings have emerged on the relationship between demographic variables and caregiver outcomes.

First, the majority of studies show that female caregivers experience higher levels of distress and depression than do male (Pruchno & Resch, 1989b; Fitting et al., 1986; Schulz et al., in press). Second, as was the case for stroke caregivers, being married to and living with patients is also associated with negative outcomes for caregivers. Third, son caregivers, although rare to begin with, tend to exhibit the least adverse effects.

Although conclusive data on the reasons for these gender and relationship effects are not yet available, it is possible that males approach the demands of caregiving in ways that are less detrimental to their well-being. For example, they appear better able to set limits on the amount of help they provide and not feel guilty about doing so, and they tend to rely more on the support of others to provide care to patients. The relationship effect can be explained by the closer bond between caregivers and patients and the greater caregiving demands associated with living with patients.

Other variables being investigated as possible mediators of caregiving outcomes include personality attributes such as self-esteem and hostility, attitudes toward helping, nature of prior relationship between patients and caregivers, social support available to caregivers, and coping strategies used. Some of these variables were recently examined in a longitudinal study by Schulz and his colleagues (Schulz et al., in press; Williamson & Schulz, in press) who found that caregivers reporting a close relationship with patients prior to illness onset felt less burdened than those who had not been close, caregivers reporting high levels of support from others had lower levels of depression, and finally, being concerned about financial problems was a predictor of depression among male caregivers.

CAREGIVER OUTCOMES: DISTRESS, BURDEN, AND MORBIDITY

Three types of outcomes have been investigated in dementia caregiving studies. The majority of studies have documented the burdens and consequent distress associated with caring for patients with cognitive and physical impairment. More recently, researchers have turned their attention to the assessment of psychiatric morbidity effects and physical morbidity effects of caregiving. Each of these literatures is discussed below.

Psychological Distress/Burden

Much of the early literature on caregiving was aimed at documenting the burdens of caregiving. As a result, it is now well established that providing care to disabled relatives creates emotional, physical, and financial strain (Horowitz, 1985). Specific problems identified by caregivers of Alzheimer's patients include undesirable social life changes, feeling overwhelmed, developing depression and anxiety, strained relations with other family members, and general feelings that life is uncontrollable (Barnes, Raskind, Scott, & Murphy, 1981; Morycz, 1985; Rabins, Mace & Lucas, 1982; Zarit et al., 1980).

Although distress among caregivers is a characteristic feature of all caregiving situations, regardless of patient disability, it is generally believed that caring for a demented individual presents the greatest challenge of all. The cognitive impairment and unusual behavioral disorders associated with dementia create burdens that are uniquely and severely stressful to caregivers (Mace & Rabins, 1981; George & Gwyther, 1986). Frequently, families must assist the demented patient with dressing, feeding, bathing, and management of incontinence. The physical demands of providing this care are aggravated by having to witness the deterioration of a loved one's personality, a process described by caregivers as a "living death" (Haley, Levine, Brown, Berry, & Hughes, 1987). The constant, unremitting nature of the stress of caring for a relative with dementia has been called a "36-hour day" because of the seemingly endless responsibilities involved (Mace & Rabins, 1981).

Psychiatric Morbidity

Generally, two types of studies have assessed the mental health consequences of caregiving. The majority of published studies use standardized self-report inventories to measure psychiatric symptomatology such as depression. A second and more recent type of study is based on clinical assessment of the caregiver and is aimed at identifying the prevalence of actual clinical cases based on standardized assessment procedures. Each of these literatures is described below.

Self-Report Studies

In one of the first studies to examine the effects of home care on caregivers of demented patients, Grad and Sainsbury (1968) reported that the mental health of more than one half of their sample of caregivers was adversely affected. Based on interviews and ratings performed by a psychiatric social worker, one fifth of the caregivers were found to report neurotic symptoms such as insomnia, headaches, excessive irritability, and depression. Older patients with either organic or affective psychosis were most likely to cause severe problems among family caregivers. The findings of this study are consistent with the large literature showing high levels of burden associated with family caregiving, but are equivocal with respect to mental health effects associated with caregiving. Since no comparison rates of psychiatric symptomatology among noncaregivers were reported, it is difficult to evaluate the significance of the these data. It should also be noted that the sample of caregivers was selected based on patient referral to a psychiatric service. As a result, the data pertaining to caregivers have limited generalizability, as the authors suggest. Finally, the fact that the patients in this study were suffering from psychiatric illnesses would lead one to expect elevated rates of psychiatric symptomatology among related family members because of shared genetic background and similarities in environmental exposures.

The most frequently studied psychiatric symptoms among caregivers are those indicating depression or demoralization. We identified a total of 10 different standardized self-report scales that have been used in caregiving studies. The most popular is the Beck Depression Inventory (BDI) (Beck & Beck, 1972), followed by the Center for Epidemiologic Studies Depression Scale (CES-D) (Radloff, 1977), the Hopkins Symptom Checklist-90 (SCL-90) (Kinney & Stephens, 1989), the General Health Questionnaire (GHQ) (Goldberg & Hillier, 1979), and a number of less well-known instruments such as the Leeds Depression Scale (Eagles, Beattie, Blackwood, Restall, & Ashcroft, 1987) or the Wiggins Depression Inventory (Fitting et al., 1986). The advantage of using these scales is that they have well-established psychometric properties and, in most cases, age- and gender-based population norms. The availability of base rates makes it possible to assess the extent to which caregivers exceed normal distress levels.

Most studies using standardized instruments show elevated depression rates among caregivers when compared to either age- and gender-based population norms or noncaregiving control groups. All studies using the BDI report elevated rates of depression among caregivers. The range of scores among researchers using the BDI Short Form is 4.9 (Kiecolt-Glaser, Glaser, Shuttleworth, Dyer, Ogrocki, & Speicher, 1987) to 11.2 (Gallagher, Wrabetz, Lovett, Del Maestro, & Rose, 1989), with three studies reporting rates above 10 (Fiore, Becker, & Coppel, 1983; Dura, Haywood-Niler, & Kiecolt-Glaser, in press; Gallagher et al., 1989). The recommended cut off scores for determining mild, moderate, and severe depression for the short form of the BDI are 5, 8, and 16, respectively (Beck & Beck, 1972).

Similar patterns are found in studies with CES-D scores as primary outcome measures. In six studies, scores ranged from 5.6 (Moritz, Kasl, & Berkman, 1989) to 28.9 (Stoller & Pugliesi, 1989). The modal score was approximately 17 (Pruchno & Potashnik, 1989; Pruchno & Resch, 1989a, 1989b, 1989c; Schulz et al., in press). Nonclinical elderly populations typically score between 8 and 9, and the usual cutoff score on the CES-D for being at risk for clinical depression is 16 or over. Thus the majority of caregiving studies show substantially elevated rates when compared to population norms.

Studies using the BDI or CES-D support two general conclusions. First, the more severely impaired the patient, the greater the depressive symptomatology. Second, females tend to be more depressed than males. Third, the more representative the sample is of a particular caregiving population, the lower is its depressive symptomatology. Thus caregivers of mildly impaired patients report fewer depressive symptoms than caregivers of moderately or severely impaired patients, and both wives and daughters report being more depressed than husbands or sons.

In addition to depression, researchers have used a number of more broadly based self-report instruments to assess psychiatric morbidity among caregivers. For example, Gilleard, Belford, et al., (1984) used the General Health Questionnaire (GHQ) to assess psychiatric symptomatology in three samples of caregivers of "mentally infirm" elderly persons. The GHQ is a self-administered test aimed at detecting psychiatric disorders among respondents in community settings; it yields a probability estimate of an individual qualifying as a psychiatric case (Goldberg et al., 1970). Gilleard, Belford, et al. (1984) found that between 57% and 74% of participants in the three different samples scored above the scale's cutoff for psychiatric "caseness." This compares to prevalence rates in community samples of 16% to 22% (Goldberg et al., 1970). In order to validate GHQ diagnoses, caregivers in one of the samples ($N = 45$) were interviewed by a psychiatrist using Goldberg's Clinical Interview Schedule. In addition, an independent International Disease Classification (8th edition) was carried out on the same caregivers. Comparisons between GHQ scores and clinical diagnoses yielded misclassifications ranging from 19.5% to 32% depending on the criterion used. Rates of false positive classification were generally higher for the GHQ than rates of false negative classifications. Nevertheless, there was concordance on more than 50% of the cases suggesting that a high proportion of caregivers in these studies displayed sufficient symptoms to warrant a psychiatric diagnosis. However, the generalizability of these findings is limited. The caregiver samples in all three studies were providing support to "mentally infirm" geriatric patients who were either attending, referred to, or on the waiting list of a psychogeriatric day hospital. As the authors point out, the principal reason for a referral to such service is strain on family members. Consequently, caregivers in these studies are more likely to represent the distressed end of the caregiving continuum.

In a recently published study, Anthony-Bergstone, Zarit, and Gatz (1988) used the Brief Symptom Inventory (BSI) to assess psychiatric symptomatology among caregivers of dementia patients. The BSI is a standardized scale based on the Hopkins Symptom Checklist that yields nine subscale scores indicating situational and chronic psychiatric symptomatology. It was expected that on subscales of depression, anxiety, and hostility, caregivers would score significantly higher than age and gender population norms. However, only older women (60 and over) had depression scores above comparable population norms. Older men and women as well as younger women reported high levels of hostility, and both young and older women reported high levels of anxiety. These results are generally consistent with those reported by Fitting et al. (1986) who found higher rates of depression among female than male caregivers on the depression subscale of the Minnesota Multiphasic Personality Inventory (MMPI) and with the results of Clipp and George (1990; also, George & Gwyther, 1986) showing elevated rates of psychotropic drug use among caregivers.

Clinical Assessment Studies

A number of case reports indicate that caregiving distress can be severe enough to require professional intervention (Goldman & Luchins, 1984; Lezak, 1978a). These studies, along with survey research documenting the burdens and associated stresses of caregiving, have instigated a number of studies in which standard clinical diagnostic procedures were used to assess psychiatric morbidity.

Coppel et al. (1985) assessed the prevalence of depression among 68 spouse caregivers of Alzheimer's disease patients using the Schedule for Affective Disorders and Schizophrenia interview (SADS) (Endicott & Spitzer, 1978). The SADS is a well established diagnostic procedure that uses criteria similar to those of the Diagnostic and Statistical Manual of the American Psychiatric Association (DSM-III) (American Psychiatric Association, 1980). Coppel et al. found that 41% of their sample was diagnosed as currently depressed and 40% met the criteria for a depressive disorder during an earlier phase of the illness. These rates were considerably higher that the prevalence of late-life depression in the general population which is thought to be below 10%. These rates are similar to those reported by Dura et al. (in press) who found that 30% of their caregivers of dementia patients experienced a clinical depressive disorder although only 1% of the matched controls fell into this category. Cohen and Eisdorfer (1988) also reported significantly elevated rates of clinical depression. In their study, 46 relatives of 27 patients with clinically diagnosed dementia were interviewed and classified by a psychiatrist using DSM-III criteria for depressive disorders. Of the 22 caregivers living with patients, 12 (55%) met DSM-III criteria for unipolar depression ($N = 5$) or adjustment disorder with depressive symptoms ($N = 7$). None of those living away from patients were clinically depressed. Although concordance rates between the Beck Depression Inventory and clinical diagnosis are not reported, the depressed sample had significantly higher BDI scores than the non-depressed sample.

Even higher rates of depression were reported by Drinka, Smith, and Drinka (1987). They found that 83% of 117 caregivers of dementia patients met DSM-III criteria for major depression, although it is not clear whether diagnoses were based on data from a self-report instrument, clinical interviews, or both.

To date, the most extensive study focused on the clinical evaluation of caregivers was carried out by Gallagher, Rose, Rivera, Lovett, and Thompson (1989). In their study, two groups of caregivers were recruited—one responding to local advertisements to participate in "Coping with Caregiving" classes ($N = 158$) and another consisting of volunteers with a relative enrolled in an Alzheimer's disease study ($N = 58$). All participants were given the SADS by a trained clinical interviewer and also completed the Beck Depression Inventory. Strengths of this study are that the researchers clearly document the method of case ascertainment and also report data regarding the reliability of their assessment procedures.

Forty-six percent of the "Coping with Caregiving" sample met criteria for one of three types of depressive disorder (major, minor, or intermittent), and an additional 22% had evidence of depressive features but not enough to warrant any diagnosis. Among the volunteers with a relative enrolled in an Alzheimer's study only 18% were diagnosed as being clinically depressed, and almost two thirds had no evidence of depression. Patients in the latter group were in the early stages of Alzheimer's disease. The sensitivity and specificity of the BDI were 70% and 79%, respectively, indicating that the BDI is a relatively good predictor of clinical depression.

To summarize, the literature on psychiatric morbidity is suggestive but not conclusive. There exists strong evidence for increased symptom reports for depression and demoralization among those caregivers studied, as well as support for increased clinical psychiatric illness among some caregivers. It is important, however, to keep in mind the criterion problem of distinguishing normal distress from psychiatric illness (Becker & Morissey, 1988). Periods of grief, despair, helplessness, and hopelessness may be much more common among caregivers. These periods of extreme distress are usually circumscribed enough to enable caregivers to retain a reasonably problem-focused orientation in coping with their own and patients' needs. Becker and Morissey (1988) have argued that severe, chronic stresses associated with Alzheimer's caregiving are unlikely to precipitate a major depressive disorder except in predisposed persons. They further contend that many depressive-like reactions in caregiving spouses should be categorized under DSM-III-R's "minimally articulated Code V: Conditions Not Due to a Psychiatric Disorder." This view is consistent with the conclusion reached by Fitting et al. (1985) that, "it is our impression that most caregivers reporting depressive symptomatology are experiencing a 'transient dysphoric mood' and not major depression" (p. 250).

Despite the overwhelming evidence for increased psychiatric symptomatology, all of these studies combined provide little evidence about the population prevalence or incidence of either symptomatology or clinically defined psychiatric conditions attributable to caregiving. Samples in almost all studies reported are biased toward those caregivers likely to be more distressed. Although studying this segment of the caregiving population is important, estimates of the extent of psychiatric morbidity among samples representative of caregivers in general are needed as well.

Physical Morbidity

Given the large literature linking stress to physical illness (e.g., respiratory diseases, hypertension, and cardiovascular disease), one could reasonably predict that caregivers should have higher rates of physical illness because they are chronically exposed to high levels of stress. Indeed, the caregiver has frequently been referred to as the "hidden patient" (Fengler & Goodrich, 1979).

Three types of outcomes have been examined as indicators of illness effects among caregivers. The most frequently used measures are self-reports of physical health status, illness, and illness-related symptoms. A few studies have examined health care utilization as an indicator of physical morbidity and one study assessed immune function as an indicator of susceptibility to disease.

Self-Report Studies

Although self-report studies consistently show poorer health among caregivers than age matched peers, it is difficult to draw causal inferences from these data. Stone et al. (1987; U. S. House of Representatives, 1987) found that caregivers perceive themselves in poorer health than do age peers in the U. S. population. In 1982, one third of female caregivers aged 45 to 64 reported their overall health in 1982 as fair or poor compared with slightly more than one fifth of all females in the same age group. The disparity between elderly female caregivers and females of all ages was considerably smaller, but male caregivers at all ages were much more likely to rate their health as fair than were age peers in the U. S. population. Caregivers are also more likely than age peers in the general population to report adjusted family incomes below the poverty line. It is possible, therefore, that lower reported health of caregivers is the result of lower income.

Haley, Levine, Brown, Berry, and Hughes (1987; see also, Haley, Levine, Brown, & Bartolucci, 1987; Haley, Brown, & Levine, 1987) also found that caregivers reported more chronic illness and poorer overall health than a group of matched noncaregivers. It is difficult to draw conclusions from these results, however, because of the inconsistent pattern of results in the self-report data and because the control group had significantly higher income.

Other possible explanations for self-report health findings are suggested by the results of a study carried out by Satariano et al. (1984). They surveyed 678 elderly individuals and found that ill-health of one spouse was a strong predictor of poor health in the other spouse. Respondents whose spouses recently had been ill were more likely to report ill health than were respondents whose spouses were healthy. These findings could be attributable to the stresses of caregiving but also could be due to other factors such as selective mating, shared environmental exposure, or contagion.

There is evidence, however, that some caregivers perceive that providing care is detrimental to their health. Snyder and Keefe (1985) reported that approximately 70% of the caregivers they polled reported a decline in physical health because of their support role. They also noted weak, but significant, positive correlations between level of patient disability and occurrence of caregiver health problems and between length of time in the caregiving role and likelihood of reporting health problems. Chenoweth and Spencer (1986) found that ill health was cited by 21% of caregivers as a reason for institutionalizing their patient. Specific conditions cited were fractures from falls, heart attacks, ulcers, "nervous breakdowns," and prolonged illnesses due to exhaustion.

Health Care Utilization Studies

Results of the few studies reporting health care utilization data are inconsistent. Haley et al. (1987) found that caregivers indicated more frequent physician visits and more prescription drug use than a matched group of noncaregivers. In contrast, other studies have failed to find that caregivers use more medical services than either large random samples of community dwelling older adults (George & Gwyther, 1986) or a matched control group (Kiecolt-Glaser et al., 1987).

Because the demands of caregiving may limit the opportunity to seek professional health care, it is unclear whether one should expect to find increased utilization among caregivers. Perhaps the place to look for utilization effects is shortly after the caregiving role has been relinquished either through institutionalization or death, when caregivers are better able to attend to their own needs.

Immune Function Studies

Although evidence for the influence of caregiving stress on physical health is equivocal, there is some indication that caregiving stress affects immune functions that may mediate physical illness. Immune function can be impaired by stressful life events such as death of a spouse or divorce (Bartrop, Lazaras, Luckhurst, Kiloh, & Penny, 1977; Schleifer, Keller, Camerino, Thornton, & Stein, 1983), and in a recent study, Kiecolt-Glaser et al. (1987) related immunosuppression to chronic stress among family caregivers of dementia victims. A comparison of 34 caregivers of Alzheimer's disease patients with 34 matched controls showed that caregivers not only reported higher levels of depression, lower life satisfaction, and lower mental health, but also had poorer immune responses. These results were not attributable to the effects of nutrition, sleep, or other health-related behaviors. These authors suggest that their data provide a "best case scenario" because their caregivers were well educated and had relatively high incomes. However, like many other caregiving samples, this one was recruited in part from Alzheimer's support groups and consequently may have been biased toward the distressed end of the continuum. Moreover, although caregivers were more distressed and showed poorer immune function than controls, no results were reported demonstrating that self-report and immune function data are correlated or that immune function is related to other indicators of health status. Studies now underway will undoubtedly shed more light on the relationships among caregiving stress, perceived health, and immune function.

In conclusion, the available data clearly indicate that providing care for a demented individual is frequently an extremely distressing experience, although it has been difficult to distinguish between the stress associated with providing care from the distress that results from witnessing the decline of a loved one. The literature on psychiatric and physical morbidity effects of caregiving is more equivocal. There exists strong evidence for increased symptom reports for depression and demoralization among those caregivers studied, as well as support for increased clinical psychiatric illness among some caregivers. The existing literature tells us little, however, about the population prevalence or incidence of clinically significant psychiatric conditions attributable to caregiving. Studies of the physical health effects as assessed by self-report, health care utilization, and immune function are suggestive of negative health effects but not conclusive.

7

Caregiving in
Chronic Mental Illness

INTRODUCTION

Mental illness is a significant problem that affects patients, their families, and the broader community. The most recent data on the extent of overall mental illness in the United States comes from the Epidemiology Catchment Area (ECA) Program, a collaborative research study funded by the National Institute of Mental Health. Data collected in five sites show prevalence rates of mental illness ranging from 16.8% to 23.4% of the population. Based on these data, it is estimated that almost 30 million (29.4) Americans or 18.7% of the population suffer from mental illness in any six-month period (Goldstein, E. G., 1987).

Only a small proportion of individuals suffering from mental illness, however, are classified as chronically mentally ill. Accurate figures concerning the extent of chronic mental illness in the United States are complicated by the deinstitutionalization movement, which caused shifts in the patterns and locus of mental health care, making it difficult to count this population. An additional problem is the lack of consensus on the boundaries as to what constitutes chronic mental illness. Estimates of the number of individuals who can be classified as chronically mentally ill range from 1.2 million to 5 to 7 million persons in the United States, with the National Institute of Mental Health estimating the population more conservatively at from 1.7 million to 3 million persons (Talbott, 1988). An even more conservative estimate of the chronically mentally ill population (between 1.7 million and 2.4 million individuals in the United States) is provided by Goldman (1984; Goldman, Gattozzi, & Taube, 1981). Of this number, up to 1.5 million chronically mentally ill persons live in the community and 900,000 are in institutions (Goldman et al., 1981).

The costs of mental illness to society and families are considerable. The U. S. General Accounting Office estimates that the cost of mental illness in the United States in 1974 was $36.7 billion, including both the direct treatment costs and the economic losses (U.S. General Accounting Office, 1977a). Studies indicate that families exhibit high tolerance toward their mentally ill family member, but often it is at considerable price to the family. Family burdens of caregiving are persistent and pervasive. A review by the Group for the Advancement of Psychiatry (1978) of where patients go upon discharge revealed that in the 1960s and 1970s almost three fourths (72%) of patients in the United States returned to their families to live. Of those returning to relatives, 50% returned to a spouse, 30% to live with parents, and 20% with other relatives. There was a similar pattern revealed in England. Today, only 25% of patients return to their families, with the rest going to live in other community settings; yet even this percentage represents a considerable number of patients (Group for the Advancement of Psychiatry, 1978; Talbott, 1988). For example, it has been estimated that approximately 150,000 to 170,000 chronic patients return to their homes on an annual basis. There are, however, no national prevalence estimates of the number of chronically mentally ill individuals who are currently living with their families (Goldman et al., 1981).

A number of researchers believe that deinstitutionalization has led to a greater burden on families today because many patients who would have been hospitalized in the past are now treated in community based programs instead. Patients may not follow through and utilize community services, however, and in most states they are not legally required to do so. In addition, because length of hospitalization has shortened, many patients are returning to the communities, and to their families, with severe emotional problems (Pepper & Ryglewicz, 1984).

THE POLICY OF DEINSTITUTIONALIZATION

Current issues regarding characteristics and treatment of the chronically mentally ill and issues pertaining to family burden are very much influenced by deinstitutionalization policies that began more than 25 years ago. Deinstitutionalization of the mentally ill has been a national goal since the passage of the Community Mental Health Centers Act in 1963. The reasons for this policy were many: concern over lack of treatment and proper care of the mentally ill in state institutions; development of new treatment philosophies that favored community based care; development of psychotropic drugs and new treatment technologies; availability of federal funds for income support of mental patients and for community based treatment facilities; cost savings to states in transferring patients from totally state funded mental institutions to other types of facilities whose lower costs were assumed in part by the federal government; more restrictive state commitment laws; and expansions of constitutional rights of the mentally ill, such as the "right to treatment" (U.S. General Accounting Office, 1977a).

This movement led to tremendous changes in the locus of treatment for the chronically mentally ill. Between 1955 and the present, the population of state mental hospitals decreased 77% from a high of 558,922 in 1955 to a low of 126,359 in 1981 (Segal, 1987). In 1955, three out of every four persons receiving mental health care were treated as inpatients; presently the situation is reversed, with three out of four persons receiving mental health care being treated as outpatients. Talbott (1981, 1988) suggests, however, that the policy of deinstitutionalization should more accurately be called "transinstitutionalization" because the number of institutionalized persons has remained constant over several decades, only their presence in particular institutions has changed. Thus there has been no reduction in the number of mental patients in hospitals, only a shift in treatment locus. For example, while there has been a 35% reduction in admissions to state mental hospitals, this has been almost entirely offset by a 32% increase in admissions to general hospitals (Talbott, 1981). A two-thirds decline in state mental hospital population has been countered by a tripling of the population of mental patients in nursing homes (Talbott, 1988).

There have also been "revolving door" admissions to state mental hospitals: brief hospitalizations leading to steadily growing admission and readmission rates. Segal reports that in 1950 state and county mental hospitals had 512,501 residents and 152,286 admissions, a ratio of .297 admissions for every resident. By 1970, there were 348,511 admissions and 337,619 residents, for a ratio of 1.4 admissions for every resident. This ratio increased to 1.74 in 1974 and to 2.83 by 1981 (Segal, 1987). Between 1970 and 1980, the median days of stay per admission to state and county mental hospitals decreased by almost half (44%) from 41 to 23 days. Concerning diagnosis, the most frequent primary diagnosis for admission to state and county mental hospitals was schizophrenia, compared to affective disorders for admission to private psychiatric hospitals and alcohol-related disorders for admission to VA hospitals (Rosen et al., 1987).

By the mid 1970s, there was much concern expressed concerning the problems of deinstitutionalization, with major critiques offered by the U.S. General Accounting Office (1977a), Group for the Advancement of Psychiatry (1978), and the President's Commission on Mental Health (1978). Among the major problems cited were increased stresses on families caused by patients' returning home to live with the family, often without adequate community based services; the continuing high admission rates to mental hospitals and escalating readmission rates noted above; inadequacies of community care; lack of coordination between hospital and community based services; lack of management systems to ensure adequacy and appropriateness of patient placement; inappropriate institutional placements (i.e., nursing homes) for many patients; and the lack of coordination, planning, and priority setting on the national and state levels to address the needs of this population group. For many chronically mentally ill patients, deinstitutionalization has meant being "dumped" into communities to live in single room occupancy hotels, boarding homes, or apartments, often without adequate necessities of life and needed daily living supports.

NATURE AND EXTENT
OF CHRONIC MENTAL ILLNESS

Defining the Population

Chronically mentally ill individuals suffer emotional disorders that are severe, long-standing, and interfere with such functional capacities as self-care, interpersonal relationships, work, and education. They often require prolonged institutional care and continued assistance in order to live successfully in the community. Goldman and colleagues, in a background paper prepared for "The U.S. Department of Health and Human Services' National Plan for the Chronically Mentally Ill," attempt to delimit this population more precisely. Building on the work on Minkhoff (1978), they developed a definition of chronic mental illness that is based upon three dimensions—diagnosis, disability, and duration. This definition also appears in "National Plan for the

Chronically Mentally Ill." The specificity, detail, and length of this definition attest to the effects of changing treatment modalities for this population. They state that:

> The chronically mentally ill population encompasses persons who suffer certain mental or emotional disorders (organic brain syndrome, schizophrenia, recurrent depressive and manic-depressive disorders, paranoid and other psychoses, plus other disorders which may become chronic) that erode or prevent the development of their functional capacities in relation to (three or more of) such primary aspects of daily life as personal hygiene and self-care, self-direction, interpersonal relationships, social transactions, learning and recreation, and that erode or prevent the development of their economic self-sufficiency. Most such individuals have required institutional care of extended duration, including intermediate-term hospitalization (90 days to one year in a single year), long-term hospitalization (one year or longer in the preceding five years) or nursing home placement on account of a diagnosed mental condition or a diagnosis of senility without psychosis. Some such individuals have required repeated short-term hospitalization (less than 90 days), have received treatment from a medical or mental health professional solely on an outpatient basis, or—despite their needs—have received no treatment in the professional care system. Thus included in the population are persons who are or were formerly "residents" of institutions (public and private psychiatric hospitals and nursing homes), and persons who are at high risk of institutionalization because of persistent mental disability. (Goldman et al., 1981, p. 23)

Numbers and Characteristics of the Chronically Mentally Ill

Using this definition as a framework and reviewing previous epidemiological studies, Goldman and associates provide estimates of the number of the chronically mentally ill population in the United States based on data from 1973-1977. Although these estimates are based on data at least 12 years old, they represent the only data currently available that provides an unduplicated count of the population at about the same point in time (Goldman & Manderscheid, 1987). They estimate the institutionalized mentally ill population at 900,000, of which 150,000 are in mental health facilities (length of stay of one year or more) and 750,000 are in nursing homes. Estimates of the number of chronically mentally ill individuals in the community range from

800,000 to 1,500,000. Of this number, 800,000 are severely disabled (those with a mental disorder unable to work at all and those who could work only occasionally) and 700,000 are moderately disabled (those whose work, including housework, was limited by a mental disorder). Of the severely mentally disabled group, about 12% represent an intermediate length-of-stay hospitalization, that is, individuals who remained in the hospital for more than 3 months but less than 12 months following admission. Estimates of mental health service use by the remaining 88% of this population of the severely mentally disabled in the community tend to be less accurate. Of these chronic patients, Goldman and associates believe that 200,000 are readmissions to state and county mental hospitals for less than 90 days, another 100,000 are patients being treated in community mental health centers, with the balance being cared for in other community settings (Goldman et al., 1981; Goldman & Manderscheid, 1987). Patients who are readmitted to mental hospitals for short stays tend to be younger and more transient than patients who are institutionalized for a year or longer (Talbott, 1988).

Concerning diagnosis, the authors indicate that between 500,000 and 900,000 chronically mentally ill individuals suffer from schizophrenia; 600,000 to 800,000 suffer from chronic and severe depression; psychosis in the elderly, which is primarily organic brain syndrome and primarily chronic, represents between 600,000 and 1,200,000 persons (Goldman et al., 1981). It should not be assumed that all of these individuals are receiving treatment. Dohrenwend (1980) notes that only about 25% of those who have clinically significant mental disorders have ever received treatment from mental health professionals. Among those with the most severe disorders, such as schizophrenia, it is estimated that one in five have never received mental health treatment.

Pepper and Ryglewicz (1984) note that the characteristics of the chronic patient have changed over time. When deinstitutionalization initially began, the typical patient released to the community had been in an institution for a considerable period of time. Today, the focus has changed to include a new component of the chronically mentally ill population, that is, young adults between the ages of 18 and 35 whose emotional disorders have been treated in the community and not in the hospital. In fact, Pepper and Ryglewicz indicate their belief that young adults whose psychological and social functioning is extremely impaired, yet who have lived most of their lives in the community and not in institutions, present particular problems for mental health treatment and that their needs should be considered as a priority in treatment. Because of the shift in treatment locus, they also present more of a burden to their families than did their hospitalized forebears.

Similarly, Talbott (1988) notes that about one third of clients served by programs for chronic patients have previously never been in a state hospital or in any mental health facility, yet their symptoms of chronicity are similar to those of long-term hospitalized patients. Talbott also notes that there is a danger of lack of service for this population group since many programs rule out never-hospitalized patients.

EFFECTS OF CHRONIC MENTAL ILLNESS ON PATIENTS

An overview of the effects of chronic mental illness on patients will help provide a fuller understanding of the sometimes devastating consequences that this illness can have on family members. Rather than trying to discuss all of the major diagnostic disorders of the chronically mentally ill—schizophrenia, depressive disorders, and organic brain syndrome—the focus here will be on schizophrenia because of its special significance among younger chronically mentally ill patients and because a number of treatment and self-help interventions for family caregivers pertain especially to this disease.

Approximately 500,000 to 900,000 chronically mentally ill individuals have a diagnosis of schizophrenia (Minkhoff, 1978). It is a chronic mental disorder whose onset usually appears in late adolescence or early adulthood, but the disorder also may begin in middle or late adult life. During the active phase of the illness psychotic symptoms are present and limit functioning in such areas as work, social relations, and self-care. Symptoms may be positive, such as hallucinations, delusions, or thought disturbances (e.g., loosening of associations); negative, such as lack of goal-directed behavior or blunting of affect; or disorders of interpersonal relationships, such as social withdrawal or emotional detachment (Strauss, Carpenter, & Bartko, 1974). The positive symptoms of schizophrenia often require hospitalization; however, negative symptoms such as social isolation and withdrawal, being more persistent over time, can be a source of greater burdens to families (Lefley, 1987).

Although the effects of this illness vary among patients, the pathological processes are often of long duration and schizophrenics rarely return to full premorbid functioning. Of those affected by schizophrenia, approximately 50% will experience some form of disability with residual impairment on an intermittent basis throughout their lifetime, and 25% will never recover from their initial illness episode and will require care for the rest of their lives. During the first few years of the disorder, residual impairment often increases between episodes (American Psychiatric Association, 1987; Carpenter, 1987; Keith & Matthews, 1984).

Lefley (1987) notes that one result of mental illness upon patients is the reaction of the patients to their deviance. Patients are aware of the effects of the illness upon them—i.e., lack of skills, reduced productivity, and poor prospects for the future. Such awareness, however, doesn't help them address these deficits, since change may be too threatening for many patients.

Summarizing the effects of schizophrenia on the patient, Carpenter (1987) states the following:

> The mind loses the intimate connectedness between thought and emotion, and mental life is often resplendent with disordered perceptions, false ideas, and lack of clarity in logic or thought. Aberrant motor and social behavior are manifest. The patient's place in society erodes in an interactive process reflecting the incapacity to engage and sustain social bonds and society's reaction to the social and personal deviancy caused by the illness. The illness strikes at the very heart of what we consider the essence of the person. Yet, because its manifestations are so personal and social, it elicits fear, misunderstanding, and condemnation in society instead of sympathy and concern. (p. 3)

EFFECTS OF CHRONIC MENTAL ILLNESS ON FAMILIES

This section examines the effects of chronic mental illness on families. We begin with a discussion of etiological theories of schizophrenia and the effects of these theories on how families have been viewed by mental health professionals. This is followed by an examination of the meaning of mental illness for families; a review of research findings pertaining to burdens of families; an overview of the problems and

needs of families of the mentally ill; and a discussion of family interaction patterns and recidivism.

Causal Theories of Schizophrenia
and the Family

A full understanding of the issues facing families of the mentally ill
today is predicated upon an historical understanding of the role of
family and of community in the mental health field. Unlike caregivers
of other diseases discussed in this book, family caregivers of the
mentally ill have been blamed as causal agents of the disease. Thus the
burdens experienced by the caregivers as a result of their caregiving
role have been magnified as a result of these theories. In addition, these
theories ascribed to by mental health professionals have affected the
ability of family caregivers to obtain needed professional supports.
Relationships between mental health professionals and family members
have not been generally supportive, although this is now beginning to
change.

The mental health system in the United States has taken conflicting
and confusing approaches to the role of family and the role of community in service delivery over the past 150 years. At times, family and
community have been seen as the problem, at other times as a potential
solution. Although there has been a gradual shift toward community
based care for the mentally ill, only recently has there been a revision
in theories that saw families as etiological agents in the development
of mental illness.

Beginning in the 1930s and 1940s, new theories of the etiology of
schizophrenia developed that saw families as causal agents of the
disease. In 1948, Fromm-Reichmann published her theory that the
origins of schizophrenia lay in the interaction between infant child and
mother in which the mother consciously expressed feelings of rejection
to her child (Hatfield, 1987b). This theory and other subsequent work
served as the basis of mental health professionals' view of families of
the chronically mentally ill and colored their interaction with these
families for the next three decades. As a consequence, families of the
chronically mentally ill have felt labeled, blamed, and rejected by
mental health professions. Only recently, as new theories of the cause
of schizophrenia have developed, have the attitudes toward each other
of both family members and professionals begun to change (Beels &
McFarlane, 1982).

The Meaning of Mental Illness
for Families

There has been very little research pertaining to the attitudes and beliefs that families have about their mentally ill family members (Clausen & Yarrow, 1955; Kreisman & Joy, 1974; Terkelson, 1987a; 1987b; Yarrow, Schwartz, Murphy, & Deasy, 1955). In one of the earliest examinations of this area, Yarrow et al. studied the cognitive and emotional problems that wives experience in the initial stages of coping with the mental illness of their husbands. Yarrow et al.'s work is based on analysis of a small number of clinical cases. According to the authors, the wife initially notices new and different behavior and tries to account for it. At this early stage, her views shift back and forth as to whether or not a problem exists and whether or not the behavior is normal. Defenses are mobilized that prevent seeing the behavior as deviant; these defenses may include reactions of denying, attenuating, balancing, and normalizing the husband's problems. Eventually a point is reached when the wife believes that a problem does exist and it is one she cannot cope with by herself. At this point, the problem is not necessarily seen as one of mental illness, but rather a physical problem, a "character" problem, or perhaps an environmental problem. Variables that affect the recognition of the problem at this stage pertain to the threatening nature of mental illness as perceived by the spouse: possible roles of the spouse in the development of the disorder, need to change satisfactory patterns of relating to the ill spouse, and recognition of one's future as the spouse of a mental patient.

In an extension of this work, Terkelson (1987b) identifies five principal variables, as follows, that attempt to explicate differences among relatives in defining the meaning of mental illness in their family member: extensiveness of relatives' involvement with the patient's daily life; relatives' theories about causation, symptoms, and outcomes; the natural history and stages of the illness; the relative's personality and life history (including prior experiences with mental illness); and relatives' interactions with other informal and formal network members.

The first variable, extensiveness of involvement with the patient, is the most important one. Relatives closest to the patient are most affected by the patient's behavior and experience the most burden. Other members of the household may try to insulate themselves from the patient and his or her behavior and in so doing may be of less assistance to the primary family caregiver. One's perception of etiology can affect the response of family members. If one's view of mental illness is biological, for example, he or she will be less likely to blame family members or oneself for deviant behaviors. If an interpersonal explanation is adopted, there may be more tension within the family since the family is divided into accusers and accused.

The feelings of relatives about mental illness are invariably affected by the fluctuating cycles of the illness itself. Relatives who understand and can accept an acute deterioration in functioning may be less able to understand and accept that the patient is still sick during remission and residual phases of the disease. One pronounced difficulty for families is dealing with loss of affectional responses by the patient. This may not be perceived as illness-related and may cause emotional strains throughout the family system.

Other variables that affect relatives' responses to mental illness include their age, their individual coping capacities and psychological hardiness, and their prior experience, if any, with mental illness. Finally, response to mental illness is affected by social network variables. Family members often feel isolated as the extent of involvement of outsiders with the ill family member diminishes over time and as the burden of the primary caregiver grows over time. Interactions of family members with mental health professionals who see the family members as causal agents in the disease can also have a negative and disturbing effect on families, although this is changing, as indicated above.

Psychosocial Effects of Mental Illness on Families

About 15 years ago, in a comprehensive review of the literature on families of the mentally ill, Kreisman and Joy (1974) indicated that little research had been conducted that examined the needs and burdens of families of the mentally ill. Although additional research has been published in this area since the Kreisman and Joy study, these newer studies have been cross-sectional in design and have utilized small, unrepresentative samples. Thus significant gaps remain in our knowledge of the variables affecting caregiver burden in families of the mentally ill and in the relationship between burden, especially over a substantial number of years, and caregiver health and mental health status.

There are a number of limitations in the existing research. The focus of research attention has often been on ways to prevent or decrease patient recidivism. Thus, in a number of studies, the family's needs have been examined only in relationship to their effect upon patient recidivism. As a result, families' needs in and of themselves have not received comprehensive attention. Overall, the extant research on families of the mentally ill have the following limitations: most studies are cross-sectional and do not examine variables that affect changes in burden levels over time; study samples are not representative of caregivers overall (many recent studies, for example, have focused on white, middle-class samples); many studies utilize self-report data and do not use standardized scales; there has been very little examination of the effect of burden levels upon caregiver health and mental health status, nor, in fact, has the stress-coping model utilized in caregiver research with many other population groups been applied to caregivers of the mentally ill; little attention has been paid to an examination of variables affecting burden such as length of illness, place of residence of the patient, relationship of the caregiver, and so forth; and there has been little examination of the effects of various interventions upon caregiver burden.

The first studies focusing, at least in part, on caregiving burdens of family members of mental patients were conducted in England (Brown, Bone, Dalison, & Wing, 1966; Grad & Sainsbury, 1963; Hoenig & Hamilton, 1969; Sainsbury & Grad, 1962; Waters & Northover, 1965), with several similar studies in the United States being conducted shortly thereafter (Davis, Dinitz, & Pasaminick, 1974; Freeman & Simmons, 1963; Pasaminick, Scarpetti, & Dinitz, 1967).

Later studies in the United States were focused primarily on the identification of the types and amounts of burdens experienced by family caregivers, the coping strategies used by these caregivers, and the identification of problems that families experienced when interacting with mental health professionals. These more recent studies were drawn from caregivers of treatment program patients (largely working to lower class) as well as from the membership of self-help groups for families of the mentally ill (largely middle class). They served to focus attention on the unmet needs of these caregivers as well as upon changes that mental health agencies and professionals should make to better serve families of the mentally ill (Crotty & Kulys, 1986; Doll, 1975, 1976; Francell, Conn, & Gray, 1988; Hatfield, 1978, 1979a, 1979b, 1981; Kint, 1978; Thompson & Doll, 1982).

The findings of the English studies will be reported first, followed by the early and later American ones, with consistencies and inconsistencies between research in the two countries noted as appropriate. The focus of the early studies in both England and the United States was an examination of factors affecting recidivism of patients and/or the comparative effects of community based versus hospital care. Thus burdens on the family caregiver were studied as an adjunct of patient care. These earlier studies utilized scales to measure burden, often at more than one point in time, and they measured variables that were associated with levels of burden and with recidivism. As indicated above, much of the later studies in the United States focused primarily on the needs of the family caregiver per se. However, as we will see, methodologies and sampling strategies of these later studies are weaker and more limited than the early research reported below.

Patient Studies in England

The work by Grad and Sainsbury (Grad & Sainsbury, 1963; Sainsbury & Grad, 1962) examined the effects on families of home care, as compared with hospitalization, of the mentally ill. This research was important because Grad and Sainsbury were the first researchers to conceptualize and measure "burden" in caregivers of the mentally ill. Over a one year period, clinical and social data were collected from patients and families referred to a community service that offered either home care for the mentally ill in Chichester, England, or a hospital based service in Salisbury, England. Interviews were conducted with every second patient and family in Chichester (271 cases) and every fourth patient and family in Salisbury (139 cases). The effects of the patient's illness on the family were rated by in-person interviewers in the following areas: family income and employment, social and recreational activities of the family, domestic routine, children in the home, health of household members, and relationships with neighbors.

The authors report that over half (61%) of all families had suffered some hardship at home because of the patient's illness, with this hardship being severe in 20% of the families. Over half of the respondents reported excessive anxiety due to worry about the patient, while a fifth reported concern over the patient's neurotic symptoms. One third of the respondents reported restrictions of social and leisure activities and upsets in domestic routine. Patient behaviors found to be most upsetting included the patient's constant focus on bodily complaints, concern about the possibility of patient suicide, and ongoing demands by the patient. A quarter of the sample reported income reductions of at least 10%, with 10% of the sample reporting income reductions of more than half. Children were disturbed in one third of the families, and in one quarter of the families someone had to stay away from work to care for the patient.

The degree of caregiver burden was not related to the length of patient's illness per se, but instead to symptomatology. Specifically, the following symptoms were related to a rating of severe burden—aggression, delusions, hallucinations, confusion, and inability to care for oneself. Burden was also related to household size and the patient's living status. In families with children, where the spouse was the caregiver, the burden was greater. Burden was also greater when the patients lived alone as compared with living in lodges, boarding houses, or hotels.

As the authors indicate, problems in managing the mentally ill are most associated with inpatient care. Almost all (88%) of inpatients' families had difficulties in coping as compared with almost half (44%) of home care families. In two thirds (65%) of the inpatients' families and one quarter (26%) of the home care families, these difficulties were severe. There was also an association between burden levels and admission for services. More than two thirds of those patients who were rated a "severe burden" had been admitted to a hospital, and one fifth (19%) of the outpatients had also been a "severe burden" and an additional 38% were "some burden." There were a number of families experiencing similar problems, however, who continued to care for the mentally ill relative in the community.

The authors then examined the effects of community based services on burden levels of family members, with burden being measured before and one month after admission to treatment. Findings showed that both groups reported significant declines of burden levels, 44% in the hospital group and 35% in the community care group. These differences were not statistically significant. There were no significant differences between the two types of treatment; thus community care was not placing a higher burden on families than hospital based care. It should be noted, however, that the home care services group in this study received ongoing visits and support from the mental health program in a much more comprehensive manner than is usually provided by mental health services in the United States.

Mental health systems in both England and the United States have historically failed to provide adequate follow-up services for former patients and their families. Studies by Waters and Northover (1965), Brown, Bone, Dalison, and Wing (1966), and Hoenig and Hamilton (1969) examined the effects upon families of having a formerly hospitalized family member return to live with them.

The effects of lack of attention to the needs of families after discharge of patients was reported in a study by Water and Northover (1965). The authors conducted a follow-up study of 42 male schizophrenics 24 to 52 months after release from a mental hospital in England. Three quarters (76%) of the patients received after care services. Of this group, after care services were usually given to the patient only (71%), rather than to the patient and family members. One quarter of the families were found to be experiencing moderate or severe hardship as a result of the patient's difficulties, yet almost two thirds (63%) of this group received no direct support.

Brown et al. (1966) reported the results of a five year follow-up study of 339 schizophrenic patients in England who returned to live with their families. The patients represented a working-class to lower-class group, with two thirds of the patients having skilled manual or semi-skilled occupations. Findings showed that relatives tended to welcome the patients and were tolerant and sympathetic toward patient behavior. The investigators believed, however, that family members tended to underrepresent the amount of trouble and distress caused by the patients' discharge: in part because of lowered expectations for patients and for their family life, and in part because they were influenced by the patients' current condition—if they were well now, the past seemed better.

Findings showed that during the last six months of the follow-up period, one quarter (27%) of relatives of patients who had been hospitalized once reported moderate to severe distress, although almost half (49%) of relatives of patients with multiple hospitalizations reported moderate to severe stresses. Specific problems reported by caregivers were similar to the Grad and Sainsbury study reported above. Almost half (46%) of the caregivers reported worry about the patient, over one third (39%) reported their own health to be negatively affected, and the same percentage reported negative affects on children in the family. Almost one third (31%) had leisure or entertainment activities curtailed, and financial problems were reported by over one quarter (29%) of the sample. In general, caregivers of patients with multiple admissions reported more serious problems. Yet, despite these problems, only 12% of the respondents reported wanting the patient to be hospitalized or to live elsewhere.

Hoenig and Hamilton (1969) also examined the effect of home based care on patients' households. Newly accepted patients of two psychiatric units in England were followed for a four-year period. Building on the work of Grad and Sainsbury, Hoenig and Hamilton examined caregiving burdens in a more sophisticated manner than in previous research. Objective burden was defined to include certain specific effects on the daily life of the household or the occurrence of certain abnormal behavior in the patient. Subjective burden was based upon the respondents' view of whether or not they were carrying a burden during the four years of the study.

Findings showed the presence of objective burden in over half (56%) of the households. Burden was not correlated with demographic and socioeconomic characteristics of the caregiver but was related to who the caregiver was and to length of illness. More burden was reported in the conjugal than in the parental home, and the longer the illness, the greater the likelihood of objective burden.

The degree of subjective burden reported was less than might be expected. In almost one quarter (23.6%) of households where the patient had caused objective burden, there was no reporting of subjective burden. This finding of tolerance of caregivers toward their levels of burden is similar to that reported above by Brown et al. There were differences in burden tolerance by type of caregiver, however, with parental homes reporting less objective but more subjective burden. Parents are thus apparently less able to tolerate a sick family member than are other types of caregivers. There was also a difference in subjective burden by social class with lower-class homes experiencing less subjective burden. This latter finding contradicts research in the United States, which reports less tolerance of the mentally ill by the lower socioeconomic class (Myers & Bean, 1968). Subjective burden leveled off over time after the second year as households made some adjustments in relation to their mentally ill family member.

We have seen that the above research examined the effects on patients and families of institutional versus community based care; later research began to focus on the effects of short-term versus standard length hospitalization. The first of these studies was reported in the United States in the mid-1970s. The first study in England was reported by Hirsch, Platt, Knights, and Weyman (1979) who interviewed 127 patients upon admission for inpatient psychiatric care. Random assignment placed 70 patients in the brief care group, and 57 patients were assigned to standard care. Follow-up data are available from 106 patients. Patients and families in the brief care group were told that the patient would probably be discharged within eight days. Data were collected from the patient and caregiver at three times—just prior to admission, 12 to 14 days after admission, and again three months later. The median lengths of stay were 9 days in the brief care group and 17 days in the standard treatment group. Findings showed that about four fifths of the patients in each group were improved after three months regardless of length of hospital stay. In both groups there was major improvement in patient behavior, social performance, and adverse effects on family members between the first and second data collection points with no further significant improvement between the two week and three month interviews. There were no significant differences between the brief and standard care groups on these measures, nor were there any significant differences between the groups in changes in levels of caregiver distress (burden) from the patient's behavior, social performance, or adverse effects on family members. Thus the authors state, similar to the earlier Herz, Endicott, and Spitzer (1976) study in the United States, that there was no adverse effect upon patients or families as a result of shortened hospital stays. A limitation of this study is that the length of hospitalization for both groups was short and both could be defined as short stay.

Patient Studies in the United States

Freeman and Simmons (1963) report findings from the Community Health Project, which was initiated in 1953, concerning family variables affecting rehospitalization of former mental patients. In this study, the dependent variable is rehospitalization rates rather than burden. The study is included here because of its importance in identifying variables, such as patient behavior, that are key components of caregiver burden. The study's findings pertaining to tolerance of deviance is also important in the identification of predictors of burden.

Families (N = 649) were interviewed very soon after the patient left the hospital and then again one year later if the patient was not rehospitalized during this period. Families stated that the reason for return of the patient to the hospital related to the presence of bizarre symptoms in the patient (this is similar to findings in the Pasaminick et al. [1967]

study reported below). Thus the difference between successful and unsuccessful patients related more to affective behavior than instrumental role performance.

Freeman and Simmons indicate that in their previous research they concluded there were differences in tolerance of deviance in different types of families. For example, it was felt that spouses were less tolerant than parents of inadequate instrumental performance and that their mentally ill spouses who could not perform adequately were more likely to return to the hospital. The previous hypothesis was subsequently revised as a result of the authors' 1963 study such that the relationship between posthospital performance and family type was felt to be determined by the influence family members have on performance levels of other family members regardless of whether the family has an ill member. Thus the differential demands and expectations of family members in different types of family settings (i.e., parental, conjugal) are key variables that affect pre- as well as posthospital performance of the patient.

As in the Brown et al. (1966) study reported above, in almost all (95%) of the families, respondents wanted the patient to live in the household. For patients who were not rehospitalized, personal problems in managing the patient diminished over time. The authors reported little stigma as defined by shame or disgrace of hospitalization, interpreting any stigma as due more to the patient's observable behavior. The authors conclude their study by noting their belief that social and psychological characteristics of families have little or no relevance to the process of rehospitalization. As we will see below, however, recent research in England and the United States on families with high expressed emotion cast doubt upon this assertion.

Pasaminick et al. (1967) reported on an experimental home care program to treat schizophrenics in the community. Of the 152 state hospital patients who were studied, 57 were randomly assigned to a drug home care group, 41 to a placebo group, and 54 to a hospital control group. The treatment program consisted of home visitation by nurse in addition to drug medication. Patients in the study were relatively young (mean age: 36.6 years), predominantly white (67%), female (68%), and lower socioeconomic status. Burden levels of caregivers were examined at intake using a scale that included 22 facets of patient behaviors that represented potential problems at home and in the community. Identified burdens were considerable, with over half of the respondents in all three groups reporting major burdens pertaining to general worry and concern about the patient, odd speech and behavior patterns, and patients being noisy or wandering during the night. These findings were similar to a study of middle-class caregivers by Biegel and Yamatani (1986), using the same burden scale, that also found high levels of overall worry about the patient. Relatives in the Pasaminick et al. study indicated significant improvement in burden levels between intake and the sixth month of the project, with reductions tapering off after six months. In all probability this was a reflection of the program's ability to address initially the most acute behavioral symptoms and signs. As we have seen above, however, chronic mental illness tends to be marked by periodic rehospitalizations and changes in patient behavior over the course of the illness. Therefore burden levels fluctuate considerably in the long run; a follow-up to the original study, as reported below, demonstrates this very point.

This study did not provide support for the earlier claim by Freeman and Simmons that there were variations in rehospitalization by family type. Pasaminick et al. (1967) found no differences in rehospitalization between patients returning to conjugal as opposed to parental settings. The major study finding was that acutely psychotic patients could be cared for at home successfully if drug medication was also utilized. Patients were rehospitalized only when their behavior became too bizarre or intolerable and relatives felt they could no longer cope with the patients.

Davis et al. (1974) reported results of a follow-up of patients and significant others of the above study in 1969, five years after the original study had ended. Findings showed that the positive impact of home care lasted at best from six months to one year after the project ended and that the benefits of home care eroded over time. This finding is not reflective of the failure of the "treatment program," rather it is a reflection of the continuing need of patients and families for specialized services over time.

The researchers report that the eight years of the study demonstrate the continuing problems that families experience in caring for a schizophrenic relative. Families worry about their ill family member, they are upset by the patient's bizarre behavior, and they frequently commit them to state and private treatment facilities. For example, at the follow-up interview in 1969, using the same burden scale originally administered, one half of families indicated the patients were a source of worry, almost half (44%) found them uncooperative, over one third (39%) found patients to be talkative and restless, 37% stated that the patients spoke and behaved oddly, 34% found patients to be a trouble at night, and 30% reported the patients' dependency to be a strain. The most frequently cited and most problematic behaviors related to bizarre ideation, speech, and action and resultant noncooperativeness with the family. These results become even more significant when one realizes that families had been dealing with these problems, for better or worse, for at least the eight years of the study. Thus cumulative effects of individual and overall burden levels need to be considered as well as static levels of burden at any single point in time.

Herz et al. (1976) report results of the first controlled study that examined the effects on families of brief versus longer hospital stay. One hundred seventy-five newly admitted psychiatric inpatients who had families were randomly assigned to either a standard inpatient care, brief hospitalization followed by transitional day care if needed, or brief hospitalization followed by discharge to the community. Patients in all three groups were offered outpatient therapy. Data were collected through the Family Evaluation Form, consisting of 455 items grouped in 45 scales, at admission, at three weeks and at 3, 6, 12, 18, and 24 months after treatment. Unlike the Hirsch et al. (1979) study in England reported above, there were considerable differences in the length of stay between the brief and standard care groups. The mean length of stay was 11 days in the brief hospitalization groups and 60 days in the standard hospitalization group.

Overall findings show very few statistically significant differences on any of the measures among the three treatment groups, although numerous contrasts were made. The researchers did find that brief hospitalization did place an additional burden on some families at three weeks. However, over four fifths (82%) of families of brief-care patients at three weeks wanted the patient at home, with only 13% believing the patient should be in the hospital. Positive effects of brief hospitalization on family functioning include earlier resumption of occupational roles and reduced financial burden. The authors caution that these findings may only be applicable to programs that offer inpatient services as part of a continuous broader treatment care program. As such, the findings support Davis et al. (1974) above in the need of patients and families for ongoing care. The authors also note, as many of the studies above indicate, burden of family caregivers is ongoing and pervasive. Although this burden tends to be the greatest just prior to hospitalization, the burden does not disappear after the patient improves and is back in the community.

Caregiver Studies in the United States

The mid-1970s saw an increasing number of studies focused on the burden of caregivers (Crotty & Kulys, 1986; Doll, 1975, 1976; Hatfield, 1978, 1979a, 1979b, 1981; Kint, 1978; Kreisman, Simmons, & Joy, 1979; Thompson & Doll, 1982). First, we will examine studies of caregivers of present and former patients of treatment programs, largely working-class to lower-class samples, and then look at findings from surveys of members of self-help groups of families of the mentally ill, largely middle-class samples.

Doll (1975, 1976) and Thompson and Doll (1982) report results of a cross-sectional study of patients and caregivers of a psychiatric rehabilitation program in Cleveland, conducted between 1972 and 1975. The response rate was 89%. A random sample of 125 family members was interviewed six months after the patient returned home. The resultant sample was predominantly female (66%), white (58%), and represented the two lowest social classes, IV and V, on the Hollingshead-Redlich Two Factor Index of Social Position. The median age of the former patients was 37, with over half of them having had three or more previous hospitalizations. Burden was examined both from an objective perspective, disruption of family life caused by the former patient, as well as a subjective perspective, the emotional costs that the patient's presence has on the family.

Findings show that almost three quarters (73%) of families reported being adversely affected by the patient in one or more ways. Almost half (46%) of the families were experiencing "moderate" levels of burden, with over one quarter (27%) experiencing "severe" burdens. Specific burdens included being forced to provide supervision that would not otherwise be necessary. Half the families reported the following burdens: financial hardship (38%), interference with family routines (30%), neglect of the caregivers' responsibilities to other family members (30%), and strained relationships with neighbors (20%). Concerning subjective burden, the authors state that the levels of embarrassment of families was twice that reported by Freeman and Simmons above, indicating either that family members were now more willing to report feelings of embarrassment or the levels of embarrassment were actually higher than previously reported. Almost three quarters (74%) of families reported feeling chronically overloaded and strained. However, this feeling of overload was accompanied by lower levels of feeling trapped (42%) or of intense resentment (13%).

Although only a very small number of families wished to exclude the former patient (7%), one quarter (27%) tried to isolate themselves from the patient at least to some extent. The data indicate that the proportion of families with severe objective burden (27%) was nearly twice the proportion of families with severe subjective burden. These findings reinforce the findings of the patient studies above that families accept the mentally ill family member and provide care but often at tremendous cost to themselves.

Further analyses were conducted to examine the correlates of burden. There was no relationship found between the patient's or respondent's demographic characteristics. As might be expected, subjective burdens were correlated with the psychiatric condition of the patient. Respondents reporting more patient symptoms and a higher number of previous hospitalizations also reported higher levels of subjective burden. Subjective burdens, however, were reported even when the patient had few behavioral symptoms. Objective burden was also correlated with the psychiatric condition of the patient.

In contrast to the above study and to the findings concerning burden reported above and in the other studies we have reviewed, Crotty and Kulys (1986) report low levels of burden on family caregivers. A sample of 56 schizophrenics and 56 significant others identified by the patients were interviewed in a cross-sectional study. The sample was drawn from an urban, outpatient community mental health center that serves an ethnically mixed, working-class community. The sample was almost entirely white, with the median age of patients being 42 years. Over four fifths (83%) had at least one hospitalization in the past three years. The mean age of the significant others was 59, with most (70%) being women and with half being the patients' mothers or sisters. Burden was assessed using a nine item scale that measured the impact of the mentally ill relative upon the caregiver and family. Findings show that caregivers reported only mild levels of burden, with only two of the nine items registering high levels of burden. One fifth of the respondents reported the patient as not burdensome at all on all nine variables. Examining the correlates of burden, the findings showed that household size was the only significant demographic variable. Smaller households reported more burden than larger households. Unlike findings from previous research, there was no correlation between caregiver burden and treatment variables. There was a correlation, however, between patients' support networks and caregiver's burdens. Caregivers who perceived that the patient had more supportive relationships reported lower levels of burdens.

In the late 1970s, Hatfield (1978, 1979a, 1979b) reported the results of a cross-sectional survey of members of a self-help group for families of schizophrenics that examined issues pertaining to caregiver burden and coping. The study sample represented a self-selected group that was largely white and middle-class. The response rate to the mailed questionnaire was 43%. Almost all respondents (85%) were parents of schizophrenic patients, with the remaining 15% being siblings, spouses or other close relatives. Over half of the patients (57%) were living at home at the time of the study, with one quarter (26%) living in their own or in group homes, and 17% were hospitalized.

Findings showed that caregivers reported considerable levels of burden: 65% of respondents reported stress, 30% reported anxiety, 24% reported resentment, and 22% reported grief and depression. Respondents were given a list of 20 items pertaining to patient behavior and asked to rate the degree of disturbance of each. Six items were rated as somewhat or very disturbing by at least 50% of the respondents as follows: behaviors relating to poor task functioning (lacks motivation [79%], handles money poorly [70%], poor grooming and personal care [67%], forgets to do things [61%]); behaviors related to intrusive and disturbing behavior (unusual eating and sleeping patterns [64%]); and behaviors that are bizarre or abnormal (talks without making sense [63%]).

Kint (1978) reported results of a mailed survey to family members of schizophrenics who were members of the American Schizophrenia Association, an organization sponsored by the Huxley Institute for Biosocial Research whose treatment modality is based on megavitamin therapy for schizophrenia. This study sample was also highly educated and middle class. The respondents were middle-aged although their schizophrenic family members were in their 20s and 30s. Over half of the patients had been ill for ten years or more. Family members reported that their major problems were finding effective treatment (89%) and worry (84%). Respondents reported that patients had an average of 10 subjective symptoms. Most disturbing were altered sense perceptions, emotions, and thinking and certain physical symptoms. Behavioral problems that were of most concern included withdrawal from others and unusual eating and sleeping patterns. Social and emotional burdens of families included: disruption of family life (77%), social life and employment patterns of patients (48%), patient living arrangements

(33%), and financial burdens (almost one third). As was the case in the patient studies reported above, levels of reported stigma were low (only 15% of respondents reported this as a problem) although the level of guilt was fairly high (45%).

Kreisman et al. (1979) reported results of a survey of 143 middle-class family caregivers. Findings were consistent with the Hatfield and Kint studies. Four fifths of the caregivers reported worrying about the patient, and difficulty finding effective treatment. Three quarters reported disruption of family life, and over 60% reported financial problems and employment and social life problems for the patient. Feelings of guilt and stigma were similar to the Kint study—41% of caregivers reported feeling guilty and only 20% reported problems of stigma. Major behavior problems of the patient included withdrawal (77%), failure to consider the future (54%), and suicide attempts (38%).

The results of these three studies need to be interpreted with caution because the study samples are not representative of caregivers in general. The studies did not utilize standardized burden scales, nor did they report any correlations of demographic and patient functioning data with reported levels of burden. It is therefore possible to compare these findings to previous work only in general terms.

A later exploratory study by Hatfield (1981), using a subsample of 30 respondents from the above study sample, examined coping effectiveness over a 30-month period. Three components of coping effectiveness—emotional mastery, cognitive skill, and need fulfillment—were rated separately for each respondent and then combined to form a single rating of coping effectiveness that was subsequently split into three categories: high, moderate, and low coping. This study was the first nonpatient study to examine coping over time and to explore the relationship between coping capacity and patient functioning. The sample is small, however, no reliability coefficients were reported for the coping scale, and coping data were reported at only one time point, so the findings need to be interpreted cautiously. Hatfield reported a decrease in stress by caregivers over the three years of the study but little change in coping effectiveness during this time period, although no data were provided to support this assertion. She hypothesizes that the lack of change in coping effectiveness may be due to lack of sensitivity of the coping instrument or to the fact that because caregivers provide care over a long time period, a three-year period may not be sufficient to show change in coping skills, especially because the sample did not include caregivers of patients in the very early stages of illness when coping changes might be expected to be more rapid. The study raises a number of questions for future research that implicitly suggest the need for longitudinal studies with larger samples and more complete data collection measures.

Specific Problems and Needs of Families of the Mentally Ill

As we have just seen, relatives of the mentally ill shoulder a significant amount of caregiving responsibilities, often with inadequate assistance from mental health and human service professionals and agencies. The burdens of such caregiving are multiple and pervasive and often contribute to feelings of guilt, resentment, worry, grief, and depression. Significant issues and problems facing caregivers of the mentally ill cited in the research and practice literature include the following:

- Managing their mentally ill relatives' symptomatology and behaviors

Families need practical management techniques for addressing some or all of the following patient symptoms: hallucinations, irrational or blocked thought content, suspiciousness, inappropriate affect, social withdrawal, isolation, unusual beliefs, or mood swings. Assistance is also required in managing intrusive and disturbing behaviors including: unusual eating and sleeping habits, aggression toward self and others, deviant sexual behavior, and argumentativeness. Lamb (1982) notes that part of the difficulty facing families is that patient behavior is often unpredictable and that families never know how a particular situation will affect a patient at a particular time. Patient reactions may sometimes include violent behavior. Spaniol and Jung (1983) conducted a national survey of members of self-help groups affiliated with the National Alliance of the Mentally Ill. They note that families cite the management of disturbing behavior as the most frequent reason for rehospitalization, a finding supported by the Freeman and Simmons (1963) study reviewed above.

- Isolation of caregivers of the mentally ill due in part to the "stigma" of mental illness

Leff (1983) notes that family caregivers lack intimate relationships that can be called upon for emotional support. Family members often feel a sense of shame or guilt, partly because of feelings of self-blame, partly because the patient's condition carries with it a stigma (Biegel & Yamatani, 1986; Kint, 1978; Kreisman et al., 1979). These feelings may cause them to withdraw from others in their social circle. Additionally, the behavior of the patients may cause relatives and friends to avoid visiting the household or to avoid any discussion about the emotional difficulties the caregiver may be facing. The net result is that when family caregivers most need others for social support, there are few, if any, individuals available to share the load.

- Interference with personal needs of family members.

Families report that providing care for a mentally ill family member is disruptive of family life and may cause strained family relationships (particularly among siblings), financial hardship, neglect of personal needs, lack of leisure time and stress related health problems (Doll, 1975, 1976; Kreisman et al., 1979; Thompson & Doll, 1982). Lamb (1982) notes the all-encompassing burden of providing care for a mentally ill relative and that even leaving the house to do some light shopping requires making arrangements for someone to watch the patient. As Lamb states, "The relatives may not only become the jailers, but, in effect be in jail themselves" (p.92).

- Inability of the patient to carry out the tasks of daily living

Patients may be unable to take responsibility for their own grooming and hygienic functions, and they may not be able to perform their share of household tasks. Grad and Sainsbury (Grad & Sainsbury, 1963; Sainsbury & Grad, 1962) found that caregivers' rating of severe burden was correlated with patients' inability to care for themselves. The latter issue may be more of a problem in low socioeconomic status households that are unable to pay others for the performance of these tasks.

- Proper use of medication

The adherence by patients to a medication regimen is a major concern of families. Spaniol and Jung (1983) found that drug management was a key need of families and that monitoring of medication was inade-quate and infrequent. In their national study of members of self-help groups for the mentally ill, drug medication was cited as an area of treatment needing the most improvement, with over half of the respondents (52%) dissatisfied with medication services.

- Mental health professionals are often seen by families as not helpful and may make the families feel blamed as a causal agent of the patient's disease

Family members complain that they have insufficient knowledge and information about mental illness—its treatment, the availability of services, and practical management techniques. For example, Holden and Lewine (1982) conducted a mail survey of 500 family caregivers with a 41% response rate. Respondents were largely middle class and predominantly female. The authors found that a majority of family members (54%) reported that mental health professionals had not involved them in the treatment of their ill family members, and two thirds (66%) reported dissatisfaction with the frequency of contact with professionals. One third of the respondents (32%) reported that they were given a diagnosis from 2 to 11 years after the initial breakdown.

Even when families actively seek out information, they rarely receive it in any sufficient quality or quantity. For example, a study by Hatfield (1978, 1979b) of families of the mentally ill found that families complained that mental health professionals only offered insight oriented therapy, but did not give families what they wanted, a clear explanation of the patient's illness, practical help concerning how to handle patient behavior, and referral to appropriate community resources. Caregivers were asked to indicate the kinds of services and supports they needed. The first two choices related to enhancing their knowledge—57% wanted assistance in becoming more knowledgeable and understanding of the patient's symptoms, and a similar percentage of caregivers (55%) wanted specific suggestions for coping with the patient's behavior. Similarly, Kreisman et al. (1979) reported that families believe they would benefit most from specific suggestions for coping with the patient's behavior and second by a knowledge of symptoms so that they could better understand the patient's behavior.

In fact, families often find other sources of assistance more effective than the help of professionals. Hatfield (1979b, 1981) found that families rated professional help much less positively than the help of parents of other schizophrenics, self-help groups, or friends and relatives. Spaniol and Jung (1983) asked respondents in their survey to report the level of satisfaction or dissatisfaction with seven professional activities: practical advice, information about the illness, emotional support, referral, treatment coordination, attitude toward the family, and attitude toward the ill member. The most frequently occurring response was "very dissatisfied" in the first five activities listed above. Similar to the Hatfield finding above, they report that one third of the sample (32.6%) stated that the self-help group was their most important source of support, as compared to one fifth (19.6%) of the sample that cited mental health professionals as their most important source of support. Similarly, self-help groups were cited to a greater degree than mental health professionals as the most helpful for learning information.

A recent study by Francell et al. (1988) provides additional evidence that supports the findings of these earlier studies. Family caregivers indicate a variety of problems in their interactions with the mental health system including a lack of information, communication problems with mental health professionals, lack of involvement in treatment decisions, and conflicts around their roles as patient advocates.

FAMILY INTERACTION PATTERNS AND RECIDIVISM

As we have seen in the preceding review of research studies, investigators have been concerned with factors affecting rehospitalization of patients and also with caregiver burden. These two concepts are very much interrelated. We know, for example, that the management of disturbing behavior is related to rehospitalization and also to caregiver burden. It is important, therefore, to obtain a better understanding of the factors affecting patient behavior with a goal of better managing and controlling such behavior. This can reduce rehospitalization rates as well as caregiver burden. In fact, one of the major concerns of researchers over the last 30 years has been the identification of factors that are associated with relapse and rehospitalization of the chronically mentally ill. The best predictor of relapse or poor clinical course has been found to be noncompliance with antipsychotic medication (Goldstein, M. J., 1987). A number of researchers have also been examining the role of psychosocial factors in recidivism. Although earlier claims that families caused schizophrenia have now been discarded, there is research to suggest that particular family interaction patterns, specifically high expressed emotion, is correlated with significantly higher rates of patient relapse.

The first research in this area began about 30 years ago at the MRC Social Psychiatric Unit, Institute of Psychiatry, London, in an attempt to get a better understanding of the factors influencing patient success in the community. It was found that patients who returned home and lived with relatives who were highly emotionally involved with them— emotional overinvolvement, hostility, number of critical comments— were more likely to suffer a relapse of florid symptoms, even after controlling for psychiatric state at time of discharge (Brown, 1959). This concept is now called expressed emotion (EE).

In a later study, Brown and colleagues (Brown, Birley, & Wing, 1972) found that the level of emotion expressed by relatives at the time of hospital admission was strongly correlated with symptomatic relapse during the nine months following discharge. The authors further found that the association between high EE and relapse is independent of other variables, such as schizophrenic symptoms, age, gender, and lack of regular medication that also have been found to be associated with higher relapse rates (Brown et al., 1972). These original studies have since been replicated by other researchers (Anderson, Hogarty, & Reiss, 1980; Falloon, Boyd, & McGill, 1984; Falloon et al., 1982; Liberman, Wallace, Vaughn, Snyder, & Rust, 1980; Vaughn & Leff, 1976a, 1976b, 1981a, 1981b; Vaughn et al., 1982). In reviewing these subsequent studies, Platman (1983) indicates that they show that relapse rates in high EE families varied between 48% and 62%, in contrast to low EE families, which had relapse rates between 9% and 21%. M. J. Goldstein, (1987) and Hatfield, Spaniol, and Zipple (1985) caution against simplistic utilization of the EE typology, noting that high EE attitudes and negative affective behaviors toward patients probably have complex origins. Hatfield et al. (1985) also fear that the high EE concept can label families negatively and therefore increase levels of alienation between families and professionals which, as we have seen, historically have been high. They also suggest that since EE levels are usually taken upon hospital admission, a very stressful and confusing time for relatives, it may not be an accurate reflection of the caregivers' usual level of interaction with the patient in the natural home environment.

Future research in this area should examine not only the natural course and history of the schizophrenic disorder but also the natural coping processes used by family members utilizing vulnerability-stress-support models that have been used with other caregiving populations. As will be seen in Chapter 8, a number of educational and behavioral interventions have been developed that attempt to reduce rates of recidivism, and therefore also family caregiver burden, by reducing levels of high EE.

SERVICES AVAILABLE
FOR PATIENTS AND FAMILIES

It is widely recognized that chronically mentally ill patients have needs, such as vocational training, housing, and socialization, that go beyond mental health treatment per se. The wide ranging unmet needs of the chronically mentally ill were identified by the U.S. General Accounting Office in its 1977a report and in the 1978 report of the President's Commission on Mental Health, among other studies. In the late 1970s, to help address these unmet needs, the National Institute of Mental Health began the Community Support Program that focuses on adults 18 years and older whose severe mental or emotional disorders impair their ability to function in the community (Tessler, Goldman, & Associates, 1982). The purpose of this program, which is operated as a federal-state partnership, is to develop a comprehensive range of programs and services for chronically mentally ill adults to better enable them to function in the community. Program components include: outreach; assisting clients to apply for entitlements and to obtain needed housing, clothing, food and medical care; provision of adequate mental health services; emergency and comprehensive psychosocial services; rehabilitative and supportive housing; consultation and education; advocacy; and strengthening of informal systems of care. These services are available to patients on a long-term basis, given the chronic nature of their disease.

In addition to the "medically" based mental health treatment services, which are offered through community mental health centers, there are a number of rehabilitation programs for chronically mentally ill persons in which the service recipients are referred to as members instead of clients or patients and which do not utilize the medical model. There is also a growing number of peer support and self-help programs for patients run by mental health consumers (patients).

As we have indicated earlier, families of chronically mentally ill patients often report that mental health professionals do not involve caregivers in the treatment of their ill relative or help address the caregivers' needs. There is some evidence that this is now changing. There are a variety of interventions that directly involve family members, ranging from information and educational programs, family therapy, psychoeducational programs, and professionally led support groups to self-help groups. Educational programs were developed by mental health agencies in acknowledgment of families' expressed need for information about mental illness and about ways of coping with this disease. These programs may be organized as a series of lectures, small group discussions, or agency led support groups.

Many therapeutic interventions exclude families. In contrast to these models, Leff's (1979) family therapy approach includes only family members and not patients. It is derived from his research on expressed emotion (EE). Group therapy sessions are held with both low and high EE families in the same group. Families are taught to avoid intrusive behavior, to allow the patient distance, to cope with crisis more effectively, and to provide a calming environment for the patient. The psychoeducational approach of Anderson, Hogarty, and Reiss (1981), which is also based on EE research, is less therapy per se than it is providing information and teaching behavioral change to reduce high EE levels.

There is now a large network of self-help groups for families of the mentally ill, most of which have been organized within the last decade. Many of these groups are affiliated with the National Alliance for Families of the Mentally Ill. Sometimes these groups are formally sponsored and initially organized through the support of mental health agencies; at other times they are independent of, in some cases stridently so, mental health centers.

It is important that interventive strategies to assist family caregivers recognize that caregivers' needs are, in part, a reflection of the stage of the patient's illness. For example, research by Abramowitz and Coursey (1989) indicates that practical information about interacting with a schizophrenic family member is most helpful earlier in the illness, with interpersonal support from other caregivers becoming more important at later illness stages.

RESEARCH ON FACTORS
AFFECTING CAREGIVER STRESS

The previous sections of this chapter discussed the psychosocial effects of mental illness upon families, identified specific problems and needs of families of the mentally ill, and discussed the relationship between family interaction patterns and recidivism. In this section, using the theoretical model presented in Chapter 2, we will summarize the literature on the variables predicting stress in caregivers of the mentally ill. Our discussion will be both a reframing of issues discussed earlier in a somewhat different context and also the presenting of some new material. The limitations of the existing caregiver literature in this field, which was discussed earlier, needs to be reemphasized because the existing gaps in the literature prevent a full understanding of the variables effecting caregiver stress.

Objective Stressors

Levels of caregiving burden, which was identified in some studies as an outcome variable and in others as a predictor variable, were found to be related to the severity of symptomatology, to the decision of the family to seek inpatient treatment for the patient, and to the number of previous hospitalizations (Brown et al., 1966; Doll, 1975, 1976; Grad & Sainsbury, 1963; Pasaminick et al., 1967; Sainsbury & Grad, 1962; Thompson & Doll, 1982). In contrast, Crotty and Kulys (1986), in a study of working-class caregivers reported above, found relatively low levels of caregiver burden and no correlations between caregiver burden and treatment variables. It should be noted that while there is consistency in the above findings (except for Crotty & Kulys, 1986), burden was not measured consistently in the various studies. In some cases there was one overall measure of burden, and in other cases burden was divided in objective burden, pertaining to disruptions in family life, or subjective burden, defined as emotional costs of the patient's presence on the caregiver and family.

There is some disagreement as to whether burden is also related to the length of illness per se, with Sainsbury and Grad (1962) finding no such relationship but Brown et al. (1966) reporting that the longer the illness the greater the chance of finding objective burden. In the latter study, there was no indication whether or not severity of symptoms was controlled in examining length of illness upon levels of caregiving burden. As noted in previous sections, family caregivers of the mentally ill are affected by both the episodic and enduring nature of the patient's illness. Although levels of caregiver burden change over time, Pasaminick et al.'s (1967) research demonstrates that such burden can continue over many years. Thus the relationship between burden and objective stressors needs to be further examined using longitudinal designs to obtain a fuller understanding of the relationship between these variables.

Contextual Variables

A number of studies of caregiver burden have examined the relationship between caregiver burden and various demographic, socioeconomic, and household characteristics. Although there have been several studies that have examined the role of social support in caregiver functioning, there have been no empirical studies that have examined the effect of the previous relationship between caregiver and patient on caregiver distress. We will begin our discussion with caregiver characteristics and then turn to an examination of the role of social support.

Research findings concerning the relationship of caregiver and patient demographic and socioeconomic characteristics and caregiver burden are inconsistent. Doll and associates (Doll, 1975, 1976; Thompson & Doll, 1982) report no relationships between patient and caregiver characteristics and caregiver burden, although Crotty and Kulys (1986) report a relationship between caregiver burden and household size such that smaller households experience more caregiver burden. Hoenig and Hamilton (1969) report no significant relationships between caregiver demographic and socioeconomic characteristics and objective burden, but do report a relationship between subjective burden and socioeconomic status of the caregiver such that lower-class caregivers report experiencing less subjective stress.

Several studies examined caregiver relationship and levels of burden on rehospitalization rates. Hoenig and Hamilton (1969) reported finding a correlation between caregiver burden and the relationship of the caregiver to the patient. More objective burden was reported in the conjugal than parental home, with the parental home reporting less objective but more subjective burden. The authors interpreted this finding to mean that parents are less able to tolerate mentally ill family members than are other types of caregivers. Other researchers have examined the correlation between relationship of the caregiver and rehospitalization rates. Pasaminick et al. (1967) did not find variations in rehospitalizations by caregiver relationship, although Freeman and Simmons (1963), in a revision of an earlier hypothesis, believe that the relationship between posthospital performance and family type is determined by the influence family members have on the performance levels of other family members. Thus it is felt that different types of family settings, i.e., parental and conjugal, create differential demands on and expectations of family members and that this affects prehospital as well as posthospital patient performance.

Although social support networks of mentally ill persons have been examined in a number of studies during the last decade, much less attention has been paid to social support systems for caregivers of the mentally ill. Concerning patients, findings have consistently showed that the social networks of mentally ill persons are more constricted and unidimensional than networks of normal persons. In fact, the nature of schizophrenia, in particular, is such that it interferes with individuals' ability to form and sustain relationships (Beels, 1978; Crotty & Kulys, 1985). Utilizing a sample of lower-middle-class white schizophrenics and their primary caregivers, Crotty and Kulys (1985) report that the patients reported significantly larger and more supportive networks for themselves than the caregivers reported for the patients. The authors hypothesize that the findings indicate negative perceptions by caregivers of patients' levels of functioning which might in turn adversely affect their actual performance levels. If this hypothesis is indeed true, then lowered patient performance might in turn affect levels of caregiver burden. Additional research is needed with broader samples of caregivers and patients to examine this issue further.

The role of social support and caregiver burden has been researched on only a very limited basis, and such examinations have not tested the statistical relationship between these two variables (Biegel & Yamatani, 1986; Leff, 1983). Rather, the sense of isolation, lack of intimate relationships, and withdrawal from others by caregivers have been identified, as well as the tendency of relatives and friends to avoid visiting the caregiver's household. Biegel and Yamatani (1986), in a study of predominantly middle-class members of self-help groups for families of the mentally ill, found that even caregivers who reported strong overall systems of social support identified the lack of social support, or anybody to talk to, concerning the specific problems and needs they experienced as caregivers of the mentally ill.

In conclusion, the literature examining predictors of caregiver distress has identified a number of variables that contribute to caregiver burden. As we can see, however, the present data are far from conclusive. Given the episodic and enduring nature of mental illness, the cross-sectional data that have been reviewed in most of the above studies is very limited in its ability to provide an accurate picture of caregiver distress. Further research using the stress-support-coping theoretical framework is needed. Such studies should be longitudinal, utilize measures with established levels of reliability and validity, and involve larger and more representative samples of caregivers and patients than the extant research does.

8

Common Factors
Affecting Family Caregivers

The preceding chapters have considered the variables found to be associated with psychosocial outcomes for family caregivers of patients with cancer, stroke, heart disease, mental illness, and Alzheimer's disease. It should be noted that the research literature reviewed for each of these health arenas has developed in isolation, building almost exclusively upon prior illness-specific studies in that specific health arena. Links with research on other chronic illnesses have been virtually ignored. As a consequence, findings regarding caregiver problems are viewed as if they are unique to that illness, yet both the general perspectives on chronic illness presented in Chapter 1 and the theoretical model presented in Chapter 2 suggest that a common group of predictors may relate to caregiver outcomes across disease categories. If this model can be confirmed we will have a clearer understanding of general factors affecting the adaptations of family caregivers. That is the goal of this chapter.

Thus far, the growing literature on psychosocial adjustment of caregivers has explored only some of the variables that may be associated with caregiver outcomes. Obviously, the gaps in current studies impede empirical testing of the entire theoretical model presented in Chapter 2. Despite this limitation, we can already begin to see some consistencies across diseases in the predictors of psychosocial adjustment for family caregivers. We will identify these variables in this chapter. We will also discuss additional variables that have emerged as salient in one or another of the chronic illnesses explored, but have not been found as consistently across illnesses.

Before turning our attention to the task of synthesizing the variables that have been found to predict caregiver outcomes across chronic illnesses, the reader should be reminded of the limitations surrounding this effort. As we have noted, some health arenas have barely begun to examine the predictors of caregiver outcomes suggested in our theoretical model. Furthermore, rarely has the same set of variables been studied across all the illness categories we have discussed. We must thus anticipate the absence of parallel data for all five chronic illnesses. Even when we see parallel patterns across illnesses, the variables identified could simply have been those more easily studied, such as gender or age, rather than those that may be the strongest contributors to caregiver strain.

Unfortunately, in many instances where we do have comparative data across diseases, the patterns are often inconsistent. Thus findings may show a predictor to be associated with caregiver strain in one illness, while showing no association, or a different pattern of relationship, in another. For example, higher social status has been found to be associated with greater caregiver strain in mental illness and heart disease, while lower socioeconomic status predicts greater strain for caregivers of stroke patients. Before concluding that SES operates differently for these two illnesses, we must compare the methodologies of each study. It might be that conflicting findings may have emerged because of differences in measurement, sampling, or study design.

One further methodological dimension central to our effort needs to be highlighted here. We are concerned with understanding the factors that affect the psychosocial outcomes of caregivers, yet the definition and measurement of our key dependent variable remains elusive. As we have already seen in Chapter 2, there is little consistency in current conceptualizations and measures of the psychosocial outcomes of caregiving. Thus we must consider the outcome domains defined in current research on the impact of the caregiving role.

The theoretical model presented in Chapter 2 defines the relevant dependent variable endpoints as enduring changes in some aspect of caregivers' life circumstances, including their decision to institutionalize the patient (when this is a possible option), role changes in other sectors of their lives, and physical or psychiatric morbidity. Such clear enduring outcomes would show the long-term impact of caregiving on the person's ability to maintain other areas of functioning. Thus an enduring outcome may be viewed as any decline in a caregiver's functional status to a level that is viewed as clinically problematic and requiring possible professional intervention. At this point society may incur the added social cost of treating the caregiver as well as the patient.

While these enduring changes in caregiver status may be the outcomes of greatest relevance to our theoretical model, as well as to society, they have rarely been incorporated into the research studies currently available. Instead, most current studies of caregivers measure outcomes by using indicators of psychological distress or reduced well-being. These standard measures of psychological adjustment tap only the immediate and shorter term costs of their role. As a consequence, this discussion will focus almost exclusively on known predictors to caregiver distress.

Although the above caveats impose some constraints on our ability to implement the comparative task we are undertaking here, there is one positive implication that should be emphasized. When we find a predictor that relates to caregiver outcomes similarly across disease categories, we can have great confidence that it is a consistent factor affecting caregivers in all the chronic illnesses discussed here. We can also have reasonable confidence that it may be generalizable to other caregiver populations. Thus, while pattern divergences are difficult to interpret, pattern convergence across illness categories represents strong confirmation of that aspect of the theoretical model.

Keeping these cautions in mind, we will now discuss the commonalities among predictors of caregiver outcomes across illness categories. Following the theoretical model, we will first explore the objective stressors related to the patient's illness characteristics, and then turn our attention to the contextual factors that may mediate the direct impact of illness.

OBJECTIVE STRESSORS—PATIENT CHARACTERISTICS

Illness Severity

There is a remarkable convergence across all illness categories on one objective stressor that is central to the amount of strain experienced by caregivers. In general, the more severe the illness, the greater the emotional impact on the caregivers. This consistent pattern is not surprising. It is, however, striking that it echoes across illnesses that differ greatly in their symptomatology, pattern of onset, and trajectory.

It is also notable that this pattern prevails despite enormous differences in the extensiveness and types of caregiving tasks required.

There are hints in the literature that caregiver outcome is not a simple direct consequence of the amount of caregiving demands. Many studies have found little relationship between family members' objective caregiving activities and their perceived burden. The consistent impact of the severity variable across diverse illnesses suggests a more complex process. Family members may, at least in part, assess the patient's plight relative to others in that illness category. The amount of strain they experience may be partially explained by their relative assessment of illness severity, in addition to the effects of other characteristics of the illness and its caregiving demands. In short, social comparison processes may be a mediating mechanism in caregivers' assessments of their own hardships.

Within particular illnesses, the data suggest some specific indicators that family members may use in assessing relative severity. In heart disease and mental illness, families of patients who had prior hospitalizations were more distressed than others. More surprisingly, and in keeping with a social comparison interpretation, families of coronary patients that return to full activity either very early or very late are more distressed than families with more normative recovery periods. And families of cancer patients whose diagnoses indicate more advanced stages of the disease or worse prognoses show more emotional symptomatology. Also for cancer, the approach of death in the terminal period represents another peak in caregiver distress.

The impact of illness stage in cancer caregiver distress suggests that, in addition to illness severity, other aspects of the chronic illness may affect caregiver outcomes. As previously discussed in Chapter 2, the concept of disease stage is elusive when it is applied across illnesses differing markedly in disease course, time duration, visibility, and trajectory. Can stages in coronary disease or stroke, where recovery increases over time, be compared to the inevitable downward course of Alzheimer's disease, or the uncertainty of cancer? Furthermore, the stage concept may not be even appropriate to all chronic illnesses. Mental illness, for example, may be classified by diagnosis and whether it is acute or chronic, but does not appear to have clear stages.

Considering these difficulties, it is not surprising that most researchers have not included illness characteristics other than severity. One simple indicator of illness course has been used across some health arenas, however. Studies of caregiving for patients with cancer and mental illness have studied the impact of time since diagnosis. Unfortunately, in both these research arenas, it appears that caregiver adjustment does not vary simply with time since diagnosis. Thus future researchers may have to develop measures of variables capturing some of the other, more complex, dimensions of illness discussed above. Such measures may be necessary to determine which additional objective disease characteristics may impact on caregiver well-being.

Suddenness of Onset

In addition to severity, one additional illness course dimension has been found to consistently predict caregiver impact. A number of studies across health arenas have found that the suddenness of illness confrontation contributes greatly to family distress. In each of the illnesses with either a sudden onset (heart attacks or stroke) or a sudden diagnosis (cancer), caregivers' stress was most pronounced during the early acute stage of the illness. For these families, the illness represented a major family crisis, with its heightened stress consequences. Disequilibrium and disruption were at their peak during this initial period, as families attempted to cope with the diagnosis and its life-altering implications. In contrast, mental illness or Alzheimer's disease do not appear to show this pattern of caregiver stress peaking after diagnosis, perhaps because these diagnoses usually occur after families have gradually became aware of worrisome behavioral changes in patients.

Patient Change

In addition to the impact of the objective illness variables of severity and suddenness, the reactions of family members also seem to depend on the degree to which the illness impacts on the patient. In physical illnesses like heart disease and cancer, the patient's own distress correlates significantly with the distress of those who care for them. The degree of family reaction in other illnesses is related to patient behavioral changes or symptom manifestation. For example, stroke victims with greater personality change, and Alzheimer's patients with more memory or communication problems, evoke more distress in families. (The finding that brain cancer represents the most stressful disease site for families may be attributable to the greater personality and behavioral changes associated with this form of cancer.)

Although one can infer from the above findings that greater patient change contributes to greater family distress, the source of this pattern is uncertain. As discussed above, greater patient change may be viewed by caregivers as an indicator of greater severity of a patient's illness. This perception may contribute to more negative social comparison judgments regarding the patient's health status. Families also could be reacting to the loss of accustomed patterns of behavior by the patient, which creates the need for other members to assume responsibility for tasks formerly performed by the patient. In addition, families may feel confusion and uncertainty about how to respond to the patient's illness-induced needs (both physical and psychological).

In conclusion, the patient illness characteristics that seem to be reliably associated with family caregiver strains are (a) greater illness severity, (b) suddenness of onset, and (c) greater changes in preexisting patient behaviors. While the theoretical model views these as objective stressors, the discussion above suggests that objective variables also may have affective and cognitive meanings for caregivers that affect their reactions.

CONTEXTUAL VARIABLES (MEDIATORS)

In addition to the objective characteristics of the patient's illness discussed above, our theoretical model suggests that a number of other variables mediate the caregiver's reaction. The research literature has studied a number of these contextual variables. Most frequently, studies have included a number of caregiver demographic factors, which we will examine first in this section. In addition, some studies have examined preexisting caregiver psychosocial status as another factor affecting their response. Finally, a few studies have incorporated a broader family system framework and examined such factors as the relationship quality between caregiver and patient, family life stage, and the social supports available to the caregiver as additional mediating variables.

Demographic Factors

Demographic factors are the workhorse variables of social science. Because they are easily measured and predictive of many other outcomes, they tend to be included in most research studies. Therefore, it is no surprise that health researchers have examined a variety of caregiver background factors expected to predict distress.

Gender. Across all illness categories, women caregivers have been found to show significantly higher levels of distress than men; however, interpreting this consistent pattern of greater caregiving impact on women is not straightforward. It would seem reasonable to attribute women's greater distress to their greater investment in all family caregiving and nurturing roles. Thus they may feel more role responsibility for caring for an ill family member. Another gender difference, however, complicates this straightforward interpretation. Women, regardless of life status, typically score higher than men on measures of psychological distress. Thus women may generally feel greater distress and depression when compared to men or, alternatively, at least be more willing to reveal their distress. Williamson and Schulz's (in press) recent study of 174 Alzheimer's caregivers specifically discusses these issues. They argue that the caregiver gender differences they obtained exceed general population norms, suggesting that at least some of the difference in impact of caregiving for men and women is a direct consequence of caregiving per se. They also suggest a number of social role processes that could account for gender differences in caregiving impact, including more nurturing tasks undertaken by women that restrict other role activities, and greater feelings of repayment for past care that sustain men in their caregiving activities. However, further clarification of these possible underlying processes awaits future research.

Type of Role Relationship with Patient. In addition to gender differences, other demographic factors have been investigated with less clear results. Spouses showed more severe reactions than nonspouse family caregivers (mainly children) in studies of mental illness, Alzheimer's disease, stroke, and cancer. Alzheimer's research suggests that spouse distress may be related to their greater likelihood of living with the patient, because, in general, caregivers who live with the patient show more distress than those who do not. However, the study by Young and Kahana (1987) of caregivers of heart attack patients showed a more complex pattern. While spouses in their study showed more physical and mental health symptoms than did nonspouse caregivers (mainly daughters), echoing the above pattern of greater impact for spouses, they also felt less burdened by the demands of caregiving. This study suggests that spouses may be more emotionally and physically distressed by their mates' illness, but less resentful of the care demands imposed by the illness. In contrast, other family members may be less emotionally reactive to the illness threat, but more resentful or stressed by the tasks of caregiving. Young and Kahana suggest that spouses define their roles to encompass looking after the other "in sickness and in health." Other categories of caregivers, however, may not define this expectation as clearly. For example, adult children may rarely antici-pate in advance the need to care for their own parents. An alternate interpretation, suggested by Neugarten's (1968) concept of the social clock, is addressed more fully in our later discussion of the impact of family life stage on caregiver distress.

For the mentally ill, parental caregivers feel more subjective burden than do other categories of caregivers, although their objective burden is lower. Since mental illness has an earlier average age of onset than most other chronic illnesses, it may have greater numbers of parental caregivers than most chronic illnesses discussed here. This finding raises a number of issues that may need to be pursued in future research. First, do parents show similar distress as caregivers for other illnesses, or is it the specific nature of chronic mental illness that evokes this reaction? If it is a general pattern, is parental distress attributable to the shattering of hopes for their children's future, or some other aspect of their role?

The above findings on the greater burden felt by spouses and parents have another interpretation. These studies may be confounding role effects with age effects. Thus older caregivers may generally find it harder to offer care than those who are younger. In illnesses having a late onset, such as Alzheimer's disease, cancer, and coronary disease, spouses and children are the most likely caregivers. Such studies show that older caregivers, i.e., spouses, feel greater emotional distress. Caregivers of the mentally ill who are parents are also likely to be older than other categories of caregivers. Future studies need to isolate the impact of role, controlling for other age-related effects, in order to clarify the current ambiguity regarding interpretation of role effects.

Beyond the consensus on gender, and the near consensus on spouse caregivers, other demographic variables reveal more limited patterns of association with caregiver stress. For example, poorer health has been found to predict worse caregiver reactions in stroke and cancer, but has not been established in other illnesses. And caregivers of the mentally ill who live in smaller households feel more burdened than do those living in larger households.

Age and Socioeconomic Status. At least two other variables, age and socioeconomic status, have shown contradictory patterns across illnesses. Younger caregivers of cancer or coronary patients experience greater distress than their older counterparts, but the opposite pattern has been found for stroke caregivers. Similarly, higher socioeconomic status has been associated with greater caregiver symptomatology in mental illness and coronary disease research. Once again, however, the limited findings on stroke victims find greater distress in lower SES caregivers.

In viewing the more extensive studies of illnesses other than stroke, it is possible to develop a theory of differential expectations to account for the greater difficulties of younger and higher SES caregivers. These categories of caregivers may have greater reason to expect their lives to unfold easily. They may also have greater belief in their own ability to control their lives. As a consequence, they may experience more emotional distress when someone they love becomes seriously ill. However, they may also have greater resources to deal with the longer term care demands of illness than would older, lower SES caregivers. It should be noted that if further research supports the countervailing findings of the stroke caregiver study of Schulz et al. (1988), more complex patterns of interaction between caregiver characteristics and illness category may be evident.

There may be another possible reason for the discrepancy between Schulz et al.'s (1988) study and the others discussed above. Most studies of cancer and coronary caregivers occur during the early diagnostic and hospital periods. At this point, emotional distress is at its peak. During this period, younger and higher SES family members show more emotional strain. In contrast, research on stroke patients follows families during longer term rehabilitation efforts. Here the physical demands on caregivers are high, compared to the more limited care needs of recovering coronary and cancer patients. At this point, families may be more preoccupied with longer term care implications of patient disability. Older caregivers, and those with lesser economic resources, could have greater difficulty meeting the physical care needs of stroke patients during this period. In order to further explore the possible sources of discrepancy in the above findings, one would need to look more carefully at the specifics of sample selection and the point of data collection relative to disease onset, as well as the measures of caregiver burden used in each study.

In summary, we have consistent evidence that women caregivers exhibit greater stress symptoms across all illness categories examined. We have reasonable evidence that spouses show more distress than other caregivers, as do caregivers in poorer health themselves. And there is some evidence of the impact of age and SES on caregiver burden, but the direction of these effects varies by illness category.

Preexisting Psychological Factors

Very few studies have included measures of caregiver mental health or life stressors prior to patient illness. Yet these preexisting emotional resources may be seen as the bedrock of an individual's response to all stress situations. There is some suggestive evidence from coronary research that caregivers with higher psychological adjustment scores prior to illness onset withstand the stress better than those scoring lower. There is also some evidence in the cancer research discussed that the presence of other life stressors exacerbates a caregiver's reactions to the patient's illness. Thus the limited data currently available suggests that the preexisting quality of a person's life and emotional resources may contribute to his or her ability to weather a family health problem. These data, however, are based on retrospective reports of these preexisting life status variables, and may be subject to recall biases.

Relationship Quality

Thus far, the quality of the preexisting relationship between caregiver and patient has been minimally studied. However, the few studies of cancer and coronary patients that have focused on the marital dyad have found that spouses with better preexisting relationships respond better to caregiving demands. On a variety of indicators, couples with greater marital cohesion and better communication withstood the onslaught of cancer or heart attack better than other couples. In these illnesses, caregiving spouses in better marriages showed fewer emotional symptoms than those in poorer marriages. In fact, the bonds often tightened as the couple rallied to overcome the illness. Studies of a broader sample of Alzheimer's caregivers (both spouses and nonspouses) confirm that those with better prior relationships felt less burdened by the demands of caregiving. Thus it may be that those who have received more positive gratification in their prior relationship with the patient may feel more motivated to provide care.

Although caregivers in better relationships may be less affected by caregiving demands, they may have more trouble coping with the ultimate loss of the patient. It should be recalled that Vachon et al. (1982) found that spouses in better relationships had greater difficulties in terminal stages of cancer and in widowhood. This study suggests that illness stage and trajectory need to be considered in future studies of relationship factors and caregiver adjustment. We may therefore speculate that caregivers in better relationships may be better able to deal with patient's illness demands during earlier illness stages. The threat of loss, however, may impact more strongly on those in closer relationships. Obviously more research is needed across diseases and prognoses to examine this pattern more closely.

Family Life Stage

Some social scientists have speculated that a family's life stage exerts major impact on its reaction to the illness of a family member. They argue that relationships and role expectations in a family shift as marriages evolve. As a consequence, chronic illness presents different challenges for spouses and children at different points in the family life cycle.

Neugarten's (1968) concept of the social clock extends this perspective still further. Neugarten suggests that childhood socialization leads members of each society to expect that they will encounter certain life events at specific periods of their lives. When our lives conform to these age-linked role expectations, we can anticipate and prepare for expected transitions. We also have the support of many in our age cohort who are experiencing similar transitions. When we experience such events "off time" we may be unprepared for them, and have fewer people around us with whom to share our problems. Consequently, psychosocial adjustment may be more difficult. If we apply Neugarten's social clock concept to issues of chronic illness, we may speculate that spouses may be best prepared to deal with illness in later years, when it occurs on schedule. It is not clear whether children anticipate as clearly the need to care for aging parents, although this increasing social trend has achieved greater media attention in recent years. However, family members are never socialized to expect responsibility for caregiving tasks in their younger years, nor, by and large, are parents prepared to give care to their adult children. The unanticipated nature of these demands may contribute to caregiver difficulties.

Rolland (1988) presents a conceptual model of the family impact of illness that postulates family life stage as a critical factor in their reaction. In direct support of this perspective at least one study of families of cancer patients found greater emotional distress for spouses with younger children. Further, more indirect support for the impact of family life stage comes from the previously cited data on age effects, which also found more distress for younger spouses of cancer and coronary patients. Rolland also links concepts related to stress points in family evolution, often related to children's arrivals and departures, to the family's ability to handle the strain of chronic illness. Since research cited above has suggested that other life stressors reduce a caregiver's resources for dealing with a chronic health problem, there is further indirect evidence supportive of Rolland's model. More research is needed, however, to strengthen Rolland's argument for the centrality of the variable of family life stage.

Social Support

In addition to the above variables relating to family cohesiveness and life cycle stresses, one additional interpersonal factor has appeared in the literature. The social support available to caregivers has been found to affect their well-being in cancer, stroke, and coronary studies. So far these studies are few in number and have not been replicated in the other chronic illnesses discussed here. One recent study (Sistler, 1989) compared a small sample of Alzheimer's caregivers with caregivers of physically impaired spouses and with unimpaired older couples. Sistler found a complex pattern of data showing Alzheimer's caregivers to be significantly more likely to seek social support and to engage in wishful thinking than the other groups. Illness related differences in coping style, however, did not affect caregiver well-being. Greater use of social support, wishful thinking, or problem solving coping did not result in better caregiver outcomes. Sistler suggests that her small study raises questions regarding the assumption that social support and problem solving coping impact positively on caregiver adjustment.

As this chapter indicates, overall, we currently have only limited data on variables associated with caregiver distress (See Figures 8.1 and 8.2). The objective stressor of illness severity is a strong and consistent predictor of caregiver distress, followed by factors indicating greater

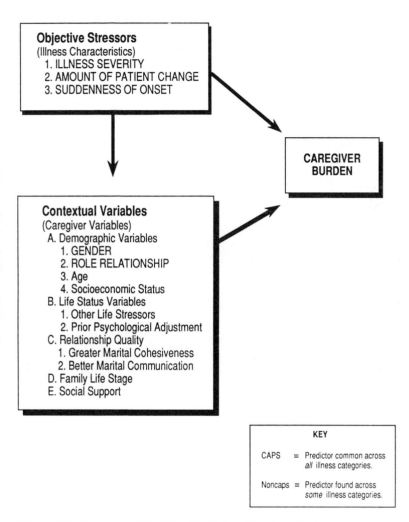

Figure 8.1. Summary of Variables Predicting Caregiver Strain

patient impact and suddenness of caregiver awareness. When we examine contextual variables that relate to the caregiver's status, the demographic variable of gender is the only one consistently and strongly associated with distress, with females much more likely to show strain. Less consistently, spouses, others who live with the patient, those in

	CANCER	HEART DISEASE	STROKE	ALZ-HEIMER'S DISEASE	CHRONIC MENTAL ILLNESS
Objective Stressors					
1. Illness Severity	X	X	X	X	X
a. Prior Hospitalization		X			X
b. Length of Recovery Period		X			X
c. Degree of Impairment/Illness Stage	X		X	X	X
d. Prognosis	X				
e. Caregiving Demands	X				
f. Time since diagnosis	X (some studies)				X (some studies)
2. Amount of Patient Change or Distress	X	X	X	X	
3. Suddenness of Onset	X	X	X		
Contextual Variables					
A. Demographic Variables					
1. Gender	X	X	X	X	X
2. Caregiver Role-Relationship to Patient		X (non-spouses)	X (spouses)	X (spouses)	X (parents)
3. Health of Caregiver	X		X		X
4. Size of Household					X
5. Age of Caregiver	X (younger)	X (younger)	X (younger)		
6. Socioeconomic Status		X (higher SES)	X (lower SES)		X (higher SES)
7. Work Status of Caregiver	X				
B. Life Status Variables					
1. Other Life Stressors	X			X (financial concerns)	
2. Prior Psychological Problems		X			
C. Relationship Quality	X	X		X	
D. Family Life Stage	X				
E. Social Support	X	X	X	X	

Figure 8.2 Variables Found to be Related to Caregiver Strain by Illness

worse health, and possibly those of higher SES and younger ages also react more strongly. Beyond that, there is scattered evidence that personal variables such as preexisting well-being and life stressors, and such relational factors as marriage quality, family life stage, and social support may also affect caregiver reactions.

9

The Outcomes of Interventions
for Caregivers

In the previous chapters of this volume we have provided an overview of family caregiving and traced the reasons for its development as a significant public policy issue; offered a number of theoretical perspectives to help in understanding the caregiving process and its effects upon caregivers; and reviewed research studies on the effects of caregiving, first by disease and second across diseases in an integrative fashion. We now turn our attention to a separate body of caregiving literature consisting of evaluative studies of programs and services—interventions—that have been developed to assist caregivers in the performance of their caregiving roles.

The explosion in the professional literature about caregiving over the past decade has included the publication of a large number of articles and book chapters about caregiver interventions. Some of these intervention modalities, such as respite care, a direct service, have been developed specifically for caregivers. Other modalities, such as self-help or support groups, have previously been widely used with a large number of diverse noncaregiver population groups and have been adapted to emphasize the needs of caregivers.

The focus of this chapter is an examination of the empirical evidence concerning the effectiveness of interventions that are designed to help caregivers adjust and cope with their caregiving status, to improve the ability of caregivers to meet patient needs, to prevent or reduce caregiver burden, and to prevent or reduce the deleterious effects of stress on the health and mental health status of caregivers. The organizing strategy for our discussion of caregiver interventions will be by type of intervention rather than by disease, although we will examine the degree to which particular intervention modalities have been utilized for different diseases. Our discussion will be guided by four central questions. First, what are the nature and characteristics of interventions for caregivers and how widely have particular intervention modalities been utilized with caregivers of Alzheimer's disease, cancer, heart disease, mental illness, and stroke patients? Second, are caregiver interventions effective in preventing or reducing caregiver distress? Third, are there differences in the effectiveness of caregiver interventions by intervention modality or by disease? Fourth, what can we learn from the strengths and weaknesses of existing caregiver intervention research to help guide the next generation of research studies?

We have organized the intervention studies into the following three categories:

Support group interventions. A group intervention designed to provide caregivers with emotional support, informational support, and enhancement of coping skills. These groups are either professionally led (usually time limited, 8 to 15 sessions) or peer led (usually of an ongoing nature). There is a strong emphasis on sharing of feelings, experiences, and coping strategies among group members.

Educational interventions. A group intervention with emphasis on the provision by professionals of information and/or skills to better enable caregivers to meet their needs. Educational interventions can be divided into three types: cognitive information only, cognitive information plus self-enhancement and/or behavioral management skills, and self-enhancement and/or behavioral management skills only.

Clinical or direct service interventions. A treatment oriented intervention that includes a wide variety intervention submodalities such as counseling/therapy, respite, behavioral/cognitive stimulation, hospice, day hospital, and general psychosocial interventions.

We will also separately examine intervention studies that cut across one or more of the above three intervention modalities. It should be noted that there is some overlap between categories, especially between the support group and educational interventions. Support groups always include an informational component. Indeed, when asked what they find most beneficial about support groups, members often cite both the opportunity for informal sharing with others in the same situation, and information they acquired about their relatives' disease and the management of that disease. Placement of interventions that have both informal support and educational components into the support group or educational intervention categories was based on which component seemed to be the primary focus of the intervention. As will be seen below, however, the educational intervention category also includes a number of studies focusing on behavioral change and behavioral management that are very different from support group interventions.

Each intervention modality will be discussed in terms of six variables—intervention description, type of disease, research design, subjects, measures, and findings (See Appendix, Tables A.1 through A.4 for a brief summary of each individual study). Studies are classified in this chapter as intervention group only, comparison group, or experimental design. Intervention group only studies utilize only an intervention group and make no attempt to compare the effects of the intervention with other comparison groups. Comparison group designs utilize at least two groups; one group receives the intervention, and the second group, which is used for comparison purposes, receives no intervention or receives treatment as usual. In this design, individuals are not randomly assigned to treatment or nontreatment conditions. Experimental designs utilize two or more groups. Subjects are randomly assigned to the experimental group that receives the intervention, or to the control group that receives no services or services as usual. Data collected in each of these designs may occur only after the intervention (posttest only) or both before and after the intervention (pre- and posttest). Some studies include multiple posttests, collected at the end of the intervention and also at one or more subsequent time periods, such as at 3 months, 6 months, or 12 months postintervention.

Comparison group and experimental designs are difficult to do in field settings and as a result tend to be reported in the literature less frequently than intervention group only designs. An encouraging sign in caregiver intervention research is the increasing use of comparison group and experimental designs, most of which have been reported in the literature only in the last several years.

The discussion of measures includes nonstandardized, generally open-ended, consumer self-report measures (i.e., What did you like best about the group? What was most helpful?, etc.), standardized self-report measures (used to assess burden, self-esteem, depression, etc.), and behavioral indicators of functioning. Our discussion of standardized outcome measures will be organized using the theoretical framework presented in Chapter 2, with variables being divided into the following categories: objective stressors, perceived stress, contextual variables (caregiver characteristics and relational variables), and enduring outcomes (physical morbidity and psychiatric morbidity).[1] In general, intervention studies utilize these variables as dependent variables, but several exceptions should be noted. Contextual variables such as such as age and gender of the caregiver, and relationship of caregiver to patient, are not capable, of course, of being manipulated by the intervention. In addition, while some objective stressors, such as patient symptoms and behaviors, are capable of being changed by interventions with patients of some diseases (i.e., Alzheimer's disease or chronic mental illness), other objective stressors, such as stage and/or length of the illness, are not manipulable at all.

In order to locate published materials about interventions for caregivers, a comprehensive analysis of the caregiving literature was undertaken. Searches of the Family Resources, Medline, Mental Health Abstracts, and Psychological Abstracts computer data bases were conducted (and the personal libraries of the coauthors were also examined) for relevant materials. A total of 138 articles and book chapters were located that met two criteria. First, the publications were focused on interventions for family caregivers of patients with Alzheimer's disease, cancer, chronic mental illness, heart disease, or stroke (some studies included a wider target population than the five diseases featured in this volume). Second, the publications contained information about the outcome of these interventions.

Of these 138 publications, 32% (43) included only clinical observations of program outcome by the study staff and did not include any data collected from program participants themselves. These materials will not be reviewed in this chapter because of our intention to focus only on studies that provide empirical data from program participants. Nevertheless, because these publications contain information that may be useful to the readers of this volume, we have included a listing of the clinical observation outcome studies in the Appendix (see Table A.5). Of the remaining 95 publications, 17 are literature reviews (see Appendix, Table A.6), and 78 are articles and book chapters representing a total of 54 different outcome studies, which will be reviewed in the following sections.

SUPPORT GROUP INTERVENTIONS

Support group interventions, as defined earlier, are designed to provide caregivers with emotional support, informational support, and enhancement of coping skills with emphasis on the sharing of feelings, experiences, and coping strategies among group members. There was considerable variation in the organization, structure, and functioning of the support groups in the 13 studies that were reviewed (See Table A.1).[2] In slightly more than one half of the studies (seven), the support groups were ongoing. Of this number, however, only three groups were peer led, with the remainder being either professionally led or co-led by professionals. Thus only a few studies were of groups that meet the traditional definition of a self-help group, that is, a group that is led by a peer leader and is an ongoing entity.

The six studies of time limited interventions varied from 8 to 15 sessions. The groups generally met on a weekly basis for about one and one-half to two hours per session. The Toseland, Rossiter and Labrecque (1989) study is unique in that it compared the effectiveness of peer led and professionally led time limited support groups for caregivers of the frail elderly.

Purposes of the support groups studied related to the provision of emotional support, informational support, and enhancement of coping skills and included the following goals: to reduce emotional isolation, anxiety, and fear of families and allow them to develop supportive networks; to provide a safe atmosphere for expressing negative emotions; to give and receive advice and support from others in the same situation; to address gaps in knowledge and to provide information and techniques useful for the caregiving role; to develop needed coping skills, and to learn from others how to cope more effectively.

Type of Disease

The majority of studies were of caregivers of the mentally ill, with a few studies of caregivers of Alzheimer's disease and cancer patients also included. There were no empirical studies of support groups for caregivers of heart disease or stroke patients. If outcome studies having clinical observations of outcome but no empirical data are included, however, there are several studies of support groups for heart disease patients. Thus this intervention modality crosscuts four of the five chronic disease groups discussed in this volume, with caregivers of stroke patients being the only unrepresented group.

Research Design

By and large, research designs utilized in studies of support groups were rather weak, especially as compared with designs utilized with other intervention modalities for caregivers. Of the 13 studies, only 1 utilized a comparison group design and 1 utilized an experimental design. Thus the findings of the support group intervention studies as a whole have to be interpreted with extreme caution.

Subjects

Though not all studies provided sufficient information about study subjects, several patterns were clear. As would be expected, most subjects were women. Some studies included a range of caregiver familial roles, while others, like the Toseland et al. (1989) study, were restricted to one familial role—daughters or daughters-in-law. Naturally occurring self-help groups tend to be predominantly middle class. Therefore, it is not surprising that some studies reviewed contained principally middle class subjects. Several studies, however, indicated that their subjects represented a wide range of socioeconomic status groups. Insufficient descriptions of study subjects prevent us from providing a complete description of the characteristics of the support group intervention subjects. Most studies had more than 40 subjects per group while four studies had 20 subjects or less per group. In general, relatively small sample sizes limited the kinds of statistical analyses the authors were able to undertake.

Measures

A wide variety of measures have been used as outcomes in support group intervention studies. The majority of studies used only nonstandardized outcome measures to assess the effects of the group (Barnes et al., 1981; Craig, Hussey, Parsons, & Seamans, 1985; Gonyea, 1989; Johnson & Stark, 1980; Katschnig, Konieczna, & Sint, 1985; Plant et al., 1987; Rose, Finestone, & Bass, 1985; Thornton, Plummer, Seaman, & Littmann, 1981). Most typically this was a consumer satisfaction survey that used a combination of open and closed ended questions to assess the members' perceptions of the benefits of the group, what they liked most/found most useful, what they liked least/found least useful, what they gained from the group, and what they wanted but did not receive. This information was supplemented in several studies (Barnes et al., 1981; Rose et al., 1985) by clinical observations and audiotapings of group meetings.

A smaller number of other studies primarily used standardized measures to examine group outcomes, although these studies sometimes also assessed consumer satisfaction using the techniques identified above. In most cases these studies used a combination of two or more standardized outcome measures. Principal outcome measures utilized included patient functioning and symptomatology (Biegel & Yamatani, 1986, 1987; Greene & Monahan, 1989; Potaszynik & Nelson, 1984; Toseland et al., 1989); burden (Biegel & Yamatani, 1986, 1987; Greene & Monahan, 1989; Potaszynik & Nelson, 1984; Toseland et al., 1989); social support/helpfulness of group participants (Biegel & Yamatani, 1986, 1987; Potaszynik & Nelson, 1984; Toseland et al., 1989); and affect balance, anxiety, depression, hostility, and self-esteem (Greene & Monahan, 1989; Lazarus, Stafford, Cooper, Cohler, & Dysken, 1981; Toseland et al., 1989). In terms of the model described in Chapter 2, these outcomes can be classified as falling into four categories. Patient functioning and symptomatology can be classified as objective stressors; social support can be considered a contextual variable; burden is perceived stress; and affect balance, anxiety, depression, hostility, and self-esteem are examples of enduring outcomes.

Findings

Overall, findings clearly and strongly demonstrate that support group participants are very satisfied with their group experience and report a number of benefits resulting from their group participation. When standardized instruments are used to measure the effects of the groups in relieving caregiver distress, however, the findings are much less persuasive. The results demonstrate that satisfaction with the group experience is not necessarily correlated with change in patient symptomatology or caregiver burden, health or mental health status. These findings are generally consistent with Toseland, Rossiter and Labrecque's (1989) earlier review of support group interventions for family caregivers of the frail elderly.

In response to nonstandardized consumer self-report measures, study subjects reported generally high levels of satisfaction with group participation. Benefits of participation, as cited by the subjects, included the following: improved family communication and family relationships, reduced isolation, and improved understanding of the disease. When asked to indicate the most helpful aspects of the group, emotional support and informational support were cited about equally. For example, subjects in Biegel and Yamatani's (1986) study of self-help groups for families of the mentally ill cited education and information, advocacy, and emotional support as the most helpful aspects of the group. Similarly, subjects in Barnes et al.'s (1981) study of an eight- week support group for Alzheimer's disease patients cited improved understanding of Alzheimer's disease and the sharing of feelings and sense of support and acceptance by others as the most important benefits of group participation.

When asked to indicate how participation in the group had changed them, subjects in Rose et al.'s (1985) study of a support group for relatives of psychiatric patients reported a number of positive changes in their lives including becoming more involved with work, more accepting of the limitations of the patient, increased ability to express negative emotions, and improved ability to make decisions. A majority of subjects in Plant et al.'s (1987) study of a hospital based support group for cancer patients, families and friends in London, England, reported increased happiness, being more relaxed, and being able to better cope with the disease.

Biegel and Yamatani (1987) analyzed the relationship between the frequency of help-giving activities and satisfaction with a self-help group for families of the mentally ill. The most frequently occurring group activities, such as catharsis, explanation, and normalization were related to nondirective, nonthreatening aspects of social support. The least frequently occurring activities were those that were more threatening and focused on behavioral change. There was a moderate correlation between the nondirective, nonthreatening activities and members' satisfaction with the group.

Standardized self-report measures were used in studies of caregivers of the mentally ill, Alzheimer's disease patients, and the frail elderly (Biegel & Yamatani, 1986, 1987; Greene & Monahan, 1989; Lazarus et al., 1981; Potaszynik & Nelson, 1984; Toseland et al., 1989) to examine the effects of the intervention upon patient functioning, the extent of caregiving, burden, caregiver characteristics, social support, and a range of mental health outcomes (affect balance, anxiety, depression, hostility, psychiatric symptomatology, and self-esteem). Significant effects in the predicted direction were only found in about half of the analyses.

Only two studies, both with caregivers of the frail elderly, reported analyses of the effects of the intervention upon objective stressors. Neither of these studies reported any intervention effects upon the hours and extent of caregiving, or upon patient IADL, ADL, behavioral, or psychological problems. Two studies of caregivers of the mentally ill examined objective stressors but did not evaluate the effect of the intervention upon these stressors.

Biegel and Yamatani (1986, 1987) report an inverse relationship between objective stressors and perceived helpfulness of the support group. Subjects reporting greater problems in patient functioning (more rehospitalizations) found the support group to be less helpful. Potaszynik and Nelson (1984) found that patient symptomatology was correlated with both objective and subjective burden in bivariate analyses. Hierarchical multiple regression analyses were conducted in which symptomatology and either supportiveness of the self-help group or the total satisfaction with one's social network were regressed on both objective and subjective burden. Findings show that the objective stressor, patient symptomatology, accounts for most of the variance in both objective and subjective burden. Supportiveness of the self-help group was a significant predictor of objective burden but contributed less to R^2 change than did patient symptomatology.

Toseland et al. (1989) report that neither the peer led nor professionally led interventions had a significant effect on the hours or extent of caregiving. Greene and Monahan (1984) utilized multiple regression analyses to assess the effects of a number of caregiver and care receiver characteristics on short- and long-term levels of anxiety, depression, hostility, and burden. Objective stressors that were examined included IADL, ADL, and psychological and behavioral problems of the care recipient. Although the results show that the intervention had significant short-term treatment effects in reducing anxiety and depression, and a significant long-term effect in reducing anxiety, objective stressors did not predict changes in any of the significant dependent variables.

Four studies collected data on levels of perceived stress/burden. Only two of these studies, however, (Greene & Monahan, 1989; Toseland et al., 1989) examined the effects of the intervention on reducing levels of burden. Neither study found that the intervention had a significant effect on reducing burden levels, although the Greene and Monahan study found a marginal effect of an Alzheimer's disease support group (significant at the .1 level). Potaszynik and Nelson (1984) found an inverse correlation between objective and subjective burden levels and satisfaction with the support of the self-help group.

There was little examination of contextual variables in the studies that utilized standardized outcome measures. Greene and Monahan (1989) was the only study that looked at caregiver characteristics (age, gender), and Potaszynik and Nelson (1984) and Toseland et al. (1989) were the only studies that looked at any relational variables (social support). As stated above, the results of Greene and Monahan's study show that the intervention had significant short-term treatment effects in reducing anxiety and depression, and a significant long-term effect in reducing anxiety; however, neither age nor gender predicted changes in any of the significant dependent variables.

Toseland et al. (1989) used social network size as a dependent variable in their study of the effects of peer led and professionally led support groups for family caregivers of the frail elderly. They found that participants in both treatment groups reported significant increases in social network size as compared with the control group. Potaszynik and Nelson (1984) did not examine the effect of the intervention on changing social network size but rather the relationship between total network size, satisfaction with the total network, network density, and supportiveness of the self-help group. They found that satisfaction with the total network was positively correlated with density and with supportiveness of the self-help group, and negatively correlated with total network size. They also found that satisfaction with the total network was negatively correlated with both objective and subjective burden. Subjects reported experiencing less burden when they had small, dense networks and when they were satisfied with the support of their total network and the support of their self-help group.

Significant effects of the intervention in changing enduring psychiatric outcomes were found in two out of the three studies that examined such outcomes. Greene and Monahan (1989) found that a short-term support group for caregivers of the frail elderly significantly reduced levels of anxiety and depression, but had no effect on levels of hostility. Toseland et al.'s (1989) study of support groups for caregivers of the frail elderly examined well-being (Bradburn Affect Balance Scale-BABS) and psychiatric symptomatology (Brief Symptom Inventory-BSI, Global Severity Index, Positive Symptom Index, and Positive Symptom Distress Index). Findings show that participants in both treatment groups reported a statistically significant increase in well-being as measured by the BABS while the control group subjects reported a decrease in well-being. Similarly, as compared with control group participants, treatment group participants reported statistically significant reductions in psychiatric symptoms as measured by both the Global Severity Index and the Positive Symptom Index, with no significant differences on the Positive Symptom Distress Index. There were statistically significant differences between the treatment and control groups on three of the nine subscales of the BSI, with the other six scales showing greater, but not statistically significant, changes in the treatment groups than in the control group. On the other hand, Lazarus et al. (1981) reported no significant effects of a short-term Alzheimer's disease caregiver support group on enhancing self-esteem or in reducing levels of anxiety or depression.

In summary, support group intervention studies utilized generally weaker types of designs than those that, as we will shall see, were utilized in studies with other caregiver intervention modalities. Most studies tended to rely only upon nonstandardized self-report consumer satisfaction measures. Self-help group members report high levels of satisfaction with group participation, yet the groups did not demonstrate an ability to reduce the levels of objective stressors or caregiving burden. It should be noted, however, that significant effects of the intervention in reducing some enduring outcomes were found in several studies of caregivers of the frail elderly that utilized comparison group and experimental designs.

The finding that satisfaction with group participation is not necessarily linked with changes in levels of caregiver distress may be a reflection of the fact that caregivers are satisfied with the group for reasons that have nothing to due with felt changes in personal distress. Caregivers often feel grateful that someone pays attention to their needs and shows interest in their problems. Participants may also be satisfied with the support group because they feel positive about the agency/organization sponsoring the group, or they may like and appreciate the professional staff working with the group. In fact, data collection methods utilized in many of these studies may bias the results because the support group staff usually also are involved in data collection. Respondents who like the group's staff members are more likely to report positive satisfaction with the group when these same staff members are the ones asking their opinions about the intervention. In addition, caregiver satisfaction with support groups is probably related in part to just having the opportunity to meet and talk with others in a similar situation.

Although the number of studies is too limited to draw definitive conclusions concerning differences in effects of the interventions by disease, the two interventions with caregivers of the frail elderly found stronger intervention effects using standardized outcome measures than did the one study of caregivers of Alzheimer's disease patients. These differences may be due to the special burdens associated with the nature and effects of Alzheimer's disease.

EDUCATIONAL INTERVENTIONS

Educational interventions emphasize the provision by professionals of information and/or skills, usually in a group format, to better enable caregivers to meet their needs. As was the case with support group interventions, there was considerable variation in the purpose and function of educational interventions in the 14 studies that were reviewed (See Table A.2).[3]

Interventions varied in the degree to which they focused upon cognitive and skill development areas and can be classified into three principal types: cognitive information only, cognitive information plus self-enhancement and/or behavioral management skills, and self-enhancement and/or behavioral management skills only.

Cognitive information only interventions were reported in studies with caregivers of cancer, mentally ill, and stroke patients (Abramowitz & Coursey, 1989; Barrowclough et al., 1987; Cozolino & Nuechterlein, 1986; Evans, Funkenstein, & Albert, 1989; Pohl, 1980; Schulz, House, & Andrews, 1986; Shapiro, Possidente, Plum, & Lehman, 1983; Smith & Birchwood, 1987). All studies used a group format, with groups meeting for from two to eight sessions, generally on a weekly basis, with the Pohl study being a four-day intervention, one hour per day for four consecutive days.[4] Topics covered in these cognitive information interventions included providing information about the nature of the disease and/or physical disability, medication, management of patient behaviors, and community resources.

Several studies focused on interventions that included both cognitive information as well as the enhancement of caregiver skills with caregivers of Alzheimer's disease patients and the mentally ill (Glosser & Wexler, 1985; Kahan, Kemp, Staples, & Brummel-Smith, 1985; Leff, Kuipers, Berkowitz, Eberlein-Vries, & Sturgeon, 1986;[5] Pohl, 1980). The Glosser and Wexler, and Kahan et al. studies with caregivers of Alzheimer's disease patients were time limited group interventions of eight weekly sessions each. In addition to the provision of information about the disease and its management, caregivers were taught patient management skills in the Glosser and Wexler study and stress management skills in the Kahan et al. study.

The Leff et al. (1986) study, which is reported in a series of seven papers by Leff and his colleagues, focused on caregivers of relatives with schizophrenia. This is a comprehensive intervention over a nine-month period that is focused both on cognitive information and on behavioral change. Caregivers are first given a series of in-home lectures (two to four sessions) focusing on disease etiology, treatment, and management. Then a relatives' group is formed that meets on a bi-weekly basis. The purpose of this group is to help alter coping styles so that families with high expressed emotion (EE) can be helped to change their behavior to more closely resemble caregivers with low EE. The intervention also includes a maximum of 25 home-based family sessions for patients and their relatives. Patients also receive medication.

Behavioral management skills were the primary focus of studies of caregivers of Alzheimer's disease patients and the frail elderly (Lovett & Gallagher, 1988; Robinson, 1988). The Robinson study of caregivers of Alzheimer's disease provided a four session social skills training program with emphasis on the enhancement of assertive behaviors and on social network building skills. The Lovett and Gallagher study of caregivers of the frail elderly consisted of 10 two-hour sessions with two different intervention groups. One group received self-change skills focused on increasing life satisfaction, whereas the second group was focused on the enhancement of problem solving skills.

One study compared two of the above educational intervention modalities. The effectiveness of a ten session cognitive information versus information plus stress management skills was evaluated in a study with caregivers of Alzheimer's disease patients (Haley et al., 1987; Haley, 1989). Both groups received information about Alzheimer's disease and behavioral management, and the latter group also received training in progressive relaxation and skills for managing stressful situations.

Type of Disease

Educational interventions cut across disease classifications, as was found above for support group interventions. Four of the five diseases were represented in the educational interventions that were reviewed; there were no educational interventions for caregivers of patients with heart disease. Again, as was the situation with support group interventions, the majority of studies are of caregivers of the mentally ill. About one quarter of the studies are of caregivers of Alzheimer's disease patients, with there being one study each of caregivers of cancer and stroke patients.

Research Design

Designs utilized in studies of educational interventions were much stronger as a whole than were the designs used in studies of support group interventions. Almost one half of the studies used experimental or comparison group designs.[6] Thus findings of the educational intervention studies as a whole can be accepted with greater confidence than the findings of the support group interventions studies reviewed above.

Subjects

Subjects in almost four fifths of the studies were family members of patients in a health care or mental health care facility, with subjects in several studies being recruited through self-help groups for Alzheimer's disease patients or caregivers who utilized adult day care services in the community. Thus the subjects examined are not representative of caregivers in general. In actuality, procedures used to identify caregivers of patients in health/mental health care settings varied from inviting caregivers who were recommended by the program's staff, to open invitations to all caregivers of patients. Given these various criteria, as well as the refusal rates of invited caregivers, caregivers may not be fully representative of caregivers of patients in the facilities studied.

As was the case with support group interventions, studies did not always provide data on the demographic and socioeconomic characteristics of the study populations. Subjects in the studies of caregivers of Alzheimer's disease patients, as expected, tended to be mainly wives and daughters, and caregivers of patients with mental illness were primarily parents. Women predominated in both groups. Only a few studies provided information on socioeconomic characteristics of the study subjects, with the subjects being either primarily middle class or heterogeneous in nature. The number of subjects in each study ranged from 10 to 107. Intervention group only studies had a mean of over 30 subjects per study. The number of subjects per group in comparison group and experimental group studies only ranged from 9 to 22, with most studies having less than 20 subjects per group. While such subject sizes are not unexpected given the practical difficulties of mounting caregiver intervention studies, the relatively small sample sizes tended to limit the kinds of statistical analyses that could be conducted.

Measures

As was the case with support group interventions, a wide variety of measures have been used as outcomes in educational interventions. A few studies used only nonstandardized measures of group effectiveness (Cozolino & Nuechterlein, 1986; Glosser & Wexler, 1985; Pohl, 1980; Schulz et al., 1986). Typically this consisted of written posttest evaluations by group members to assess the effects of the intervention and/or member satisfaction with their group. Some of these instruments were open-ended, although others used Likert scaled questions. None of these studies utilized standardized outcome measures with established reliability and validity. It should be noted, however, that compared with support group interventions, a much smaller percentage of educational intervention studies relied only upon nonstandardized outcome measures.

The majority of studies primarily used standardized measures to examine group outcomes, although these studies sometimes also assessed consumer satisfaction using open- or closed-end questions. In most cases studies used a combination of two or more standardized outcome measures. The major outcome measures utilized in these studies included increase in caregiver knowledge and skills (Barrowclough et al., 1987; Evans & Held, 1984; Kahan et al., 1985; Leff et al. 1986; Shapiro et al., 1983; Smith & Birchwood, 1987; Robinson, 1988), burden (Abramowitz & Coursey, 1989; Kahan et al., 1985; Lovett & Gallagher, 1988; Robinson, 1988; Smith & Birchwood, 1987), family functioning and social networks (Haley et al., 1987; Lovett & Gallagher, 1988; Robinson, 1988; Shapiro et al., 1983), and depression, life satisfaction, patient institutionalization, self-efficacy, or self-esteem (Abramowitz & Coursey, 1989; Haley, 1989; Haley et al., 1987; Kahan et al., 1985; Lovett & Gallagher, 1988; Robinson, 1988; Smith & Birchwood, 1987). None of these studies examined the effects of the intervention on such objective stressors as patient functioning or symptomatology.

The study by Leff et al. (1986) used expressed emotion as its principal outcome measure. This variable does not easily fit within the stress-coping-support theoretical framework used in this volume.

Therefore, outcomes pertaining to this variable will be separately discussed in the outcome section below.

Findings

There is strong consensus across most studies, using both open-ended self-reports and quantitative data collection instruments, that educational intervention participants gain valuable knowledge and in some case useful skills from group participation. As was the case with support group interventions, however, the effects of the groups on caregiver distress levels is less clear-cut.

In studies of caregivers of Alzheimer's disease patients, cancer patients, individuals with mental illness, and stroke patients (Barrowclough et al., 1987; Cozolino & Nuechterlein, 1986; Evans & Held, 1984; Glosser & Wexler, 1985; Leff et al., 1986; Pohl, 1980; Schulz et al., 1986; Shapiro et al., 1983; Smith & Birchwood, 1987) researchers found that participants' evaluations of their experience were quite positive. Benefits of participation included the following from the subjects' perspectives: increased knowledge, the provision of practical information, reduced anxiety, improvements in family communications, and helpful interaction with group members in learning new problem solving skills.

Results concerning the level of knowledge increase, measured with a quantitative instrument before and after the intervention, were generally positive, although perhaps not quite as positive as participants' self-reports through open-ended data collection mechanisms. Evans and Held's, (1984) study of stroke caregivers found an increase in knowledge score from 43% to 63%, pretest to posttest. Only Shapiro et al.'s (1983) intervention with caregivers of the mentally ill found that the group experience had no effect upon knowledge levels.Of the other three intervention studies of caregivers of persons with mental illness, Leff and colleagues (1986) were least positive about the cognitive effects of the intervention, reporting that subjects retained little cognitive knowledge, with most retention about diagnosis and least information retention concerning patient management. Robinson's (1988) intervention study of Alzheimer's disease caregivers did not find a significant effect for the intervention in skill development by subjects.

Leff et al.'s (1986) cognitive plus skill development experimental study utilized level of expressed emotion (EE) and patient recidivism rates as primary outcome measures. Findings showed that 9 out of 12 treatment families showed either reduced EE levels or reduced face to face contact (75% success rate). Nine month follow-up data showed an 8% to 9% relapse rate for treatment group patients versus a 50% relapse rate for control group patients. Findings at the two-year follow-up show a 14% relapse rate among treatment families in which the patient remains on medication, and in which face to face contact or EE levels were reduced (excluding suicides), and a 78% relapse rate among control group patients in which family contact time remained stable. Thus, according to the authors, findings show support for both the causal influence of high EE on relapse as well as the protective effects of reduced social contacts between patient and relative.

Standardized self-report measures were used in studies with caregivers of Alzheimer's disease patients, the frail elderly, and individuals with mental illness that examined the effects of the intervention upon perceived burden, family functioning, social support/social network, depression, life-satisfaction, morale, self-efficacy, self-esteem, and trait anxiety (Abramowitz & Coursey, 1989; Haley, 1989; Haley et al., 1987; Kahan et al., 1985; Lovett & Gallagher, 1988; Robinson, 1988; Shapiro et al., 1983; Smith & Birchwood, 1987). Significant effects were found in one half of the analyses.

None of the above studies examined the effect of the interventions on objective stressors. Overall, findings of the effect of the educational groups upon perceived stress/burden were mixed; however, in general, the educational interventions had greater effects on the reduction of stress/burden than did the support group interventions previously reviewed. Studies of educational interventions for family caregivers of persons with mental illness showed significant effects in reducing levels of stress/burden. Abramowitz et al.'s (1989) study of a six-week cognitive intervention showed that the experimental group after the intervention had significantly less personal distress and family disruption than did the control group. The intervention had no effect upon life upset or negative feelings toward the patient. Smith and Birchwood (1987) compared the effects of a four-week group cognitive intervention led by a therapist with a group that received cognitive written materials through the mail. Results show significant reductions in burden for both groups at the six-month follow-up, though there were no significant effects at the posttest immediately after the end of the intervention.

On the other hand, educational interventions with caregivers of Alzheimer's disease patients reported conflicting findings, and no significant differences were found in an educational intervention with caregivers of the frail elderly. Kahan et al.'s study of an eight-week cognitive and skill building intervention for caregivers of Alzheimer's patients found that the experimental group showed a significant reduction in burden as compared to the control group. Robinson's (1988) four session skill building intervention for caregivers of Alzheimer's patients, however, showed no differences in posttest means between the experimental and control group on levels of burden. Lovett and Gallagher's 20 session skill based intervention for caregivers of the frail elderly showed no effect on reducing perceived stress though, as we will see below, significant enduring outcome effects were found.

As was the case with support group interventions, there was little focus on contextual variables in the studies that utilized standardized outcome measures. Relational variables were examined in studies by Shapiro et al. (1983), Lovett and Gallagher (1988), Haley et al. (1987), and Robinson (1988) with caregivers of Alzheimer's disease patients, the frail elderly, and individuals with chronic mental illness. All of the above studies, except for Lovett, utilized social network/social support as an outcome variable with no significant intervention effects found for social network/support enhancement in any of these studies. The Shapiro et al. study also looked at another relational variable, family functioning, but again found no significant intervention effects. Lovett and Gallagher (1988) did not find any significant relationships between the number of persons who provide positive support and levels of stress, morale, or depression.

Educational intervention studies with caregivers of Alzheimer's disease, frail elderly, and individuals with mental illness utilized one or more enduring outcome measure (Abramowitz & Coursey, 1989; Haley 1989; Haley et al. 1987; Kahan et al., 1985; Lovett & Gallagher, 1988; Robinson, 1988; Smith & Birchwood, 1987). Three of these studies found significant effects on at least one enduring outcome measure, one study found short-term but no long-term effects, and two studies found no significant effects at all. Both intervention studies with caregivers of persons with mental illness showed some intervention effects. The experimental group in Abramowitz and Coursey's (1989) six-week cognitive intervention showed a decrease in trait anxiety but no effect on levels of self-efficacy. In contrast, Smith and Birchwood's (1987) four-week cognitive intervention showed a decrease in depression lev-

els for both the education and mail groups at posttest. However, this
effect dissipated and returned to baseline at six months.

Of the three Alzheimer's disease intervention studies, Kahan et al.
(1985) found a small but significant intervention effect in the reduction
of depression levels, with the other two studies finding no significant
intervention effects on levels of self-esteem or life satisfaction and
depression. Lovett and Gallagher's (1988) intervention study with caregivers of the frail elderly examined the effect of the intervention on
self-efficacy, depression, and morale. Findings showed that the experimental group had a significant decrease in the level of depression and
an increase in the level of morale with no effect of the intervention on
the level of self-efficacy.

In summary, educational interventions varied considerably in purpose and format, ranging from cognitive interventions, to cognitive and
skill building, to skill building only. This intervention modality was
utilized with caregivers of Alzheimer's disease, cancer, mental illness,
and stroke patients. As was the case with support group interventions,
group participation was evaluated very positively in subjective assessments of their experiences by group members. When standardized
measures were used to assess the effect of the intervention on caregiver
distress, however, the results were much more equivocal. As was the
case with support group interventions, stronger intervention effects
were found with studies of caregivers of persons with mental illness
than were found with caregivers of Alzheimer's disease patients.

Overall, the findings of the educational intervention studies provide
little data to help us assess whether some educational approaches are
more effective than others. In fact, only Smith and Birchwood's (1987)
study of a cognitive intervention for caregivers of persons with mental
illness compared different intervention approaches, in this case, a group
intervention versus sending educational materials through the mail. As
noted earlier, there is overlap between the support group and educational interventions in that support group interventions also contain an
informational support component. In addition, there can also be overlap
in the opposite direction with the educational intervention containing
an emotional support component if the intervention is group based. In
fact, standardized measures of caregiver distress may not be able to
tease out effects caused by the information component from effects
caused by the emotional support component of interacting with others
in the same situation. Further research is needed to clarify these relationships.

CLINICAL/DIRECT SERVICE INTERVENTIONS

Clinical interventions, direct treatment oriented services, the most prevalent type of caregiver intervention found in the literature, were reported with caregivers of Alzheimer's disease, cancer, mental illness, and stroke patients. The 24 different clinical intervention studies reported here varied much more than did either support group or educational interventions and can be broadly categorized into six different types: counseling/therapy, respite, behavioral/cognitive stimulation, hospice, day hospital, and general psychosocial interventions.[7] Therefore, overall findings of these studies need to be examined cautiously because of the heterogeneity of the interventions.

Over half of the interventions were represented in the counseling/therapy classification (Christensen, 1983; Croake & Kelly, 1985; Davies, 1981; Falloon et al., 1984;[8] Goldberg & Wool, 1985; Heinrich & Schag, 1985; Kopeikin, Marshall, & Goldstein, 1983;[9] Kottgen, Sonnichsen, Mollenhauer, & Jurth, 1984; Mills, Hansen, & Malakie, 1986; Snyder & Liberman, 1981). All four illnesses represented in clinical interventions were included in one or more of these counseling/therapy interventions.

There was considerable variation among the counseling/therapy intervention studies that were most often designed for caregivers of individuals with mental illness. These programs varied in length from ten weeks to two years and tended to include patients as well as caregivers and other family members. Counseling/therapy intervention studies for caregivers of cancer patients varied from a four week couples treatment following mastectomy to a 12 session, six month social support counseling intervention for patients and families. The one stroke counseling/therapy intervention study involved life review therapy for spouses and adult children of stroke patients and included at least six sessions.

Respite care studies (Geiser, Hoche, & King, 1988; Lawton, Brody, & Saperstein, 1989; Lundervold & Lewin, 1987) focused upon caregivers of Alzheimer's disease patients and individuals with mental illness. The Alzheimer's disease respite care intervention studies included in-home, out-of-home, formal, and informal respite care services, whereas the mental illness respite care intervention study focused only on short-term inpatient psychiatric respite care.

Behavioral/cognitive stimulation interventions were reported with caregivers of Alzheimer's disease patients and caregivers of mentally and physically impaired elderly persons (Pinkston & Linsk, 1984; Pinkston, Linsk, & Young, 1988; Quayhagen & Quayhagen, 1989), while two studies examined day hospital programs for Alzheimer's disease patients (Gilleard, Gilleard, & Whittick, 1984;[10] Winogrond, Fisk, Kirsling, & Keyes, 1987).

Studies by Reifler and Eisdorfer (1980) and Theorell, Haggmark, and Eneroth (1987) with caregivers of Alzheimer's disease and cancer patients can be broadly categorized as psychosocial interventions. The Reifler and Eisdorfer study with caregivers of Alzheimer's disease patients included comprehensive clinic and in-home assessment interviews followed by a broad range of treatment recommendations and follow-up treatment. Little information was given concerning the nature of the "psychosocial intervention" in the Theorell et al. intervention with families of cancer patients. Finally, Godkin, Krant, and Doster (1983-1984) report on findings from a study of living spouses of deceased cancer patients who received care in a hospice program.

Type of Disease

As was the case with support group and educational interventions, clinical interventions cut across disease categories, with all diseases except heart disease represented in these intervention studies. Again, the majority of studies were of caregivers of individuals with mental illness, with about the same number of studies of caregivers of Alzheimer's disease patients and of caregivers of cancer patients. There was one study of stroke caregivers and two studies of mentally and physically impaired elderly.

Research Design

In general, the designs used in clinical/direct service interventions were stronger than those used in both support group and educational interventions. Although the educational interventions had a higher percentage of experimental designs than did the clinical intervention studies, four times as many clinical intervention studies used comparison group designs as compared with educational intervention studies. Overall, one half of clinical intervention studies used comparison group or experimental designs, as compared with less than half of educational interventions and only a few support group intervention studies.

Subjects

Subjects in over four fifths of the clinical intervention studies reviewed were family members of patients in a health care or mental health care facility. Subjects in several studies were recruited through local Alzheimer's disease and Related Disorders Association chapters, community agencies, Alzheimer's disease research centers, or senior center programs. Thus, as was the case with subjects in the educational intervention, subjects in these intervention studies are not representative of caregivers in general.

As was also the case with support group and educational interventions, studies usually did not provide adequate data on the demographic and socioeconomic characteristics of the study populations. In common with the intervention modalities previously reviewed, caregivers of persons with mental illness tended to be mainly parents and spouses, especially wives, and children tended to predominate in intervention studies with the other diseases. The total number of subjects in each study ranged from 1 to 632. Intervention group only studies had a mean of almost 50 subjects per study. The number of subjects per group in comparison group and experimental studies, however, ranged from 6 to 317, with most studies having less than 20 subjects per group, as was the case with educational interventions.

Measures

A diversity of outcome measures were used in the clinical intervention studies that were reviewed. Unlike either support group or educational intervention studies, however, very few studies relied only upon nonstandardized measures of group outcomes. The two studies that relied exclusively upon such measures used questionnaires that were mailed to group participants at the conclusion of the intervention. These questionnaires asked the subjects their perceptions of the effects of the group upon them and/or their ill family member.

Almost all studies primarily used standardized measures to examine group outcomes. The range of measures used was broader than either of the two intervention modalities previously discussed, with particular studies typically using multiple outcome indicators. Principal outcome measures used by studies can be classified as follows:

Objective Stressors. Children's behavior, patients' behaviors and symptoms (Croake & Kelly, 1985; Falloon et al., 1984; Gilleard,

Gilleard, & Whittick, 1984; Kopeikin et al. 1983; Lawton et al., 1989; Lundervold & Lewin, 1987; Pinkston & Linsk, 1984; Pinkston, Linsk, & Young, 1988; Winogrond et al., 1987)

Perceived Stress/Burden. (Falloon et al., 1984; Gilleard, Gilleard, & Whittick, 1984; Lundervold & Lewin, 1987; Winogrond et al., 1987; MacCarthy et al., 1989; Quayhagen & Quayhagen, 1989; Pinkston & Linsk, 1984; Lawton et al., 1989)

Contextual Variables. Age of caregiver, social support, family cohesion and conflict (Gilleard, Gilleard, & Whittick, 1984; Mills et al., 1986; MacCarthy et al., 1989; Pinkston & Linsk, 1984)

Enduring Outcomes. Anxiety, depression, prolactin levels in the blood (associated with psychological exhaustion), psychiatric status, self-esteem (Christensen, 1983; Gilleard et al., 1984; Goldberg & Wool, 1985; Heinrich & Schrag, 1985; Kopeikin et al., 1983; Lawton et al., 1989; Lundervold & Lewin, 1987; Pinkston, Linsk, & Young, 1988; Quayhagen & Quayhagen, 1989; Theorell et al., 1987; Winogrond et al., 1987)

Other Outcomes. Expressed emotion (Falloon et al., 1984; MacCarthy et al., 1989) and patient rehospitalization rates (Croake & Kelly, 1985; Falloon et al., 1984; Geiser et al., 1988; Kopeikin et al., 1983; Kottgen et al., 1984).

Findings

Overall, findings of the effects of clinical interventions using standardized outcomes fail to show consistent results in favor of the intervention. The strongest effect of clinical interventions was found upon objective stressors, with more than one half of the studies finding significant effects in the hypothesized direction. This was slightly greater than was found with support group interventions (no educational interventions examined objective stressors).

The weakest effect of clinical interventions was found in relationship to perceived burden and enduring outcomes, with significant effects found in only slightly over one third of the studies on these outcome variables. This compares with two thirds of the support group and educational interventions finding significant effects on enduring outcomes. Over one half of the educational interventions found significant intervention effects on perceived burden, with no effects found in the support group studies (only two studies examined this variable).

As was the case with support group interventions, findings concerning the effect of the intervention upon objective stressors with caregivers of dementia patients, the frail elderly, or persons with mental illness was mixed, with four studies, all involving caregivers of Alzheimer's disease or dementia patients, reporting no significant effects and five studies reporting significant effects in favor of the intervention (Croake & Kelly, 1985; Falloon et al., 1984; Gilleard, Gilleard, & Whittick, 1984; Kopeikin et al., 1983; Lawton et al., 1989; Lundervold & Lewin, 1987; Pinkston & Linsk, 1984; Pinkston, Linsk, & Young, 1988; Winogrond et al., 1987). It should be noted, however, that four of the five studies showing significant effects of the intervention on objective stressors utilized intervention group only research designs. Therefore these findings should be taken with some caution.

Three of the studies finding significant effects were with family caregivers of persons with mental illness. Croake and Kelly's (1985) intervention group only design, a 14 session family therapy intervention for schizophrenic and depressed veterans and their families that had a major emphasis on changing children's behavior, reported a decrease in misbehavior. Kopeikin et al.'s (1983) experimental study of a six-week outpatient psychological and pharmacological treatment focusing on crisis oriented family therapy found that all four treatment groups showed fewer symptoms at the six-month follow-up period. Subjects in Falloon et al.'s (1983) three subject study showed improved communications skills at ten weeks. Finally, Pinkston & Linsk's (1984) and Pinkston, Linsk, & Young's (1988) behavioral intervention with caregivers of the mentally and physically impaired elderly showed that the intervention was effective in improving about three quarters of the targeted patient behaviors.

The impact of clinical interventions on perceived stress/burden was evaluated in studies with caregivers of Alzheimer's disease patients, persons with mental illness, and the impaired elderly (Gilleard, Gilleard, & Whittick, 1984; Lundervold & Lewin, 1987; Winogrond et al., 1987; Falloon et al., 1984; MacCarthy et al., 1989; Quayhagen & Quayhagen, 1989; Pinkston & Linsk, 1984; Lawton et al., 1989). The majority of studies found that the intervention had no significant effects on changes in level of perceived stress/burden, with only Gilleard, Gilleard, & Whittick, (1984), Falloon et al. (1984) and Quayhagen and Quayhagen (1989) reporting significant treatment effects. Gilleard, Gilleard, and Whittick,'s (1984) intervention group only study of the effects of a psychogeriatric day hospital for dementia patients showed that a reduction in caregiver strain was related to a greater impact of day care. Quayhagen and Quayhagen's (1989) comparison group study of a home based program of cognitive stimulation for Alzheimer's disease patients and caregivers found that caregiver burden levels for the treatment group were maintained over time, while the comparison group increased in perceived burden. Falloon et al.'s experimental study of behavioral family intervention for patients with mental illness and their families found a reduced level of burden in caregivers of the family treatment patients.

Only a few studies, with caregivers of dementia patients, persons with mental illness, and the impaired elderly, examined the impact of the intervention on changes in contextual variables (Gilleard, Gilleard, & Whittick, 1984; Mills et al., 1986; MacCarthy et al., 1989; Pinkston & Linsk, 1984). Three of these studies were intervention group only designs, so findings need to be interpreted with caution. Gilleard, Gilleard, & Whittick (1984) was the only study that reported findings concerning the relationship of caregiver characteristics to outcome. They reported that age of the caregiver was not related to the caregiver's subjective evaluation of the benefits of the intervention. The other three studies looked at relational contextual variables. Pinkston et al. found that the intervention had no effect on social support as measured by contact with family, contact with close friend, and desired social activities. MacCarthys et al.'s (1989) study of a psychoeducational group focused on reducing EE levels for families of persons with mental illness, found that the experimental group showed more changes in coping styles than the control group. Mills et al.'s (1986) study of a similar intervention, focused on enhancing communication and reducing conflict, found that family cohesion scores were up slightly and family conflict scores were down slightly in this intervention group only study.

A large number of studies examined the impact of clinical interventions on enduring health and mental health outcomes with caregivers of Alzheimer's disease patients, cancer patients, impaired elderly, and individuals with mental illness (Christensen, 1983; Gilleard, Gilleard, & Whittick, 1984; Goldberg & Wool, 1985; Heinrich & Schrag, 1985; Kopeikin et al., 1983; Lawton et al., 1989; Lundervold & Lewin, 1987; Pinkston et al., 1988; Quayhagen and Quayhagen, 1989; Theorell et al. 1987; Winogrond et al., 1987). Almost two thirds of the studies found that the interventions examined had no effect on any of the enduring outcome measures utilized, while four of the studies reported significant findings on at least one of the enduring outcome measures utilized.

Christensen's (1983) experimental study evaluated the effects of a four week structured couples treatment intervention to alleviate psychosocial discomfort following the effects of mastectomy. He found that the treatment had a significant effect in reducing depression levels of wives but not of husbands. No significant effects of the treatment on self-esteem or anxiety were found for either wives or husbands. Theorell et al.'s (1987) comparison group study of a comprehensive clinical program for close female relatives of cancer patients who subsequently died found no differences in psychiatric scores between the treatment and comparison groups during the treatment period, but did find that prolactin levels in the blood tended to be lower for treatment group relatives. Kopeikin et al.'s (1983) experimental study of a six-week outpatient psychological and pharmacological treatment focusing on crisis oriented family therapy found that all four treatment groups showed fewer psychiatric symptoms. Finally, Quayhagen and Quayhagen's (1989) study of Alzheimer's disease caregivers found that the treatment group maintained its level of affective symptoms over time whereas the symptoms of the control group increased over time. The intervention had no significant effects on well-being levels.

Studies of caregivers of individuals with mental illness found the intervention had positive effects on reducing caregiver levels of expressed emotion—EE (Falloon et al., 1984; MacCarthy et al., 1989). Falloon and colleagues (Falloon et al., 1984) report the results of two intervention studies. The first was an intervention group only study of family caregivers and patients with mental illness (three subjects living with high EE relatives) that involved a comprehensive behavioral approach focusing on skills training and family therapy. Findings showed a short-term reduction in parental EE ratings. The second study by Falloon and colleagues was a 14 subject comparison group study evaluating the effects of insight-oriented family therapy plus holistic health therapy, behavioral family therapy and social skills training, and standard state hospital treatment. Findings showed a 60% decrease in critical comments or lower EE in the treatment groups versus a 16% decrease in critical comments in the control group. There were also significant differences in patient relapse rates, with a 21% relapse rate among treatment patients at the nine-month follow-up versus a 56% relapse rate among control group patients.

MacCarthy et al.'s comparison group intervention examined the effect of a psychoeducational group led by a professional team. Findings showed that the experimental group showed a decrease in high EE that approached, but was not, statistically significant. There was a statistically significant change in critical comments, with a decrease in the number of such comments in the experimental group and an increase in the control group. There were no significant differences between the groups in the level of overinvolvement.

Studies of caregivers of individuals with mental illness found consistent effects of the intervention upon patient recidivism levels (Croake & Kelly, 1985; Falloon et al., 1984; Geiser et al., 1988; Kopeikin et al., 1983; Kottgen et al., 1984). The Kopeikin et al. and Falloon et al. studies, involving either comparison group or experimental designs, reported significant effects of the interventions on reducing patient recidivism rates. Kottgen et al.'s comparison group intervention found effects leaning toward lower relapse rates among the treatment groups, but these effects were not statistically significant. The Croake and Kelly and Geiser et al. studies, which did not have comparison or control groups, both reported treatment effects in favor of the intervention.

In summary, there were a large number of clinical intervention studies using quite diverse treatment strategies. Respite care interventions, which focus on release time for the caregiver, for example, are very different in purpose and focus than counseling/therapeutic interventions in which clinical staff are directly engaged in trying to change caregiver interactions with the patient, caregiver behavior, or caregiver adjustment to caring for someone with chronic illness.

Interventions cut across all of the diseases discussed in this volume with the exception of heart disease. Research designs utilized were the strongest overall of the three intervention modalities that we have reviewed; but as was the case with the other two modalities, there were only a small number of subjects per intervention group. Studies principally used standardized measurement instruments. Findings show only weak to moderate support for the effect of the interventions, with the strongest findings related to the effect of the intervention in changing objective stressors and the weakest effect of the interventions related to affecting enduring mental and physical health outcomes.

The great diversity of clinical intervention approaches makes it difficult to draw any definitive overall conclusions about the effects of these interventions. The finding, however, that clinical interventions had the strongest effect in relationship to objective stressors is consistent with the fact that this modality, more than the other two, targeted the changing of the objective stressors as one of the goals of the intervention. On the other hand, the poor findings pertaining to lack of change in most studies in affecting levels of anxiety, depression, or self-esteem may be a reflection of the fact that the interventions were not sufficiently targeted to making changes in these areas. For example, self-esteem seems more likely to be enhanced in a support group intervention where subjects learn that their problems are not unique, and that, in fact, they may be doing quite well in adjusting to a difficult situation. Similarly, the focus of learning new skills in many educational interventions seems directly related to subjects feeling better about themselves if successful in acquiring these new skills. This suggests that interventions need to target more carefully appropriate change variables and perhaps be more realistic in the changes that can most likely be made in program participants as a result of the intervention. This finding also implies that a range of intervention modalities are needed to meet the diverse needs of caregivers.

MULTIPLE INTERVENTION COMPARISON STUDIES

A few intervention studies (Anderson, 1986; Ingersoll-Dayton, Chapman, & Neal, 1990; Montgomery, Stull, & Borgatta, 1989; Zarit, Anthony, & Boutselis, 1987) were reviewed in which treatment conditions were compared that cut across one or more of the three intervention modalities, support group, educational, or clinical/direct service, reviewed in this chapter (see Table A.4). Target populations of these studies included caregivers of dementia patients, persons with mental illness, the impaired elderly, and dependent family members (elder, disabled adult, or child).

The interventions utilized differed in all four studies. Anderson's (1986) study was a two-year treatment program for patients with mental illness and family members with high EE levels. The intervention was psychoeducational, with random assignment to one of four intervention modalities: family therapy, social skills training, family therapy and social skills training, and medication only. Ingersoll-Dayton et al.'s (1990) intervention study for employed caregivers of dependent family members included a seven-week educational seminar series on caregiving followed by participation into one of three self-selected eight-week programs—care planning, support group, or buddy system. Montgomery et al. (1989) evaluated five different treatment constellations for caregivers of the impaired elderly. Groups received various combinations of one or more treatments as follows—Group 1 (seminars, support group, consultation, respite), Group 2 (seminars, support group, consultation), Group 3 (seminars, support group), Group 4 (consultation), Group 5 (respite), Group 6 (control). Zarit et al. (1987) evaluated the effectiveness of an eight session stress management support group versus a family counseling group for caregivers of persons with dementia.

Overall, the designs utilized were strong, with three of the four studies using experimental designs, with the Ingersoll-Dayton et al. (1990) study using an intervention group only design. The number of subjects in these studies, a considerably larger number than the number of subjects in the other intervention modalities previously reviewed, ranged from 102[11] to 541, with considerably more than 20 subjects in each of the treatment groups. Subjects tended to be female, spouses, and adult children,[12] as was found in the other intervention modality studies.

All four studies utilized standardized outcome assessment measures. As was the case with the other three intervention modalities, a range of outcome measures were examined with each study using multiple outcome measures. Principal measures used included the following: objective stressors—hours of caregiving tasks, objective burden (Montgomery et al., 1989; Zarit et al., 1987); perceived burden (Ingersoll-Dayton et al., 1990; Montgomery et al., 1989; Zarit et al., 1987); contextual variables—social support (Ingersoll-Dayton et al., 1990; Zarit et al., 1987); enduring outcomes—affect, self-reported health, mental health status (Ingersoll-Dayton et al., 1990; Montgomery et al., 1989; Zarit et al., 1987); other—patient relapse (Anderson, 1986).

Overall, findings show that the interventions had little effect on any of the major outcome variables that were examined. These findings were weaker than those from any of the three intervention modalities that were previously reviewed.

Montgomery et al. (1989)[13] and Zarit et al. (1987) failed to find any effects of the intervention in changing the level of objective stressors. Montgomery did not find any effect of the intervention in decreasing the number of hours of caregiving tasks performed after controlling for caregivers whose patients became institutionalized during the course of the study. In addition, she found no differences at Time 2 between the groups in the level of objective burden. Zarit et al. (1987) examined the degree to which the intervention affected the frequency of patient behavioral problems and found no effect.

The effect of the interventions on perceived stress/burden was examined by the Ingersoll-Dayton et al., Montgomery et al., and Zarit et al. studies. Montgomery et al. found a statistically significant reduction in subjective burden between Time 1 and Time 2 for all groups except the control group. The other two studies found no significant effects of the intervention on perceived stress/burden.

The effects of the interventions on social support were examined by the Ingersoll-Dayton et al. and Zarit et al. studies, with no significant effects found in either study. However, Ingersoll-Dayton et al. found that social support approached significance in an analysis of the most helpful aspects of the care planning versus support group conditions, suggesting that the support group might be slightly more helpful as a source of emotional support than was the care planning group (no subjects in the Ingersoll-Dayton et al. study chose the buddy group intervention condition).

Ingersoll-Dayton et al., Montgomery et al., and Zarit et al. found little support for the effect of the interventions on enduring outcomes. Ingersoll-Dayton et al. found that subjects in the care planning and support group conditions showed a significant decrease in negative affect over time. However, there was no control or comparison group utilized, so we cannot necessarily attribute this change to the effects of the intervention. Montgomery, Stull, and Borgatta (1985) found no change in self-reported health by the subjects from Time 1 to Time 2 and Zarit et al. found that the interventions had no effect on change in mental health status of the caregivers.

Anderson examined the effects of the four different interventions on psychotic relapse of the patients, an outcome for patients that is highly correlated with increased stress for caregivers. She found considerable differences among the interventions at one year, with family therapy alone having the most positive impact and medication the least impact. After two years relapse rates generally increased, with patients in the social skills training and family therapy group having the lowest relapse rate and patients in the medication group having the highest relapse rate.

CONCLUSIONS

A total of 54 caregiver intervention studies were reviewed, 48 of which focused exclusively or almost exclusively on the five chronic diseases examined in this volume. The additional 6 studies were principally focused on frail or impaired elderly. More than one fifth (12) of these 54 studies utilized only nonstandardized, rather than standardized, outcome measures. Findings of these 12 subjective outcome studies were uniformly very positive, with participants overall being very pleased with the intervention regardless of the intervention modality. A number of the remaining 42 studies, which primarily used standardized outcome measures, also asked study participants to subjectively evaluate the intervention. Again, overall responses from the subjects were quite positive.

Of those studies that used standardized outcome measures, there was considerable variation among the intervention modalities in the number of studies that reported significant findings related to the effects of the intervention on objective stressors, stress/burden, contextual variables, and enduring outcomes (see Figure 9.1). It should be noted that there also was considerable variation among the studies, as previously discussed, in the strength of the design, number of subjects, and overall methodology, which is not reflected in Figure 9.1. Therefore, comparisons of the number of significant findings pertaining to particular outcomes is only a gross comparative measure. Nevertheless, we believe it is a useful one.

As can be seen in Figure 9.1, of studies that used objective outcome measures, 48% found significant effects of the intervention on enduring outcomes, 47% found significant effects of the intervention on objective stressors, 39% found significant effects of the intervention on levels of perceived stress/burden, and 25% found significant effects of the interventions on contextual variables. It is apparent from these results that subjective satisfaction by subjects with the intervention is not necessarily associated with change in caregiver short- or long-term outcomes. Almost all subjects queried were very positive about the intervention, yet levels of stress/burden and enduring outcomes were not affected in more than one half the studies.

Examining the types of outcomes by intervention modality is difficult because of the limited number of studies using particular outcome measures with specific intervention modalities. Nevertheless, it appears that there is a relationship between intervention modality and type of

TABLE 9.1. Percentage of Significant Outcomes by Intervention Modality

Modality	Objective Stressors	Stress/ Burden	Contextual Variables	Enduring Outcomes
Support Group	50% (N = 4)	0% (N = 2)	50% (N = 2)	67% (N = 3)
Educational	—	60% (N = 5)	0% (N = 4)	67% (N = 6)
Clinical	56% (N = 9)	38% (N = 8)	50% (N = 4)	36% (N = 11)
Multiple Int.	0% (N = 2)	33% (N = 3)	0% (N = 2)	33% (N = 3)
Total	47% (N = 15)	39% (N = 18)	25% (N = 12)	48% (N = 23)

reported change. Of studies that used objective outcome measures, clinical interventions had the best effects on objective stressors, educational interventions had the best effects on levels of perceived stress/ burden, support group and clinical interventions had the best effects on contextual variables, and support and educational interventions had the best effects on enduring outcomes. The finding that clinical interventions have the best effects on such objective stressors as patient behaviors and symptoms is probably due, as we stated earlier, to the fact that clinical interventions, more than the other types of intervention modalities, target the changing of objective stressors as one of the goals of the intervention. Similarly, educational interventions are perhaps the most focused intervention aimed at reducing levels of perceived stress. Further research is needed, however, with a larger number of well-designed studies to examine whether these relationships continue to hold.

Turning to an analysis of the findings by disease, there were a total of 48 intervention studies that were primarily or exclusively focused on Alzheimer's disease, cancer, mental illness, or stroke (there were no empirical outcome studies with caregivers of heart disease patients). Figure 9.2 presents an overview by disease of the number of studies, the research designs utilized, the percentage of studies using standardized outcome measures, and the number of studies using standardized outcome measures reporting significant intervention effects on objective stressors, perceived/stress burden, contextual variables, and enduring outcomes.

Overall, less than half (42%) of these 48 studies used comparison group or experimental designs, with the strongest designs being used in intervention studies with caregivers of Alzheimer's disease patients. Alzheimer's disease intervention studies also had the highest percentage of studies that used standardized outcome measures. Because of limitations in the number of studies of particular diseases that used any

TABLE 9.2. Overview of Intervention Studies by Disease

	Mental Illness	Alzheimer's Disease	Cancer	Stroke	Heart Disease	All
# of Studies	23	15	8	2	0	48
Design						
Intervention Group Only	65%	40%	50%	100%		56%
Comparison Group	17%	13%	25%			17%
Experimental	17%	40%	25%			25%
Other		07%				02%
% of studies with standardized outcome measures	74%	80%	62%	50%		75%
Findings						
Objective Stressors	100% ($N = 5$)	0% ($N = 5$)	—	—		50% ($N = 10$)
Stress/Burden	60% ($N = 5$)	50% ($N = 8$)	—	—		62% ($N = 13$)
Contextual	75% ($N = 4$)	0% ($N = 4$)	—	—		38% ($N = 8$)
Enduring Outcomes	100% ($N = 3$)	20% ($N = 10$)	50% ($N = 4$)	—		41% ($N = 17$)

of the four types of standardized outcome measures, we are limited to examining only the results for Alzheimer's disease and mental illness intervention studies.

Results of intervention studies of caregivers of Alzheimer's disease patients show that these interventions overall have the greatest effects in reducing levels of perceived stress/burden and the least effects in reducing levels of objective stressors. Results of intervention studies of caregivers of persons with mental illness show generally more positive effects than the Alzheimer's disease results and these effects cut across all four types of outcome measures. These differences in findings appear to be due in large part to the nature of the diseases and of the interventions. Alzheimer's disease is one in which patients face a progressive decline as compared to chronic mental illness, which tends to be cyclical in nature. Alzheimer's disease may be less amenable, therefore, to interventions aimed at reducing objective stressors. In addition, many of the mental illness interventions are interactional, family interventions that are focused on changing the patient's behavior through modifying how the caregiver interacts with the patient.

As this chapter indicates, there have been an increasing number of interventions for caregivers of persons with chronic illness and a trend toward more sophisticated designs and measurement methodologies. As was the case with our review of theoretical research on caregiving, however, there are many gaps in the literature that remain to be addressed by future research studies. Existing studies have many limitations including the small number of subjects, limited long-term follow-up of study subjects, little testing of the efficacy of the different types of interventions in the same study or testing of the same intervention with caregivers of patients with different diseases, little attention paid to the appropriate timing of the intervention relating to the stage of caregiving, and no attention given to examination of the differential effects of the interventions, if any, by race or ethnicity of caregiver. In addition, there was little focus on the intervention process itself. We need to know not only whether an intervention affects caregiver distress, but how it does so and whether particular parts of a multifaceted intervention are more effective than others. The concluding section of this volume presents some recommendations for enhancing theoretical and intervention research with caregivers of persons with Alzheimer's disease, cancer, heart disease, mental illness, and stroke.

NOTES

1. Most intervention studies limit postintervention data collection time periods to immediately after the intervention or up to six months later. Therefore, data collected on levels of caregiver psychiatric symptomatology or depression, for example, are really indicators of short-term rather than long-term effects of the intervention.

2. There were 13 studies reviewed, but 14 empirical papers because Biegel & Yamatani, 1986 and 1987, were based on one study. One of the 13 studies (Gonyea et al., 1989) is not an intervention study per se but rather a study of members of Alzheimer's support groups that includes a members' assessment of the perceived benefits of the group. In addition, 12 studies of support group interventions that contain only clinical observations of outcomes are listed in the Appendix but are not reviewed here.

3. A total of 21 empirical papers of educational interventions, representing 14 different studies, were reviewed (see Table 9.2). In addition, 14 studies of educational

interventions that contain clinical observations as the only outcome measures are listed in the Appendix but are not reviewed here.

4. The D. Evans et al. study did not provide information concerning the number of weeks for the educational sessions.

5. Leff and colleagues have published a number of papers on their chronic mental illness intervention studies. For simplicity, only one reference to their work is cited in the text of this chapter. See Appendix, Table A.2, for complete reference citations.

6. Authors of the Kahan et al. (1985) study did not specify whether subjects were randomly assigned to experimental or control groups. Based on the article, however, we assume this to be the case.

7. A total of 39 empirical papers of clinical/direct services interventions, representing 24 different studies, were reviewed (see Appendix, Table A.3). In addition, 16 studies that contain clinical observations as the only outcome measures are listed in the Appendix but are not reviewed here.

8. Falloon and colleagues have published a large number of papers on their chronic mental illness intervention studies. For simplicity, only one reference to their work is cited in the text of this chapter. See Appendix, Table A.3, for complete reference citations.

9. Kopeikin, M. J. Goldstein and colleagues have published several papers on their chronic mental illness intervention studies. For simplicity, only one reference is cited in the text of this chapter. See Appendix, Table A.3, for complete reference citations.

10. The Gilleard, Gilleard, and Whittick study was focused on dementia patients in general, rather than on Alzheimer's disease patients exclusively.

11. The Ingersoll-Dayton et al. study included 256 persons who attended the seminar series, but only 50 subjects attended the subsequent eight-week programs.

12. The Anderson study did not provide data about the relationship of the study subjects to the patients.

13. It should be noted that only one third of the subjects eligible for services in the Montgomery study actually used them, despite the fact that the services were free and subjects were positively encouraged to use them.

10

Future Directions:
Research and Policy

This volume began with a discussion of trends indicating reasons why family caregiving has grown to be such an important public policy issue. Based upon these trends, in the future we can expect that family caregivers will need a growing array of diversified and accessible services to assist them in the performance of their roles as the chronically ill population expands in size and increases in age, and as the demographic characteristics of the typical caregiver also undergo change. Similarly, we expect the demand for new public policy initiatives to assist caregivers, represented today most clearly by organized constituencies of family caregivers of individuals with Alzheimer's disease and developmental disability, will also increase.

Future policy and service development initiatives need to be responsive to research findings from studies of caregiver burden and interventions. Our review of theory and research in this volume suggests a number of important implications for service delivery, public policy, and future research efforts to assist family caregivers.

The present service delivery system, as well as patient and caregiver advocacy efforts, is segmented by disease. Therefore, it is not surprising that professionals, families, and patients tend to look only within their own disease when they are confronting issues and problems. An important lesson of this volume is the need to focus attention *across* as well as *within* diseases. Yet, there are growing advocacy efforts around the development of more disease-specific services and programs. Such directions are only appropriate, however, if there are greater differences than similarities among the needs of caregivers across diseases. There is some evidence, provided in this volume and by other researchers (Montgomery, Kosloski, & Borgatta, 1990), to suggest that this assumption may not be warranted. Currently, most research (and interventions) is organized by disease type. There is need for more comparative research across diseases that would allow us to determine, more than we could in this volume, the commonalities and differences in caregiver reactions to various illnesses.

To date, the empirical literature is dominated by studies that treat caregiving homogeneously, mixing types and stages of illnesses, and studies that examine single illnesses only. A fundamental understanding of the caregiving phenomenon requires that we be sensitive simultaneously to illness type and stage of the disease. Further attempts need to be made to classify illness characteristics. Rolland (1988), for example, believes that such disease dimensions as type of onset, disease course, likely outcome, and level of incapacitation are critical for an understanding of family response to chronic illness. A typology of illness dimensions that cuts across diseases would allow further testing of the centrality of these illness factors.

This needed future research effort also has implications for service planning, if caregiver status or illness stage is indeed more important than illness category. Thus, rather than interventions guided by disease, new research findings from comparative studies might suggest that interventions be guided by sources of caregiver distress or circumstances of the caregiver. Our conceptual model of caregiver distress, and the key variables found in Chapter 8 to cut across diseases, suggest the kinds of variables that could be utilized as a possible new conceptual framework for caregiver interventions. One implication of this approach is that service planning should be based upon a functional analysis not only of patient needs, but also upon an analysis of caregivers and their life circumstances—economic status, physical and mental health status, burden, relationship to the patient, roles vis-à-vis the patient, other roles, and so forth.

We believe that merged funding streams should be utilized where feasible to meet the needs of a cross-section of caregiver groups. Furthermore, where common needs of caregivers across diseases have been identified, new caregiver service delivery and advocacy organizations crosscutting diseases should be developed to advocate for needed service and policy initiatives for caregivers.

The medical basis of our health care system has a number of implications for service delivery and research. Under our current medical system, services for patients are designed, by definition, when the patient is in crisis or under active medical treatment. The needs of caregivers, in fact, often come to the attention of clinicians only when the patient is under active treatment. Thus we know much too little about the needs of patients and caregivers when the patients are not under active medical treatment and care. It is our belief that services for caregivers also need to be available when the patients are most insulated from medical treatment. In fact, it is this time period when caregivers might be most burdened and isolated.

A related issue is that services for patients, especially medical services, need to adopt a psychosocial systems approach and examine the implications of patient care recommendations not only upon the patient's health status and functioning but also its effects upon the caregiver and the entire family system. This is especially important considering the fact that caregivers are often asked to provide complex medical treatment and to administer medications to patients returning home to live with the caregiver after leaving the hospital. One way of addressing this issue is to conceptualize the client as the family system rather than as the patient per se. In this manner, services to caregivers would not be based only on the patient's treatment status.

The patient's illness affects not only the patient and caregiver but the entire family constellation, especially children and those family members living in the same household as the patient. All family members are impacted both by the patients' illness itself as well as by the diversion of time and emotion by the caregivers. Furthermore, caregiver tasks are often shared by family members, so burden falls on more than the primary caregiver. Current research and service delivery tends to focus exclusively on a single caregiver, rather than examine the impact of illness and caregiving needs on all family members.

As noted in the previous chapter, research findings about interventions to assist family caregivers demonstrate that generally caregivers like these services very much and that most caregivers feel better as a result. Though burden levels are sometimes decreased and caregiver mental health functioning is sometimes increased, interventions are more effective at making caregivers feel better than they are at improving short- or long-term functioning. These findings should, however, be viewed in a positive light because the interventions tested are usually fairly modest in scope and are generally not tailored to fit the circumstances of particular caregivers. Interventions are often developed based on the premise that all caregivers are, by definition, burdened. Therefore, service planners often assume that the more services that agencies can offer the better, rather than developing services based upon specific indicators of client and caregiver need.

Intervention research (as well as service planning) would benefit from more basic research that isolates the variables affecting caregiver needs, and that analyzes these variables in relationship to intervention effects. Many caregivers can handle their caregiver roles without undue problems. We need a better way of identifying high risk caregivers who could most benefit from services. If we do not know the objective stressors and contextual variables relevant to caregiver response to interventions, we cannot tailor interventions to caregiver needs. Such research should help us find out who best benefits from what types of services at what stage of illness.

Research on the determinants of caregiver reaction and the effects of interventions to reduce caregiver distress is still clearly in its infancy. As noted throughout this volume, many methodological issues and problems remain to be addressed before clarity can be achieved. In addition to the issues addressed above, future research needs to focus on issues pertaining to improvements in sampling, advancements in study design, and standardization of major study variables.

First, we need to be more careful in our selection of samples for caregiving studies. Most studies utilize small, unrepresentative samples. Participants in almost all caregiving studies are volunteers and therefore may overrepresent individuals for whom caregiving is particularly problematic. Many studies use hospital or agency based samples in which patients are likely to be in crisis and, therefore, the patients' caregivers can be expected to have greater problems than would be found in more representative samples. Such samples are likely to overestimate the negative effects of caregiving. In addition, sufficiently large samples in future studies need to be drawn so that analyses can be conducted by race and ethnicity, since there is substantial evidence that not all individuals meet their needs and solve problems in the same way.

The use of volunteer samples may be an even more severe problem in studies where participants have been selected from support groups. It is likely that these individuals are unusual in that they are seeking to address an identified problem, feel comfortable in a group context, and have expectations that interacting with group members will be beneficial.

A second issue that cuts across all caregiving studies is the need for improvements in study designs. Much of the existing research is cross-sectional and provides valuable descriptive data about caregiving. Such studies, however, are not very useful for testing models of the type identified in the preceding chapters of this volume and, in particular, for investigating mechanisms that account for important caregiving end points. There is need for more theoretically grounded, longitudinal research studies to address this issue. When feasible, future longitudinal research studies should include studies that are prospective, with data collection points occurring before the onset of caregiving. This will help address difficulties of current longitudinal designs in evaluating, for example, changes in depression due to caregiving. Differences in depression levels between men and women reported in caregiving studies may actually be due to baseline differences between men and women before the caregiving experience. For women in particular, it would be important to examine to what extent the caregiving experience has increased existing levels of depression.

Third, improvements are needed in the conceptualization and measurement of major study variables. As noted in Chapter 2, there are a number of issues pertaining to both the measurement of burden and the measurement of enduring outcomes. To briefly summarize, burden needs to be examined from both an objective basis—tasks carried out by the disabled relative, and a subjective basis—effects of these tasks. The specific problems of caregiving need to be distinguished from the more general sources of caregiver distress, such as the anticipated loss of a loved one. Using models such as those proposed in this volume, burden needs to be distinguished from other indicators of caregiving effects such as well-being and physical and mental health status.

As we have seen in our reviews of the five illnesses discussed in this volume, many caregiving studies look only at short-term rather than enduring outcomes. The limitations of self-report inventories of physical health and mental health status have also been discussed. Such measures need to be coupled with more objective measures through use of clinical instruments, such as the DIS and SADS to assess mental disorders and ICD classifications, health care utilization data, and medication use to measure physical health. Research is needed to examine the possible relationship between types of stressors (e.g., physical versus cognitive disability) and type of health problem. We also need to develop a better understanding of the mechanisms that account for particular health effects, keeping in mind that mechanisms that account for symptom reporting, health care utilization, and disease processes may all differ from each other.

To advance our ability to study caregiver outcomes across diseases, outcome measures of caregiver burden and enduring physical health and mental health outcomes need to be standardized for each illness and, ultimately, across illnesses. Only then can we truly make valid comparisons.

Obviously, many methodological hurdles need to be overcome before we develop a comprehensive empirical base for testing the theoretical model presented in this volume. At present, however, this model can serve as a guide for future research efforts. First, untested variables can be explored in each disease area to determine further consistencies across illnesses. Later, more ambitious studies would allow us to collect parallel data across illness categories.

Currently, there are few comparative studies of chronic illnesses, and these have focused on patients, rather than caregivers. The recent Medical Outcome Study of 11,242 adults comparing outpatients with depressive symptoms to others suffering from eight major chronic illnesses (Stewart et al., 1989; Wells et al., 1989) found that patients with depressive symptoms had worse physical, social, and role functioning, more days in bed, and worse health and bodily pain than most other chronic illness categories. Only patients with advanced coronary artery disease or angina showed greater physical and functional limitations.

An earlier study by Cassileth et al. (1984) of 758 patients in six diagnostic groups also found depressed patients to show worse psychosocial status than five other chronic illness groups. However, the other illness categories did not differ significantly from each other, or from the general public. Cassileth et al.'s (1984) study then focused on exploring other factors that affected patient adjustment. They found that patients who were recently diagnosed, patients who showed great declines in physical health, or younger patients had low mental health scores across all illness categories. In their conclusion, Cassileth et al. suggested that patient adjustment was affected primarily by factors other than specific diagnosis. Our current analysis of caregiver adjustment appears to suggest a similar pattern (unfortunately, the extensive collaborative Medical Outcome Study data reported by Stewart et al. [1989] and Wells et al. [1989] did not examine the contributions of other predictors of patient adjustment).

This book has examined the difficulties of family caregivers in chronic illness and the variables that influence their response. In focusing on caregivers, we believe we are compensating for a strong bias toward patients in much of the literature. In the future, however, we may find that common factors affect the reactions of both patients and their caregivers. For example, it seems likely that objective characteristics of illness severity directly impact on both patient and caregiver, and that social support operates similarly for both. Thus we may ultimately discover that a small set of common variables affects both patient and caregiver responses to illness. A recent study by Wellisch, Wolcott, Pasnau, Fawzy, and Landsverk (1989) suggests the close interplay between patient and family adjustment. Unfortunately, this speculation must also await further exploration.

In closing, we must recognize that there are three primary actors involved with family caregiving in chronic illness—patients, family caregivers, and the health care system. The interests of these three parties are often in conflict with each other. What is in the best interest of the health care system may not necessarily be in the best interest of the patient or caregiver, such as the patient being released from the hospital because of DRG (Diagnostic Related Groups) payment restrictions. In other instances, both patient and health care providers may be consistent in attempting to keep the patient out of an institution, but this may conflict with the best interests of the caregiver. Whose interests should society pursue? We have posed a number of questions about family caregiving that we believe can be appropriately answered by future research. We recognize, however, that ultimately the caregiving field is confronted by choices concerning the value of human life and the hierarchy of rights that are primarily moral and ethical in nature.

Appendix

TABLE A.1 Support Group Interventions

Authors	Barnes et al. (1981)
Disease	Alzheimer's disease
Research Design	Intervention group only
Intervention Description	Eight week support group for families of Alzheimer's disease patients living at home. Sixteen 90-minute biweekly sessions.
Subjects	12 spouses and 3 adult children of Alzheimer's disease patients (9 women and 6 men)
Measures	Clinical observations based on analysis of audiotapes of group meetings; verbal reports by group members of benefits at end of group
Findings	Improved understanding of Alzheimer's disease most helpful benefit. Adjusted expectations of disease outcome. Sharing feelings and sense of acceptance and support by others reduced isolation. Attainment of more self-identity in relation to the patient. Help in practical problem solving
Authors	Gonyea (1989)
Disease	Alzheimer's disease
Research Design	Nonexperimental survey
Intervention Description	Mail survey of Alzheimer's support groups
Subjects	301 members of 47 Alzheimer's disease support groups in Massachusetts
Measures	Focus on groups' structure, format, composition, and perceived benefits
Findings	Respondents given list of 16 potential group benefits—asked to rate each on 3 point helpfulness scale. Respondents were very positive overall about group. Information sharing and peer support were cited as two most helpful areas. In comparison with these areas, group was rated much less helpful in addressing personal needs of caregivers—reducing guilt, coping with anger, coping with fears about the future, enhancing relationship with patient, etc.

Authors	Lazarus et al. (1981)
Disease	Alzheimer's disease
Research Design	Comparison group; pre- and postgroup evaluation
Intervention Description	10 weekly, hour long discussion group meetings co-led by two geriatric psychiatrists
Subjects	Eight family members of patients in cholinergic drug study at psychiatric institute were invited—4 participated in group, 3 did not (1 each of wife, husband, brother, and son).
Measures	(a) Family Unit Inventory; (b) Rosenberg Self-Esteem Scale (adapted); (c) Depression/Anxiety Scale—Hopkins Check-list; (d) Rotter's locus of control; (e) Goal Attainment Scale; (f) tape recorded analysis of sessions
Findings	Comparison of caregivers attending group versus those who did not attend.

No significant differences between groups at pretest.

Control group members showed no significant changes from pre- to posttest. For treatment group, no significant differences in self-esteem, anxiety or depression pre- to posttest.

Treatment group participants showed greater locus of control on posttest.

Treatment group showed significant differences on 2 of 11 measures of family unit inventory—higher score on family separateness and family's concern with success, prestige, and opinions of others was of less importance as a result of group participation.

3 of 4 participants said group helping in being able to cope

Authors	Johnson & Stark (1980)
Disease	Cancer
Research Design	Intervention group only with postgroup evaluation
Intervention Description	Open-ended information and support group for patients and relatives—3 one hour sessions per week—open discussion, medical/nursing information, and discussion of psychosocial issues
Subjects	Inpatients, outpatients, and family members; participants are self-selected; age 18-90, wide SES range; group is co-led by interdisciplinary team of professionals
Measures	14 item program assessment questionnaire (Consumer satisfaction survey)
Findings	136 patients and 152 family members participated in at least one session; 32 patients and 27 family members responded to questionnaire (40% response rate)

Participants wanted information the most, followed by an opportunity to share feelings; about 75% felt their expectations were met by the group, 75% thought the group was a helpful, positive experience.

Authors	Plant et al. (1987)
Disease	Cancer
Research Design	Intervention group only
Intervention Description	Hospital based, professionally led, monthly support group for cancer patients, families, and friends. Bereaved were also included [London].
Subjects	Participants were initially recruited from hospital patient-load and then new admissions; 18% of those invited actually participated. 42% relatives, 13% friends; 45% patients; 55% married; mean age: 50 years; median number of sessions: 2
Measures	Three page open- and closed-ended questionnaire sent to participants 3 months after first group participation and to those who attended at least one meeting
Findings	58% response rate to survey (*N*=60). Responders attended an average of 3 meetings.

Group members attended an average of 3 meetings. Group members divided about whether bereaved persons should participate.

81% received all or some of information desired, 70% felt determined to overcome cancer, 55% felt it was easier to talk about it; 64% were happier and 81% were more relaxed after attending group; 26% felt more anxious or worried and 29% felt more depressed or sad; 53% stated group helped with coping with cancer.

Authors	Greene & Monahan (1989)
Disease	Frail elderly; 14% Alzheimer's disease
Research Design	Comparison group; pre- and postgroup evaluation (before group, after 8 weeks, and at 6 months)
Intervention Description	Professionally led support groups met weekly for 2 hours over 8 weeks; 34 support groups conducted during 14 months period; group content—professionally led group discussion, educational, physical, and social skill development, and relaxation training
Subjects	Recruitment through community agencies—caregivers of frail elderly who were experiencing considerable stress, at-risk for placement of elder, and interested in participating in a support group. Also media coverage which led to self-referrals. 289 subjects, 208 in support group, 81 in the control group. Control group members' schedule did not allow for group participation. Caregivers' mean age—58 years; 86% female; 47% providing care to spouse; one quarter of caregivers were Hispanic.
Measures	Caregiver: SCL-90 subscales—global anxiety, depression, and hostility; Burden (Modified Zarit scale)

Carereceiver: ADL and IADL, cognitive dysfunction, psychological and psychobehavioral problems

Findings Multiple regression analyses for short-term effects—Results show significant treatment effects in reducing anxiety and depression. There was a very marginal effect in burden reduction and no effect of the treatment on hostility.

The same analyses were conducted at six months post- pretest. Findings showed longer term effects similar to, but weaker than, short-term changes. Significant treatment effects were found for anxiety and depression.

As with short-term changes, greater burden at pretest predicted less improvement in anxiety. Higher pretest anxiety and depression predicted less reduction in depression. There were no significant treatment effects at six months for hostility or burden. Alzheimer's caregivers showed less improvement in burden reduction at six months than did other caregivers.

Authors Toseland et al. (1989)
Disease Frail elderly
Research Design Experimental; pre- and postgroup evaluation
Intervention Description (1) Professionally led support group (*N*=18); (2) Peer-led support group (*N*=18); (3) Respite only control group (*N*=20). Support groups met two hours per week for eight weeks. Professionally led group was more structured, included a problem solving component.
Subjects Adult daughters or daughters-in-law with above average stress who are primary caregivers of a parent with chronic disabilities living in the community. Subjects recruited through media and community agencies and organizations.

150 volunteers, 71 eligible to participate of which 56 actually participated. Subjects in general were white, Christian, employed full-time, early 50s in age, and had been caregiving for 5-8 years.
Measures Caregiver outcome measures: Hours of caregiving; extent of caregiving; health; Zarit Burden Inventory; problems with caregiving; Bradburn Affect Balance Scale (BABS); Brief Symptom Inventory; informal support; formal support (Community Resource Scale); changes in personal problems (3 scales); satisfaction with group
Findings No significant changes in caregiving condition or in burden among the three groups. Participants in both treatment groups reported increased in well-being as measured by the BABS although the control group reported a decrease in well-being.

Treatment group participants differed from control group participants on three of the nine BSI subscales—somatization, obsessive-compulsiveness, and phobic anxiety.

Treatment group participants reported significant increases in social network size as compared with control group.

Participants in the treatment group reported significantly greater knowledge of community resources than did the participants in the control group.

Treatment group participants showed significantly greater improvements than did control group participants in a number of personal change areas—guilt, anger at other family members who did not help with caregiving, balancing caregiving with other responsibilities, and in relationships with the carereceiver.

Participants of both treatment groups reported high levels of satisfaction with the group.

Authors	Biegel & Yamatani (1986)
Disease	Mental illness
Research Design	Intervention group only; longitudinal; pretest and 6 months posttest self-administered questionnaire
Intervention Description	10 member led support groups; groups met monthly or twice per month
Subjects	N=45; 95% white; 73% female; 73% middle-class; 51 years mean age; 71% married; 63% parents, 14% siblings, 9% spouses.
Measures	Family Distress Scale (Burden)
	Patient functioning; helpfulness of group; satisfaction with group.
Findings	High satisfaction with group; most helpful—group as source of education and information, advocacy, and emotional support.
	Higher group participation, higher perceived helpfulness of group
	Greater hospitalizations of patient, less helpfulness of group

Authors	Biegel & Yamatani (1987)
Disease	Mental illness
Research Design	Intervention group only
Intervention Description	Same as above
Subjects	Same as above
Measures	Frequency of help-giving activities in group.
	Satisfaction with group.
Findings	Most frequent group activities were nondirective social support—emotional, affirmational, or informational.
	Least frequent activities were oriented toward behavioral change.
	Moderate correlation between most frequent activities and satisfaction with group.

Authors Craig et al. (1985)

Disease Mental illness

Research Design Intervention group only; consumer satisfaction survey

Intervention Description Ongoing support group for relatives of inpatients in psychiatric hospital. Group meets weekly and is co-led by paraprofessionals and professionals.

Subjects Relatives of patients and also some self-referred patients; 300 families have participated since 1980. An average of 20 families and 15 staff attend each week.

Measures Open-ended participation satisfaction questionnaire

Findings More than 85% of respondents said group helped families appreciate each other, communicate better, reduce isolation and improve overall family relationships; 50% indicated increased understanding, decreased criticism, and positive approach to problem solving

Authors Katschnig et al. (1985)

Disease Mental illness

Research Design Intervention group only

Intervention Description Monthly support groups for families of persons with schizophrenia (Austria)

Subjects 30-50 persons attended monthly meetings.

Measures Mailed survey sent to group members (28% response rate) $N = 79$

Findings Most useful about self-help group: 68% information about disease; 70% interaction/exchange with others; 33% practical help; 63% want more contact with psychiatrists

Authors Potaszynik & Nelson (1984)

Disease Mental illness

Research Design Intervention group only; posttest only

Intervention Description Survey of 3 self-help groups for families of the mentally ill (Canada).

Subjects Parents of a child with mental illness ($N=56$). Mean age—56 years, married, mainly mothers, wide range of education and income; 2-3 person households.

Measures Objective and subjective burden; Family Environment Scale; Social Network List (quality of support from self-help group); open-ended questions; patient symptomatology (Short Clinical Rating Scale)

Findings Satisfaction with total network was positively correlated with supportiveness of self-help group.

Amount of time spent with patient by spouse was positively correlated with self-help group supportiveness.

Less burden was correlated with small network size, density, support of total network, and the self-help group.

Open ended questionnaire—59% expressed positive attitude toward self-help group—information about disease, sharing of support and coping strategies, and common bond among members; 54% negative attitudes about professionals, 66% cited lack of appropriate information.

Authors	Rose et al. (1985)
Disease	Mental illness
Research Design	Intervention group only
Intervention Description	Professionally led support group for relatives of patients in a psychiatric unit of a general hospital; six sessions ninety minutes each.
Subjects	20 families referred to the group, 7 agreed to participate. Participants were middle-class, three parents, three spouses, and one sibling. Mean age 51 years. Professional occupations represented.
Measures	Unstructured interviews with families before start of group and after six weeks. One-way mirror observation of group sessions and audiotaping of sessions.
Findings	Members reported positive changes in their lives—becoming more involved in work, more accepting of patient's limitations, increased ability to express negative emotions, to consider alternative ways of responding to problems and hence improve decision making.

Authors	Thornton et al. (1981)
Disease	Mental illness
Research Design	Intervention group only, with postgroup evaluation
Intervention Description	Time limited support group for families; 12-15 sessions
Subjects	Family members of individuals with schizophrenia; twice as many mothers as fathers
Measures	Postgroup evaluation
Findings	Group members liked most the opportunity to share feelings with others and to discuss their concerns about the future; most discussed topic related to information about mental illness.

TABLE A.2 Educational Interventions

Authors	Glosser & Wexler (1985)
Disease	Alzheimer's disease
Research Design	Intervention group only; postgroup evaluation
Intervention Description	Timed limited group, 8 weekly sessions; goals—provide information on disease, teach patient management skills; social support through group sharing
Subjects	Total participants—54; 50% were primary caregivers; 58% adult children (87% daughters), 27% spouses (50% wives), 15% siblings/in-laws; 50% of patients were recently diagnosed; heterogeneous socioeconomic levels and geographic areas.
Measures	Written evaluation by group participants, 17 items, Likert scale
Findings	84 persons came to at least 4 sessions; 64% (54) completed evaluation questionnaire. Most helpful to members was learning problem solving skills from interaction with group members, meeting and sharing with others in a similar situation. Community resource information was less helpful than group aspects.
Authors	Haley, Brown, & Levine (1987)
Disease	Alzheimer's disease
Research Design	experimental; posttest measures at four months
Intervention Description	3 groups: education group—combination of structured and unstructured sessions; support skills group—participants trained in progressive relaxation and learned cognitive skills for managing stressful situations; control group
Subjects	Study participants recruited through Alzheimer's disease society, advertising, and community referral sources. Caregivers had at least weekly contact with patient (60 years and older). Patients scored 24 and below on Mini-Mental Status measure.
	43 subjects randomly assigned to two treatment conditions (12 dropouts from treatment leaving 17 in the support/skills group and 14 in the support group), 9 were assigned to control waiting list group.
	Patients were moderately to severely impaired, mean age—78 years. Caregivers were primarily spouses and daughters, and were middle-class.
Measures	Outcome measures: Beck Depression Inventory (BDI); Life Satisfaction Index-Z (LISZ); Elderly Caregiver Family Relationship (ECR); Health & Daily Living Form (HDLF); Social network satisfaction
Findings	Treatment group did not show any significant change after participation as compared with waiting list group on outcome measures.

Participants rated the treatment groups very highly—4.57 on a 5 point scale. Almost all participants (89% or more) rated their group as helpful on the following: learning about community resources, learning about dementia, help in learning to manage problems, and a sense of belonging.

Authors	Haley (1989)
Disease	Alzheimer's disease
Research Design	Long term follow-up to above; experimental design study; follow-up assessment 29 months after pretest
Intervention Description	Same as above
Subjects	N=48
Measures	Adjustment to patient's death, nursing home placement, or continued home care.
Findings	70% of patients of group dropouts died during follow-up versus 21% of patients of caregivers who completed groups (initial findings showed that dropouts had patients with greater impairment).

50% of caregivers who had completed group participation had placed their relative in a nursing home. Clinical interviews suggest that group participation may have facilitated nursing home placement.

Group satisfaction ratings for 38 caregivers who completed group was high—4.6 on a 5 point scale.

Caregiver depression, life satisfaction, social activity, social network, and health were stable over time (no comparison group available because all subjects were offered treatment).

Authors	Kahan et al. (1985)
Disease	Alzheimer's disease
Research Design	Experimental; pre- and posttest
Intervention Description	Eight, 2 hour weekly group educational and discussion sessions.

Education—information about Alzheimer's disease, patient management, medical and legal concerns, stress management

Discussion—skill enhancement and building, role playing, stress management training, and discussion of commonly experienced problems in caregiving

Subjects	22 family members recruited through an outpatient gerontology clinic; 18 control subjects were assigned to a waiting list.

25 were primary caregiver, 15 were other family members

Most were wives and daughters, most were 50 years and older. Most lived with patients. No significant demographic difficulties between the two groups.

Measures   Outcomes measures: Family Burden Interview (Zarit); Zung Self-rating Depression Scale; Dementia Quiz (caregiver knowledge); program rating sheet—to assess most helpful components of the intervention

Findings   Experimental group showed a significant reduction in burden as compared to control group.

Experimental subjects also showed a small but significant decrease in depression (this was mood related, not clinical symptoms of depression).

Positive correlation between knowledge and decrease in depression, only moderate correlation between knowledge and burden.

Concerning self-reports of group experience, 90% of the participants rated the group as very helpful.

Participants reported improvement in family relationship and behavioral changes regarding caregiving of the patient.

Experimental group showed significant increase in knowledge about dementia as compared to control group.

Authors   Robinson (1988)

Disease   Alzheimer's disease

Research Design   Experimental; pre- and postgroup evaluation

Intervention Description   Social skills training program—4 sessions. Emphasis on enhancement of assertive behaviors and on social network building skills.

Subjects   Convenience sample of caregivers in ADRDA chapters (*N*=20). Group included some caregivers of institutionalized elderly and some nonfamily caregivers.

11 subjects in treatment group, 9 in control group.

Measures   Caregiver outcome measures: Self-esteem scale (Rosenberg); Assertion Inventory (Gambrill and Richey); Burden (Montgomery); Social Support Questionnaire (NSSQ); consumer satisfaction evaluation

Findings   Differences between the posttest means of the experimental and control group were compared using independent t tests.

Results showed no significant differences between the groups on any of the four outcome variables. However, the scores were in the predicted direction except for discomfort (assertion) and functional social support.

Group most appreciated shared experiences and socialization with others.

Group was split between those who wanted more information and those who preferred opportunity for emotional support.

Authors	Pohl (1980)
Disease	Cancer
Research Design	Intervention group only; postgroup evaluation at 8 weeks.
Intervention Description	Educational sessions for outpatients, inpatients, and their family members—4 days per week, one hour each
	Patients are taught to be active participants in their treatment, family members learn communication skills
Subjects	1,000 participants have attended the sessions
Measures	Evaluation questionnaire
Findings	94% of participants report a significant improvement in family-patient communication.
	93% felt that personal needs related to the disease of cancer were accurately addressed.
	97% stated that they would refer others to the service.

Authors	Lovett & Gallagher (1988)
Disease	Frail elderly
Research Design	Experimental; pre- and posttest
Intervention Description	2 Psychoeducational groups and 1 waiting list control group. Each group had 10 2 hour sessions. First group: members taught self-change skills focused on increasing life satisfaction. Second group: focused on problem solving skills.
Subjects	107 caregivers of frail elderly who used adult day care, day health, or overnight respite programs
	40% of elders suffered from moderate to severe memory impairment
	Caregivers—83% female, 55% taking care of impaired spouse, 41% taking care of parent/in-law. Caregivers' mean age—59 years; 30 months as caregiver.
Measures	Outcome measures—Perceived Stress Scale; Philadelphia Geriatric Center Morale Scale; Beck Depression Inventory; Schedule for Affective Disorders and Schizophrenia (SADS); Index of Unpleasant Events; Reduction of Pleasant Events; social support; self-efficacy
Findings	Preliminary results based on 62 subjects
	Participants in both groups experienced a significant reduction in stress and an increase in morale from pre- to posttest assessment.
	Caregivers who participated in either intervention group showed decreases in depression and increases in morale. The waiting list control group experienced no change on these measures.
	Perceived stress and self-efficacy were not affected by class participation.

Authors	Abramowitz & Coursey (1989)
Disease	Schizophrenia
Research Design	Comparison group; pre- and posttest
Intervention Description	Six weekly two-hour educational sessions for family care-givers; 5 experimental groups, each consisting of 5-17 care-givers. Topics: nature of schizophrenia, medication, behavior management, and community resources
Subjects	Family members were recruited by staff from four community mental health centers

100 subjects were recruited, 63 expressed interest of which 48 were included in the study. Subjects were assigned to treatment or waiting list control based on their availability for the scheduled group meetings. Most experimental group participants were parents, women; mean age—50 years; two-thirds white, 3 person households.

Measures	Outcome measures at six weeks—State-Trait Anxiety Inventory; Relatives' Stress Scale—Personal Distress, Negative Feelings Toward the Patient, and Life Upset; use of community resources; generalized self-efficacy
Findings	No significant differences at pretest between the experimental and control groups.

Examination of posttest scores showed that experimental group had significantly less trait anxiety, less personal distress, less family disruption, and used more services than the control group.

There were no significant differences in negative feelings toward the patient, life upset, or generalized self-efficacy.

Most helpful part of the group—38% general information, 33% opportunity to talk with other group members, 29% community resource information.

Authors	Barrowclough et al. (1987)
Disease	Mental illness
Research Design	Intervention group only; pre- and posttest
Intervention Description	2 group educational sessions, one and two weeks after patient discharge; focus of group was information about schizophrenia
Subjects	24 relatives (related to 17 patients) in English psychiatric hospital; 15 relatives were parents, 6 were spouses, and 3 were other relatives. All lived with the patient at least 3 months prior to admission. Patient was expected to return to the family upon discharge.

20 relatives were high EE

Measures	Outcome measure: Knowledge About Schizophrenia (KASI) focus of instrument—degree of knowledge and effect of knowledge on relative's behavior; Camberwell Family Interview

Findings Authors report significant improvement in relatives' knowledge. Significant change for 5 of 6 areas in responses from
functionally negative or neutral before the intervention to
positive after the intervention (except for information about
medication). Relatives "low on criticism" had significantly
higher pre- and posttest scores, but not so for "low hostility"
or "emotional overinvolvement groups." Relatives of patients
with more recent onset showed lower pretest and higher posttest scores approaching, but not statistically significant.

Authors Cozolino & Nuechterlein (1986)
Disease Mental illness
Research Design Intervention group only; consumer satisfaction survey
Intervention Description 3 session group; educational program for family members
soon after hospital discharge of patient. Topics included:
Overview of schizophrenia, medication, and family stress
management
Subjects 10 family members representing 6 schizophrenic patients.
Patients were generally young and recently diagnosed.
Measures Satisfaction survey
Findings Family members were very positive about the program. Practical information was felt to be most useful. Families felt
good about their relationship with professionals but felt that
information on disease etiology and prognosis was too general or vague.

Authors Berkowitz, Eberlein-Fries, Kuipers, and Leff (1984)
Berkowitz, Kuipers, Eberlein-Fries, and Leff (1981)
Kuipers, Berkowitz, and Leff (1985)
Leff, Kuipers, and Berkowitz (1983)
Leff, Kuipers, Berkowitz, Eberlein-Fries, and Sturgeon (1982)
Leff et al. (1986)
Leff, Kuipers, Berkowitz, and Sturgeon (1985)
Disease Mental illness (schizophrenia)
Research Design Experimental; pretest, posttest; knowledge interview given
pre- and postprogram (education component) and at 9 month
follow-up. Follow-up 9 months after patients discharged
from hospital
77% success rate for follow-up with control families; 2 year
follow-up (5 of 24 patients dropped out of treatment/discon-
tinued medication)
Intervention Description Comprehensive social intervention (9 month duration) involving (a) Education: 2-4 lectures in-home on etiology,
treatment, management; (b) Relatives group: to help alter
coping styles so high EE families can more closely resemble
low EE relatives (bi-weekly meetings); (c) Family sessions:
home-based sessions (with patient and relatives) for maximum of 25 sessions (mean *N*=5.6); (d) Medication

Subjects Patients chosen over a 4 year period: 24 patients who are in face-to-face contact with relatives for more than 35 hours per week (treatment began while patients were hospitalized).

Patients at high risk for relapse: treatment—12 patients (high EE) (6 lived with spouse, 6 lived with parents); 12 relatives (high EE), 9 relatives (low EE)

Control—12 patients (6 lived with spouse, 5 lived with parents, 1 lived with sibling); 10 relatives (high EE), 5 relatives (low EE)

Measures (1) Present State Examination on confirmation of psychotic status (schizophrenia); (2) Camberwell Family Interview; (3) Analysis of taped family sessions for EE, criticism, hostility, warmth, and overinvolvement; (4) Knowledge interview (21 question format to assess effect of education program)

Findings Treatment relatives significantly reduced criticism during 9 month intervention. Control relatives had small, insignificant reduction in criticism.

Treatment relatives showed no significant decrease in overinvolvement; control relatives showed no change.

6 treatment relatives decreased contact time (<35 hours per week), and 3 control relatives did so (due to divorce, social isolation, and outside interests). Five treatment families reduced EE.

Summary: 9 of 12 treatment families showed either reduced EE or face-to-face contact (75% success rate).

9 month follow up: "Provides unequivocal evidence both for the causal influence of high EE relatives on relapse and for the protective effect of lowered social contact between patient and relative."

1 treatment patient relapsed; 6 control patients relapsed (3 of 6 were rehospitalized), 8% or 9% relapse for treatment, 50% relapse for control, 8% relapse rate for high EE families seems to correspond to rate for low EE families.

2-year follow-up: Social intervention and medication had significant benefit for treatment group; if suicide is factored in, treatment failure rate is not significantly different from control group (40% treatment/78% control), 14% relapse rate among families in which face contact was reduced, and/or where EE was reduced (excluding suicide). Compared with 78% relapse among control patients and families in which contact time remained stable.

Relatives seemed to remember little of informational content—they retained most about diagnosis but little about management. They retained their own original perception of the illness etiology.

Authors Schulz et al. (1986)

Disease Mental illness

Research Design Intervention group only; postgroup evaluation

Intervention Description Time limited group for relatives of patients in after-care program; 8 weekly sessions. Purpose of group to provide information and support to families.

Subjects Participants invited to group because they wanted information about schizophrenia or because clinical staff felt them to be at high risk

17 participants (12 mothers, 2 aunts, 1 sister, 2 fathers); 12 completed all sessions.

Measures Written evaluations by group participants

Findings Participants reported increased knowledge about schizophrenia and reduced anxiety. Clinicians noted decreased isolation, reduced guilt and increased awareness of community resources. Clinicians also reported impression that group helped reduce rehospitalizations.

Authors Shapiro et al. (1983)

Disease Mental illness

Research Design Intervention group only; pre- and postgroup evaluation

Intervention Description CMHC sponsored education and support group with 8 weekly sessions. First half of each session was didactic material presented by professionals, second half was discussion.

Subjects Patients asked permission to invite family members to a support group; only 6% of patients agreed; ten family members representing 6 patients attended regularly.

Measures Knowledge about mental illness; attitudes toward mental illness; social network; family functioning

Findings No significant differences in participants' knowledge about mental illness; no significant changes in overall attitudes toward psychiatrist, mental hospital, or mental patient. High satisfaction with group. Eight week postgroup follow-up—5 families had improvement in family functioning, 5 no change. Increase in members networks—5 had joined a self-help group.

Authors Smith & Birchwood (1987)

Disease Mental illness

Research Design Intervention group only; pre- and posttest and six month follow-up

Intervention Description 2 Groups—education group: weekly group meeting for 4 weeks led by therapist; mail group: received educational materials through the mail.

Subjects 23 families randomly chosen from patients known by hospital. Subjects lived with or had close contact (5 or more days per week) with relatives with schizophrenia. Patients had been ill for a mean of 7.9 years; 40 relatives (28 parents, 7 spouses, 5 other)

Measures   Outcomes measures: knowledge; belief in family's roles in treatment; fear; stress; burden

Findings   Knowledge—both groups showed gain, with group intervention gaining more. Gains leveled off after six months.

Belief in family's role in treatment—group intervention families increased, mail group returned to baseline in six months.

Fear—group intervention families decreased during group intervention, returned to baseline in six months. Postal group fear decreased and continued to decrease at six months.

Stress—both groups showed decreased stress at posttest with a return to baseline at six months.

Burden—both groups reported significantly less burden at 6 months follow-up as compared to pretest.

Authors   Evans & Held (1984)

Disease   Stroke

Research Design   Intervention group only; pre- and posttest

Intervention Description   Weekly 1 hour educational meetings for patients and family members conducted by OT staff. Purpose to provide clinical and health care education about stroke and to decrease anxiety.

Subjects   Current inpatients and/or family members.

43 persons anticipated in classes, 35 completed pre- and posttest evaluations.

Measures   Outcome measures—knowledge and anxiety

Findings   Knowledge—participants answered 63% correctly at posttest versus 43% at pretests.

At pretest, 46% expressed worry or fear, 94% at posttest said they felt more informed or less concerned; 89% said they knew more about stroke after the intervention.

TABLE A.3 Clinical Interventions

Authors	Gilleard, Gilleard, & Whittick (1984)
Disease	Dementia (not specifically Alzheimer's disease)
Research Design	Intervention group only. Follow-up interviews at 3-4 and 6-8 month period completed by 87 caregivers "supporters."
Intervention Description	Psychogeriatric day hospital for patients maintained in their homes
Subjects	Patients: 45 males/84 females > 75 years = 88. Referred from community. Caregivers: husband = 19; wife = 30; daughter = 49; sibling = 10; others = 21. Total 129 attendees at 4 psychogeriatric day hospitals in Scotland. Mean ages— husband (72), wife (70), daughter (50), sibling (74), other (60). Dementia $N=96$; functional $N=18$; mixed $N=15$
	31% patients still attending at 6 months; 37 patients institutionalized by 6 months
Measures	(a) Structured interview; (b) Questionnaire; (c) Ratings; (d) Retrospective diary of preceding week; (e) General Health Questionnaire (psychiatric symptoms); (f) Strain Scale—13-item scale for caregiver strain; (g) Social interaction scale—6-item scale for quality of caregiver/patient relationship; (h) Problem checklist scale—28-item scale problem severity index; (i) CAPE Information/Orientation subtest
Findings	Caregivers/supporters indicate day hospital care of most benefit to themselves and found effects increased over time.
	Caregivers/supporters indicate positive but "muted" impact on the patients; did not become more positive over time. Supporter evaluations were higher for current attendees who were eventually institutionalized. Variation within day hospital programming does not affect caregiver/supporter ratings on effect.
	Caregiver age, level of strain, or initial expressed need for help did not indicate caregiver ratings. Caregiver reduction in problems and strain was related to greater impact of day care; those who foresaw problems were less likely to see day hospital as helpful.
	Subjective ratings seem to be valid means of service evaluation.
Authors	Lawton et al. (1989)
Disease	Alzheimer's disease
Research Design	Experimental design; pretest and posttest evaluation (12 months)
Intervention Description	Informal and formal respite care services. Experimental group ($N=315$); control group ($N=317$)

Subjects Eligibility—primary caregivers of mentally impaired older persons. Recruitment through Alzheimer's caregiver support groups, local service agencies and the media (N=632); mean age = 60 years, 70% female, 72% married, 25% black, 34% employed; relationship—45% spouse, 39% children.

Measures Patient: Severity of impairment; days alive

Caregiver: Amount of informal and formal respite

Caregiver well-being: (a) Caregiving attitudes (5 scales)—subjective burden, caregiving uplifts, caregiving impact, caregiving competence, caregiving ideology; (b) Physical health; (c) Depression (CESD); (d) Bradburn Affect Balance Scale

Findings Sample characteristics very similar to two national comparison samples. Experimental group patient had a small but statistically significant longer tenure in the community (22 days)

No significant effects of assignment to experimental versus control group on caregiver well-being. Nor were there any significant effects when comparing only those in the experimental group who actually used respite with the control group. Even when level of need was controlled for, there were no significant differences between the experimental and control groups.

Significant differences between groups on extent of relief from use of respite and satisfaction with respite care.

Authors Lundervold & Lewin (1987)

Disease Alzheimer's disease

Research Design Single subject A-B design; baseline measures administered 2-4 times in-home (approximately 3-4 days apart). During first month treatment, once a week assessment (in-home). Thereafter, once a month (in-home or by mail questionnaire). In-home evaluation 3-6 months after receiving service

Intervention Description Short-term, in-home respite care (4-6 hours of care per week for period of up to 6 months). Respite provided by local senior services agency.

Subjects 4 caregivers of Alzheimer's disease patients (3 in treatment, 1 as control case)

Measures Effects of caregiver level of depression, stress, burden, health status; frequency of problem behaviors by Alzheimer's disease patient and caregiver's reaction to these problems.

(a) Beck Depression Inventory; (b) Memory Problem and Behavior Checklist (functional status of Alzheimer's disease patient); (c) Burden Interview (caregiver strain); (d) Perceived Stress Scale

Findings "Does not result in significant changes in caregiver reports of burden, depression, stress" at this level of respite care (4-6 hours per week).

Some indication of improved caregiver health rating.

No significant improvement in caregiver's social support.

Authors Quayhagen & Quayhagen (1989)

Disease Alzheimer's disease

Research Design Comparison group; pretest & posttest evaluation; families assessed prior to training and at 4 and 8 month intervals

Intervention Description Home-based program of cognitive stimulation—conversation, memory-provoking exercises, and problem-solving techniques. Families asked to work 1 hour per day (6 hours per week) with patients and to keep a log of their activities.

Subjects 24 families recruited through ADRDA and Alzheimer's Disease Research Center, 20 of which were eligible to participate; 16 dyads completed the entire 8 month study, 10 dyads in treatment group and 6 dyads in comparison group. Caregivers in the study were in their mid-60s and were highly educated.

Measures Caregiver outcomes: Well-being Burden Inventory (Zarit); Hopkins Symptom Checklist; Health Assessment Scale

Findings Patients: Significant differences between the groups on cognitive functioning of patients; patients in treatment group maintained functioning levels over time.

Caregivers: Significant difference between groups in mental health status and burden. Treatment group caregivers maintained mental health status (affective symptoms) and burden over time, whereas control group caregivers increased in symptoms and perceived burden. There were no treatment effects on caregiver well being.

Qualitative outcomes for treatment group caregivers included more effective coping methods and resources.

Authors Reifler & Eisdorfer (1980)

Disease Alzheimer's disease/cognitive impairment/dementia

Research Design Intervention group only; posttreatment mail questionnaire to family members regarding consumer satisfaction

Intervention Description Outpatient clinic providing psychiatric, medical, social, nursing, architectural evaluation, and other clinical assistance

3 phases: (1) Evaluation—3-4 assessment interviews in clinic and home (psychiatric diagnostic, family stress and social structure, and medical); (2) Treatment recommendations in areas of housing, nutrition, self-care, physical health, household tasks, emotional and mental health, financial, transportation, daily routine, family stress, and patient interference; (3) Follow-up treatment.

Subjects 68 of 82 consecutively seen patients at clinic had cognitive impairment; 48 of 68 had Alzheimer's disease; 18 of 82 had symptoms of depression. Mean age = 77 years, 56 female, 26 male. Relationships—32 daughters, 27 spouses, 14 sons. Community residing patients at time of evaluation. Mostly referred by family member; 50% of referring relatives lived with patient.

Measures Appointment keeping behavior and family evaluation of clinic's success. Services monitored on 64 patients following the initial 4 visit evaluation sessions. Institutionalization rate: (a) Kahn et al. Scale of Cognitive Impairment; (b) Dementia Rating Scale; (c) Mini-Mental State. Mail questionnaire to family 3 months after evaluation phase (21 of 30 responded = 70%).

Findings Average number of postevaluation clinic visits = 1.3.

Among initial 50 patients, only 1 failed to keep initial appointment (2%). Only 1 family failed to complete evaluation protocol.

90% families would call for further help; 90% families would recommend clinic; 71% families satisfied with overall evaluation and treatment; 38% reported improvement in patient's physical health; 24% reported improvement in patient's mental functioning; 47% families reported increased ability to cope with stress

3 of 15 patients (20%) resided in nursing home at time of mail questionnaire

Authors Winogrond et al. (1987)

Disease Alzheimer's disease

Research Design Intervention group only. Testing at time of entrance into program and 6 months following.

Intervention Description Alzheimer's disease day hospital (affiliated with hospital).

Twice per week program of physical and recreational activities. Caregivers group (participation expected for as long as patient attends day hospital)

Once per week with focus on: (a) information; (b) management techniques; and (c) peer support.

Subjects 18 patients: 11 = female; 7 = male. Median age = 71.5

18 caregivers: 9 = spouses; 5 = children; 3 = siblings; 1 = friend.

Measures Patient measures: (a) Temporal orientation; (b) Personal orientation; (c) Digit span; (d) Token test; (e) Similarities and Comprehension WAIS-R; (f) Zarit modified checklist for behavior function.

Caregiver measures: (a) Corresponding tolerance ratings to Zarit modified checklist for patient's behavior function; (b)

Caregiver burden of care (self-report inventory); (c) Life Satisfaction Index Z - caregiver morale.

Findings   Patients showed significant decline in cognitive functioning, but no significant changes in patient behavioral problems or caregiver tolerance of them.

Caregivers also did not indicate significant changes in perceived burden of care or morale; relatives of patients with highest functioning initially showed increase in burden of care and were least likely to experience improved morale.

Relatives seemed to cope better over time except for those caring for patients with higher cognitive abilities.

Authors   Christensen (1983)

Disease   Cancer (breast)

Research Design   Experimental; posttest evaluation 1 week after treatment; posttreatment self-report

Intervention Description   4-week structured couples treatment to alleviate psychosocial discomfort following mastectomy; orientation session 1 week prior to treatment.

Sessions covered: (1) Information gathering re: couple relationship. (2) Educational information/discussion re: Mildred Witkin's work on psychosocial adjustment to mastectomy. Preliminary exploration of possible behavior changes; problem solving. (3) Expressive exercises re: effects of concern on self-esteem; communication. (4) Integration of new information and adjustments thus far; future oriented with reinforcement of strengths.

Couples seen individually for each weekly session.

Subjects   20 postmastectomy patients and spouses (female mean age = 39.7; male mean age = 39.5).

Referred by various medical personnel (treatment = 10 couples, control = 10 couples)

Measures   (a) General Information; (b) Psychological Screening Inventory—identification of serious psychological disturbances; (c) Locke-Wallace Marital Adjustment Test; (d) Sexual Satisfaction Scale; (e) Beck Depression Inventory; (f) Rosenberg Self-Esteem Scale; (g) Internal-External Locus of Control Scale Revised (feelings of helplessness); (h) Spielberger State Trait Anxiety Inventory. Posttreatment self-report of treatment efficacy.

Findings   No significant difference between treatment and control conditions on any variables.

Supplemental analysis of covariance using pretest data: treatment reduced emotional discomfort in both partners, reduced patient depression, and increased sexual satisfaction for both partners. Couples "appreciated" treatment.

Authors Godkin et al. (1983-1984)

Disease Cancer (late-stage); 29% lung, 15% breast, 11% colon/rectum

Research Design Retrospective evaluation by 100 living spouses of deceased patients

Intervention Description Hospice program with 10-bed inpatient unit and coordinated home care program (university-based)

Subjects Terminally ill (prognosis of less than 6 months) cancer (de-facto) patients primarily referred by medical personnel

Patients: male $N=90$; female $N=93$; mean age = 64.3 years

Caregivers: spouse $N=100$; child $N=45$; sibling $N=13$

Other: relative $N=8$; friend $N=13$; none $N=4$

Median length in program = 30 days; 76% died in hospital; 17% died in home; 4% died in nursing home

Measures Mail questionnaires assessing (a) perceptions of Palliative Care Services (PCS); (b) perceptions of emotional support and impact on family functioning; (c) psychological well-being; (d) family preparedness for death; (e) bereavement problems

Findings 58/100 completed questionnaires (more men tended to be nonrespondents); 91% rated PCS excellent and significantly better than prior care; 70% spouses felt more supported with PCS than prior care; 84% indicated postdeath contact important for emotional support; 72% indicated families grew closer during PCS care; 81% indicated children's ability to cope with loss; 75% spouses felt safe, cared for, supported with PCS; behavior corollaries also positive; 75% indicated PCS prepared them for relative's death to high degree; 51% experienced "large/major" feelings of loss/grief. PCS may have improved health outcomes of survivors.

Authors Goldberg & Wool (1985)

Disease Cancer (newly diagnosed lung)

Research Design Experimental; randomized prospective clinical trial pretest posttest at 8 and 16 week period

Intervention Description Social support counseling for patients and families; 6-month treatment period (12 sessions following intake)

Goals: (1) development of therapeutic relationship; (2) assess problems and increase Significant Known Others's (SKO) competence and autonomy; (3) resolution of SKO's sense of loss and increase in coping mechanism; (4) anticipatory mourning process and evaluation

Subjects 42% of 191 patients participated ($N=53$) (treatment group $N=28$); mean age = 61 years. SKO (treatment group $N=27$); mean age = 47 years—mostly female, spouses, married, high school education, Catholic, varied income levels.

Measures (a) Semi-structured interview; (b) Standardized psychological tests; (c) Karnofsky Performance Status Scale; (d) Psychosocial Adjustment to Illness Scale (PAIS); (e) Profile of
Moods Scale (POMS)

Findings Hypothesis that counseling intervention would result in differential improvement in patients and SKOs not supported
by data in areas of emotional, social, or physical functioning. Outcome measures remained relatively stable over time
regardless of counseling intervention.

Authors Heinrich & Schag (1985)

Disease Cancer: lung = 16%; colo-rectal = 25%; prostate = 13%;
breast = 27%

Research Design Comparison group; pretest, posttest. Follow-up at 2 months
by telephone (4 month evaluation not completed due to pa-
tient attrition)

Intervention Description Treatment group: Stress and Activity Management (SAM);
6-week structured small group.

Patients and spouses focused on: (a) education and information; (b) relaxation exercises; (c) cognitive therapy and problem solving; (d) activity management in addition to current
available care.

Control group: Current Available Care (CAC); Comprehensive medical/psychosocial care, including mental health and
support services.

Subjects Patients: 51 of 92 eligible cancer patients at VA hospital
completed pre- and postevaluation; recruited by medical personnel; mean age = 56 years; male = 68%

Spouses: treatment group $N=12$; control group $N=13$.

No significant demographic differences between control and
treatment groups.

Consecutive patients meeting screening criteria were enrolled in the group.

Condition currently open (treatment or control) until a minimum of 5/maximum of 10 subjects were enrolled (treatment
group was first open, which was determined randomly).

Measures (a) Interviews; (b) Questionnaires; (c) Self-monitoring of behavior; (d) Karnofsky Performance Scale; (e) Cancer Information Test; (f) Psychosocial Adjustment of Illness Scale;
(g) Quality of Life (6-point scale); (h) Daily Activity Diary
(self-report of week's daily activities—physical and recreational); (i) Evaluation of Current Care—level of satisfaction
with medical/health care; (j) Symptom Checklist 90 revised
(Anxiety and Depression Subscales, Summative Global Severity Index)

Findings Patients' treatment increased knowledge over time, but no significant effect on spouse information found over time. Treatment group patients/spouses increased knowledge base and coping more than control group couples. Both groups patients/spouses showed greater adjustment over time.

No significant effect on physical/recreational activities for patients (spouses not evaluated).

Treatment patients more satisfied with help for disease-related problems.

Both spouse groups showed increased satisfaction over time with problem solving and education help; treatment spouses showed more satisfaction than control spouses.

Approximately 75% indicated relaxation, education/information and group helpful; 50% indicated activity management and problem solving helpful.

At two-month evaluation: treatment patients using stress management activities more than control patients; treatment patients more likely to meet activity goals than control patients; support for treatment efficacy and adjustment to cancer during course of illness.

Authors Theorell et al. (1987)
Disease Cancer
Research Design Comparison group; posttest
Intervention Description Total clinical services (excluding surgery): information, support, medical treatment, and psychosocial intervention
Subjects Close female relatives of cancer patients treated at Stockholm hospital/clinic. Of 96 accepting participation—36 = treatment group, mean age = 52 years; 36 = control group, mean age = 51 years. Only relatives whose family members died were evaluated—18 = treatment group, 17 = control group.
Measures (a) Karnofsky index (severity of patient's illness); (b) Psychiatric observation based on procedures of Holland and Sgroi (measuring anxiety, depression, and mental exhaustion; (c) Blood samples to measure cortisol and prolactin levels. Observations and samples were made approximately once per month.
Findings No difference in psychiatric scores between groups during treatment period; prolactin levels tended to be lower in treatment group. Prior to patient's death at terminal phase, treatment relatives had significantly elevated cortisol levels.

One to two months following patient's death, treatment relatives had significantly lower mental exhaustion scores. Grief is activated by treatment and "active mourning may have prophylactic value" to relatives.

Authors Croake & Kelly (1985)

Disease Mental illness (schizophrenia and depression)

Research Design Intervention group only; pretest and 6-week posttest evaluation; measurement before the 4th, 10th, and 14th sessions.

Intervention Description Based on Dreikur's model of family therapy, except all family members seen together; systems based (focus not on Identified Patient). Fourteen family sessions involving: (1) information gathering goal setting for children's behavior; (2) discussion re: children's behaviors; (3-4) discussion re: bedtime routines and discipline; (5-6) discussion re: eating and mealtime routines; (7-8) discussion re: school/homework; (9-10) discussion re: chores and allowances; (11-14) discussion re: family council meetings. Each session involved homework assignments during interval.

Subjects 29 schizophrenic and 31 depressed male veterans and their families seen in VA outpatient treatment over 7-year period (1975-1982). Mean age schizophrenic = 36 (male); mean age spouse = 33.4; mean number of children = 1.9; mean age depressed = 38 (male); mean age spouse = 36.3; mean number of children = 2.4

Measures (a) Rehospitalization incidents during treatment period and follow-up; (b) Attitudes Child Rearing Scale—democratic attitudes of mothers; (c) Child-Rearing Practices Scale—changes in mother's behavior and verified by father's observation; (d-e) Children's Behavior Checklist (observed and those that bothered the mother)

Findings No rehospitalization of any patient during treatment or follow-up period. Overall results indicate both diagnostic groups benefited. "Significant positive" changes noted on test measurements (items b-e)—no significant differences between the two diagnostic groups.

- decrease in authoritarian attitudes in mothers
- increase in democratic child-rearing behavior
- decrease in children's misbehavior
- decrease in degree to which mothers were bothered by misbehavior

"Diagnosis of psychosis is not deterrent to the use of Adlerian family therapy."

Authors Falloon (1985)—research design only, no outcome

Falloon (1986)

Falloon et al. (1984)

Falloon, Boyd, & McGill (1985)—outcome

Falloon, Boyd, McGill, Strang, & Moss (1981)— based on 9-month evaluation only

Falloon et al. (1982)— based on 9-month evaluation only

Falloon, Boyd, McGill, Williamson, et al. (1985)
Falloon, Boyd, Moss, et al. (1985)
Falloon & Liberman (1983)
Falloon & Pedersen (1985)
McGill, Falloon, Boyd, & Wood-Siveria (1983)—
this article reports on patient/family knowledge base,
rather than on clinical data

Disease Mental illness (schizophrenia)

Research Design Experimental measures at baseline, 3 months, 9 months, and
24 months. Monthly ratings of clinical factors. Biweekly
family interviews. Family interaction observed in controlled,
structured assessments at baseline, 3 months, and 24 months.

Intervention Description Behavioral Family Therapy: (a) Education about schizophrenia; (b) Communication skills training; (c) Problem
solving skills training; (d) Behavioral strategies for specific
problems; (e) neuroleptic medication—also crisis intervention, vocational rehabilitation. Two-year long in-home program: once per week for 1-3 months; bi-weekly for 3-9
months; once per month thereafter. Total = 40 sessions

Individual treatment: Patient-oriented, individual treatment
with neuroleptic medication, care management, vocational
rehabilitation, support, crisis intervention but no focus on
enhancing family problem solving.

Same treatment schedule for individual group.

Subjects 36 of 39 patients completed initial 9 months of treatment.
Age range 18-45 years. Patient living with or in close daily
contact with at least one parent.

18 = treatment group; 18 = control group; 24 males, 12
females. At least one family member rated high EE or other
evidence of extreme family tension. Patients considered at
high risk for relapse

54 parents completed 24 month protocol

Family treatment: 17 = mothers, 11 = fathers; Individual
treatment: 17 = mothers, 9 = fathers

Measures (a) PSE/Category GO—diagnosis of schizophrenia; (b)
Camberwell Family Interview (abbreviated); (c) Relapse
rates; (d) Brief Psychiatric Rating Scale; (e) Hopkins' Symptoms Checklist (psychiatric patient self-report questionnaire); (f) Community tenure; (g) Clinical reports, family
interview, self-report questionnaire of social functioning;
(h) Social Adjustment Scale—self-report; (i) Social Behavior Assessment Schedule (family burden); (j) Blood plasma
levels

Two-part questionnaire designed to measure knowledge
about schizophrenia (open-ended questions and multiple
choice)

Findings Both patient groups had a similar amount of psychopathology during first 9 months; however, 13 major episodes for family treatment group, while 29 major episodes for control (individual treatment group)

9 months: 10 family treatment patients in full remission; 3 individual treatment patients in full remission

2 years: 12 family treatment patients in full remission; 4 individual treatment patients in full remission or no paranoid symptoms

Therefore, "increased clinical stability" of psychopathology with family treatment

Increase in functional (work, activity) performance by family treatment patients; greater general social functioning with family treatment; reduced sense of burden in families in family treatment; fewer incidents of hospitalization and fewer hospital days for family treatment patients; increased knowledge in patients and family members at 3 and 9 month evaluations.

Authors Falloon et al. (1984)
Falloon & Liberman (1983)
Falloon, Liberman, Lillie, & Vaughn (1981)

Disease Mental illness (schizophrenia)

Research Design Intervention group only; pretest and posttest follow-up at 3 months and at 9 months

Intervention Description 1975 (London): Comprehensive behavioral approach for patient and family focusing on social skills training, family therapy, communication skills training.

15 week program with daily and weekly sessions.

15 week intervention—10 sessions of educational focus, 15 sessions on family communication and problem solving

Subjects 3 male schizophrenics living with high EE family members (patients transferred to hospital setting)

Measures (a) Camberwell Family Interview; (b) Present State Examination; (c) Personal Adjustment Role Scale (indicator of patient's social functioning); (d) STAI questionnaire—self-reported anxiety status; (e) Physiological measures (skin and heart rate); (f) Reports of progress in social skills training

Findings Reduction in parental EE rating but effects were short-term (2 of 3 parents).

Three patients showed improvement in communication skills at 10 weeks.

Improved social functioning and "consistent pattern change" in anxiety scores.

Authors	Falloon et al. (1984)
	Liberman, Falloon, & Aitchison (1984)
	Falloon & Liberman (1983)
	Snyder & Liberman (1981)
Disease	Mental illness (schizophrenia)
Research Design	Experimental: Two matched contrast groups randomly assigned
	(a) insight-oriented family therapy and holistic health therapy (*N*=14 patients, 11 relatives); (b)behavior family therapy and social skills training (*N*=14 patients, 28 relatives); (c) standard state hospital treatment (*N*=36 patients, 11 relatives) pretest and posttest evaluation
Intervention Description	14 Subject Study (no date): 9 week/9 session comprehensive behavioral approach emphasizing problem-solving, along with communication skills training and social skills training, education in format of multiple family therapy (3-4 families) including patients
Subjects	14 males living with high EE relatives, white, age range 21-35 years; average attendance for relatives—85%
Measures	(a) Schizophrenia Knowledge Index; (b) Camberwell Family Interview; (c) Present State Examination; (d) Family Conflict Inventory; (e) Present State Examination; (f) Psychiatric Assessment Scale; (g) Relapse Ratings; (h) Consumer Satisfaction Scale; (i) Brief psychiatric rating scale
Findings	Critical statements by parents (*N*=11) reduced 60%—reduced EE

8 of 11 parents change to low EE (73%); at 9-month follow-up, 3 of 14 patients relapsed (21%) compared with 56% relapse in control group; increased knowledge by patients and relatives in treatment group; significant reduction in conflict in treatment group; high consumer satisfaction.

Not able to identify specific effects of family therapy since treatment combined behavioral, individual, and family treatment.

60% decrease in critical comments in lower EE treatment group; 16% decrease in critical comments among control group.

Significant increase in knowledge base among treatment relatives.

21% relapse rate among treatment patients at 9-month follow-up; 56% relapse among control patients.

Authors Geiser et al. (1988)
Disease Mental illness
Research Design Intervention group only; pretest and posttest evaluation
Intervention Description Inpatient psychiatric respite program—two to seven day inpatient hospitalization at six to eight week intervals
Subjects Eligibility—patient must live with a family member and have a history of multiple hospitalizations. Arrangements are made for respite before the patient is discharged from the hospital; first respite is 6-8 weeks postdischarge. N=14, patient mean age—39 years, majority nonwhite
Measures Patient outcome—days of hospitalization
Findings Number of hospital days for the patients dropped from 1,240 days before participation to 615 days after program participation. There was a statistically significant decrease in the mean number of days of hospitalization from 89 to 44.

Families evaluated the program positively, but no objective data collected on effect of the program on coping or burden.

Authors Kopeikin et al. (1983)
Goldstein & Kopeikin (1981)
Goldstein (1987)—6 month results only
Goldstein, Rodnick, Evans, May, & Steinberg (1978)—
   6 month results only
Disease Mental illness (schizophrenia)
Research Design Experimental pretest; posttest follow-up at 6 months; long-term follow-up 3-6 years after treatment (58% of original aftercare group)
Intervention Description 6 week/6 session outpatient psychological and pharmalogical treatment in support of crisis-oriented family therapy focusing on: (a) identifying current stressors; (b) developing strategies to prevent stress and cope with it; (c) implementation and evaluation of strategies; (d) planning for future stresses. Two levels of medication: (a) moderate; (b) low. Four treatment groups: (a) moderate medication and family treatment; (b) low medication and family treatment; (c) moderate medication and no family treatment; (d) low medication and no family treatment
Subjects Consecutive inpatient admissions to CMHC. Patients = 103 (69% first admissions). Mean age = 23.26 years. 96/103 patients completed treatment (92%); 79% white, 75% high school education or below, 62% single.
Measures (a) New Haven Schizophrenia Index; (b) UCLA Social Adjustment Scale (estimate of premorbid adjustment); (c) Brief Psychiatric Rating Scale (psychopathology); (d) Global Assessment Scale (psychosocial functioning); (e) Relapses (regressions) requiring emergency intervention; (f) Systematic behavioral ratings; (g) Audiotape recordings of family

therapy sessions (for 21 of 52 cases); (h) Review of service utilization

Findings No patient in family therapy and moderate medication experienced relapse during 6 month follow-up; 48% of low medication and no family therapy relapsed during 6 month follow-up.

Complementary effects of family therapy with moderate medication.

Medication especially helpful for patients with poor premorbidity adjustment. Family therapy helpful to females with good premorbid adjustments.

Significantly less symptoms after family therapy; with moderate medication, patients were significantly less withdrawn. All 4 treatment groups showed less symptoms.

Long-term follow-up (3-6 years): Poor premorbid patients more likely to need long-term services (68%). Family therapy and moderate medication patients used less psychotherapy. Communication patterns seemed to be determinate of treatment outcome (positive communication—achievement; negative communication—detrimental to achievement). But, family behavior seemed not to be a predictor of treatment outcome. Strongest treatment effect during and immediately after treatment and remained significant at 6 months. Modest effects 3-6 years after treatment.

Authors Kottgen, Sonnichsen, Mollenhauer, & Jurth (1984)
Disease Mental illness (schizophrenia)
Research Design Comparison group
Intervention Description Group therapy (with separate patient groups and relative groups); 4 relatives' treatment groups; 4 patient treatment groups. Long-term groups (2 year duration); 2 patterns of treatment group: (a) patient group once per week, relative group once per month; (b) patient group once per month, relative group once per week.

Goals: (a) information; (b) reduce social isolation; (c) mainstream/normalization

Strengths-based/Positive life experience focused
Subjects 16 families (15 of whom were high EE)

Treatment: 15 patients (high EE); 1 patient (low EE)—male = 13, female = 3, relatives = 26, mothers = 14, fathers = 10, siblings = 2

Control: 14 patients (high EE); 20 patients (low EE); patient age range 18-30 years.

Measures (a) Rates of relapse 9 months after discharge; (b) Camberwell Family Interview (CFI) (18 months after discharge)

Findings 26 treatment relatives: 10 attended regularly (75% sessions); 10 attended less regularly; 5 attended occasionally (less than 40% sessions); 1 deceased

16 treatment patients: 5 attended regularly (75% sessions); 4 attended less regularly; 6 attended occasionally (less than 40% sessions); 1 refused

Tentative results (initial sessions): No significant differences among 3 patient types (high EE treatment, high EE control, low EE control) though slight tendency toward fewer relapses among treatment groups.

At follow-up, 5 of 11 treatment families were no longer high EE.

One treatment group of relatives completing 2-year program has turned into self-help group.

Authors MacCarthy et al. (1989)

Disease Mental illness

Research Design Comparison group; pretest and posttest

Intervention Description Three home visits focusing on knowledge of mental illness and treatment of patient's disorder followed by a monthly psychoeducational group led by a professional team—1½ hours per week for 52 weeks.

Group focused on issues related to expressed emotion, with a goal of reducing the number of critical comments and extent of overinvolvement.

Subjects Patients attending a psychiatric day care program at least 2½ days a week and who lived or spent at least one day a week with a relative were identified. Out of 78 high attenders, 33 patients met the study guidelines. Relatives of 13 patients of one staff team were invited to join the experimental group; 13 relatives of 9 patients agreed to participate (11 parents, 1 spouse, 1 sibling) and the relatives of 4 patients refused.

The control group consisted of 17 relatives of the remaining 20 patients.

Patients had a mean age of 36.1 years. Majority of caregivers were parents of the patients.

Measures Caregiver outcomes: (a) knowledge of mental illness; (b) expressed emotion; (c) strain; (d) coping styles

Findings The experimental group showed a decrease in high EE as compared to the control group; this difference was approaching, but was not, statistically significant. There was a statistically significant difference in change in critical comments, with a decrease in the experimental group and an increase in the control group.

There were no significant differences between the groups in warmth or overinvolvement; there were no significant differences in strain. The experimental group showed more changes in coping style than the control group. The intervention had little effect on changes in knowledge scores.

Subjects were generally positive in appraisal of the group's value to them.

Authors Mills et al. (1986)

Disease Mental illness (schizophrenia)

Research Design Intervention group only; pretest (first session), posttest (last session); 3-month posttreatment family interview

Intervention Description Family group-oriented psychoeducational program with focus on (a) structured communication; (b) conflict-resolution training. Ten sessions on weekly basis. Multi-family groups meeting for 2 hours/session. Opportunity for practice of skills learned during input portion of sessions (in various groupings).

Subjects 5 consenting families of young adults in residential facility selected (4 completed protocol). Patients: 3 male, 2 female (1 completed). Age range 25-31 years; 10 parents, 1 family of 5 ultimately withdrew from treatment.

Measures (a) Family Environment Scale "personality of person's environment" (relationship and family system; conflict and cohesion; development of growth and goals); (b) follow-up structured interview (Likert-type and open-ended) measuring (i) program effect on family communication; (information) use of communication skills presently; (ii) experiences of conflict resolution, cohesion, or organization ("subjectivity of the interview")

Findings (Based on 4 families completing protocol.) Organization scores "clearly up"; family cohesion scores "slightly up"; conflict scores "slightly down." General ratings of program helpfulness; improved communication patterns allowing for conflict resolution and greater sense of closeness.

Authors Pinkston & Linsk (1984)

Disease Mentally and physically impaired elderly

Research Design Intervention group only; pretest and posttest evaluation

Intervention Description Behavioral intervention designed to increase positive behaviors of both elderly and their caregivers and to decrease behaviors found negative by the elderly and/or caregivers.

Subjects Eligibility criteria: elderly persons (at least 60 years) with physical or mental impairment, used few services, had available family caregiver willing to participate in intervention. Referrals through hospital social work and medical staff.

51 elderly persons were referred, of which 24 were involved in program. Majority (58%) of caregivers were spouses; age range of caregivers—61-70 years.

Measures Patients: Time-sampling and behavior checklists; mental status; independent abilities; Shanas Self-Care; home activities engaged in

Caregiver: illness interference; family contact; contact with best friend; desired social activities.

Findings Contracting, cuing, or reinforcement was used in 94% of the cases, and these procedures were associated with improvement in 73% of all behaviors.

There was close to a statistically significant improvement in patient's mental status scores pre- and posttest ($p < .06$). No statistically significant improvements in independent abilities or in self-care.

Caregivers reported a statistically significant increase in home activities engaged in. There were no significant changes in family contact, contact with best friend, and desired social activities.

A longer-term follow-up, median of 8.3 months postintervention, showed that 78% of previously targeted behaviors were maintained at or above postintervention levels with only two clients moving to long-term care facilities. Clients and families rated the intervention highly in subjective evaluations of the program.

Authors Pinkston, Linsk, & Young (1988)

Disease Mentally and physically impaired elderly

Research Design Intervention group only; pretest and posttest evaluation

Intervention Description Behavioral intervention designed to increase positive behaviors of both elderly and their caregivers and to decrease behaviors found negative by the elderly and/or caregivers

Subjects Eligibility criteria: elderly person (at least 60 years) with physical or mental impairment, used few services, had available family caregiver willing to participate in intervention.

Referrals through hospital social work and medical staff.

$N=66$, mean age = 64 years; 75% female, 46% spouses; 28% adult children

Measures Patients: Time-sampling and behavior checklists; Mental Status Questionnaire; OARS

Caregivers: Family Burden Scale (Zarit); self-reported physical and mental health; kinds of help provided

Findings Patient Outcomes: Improvement observed in 76% of the targeted behaviors.

Caregiver Outcomes: No significant changes from pre- to posttest in caregiver burden, self-reported physical health, or self-reported mental health. Significant changes pre- to posttest included (1) satisfaction with current ability to learn to change their relative's behavior; (2) less embarrassed by relative's behavior; (3) average interference with family members and friends; and (4) less strain interacting with patient. Caregivers perceived their relative as more dependent after the intervention.

Authors   Davies (1981)

Disease   Stroke

Research Design   Single-subject (married couple and adult children); pre-experimental; posttreatment evaluation by staff

Intervention Description   Framework of life review therapy, modeling, and prompting techniques directed toward involving wife and adult children; treatment involved at least 6 visits during a 5-week period

Subjects   65-year-old institutionalized stroke patient and his wife with 2 adult daughters (patient also severely depressed)

Measures   (a) Beck Depression Inventory (wife and husband); (b) Reinforcement Survey schedule; (c) Family's self-report of husband's previous interests and interactions during visiting times; (d) Direct observation of behavior during visiting times and by audiotaping visiting sessions (content analyzed; (e) Visit satisfaction rating 3 times during each visiting session; completed by wife

Findings   By content analysis, patient's utterances overall and positive utterances increased with prompting. Family self-report of patient's improvement and decrease in wife's strain. Patient depression score dropped, indicating increase in positive outlook (no change score reported for spouse). Staff generally noted patient improvement. Family satisfaction with visits increased.

TABLE A.4 Multiple Intervention Comparisons

Authors	Zarit et al. (1987)
Disease	Dementia
Research Design	Experimental design; pretest and posttest evaluation (after end of intervention and 1 year follow-up)
Intervention Description	2 eight session stress-management treatment groups co-led by two therapists. One group was a support group, the other an individual and family counseling group. Subjects were randomly assigned to one of the two treatment groups or to the waiting list control group. Focus of both groups—increasing understanding of patient's disease, improving the management of problem behaviors, and helping to identify and enhance use of informal and formal supports
Subjects	184 primary caregivers recruited for study, 40 (22%) refused to participate after initial assessment, 25 (14%) dropped out before the end of treatment. Subjects completing treatment: age 62 years (mean); education: 14.4 years; 87% white; 52% spouse, 41% child
Measures	Caregiver outcomes: Burden Interview—BI (Zarit); Brief Symptom Inventory—BSI; Management of Problem Behavior—Memory and Behavior Problems Checklist (MBP); social support; assistance with caregiving tasks; caregiver's perception of the intervention
Findings	No treatment or treatment by time effects for the BI or BSI.
	No treatment effects for changes in management of problem behavior, or social support.
	Experimental group participants rated the intervention positively. Subjects rated problem solving and information components higher than general therapeutic approaches. One year follow-up results showed that subjects remained below their initial baselines on the BI and BSI although there was no long-term control group that could be used for comparison purposes.
Authors	Ingersoll-Dayton et al. (1990)
Disease	Employed caregivers of dependent family members (elder, disabled adult, child)
Research Design	Intervention group only; pretest and posttest evaluation (pretest, 7 week posttest, 15 week posttest)
Intervention Description	7 week educational seminar series on caregiving, followed by choice of participation in three 8 week programs: care planning, support group, or buddy system
Subjects	256 persons attended the seminar series, of which over one third were "anticipatory caregivers." Mean age—45 years; 85% female; 18 in care planning group; 32 in support group; no subjects chose the buddy system condition.

Measures Helpfulness of seminar series; impact on working knowledge of aging services; satisfaction with social support; caregiving worries, stress, and strain; affect (from Bradburn Affect Balance Scale)

Findings Subjects rated seminar series very positively. Knowledge of services for the aging increased; days absent from work increased.

Subjects in care planning and support groups showed a significant decrease in negative affect with no significant differences in caregiver strain.

Authors Montgomery & Borgatta (1989)

Disease Impaired elderly

Research Design Experimental design; pretest and posttest evaluation (before treatment, after 12 months, after 20 months)

Intervention Description 5 treatment groups: Group 1—seminars, support group, consultation, respite; Group 2—seminars, support group, consultation; Group 3—seminars, support group; Group 4—consultation; Group 5—respite; Group 6—control

Subjects 541 family units; self-referred through agencies or media; caregiver had to live within one hour of elder.

Elder: Median age—82 years, 67% female, majority were high school graduates and above.

Caregiver: 79% female, 59% adult children, 31% spouses, 40% employed full-time

Measures Elder: Health and functional level, living arrangement.

Caregiver: Types and extent of tasks performed. Objective and subjective burden; health

Findings Almost 1/3 of caregivers eligible for services did not use them.

Statistically significant reduction in subjective burden between Time 1 and Time 2 for all groups except the control group.

Objective burden is related to the level of impairment of the elderly person regardless of group assignment.

There was no effect of treatment upon length of time that families continued caring for their elderly relatives.

Among spouse caregivers, there were statistically significant differences in the number of months elderly persons spent in the nursing home between four of the treatment groups (not Group 4) and the control group. In each of these 4 treatment groups, persons spent more months in the nursing home than did those in the control group. The data suggest that project support services encouraged spouses to place elderly persons in nursing homes.

Authors	Anderson (1986)
Disease	Mental illness (schizophrenia)
Research Design	Experimental; periodic measures of individual and family functioning
Intervention Description	Psychoeducational program with random assignment to 1 of 4 groups: (a) family therapy; (b) social skills training; (c) family therapy and social skills training; (d) medication only
	2 year treatment program, 4 phases: (1) Connecting with family—relationship building in hospital with establishment of treatment contract; (2) 1 day educational program for 4-5 families (illness and management)—survival skills focus; (3) Family therapy (including patient) every 2-3 weeks; (4) Option for further long-term family treatment or periodic supportive intervention
Subjects	102 patients and family members with high EE; treatment group: $N=88$
Measures	Relapse (not defined)
Findings	(Based on 1 year participation)
	Family therapy alone—19% experienced psychotic relapse
	Social skills training alone—21% experienced psychotic relapse
	Family therapy and social skills training—0 experienced relapse
	Medication—36% experienced psychotic relapse
	(Based on almost 2 year participation)
	Generally, relapse rates increase in all groups
	Family therapy alone—25% relapse
	Social skills training alone—35% relapse
	Social skills training and family therapy—22% relapse
	Medication—57% relapse

TABLE A.5 Clinical Observation Outcome Studies

Support Group Interventions

Aronson, M. K., Levin, G., & Lipkowitz, R. (1984). A community-based family/patient group program for Alzheimer's disease. *The Gerontologist, 24*(4), 339-342.

Berger, J. M. (1984). Crisis intervention: A drop-in support group for cancer patients and their families. *Social Work in Health Care, 10*(2), 81-92.

Dincin, J., Selleck, V., & Streicker, S. (1978). Restructuring parental attitudes—Working with parents of the adult mentally ill.

Drescher, R. (1986). Mutual support groups for families of the mentally ill. In M. Z. Goldstein (Ed.), *Family involvement in the treatment of schizophrenia* (pp. 36-52). Washington, DC: American Psychiatric Press.

Schizophrenia Bulletin, 4(4), 597-608.

Hatfield, A. B. (1979). The family as partner in the treatment of mental illness. *Hospital & Community Psychiatry, 30*(5), 338-340.

Hatfield, A. B. (1979). Help-seeking behavior in families of schizophrenics. *American Journal of Community Psychology, 7*(5), 563-569.

Hatfield, A. B. (1981). Self-help groups for families of the mentally ill. *Social Work,* 408-413.

Jerse, M. A., Whitman, H. H., & Gustafson, J. P. (1984). Cancer in adults. In H. B. Roback (Ed.), *Helping patients and their families cope with medical problems* (pp. 251-284). San Francisco: Jossey-Bass.

Levy, L. (1981). The National Schizophrenia Fellowship: A British self-help group. *Psychiatry, 16*, 129-135.

Mishel, M. H., & Murdaugh, C. L. (1987). Family adjustment to heart transplantation: Redesigning the dream. *Nursing Research, 36*(6), 332-338.

Parsonnet, L., & Weinstein, L. (1987). A volunteer program for helping families in a critical care unit. *Health & Social Work, 12*(1), 21-27.

Vachon, M. L. S., Lyall, W. A., Rogers, J., Formo, A., Freedman, K., Cochrane, J., & Freeman, S. J. J. (1979). The use of group meetings with cancer patients and their families. In J. Tache & S. Day (Eds.), *Cancer, stress and death* (pp. 129-139). New York: Plenum Medical Book.

Videka, L. M. (1979). Psychosocial adaptation in a medical self-help group. In M. H. Lieberman & L. D. Borman & Associates (Eds.), *Self-help groups for coping with crisis* (pp. 362-386). San Francisco: Jossey-Bass.

Wiancko, D. C., Crinklaw, L. D., & Mora, C. D. Nurses can learn from wives of impaired spouses. *Journal of Gerontological Nursing, 12*(11), 28-33.

Williams, P., Williams, W. A., Sommer, R., & Sommer, B. (1986). A survey of the California alliance for the mentally ill. *Hospital & Community Psychiatry, 37*(3), 253-256.

Zarit, S. H., & Anthony, C. R. (1986). Interventions with dementia patients and their families. In M. L. M. Gilhooly, S. H. Zarit, & J. E. Birren (Eds.), *The dementias: Policy and management* (pp. 66-92). Englewood Cliffs, NJ: Prentice-Hall.

Educational Group Interventions

Anderson, C. M. (1983). A psychoeducational program for families of patients with schizophrenia. In W. R. McFarlane (Ed.), *Family therapy in schizophrenia* (pp. 99-116). New York: Guilford Press.

Anderson, C. M., Hogarty, G. E., & Reiss, D. J. (1980). Family treatment of adult schizophrenic patients: A psycho-educational approach. *Schizophrenia Bulletin, 6*(3), 490-505.

Anderson, C. M., Hogarty, G., & Reiss, D. J. (1981). The psychoeducational family treatment of schizophrenia. In M. J. Goldstein (Ed.), *New directions for mental health services: New developments in interventions with families of schizophrenics* (No. 12, pp. 79-94). San Francisco: Jossey-Bass.

Brown, D. G., Glazer, H., & Higgins, M. (1983). Group intervention: A psychosocial and educational approach to open heart surgery patients and their families. *Social Work in Health Care, 9*(2), 47-59.

Kyle, S., & Taylor, P. (1983). Developing a group for friends and families of schizophrenics: A hospital model. *Canada's Mental Health,* 14-25.

McLean, C. S., Greer, K., Scott, J., & Beck, J. C. (1982). Group treatment for parents of the adult mentally ill. *Hospital & Community Psychiatry, 33*(7), 565-568.

Steuer, J. L., & Clark, E. O. (1982). Family support groups within a research project on dementia. *Clinical Gerontologist, 1*(1), 87-95.

Clinical/Direct Service Interventions

Baker, S. R. (1984). Amelioration of phantom-organ pain with hypnosis and behavior modification: Brief case report. *Psychological Report, 55,* 847-850.

Boyd, J. L., McGill, C. W., & Falloon, I. R. H. (1981). Family participation in the community rehabilitation of schizophrenics. *Hospital & Community Psychiatry, 32*(9), 629-632.

Cohen, M. M. (1982). In the presence of your absence: The treatment of older families with a cancer patient. *Psychotherapy: Theory, Research and Practice, 19*(4), 453-460.

Cohen, M. M., & Wellisch, D. K. (1978). Living in limbo: Psychosocial intervention in families with a cancer patient. *American Journal of Psychotherapy, 32*(4), 561-571.

Creek, L. V. (1982). A homecare hospice profile: Description, evaluation, and cost analysis. *The Journal of Family Practice, 14*(1), 53-58.

Davenport, Y. B. (1981). Treatment of the married bipolar patient in conjoint couples psychotherapy groups. In M. R. Lansky (Ed.), *Family therapy and major psychopathology.* New York: Grune & Stratton.

Euster, S. (1984). Adjusting to an adult family member's cancer. In H. B. Robsek (Ed.), *Helping patients and their families cope with medical problems* (pp. 428-452). San Francisco: Jossey-Bass.

Falloon, I. R. H. (1981). Communication and problem-solving skills training with relapsing schizophrenics and their families. In M. R. Lansky (Ed.), *Family therapy and major psychopathology* (pp. 35-56). New York: Grune & Stratton.

Green, G. R., Linsk, N. L., & Pinkston, E. M. (1986). Modification of verbal behavior of the mentally impaired elderly by their spouses. *Journal of Applied Behavior Analysis, 19*(4), 329-336.

Harris, L. L., Vogtsberger, K. N., & Mattox, D. E. (1985). Group psychotherapy for head and neck cancer patients. *Laryngoscope, 95*, 585-587.

Krant, M. J., Beiser, M., Adler, G., & Johnston, L. (1976). The role of a hospital-based psychosocial unit in terminal cancer illness and bereavement. *Journal of Chronic Disability, 29*, 115-127.

Krant, M. J., Doster, N. J., & Ploof, S. (1980). Isolation in the aged: Individual dynamics, community and family involvement. Meeting the needs of the late-stage elderly cancer patient and family: A clinical model. *Journal of Geriatric Psychiatry, 13*, 53-61.

Lurie, A., & Ron, H. (1971). Multiple family group counseling of discharged schizophrenic young adults and their parents. *Social Psychiatry, 6* (2), 88-92.

Nathan, P. K. (1986). Helping wives of Alzheimer's patients through group therapy. *Social Work with Groups, 9*(2), 73-81.

Rainey, L. C. (1985). Cancer counseling by telephone help-line: The UCLA psychosocial cancer counseling line. *Public Health Report, 100*(3), 308-315.

Sands, D., & Suzuki, T. (1983). Adult day care for Alzheimer's patients and their families. *The Gerontologist, 23*(1), 21-23.

Schmidt, G. L., & Keyes, B. (1985). Group psychotherapy with family caregivers of demented patients. *The Gerontologist, 25*(4), 347-350.

Stam, H. J., Bultz, B. D., & Pittman, C. A. (1986). Psychosocial problems and interventions in a referred sample of cancer patients. *Psychosomatic Medicine, 48*(8), 539-548.

Watzlawick, P., & Coyne, J. C. (1980). Depression following stroke: Brief, problem-focused family treatment. *Family Process, 19*, 13-18.

Wellisch, D. K., Mosher, M. B., & Van Scoy, C. (1978). Management of family emotion stress: Family group therapy in a private oncology practice. *International Journal of Group Psychotherapy, 28*, 225-231.

TABLE A.6 Litertaure Reviews

Beels, C. C., & McFarlane, W. R. (1982). Family treatments of schizophrenia: Background and state of the art. *Hospital & Community Psychiatry, 33*(7), 541-550.

Bernheim, K. F., & Lehman, A. F. (1985). Psychoeducation and the family. *Working with families of the mentally ill*. New York: Norton.

Falloon, I. R. H. (1985). Family interventions in schizophrenia: Controlled research. In I. R. H. Falloon (Ed.), *Family management of schizophrenia: A study of clinical, social, family, and economic benefits*. Baltimore, MD: Johns Hopkins University Press.

Falloon, I. R. H., Boyd, J. L., & McGill, G. W. (1984). *Family care of schizophrenia: A problem-solving approach to the treatment of mental illness*. New York: Guilford Press.

Falloon, I. R. H., Pederson, J., & Al-Khayyal, M. (1986). Enhancement of health-giving family support versus treatment of family pathology. *Journal of Family Therapy, 8*, 339-350.

Goldstein, M. J., & Strachan, A. M. (1986). Impact of family intervention programs on family communication and the short-term course of schizophrenia. In M. J. Goldstein, I. Hand, & K. Hahlweg (Eds.), *Treatment of schizophrenia: Family assessment and intervention* (pp. 185-192). Berlin: Springer-Verlag.

Leff, J. P. (1980). Developments in family treatment of schizophrenia. *Advances in Family Psychiatry, 2*, 313-323.

Marder, S. R. (1981). Combining family therapy and pharmacotherapy: Literature review and methodologic issues. In M. R. Lansky (Ed.), *Family therapy and major psychopathology* (pp. 359-373). New York: Grune & Stratton.

McFarlane, W. R. (1983). *Family therapy in schizophrenia*. New York: Guilford Press.

Mosher, L. R., & Gunderson, J. G. (1979). Group, family, milieu, and community support systems treatment for schizophrenia. In L. Bellak (Ed.), *Disorders of the schizophrenic syndrome* (pp. 399-452). New York: Basic Books.

Mosher, L. R., & Keith, S. J. (1979). Research on the psychosocial treatment of schizophrenia: A summary report. *The American Journal of Psychiatry, 136*(5), 623-631.

Mosher, L. R., & Keith, S. J. (1980). Psychosocial treatment: Individual, group, family, and community support approaches. *Schizophrenia Bulletin, 6*(1), 10-41.

Northouse, L. (1984). The impact of cancer on the family: An overview. *International Journal of Psychiatry in Medicine, 14*(3), 215-243.

Strachan, A. M. (1986). Family intervention for the rehabilitation of schizophrenia: Toward protection and coping. *Schizophrenia Bulletin, 12*(4), 678-698.

Toseland, R. W., & Rossiter, C. M. (1989). Group interventions to support family caregivers: A review and analysis. *The Gerontologist, 29*(4), 438-448.

Vachon, M. L. S. (1986). Models of group intervention for cancer patients and families. In B. Stacey & M. D. Day (Eds.), *Cancer, stress, and death* (2nd ed.) New York: Plenum Medical Book Co.

Wynne, L. C. (1974). Family and group treatment of schizophrenia: An interim view. In R. Canero, N. Fox, & L. E. Shapiro (Eds.), *Strategic intervention in schizophrenia: Current developments in treatment* (pp.79-97). New York: Behavioral Publications.

References

AARP. (1989). *Working caregivers report, March 1989*. Washington, DC: American Association of Retired Persons.

AARP & The Travelers Companies Foundation. (1988). *National survey of caregivers: Summary of findings*. Washington, DC: American Association of Retired Persons.

Abramowitz, I. A., & Coursey, R. D. (1989). Impact of an educational support group on family participants who take care of their schizophrenic relatives. *Journal of Consulting and Clinical Psychology, 57*(2), 232-236.

Abrams, R. (1974). *Not alone with cancer*. Springfield, IL: Charles C Thomas.

Ahlsio, B., Britton, M., Murray, V., & Theorell, T. (1984). Disablement and quality of life after stroke. *Stroke, 15*, 886-890.

Akessen, H. O. (1969). A population study of senile and arteriosclerotic psychoses. *Human Heredity, 19*, 546-566.

American Cancer Society. (1987). *Cancer facts and figures*. New York: Author.

American Heart Association National Center. (1983). Sex and heart disease. Dallas: Author.

American Heart Association. (1988). *1988 heart facts*. Dallas: American Heart Association National Center.

American Psychiatric Association. (1980). *Diagnostic and statistical mannual* (3rd ed.). Washington, DC: Author.

American Psychiatric Association. (1987). *Diagnostic and statistical manual of mental disorders* (3rd ed., rev.). Washington, DC: Author.

Anderson, C. M. (1986). Psychoeducational family therapy. In I. Hand & M. J. Goldstein (Eds.), *Treatment of schizophrenia: Family assessment and intervention* (pp. 146-151). Berlin: Springer-Verlag.

Anderson, C. M., Hogarty, A., & Reiss, D. J. (1980). Family treatment of adult schizophrenic patients: A psycho-educational approach. *Schizophrenia Bulletin, 6*, 490-505.

Anderson, C. M., Hogarty, A., & Reiss, D. J. (1981). The psychoeducational family treatment of schizophrenia. In M. J. Goldstein (Ed.), *New developments in interventions with families of schizophrenics*. San Francisco: Jossey-Bass.

Anderson, C. M., Reiss, D. J., & Hogarty, G. E. (1986). *Schizophrenia and the family: A practitioner's guide to psychoeducation and management*. New York: Guilford Press.

Anderson, E., Anderson, T. P., & Kottke, F. J. (1977). Stroke rehabilitation: Maintenance of achieved gains. *Archives of Physical Medicine and Rehabilitation, 58*, 345-352.

Anderson, T. P., & Kottke, F. J. (1978). Stroke rehabilitation: A reconsideration of some common attitudes. *Archives of Physical Medicine and Rehabilitation, 59*, 175-181.

Anthony-Bergstone, C. R., Zarit, S. H., & Gatz, M. (1988). Symptoms of psychological distress among caregivers of dementia patients. *Psychology and Aging, 3*, 245-248.

Artes, R., & Hoops, R. (1976). Problems of aphasic and non-aphasic stroke patients as identified and evaluated by patients' wives. In Y. Lebrun & R. Hoops (Eds.), *Recovery in aphasics*. Amsterdam: Swets and Zeitlinger B.V.

Arnett, R. H., McKusick, D. R., Sonnefeld, S. T., & Cowell, C. S. (1986). *Health Care Financing Review, 7*(3), 1-36.

Arnoff, F. (1975). Social consequences of policy toward mental illness. *Science, 188*, 1277-1281.

Baider, L., & DeNour, K. (1984). Couples' reactions and adjustments to mastectomy. *International Journal of Psychiatry in Medicine, 14*, 265-276.

Bandura, A. (1977). *Social learning theory*. Englewood Cliffs, NJ: Prentice-Hall.

Barash, D. P. (1982). *Sociobiology and behavior* (2nd Ed.). New York: Elsevier.

Barnes, R. F., Raskind, M. A., Scott, M., & Murphy, C. (1981). Problems of families caring for Alzheimer's patients: Use of a support group. *Journal of the American Geriatrics Society, 29*(2), 80-85.

Barrowclough C., Tarrier, N., Watts, S., Vaughn, C., Bamrah, J. S., & Freeman, H. L. (1987). Assessing the functional value of relatives' knowledge about schizophrenia: A preliminary report. *British Journal of Psychiatry, 151*, 1-8.

Bartrop, R. W., Lazaras, L., Luckhurst, E., Kiloh, L. G., & Penny, R. (1977). Depressed lymphocyte function after bereavement. *Lancet, 1*, 834-836.

Batson, C. D., & Coke, J. S. (1983). Empathic motivation of helping behavior. In J. R. Cacioppo & R. E. Petty (Eds.), *Social psychophysiology: A sourcebook*. New York: Guilford Press.

Baum, H. M. (1982). Stroke prevalence: An analysis of data from the 1977 National Health Interview Survey. *Public Health Reports, 97*, 24-30.

Baumann, D. J., Cialdini, R. B., & Kendrick, D. T. (1981). Altruism as hedonism: Helping and self-gratification as equivalent responses. *Journal of Personality and Social Psychology, 40*, 1039-1046.

Beck, A. T., & Beck, R. W. (1972). Screening depressed patients in family practice: A rapid technique. *Postgraduate Medicine*, 81-85.

Becker, J., & Morissey, E. (1988). Difficulties in assessing depressive-like reactions to chronic severe external stress as exemplified by spouse caregivers of Alzheimer's patients. *Psychology and Aging, 3*, 300-306.

Beels, C. (1978). Social networks, the family and the schizophrenic patient: Introduction to special issue. *Schizophrenia Bulletin, 4*(4), 512-521.

Beels, C. C., & McFarlane, W. R. (1982). Family treatment of schizophrenia: Background and state of the art. *Hospital and Community Psychiatry, 33*, 541-550.

Belcher, S. A., Clowers, M. R., & Cabanayan, A. C. (1978). Independent living rehabilitation needs of postdischarge stroke persons: A pilot study. *Archives of Physical Medicine and Rehabilitation, 59*, 404-409.

Berkman, B. (1978). Mental health and aging: A review of the literature. *Clinical Social Work Journal, 6*, 230-245.

Berkowitz, L. (1972). Social norms, feelings, and other factors affecting helping and altruism. In L. Berkowitz (Ed.), *Advances in experimental social psychology, Vol. 6*. New York: Academic Press.

Berkowitz, R., Eberlein-Fries, R., Kuipers, L., & Leff, J. (1984). Educating relatives about schizophrenia. *Schizophrenia Bulletin, 10*(3), 418-429.

Berkowitz, R., Kuipers, L., Eberlein-Fries, R., & Leff, J. (1981). Lowering expressed emotion in relatives of schizophrenics. In M. J. Goldstein (Ed.), *New development in interventions with families of schizophrenics* (No. 12, pp. 27-48). San Francisco: Jossey-Bass.

Biegel, D., Shore, B., & Gordon, E. (1984). *Building support networks for the elderly: Theory and applications.* Beverly Hills, CA: Sage.

Biegel, D., Schulz, R., Shore, B., & Morycz, R. (1989). Economic supports for family caregivers of the elderly: Public sector policies. In M. Z. Goldstein (Ed.), *Family involvement in the treatment of the frail elderly.* Washington, DC: American Psychiatric Press.

Biegel, D. E., & Yamatani, H. (1986). Self-help groups for families of the mentally ill: Research perspectives. In M. Z. Goldstein (Ed.), *Family involvement in the treatment of schizophrenia* (pp. 58-80). Washington, DC: American Psychiatric Press.

Biegel, D. E., & Yamatani, H. (1987). Help-giving in self-help groups. *Hospital and Community Psychiatry, 38,* 1195-1197.

Binder, L. M. (1983). Emotional problems after stroke. *Current Concepts of Cerebrovascular Disease: Stroke, 18,* 17-21.

Block, A., Boyer, S., & Imes, C. (1984). Personal impact of myocardial infarction: A model for coping with physical disability in middle age. In M. G. Eisenberg, L. C. Sutkin, & M. A. Jansen (Eds.), *Chronic illness and disability through the life span* (pp. 209-221). Newbury Park, CA: Sage.

Bowen, M. (1966). The use of family theory in clinical practice. *Comprehensive Psychiatry, 7*(5), 345-374.

Boyd, J. L., McGill, C. W., & Falloon, I. R. H. (1981). Family participation in the community rehabilitation of schizophrenics. *Hospital and Community Psychiatry, 32,* 629-632.

Branch, L. G. (1984). Relative risk rates of nonmedical predictors of institutional care among the elderly. *Comprehensive Therapy, 10,* 33-40.

Branch, L. G., & Jette, A. M. (1982). A prospective study of long-term care institutionalization among the aged. *American Journal of Public Health, 72,* 1373-1379.

Brickman, P., Rabinowitz, V. C., Karuza, J., Coates, D., Cohn, E., & Kidder, L. (1982). Models of helping and coping. *American Psychologist, 37,* 368-384.

Brocklehurst, J. C., Morris, P., Andrews, K., Richards, B., & Laycock, P. (1981). Social effects of stroke. *Social Science and Medicine, 15A,* 35-39.

Brody, E.M. (1981). Women in the middle and family help to older people. *The Gerontologist, 21*(5), 471-480.

Brody, S. J., Poulshock, S. W., & Masciocchi, C. F. (1978). The family caring unit: A major consideration in the long-term support system. *The Gerontologist, 18,* 556-561.

Brown, G. (1959). Experiences of discharged chronic schizophrenic mental hospital patients in various types of living group. *Milbank Memorial Fund Quarterly, 37,* 105.

Brown, G., Birley, J., & Wing, J. (1972). Influences of family life on the course of schizophrenic disorders: A replication. *British Journal of Psychiatry, 121,* 241-258.

Brown, G., Bone, M., Dalison, B., & Wing, J. (1966). *Schizophrenia and social care.* London: Oxford University Press.

Bruhn, J. G. (1977). Effects of chronic illness on the family. *The Journal of Family Practice*, *4*(6), 1057-1060.

Buck, M. (1968). *Dysphasia: Professional guidance for family and patients*. Englewood Cliffs, NJ: Prentice-Hall.

Burish, T., & Lyles, J. (1983). Coping with the adverse effects of cancer treatments. In T. Burish & L. A. Bradley (Eds.), *Coping with chronic illness* (pp. 159-189). New York: Academic Press.

Callahan, D. (1988). Families as caregivers: The limits of morality. *Archives of Physical Medicine and Rehabilitation*, *69*, 323-328.

Cantor, M. H. (1983). Strain among caregivers: A study of experience in the United States. *The Gerontologist*, *23*, 597-604.

Cantor, R. H. (1978). *And a time to live: Toward emotional well-being during the crisis of cancer*. New York: Harper Colophon.

Carpenter, W. T. (1987). Approaches to knowledge and understanding of schizophrenia. In D. Shore (Ed.), *Special report: Schizophrenia 1987*. Reprinted from *Schizophrenia Bulletin, Vol. 13, No. 1*. Rockville, MD: U.S. Department of Health and Human Services, Alcohol, Drug, and Mental Health Administration.

Cassileth, B., & Hamilton, J. (1979). The family with cancer. In B. Cassileth (Ed.), *The cancer patient: Social and medical aspects of care* (pp. 233-247). Philadelphia: Lee & Febiger.

Cassileth, B., Lusk, E., Brown, L., & Cross, P. (1985). Psychosocial status of cancer patients and next of kin. Normative data from the POMs. *Journal of Psychosocial Oncology*, *3*(3), 99-105.

Cassileth, B., Lusk, E., Struse, T., Miller, D., Brown, L., & Cross, P. (1985). A psychological analysis of cancer patients and their next-of-kin. *Cancer*, *55*(1), 72-76.

Cassileth, B., Lusk, E., Strouse, T., Miller, D., Brown, L., Cross, P., & Tenaglia, A. (1984). Psychosocial status in chronic illness: A comparative analysis of six diagnostic groups. *New England Journal of Medicine*, *311*(8), 506-511.

Chekryn, J. (1984). Cancer recurrence: Personal meaning, communication and marital adjustment. *Cancer Nursing*, *7*, 491-498.

Chenoweth, B., & Spencer, B. (1986). Dementia: The experience of family caregivers. *The Gerontologist*, *26*, 267-272.

Christensen, D. N. (1983). Postmastectomy couple counseling: An outcome study of a structured treatment protocol. *Journal of Sex and Martial Therapy*, *9*(4), 266-275.

Chwat, S., Chapey, R., Gurland, G., & Pieras, G. (1980). Environmental impact of aphasia: The child's perspective. In R. Brookshire (Ed.), *Clinical Aphasiology Conference Proceedings, 1980*. Minneapolis, MN: BRK Publishers.

Clausen, J. A., & Yarrow, M. R. (Eds.). (1955). The impact of mental illness on the family. *Journal of Social Issues*, *11*.

Clipp, E. C., & George, L. K. (1990). Psychotropic drug use among caregivers of patients with dementia. *Journal of the American Geriatric Society*, *38*, 227-235.

Cohen, C. (1978). Three-year follow-up study of stroke patients at the Medical College of Virginia. *Southern Medical Journal*, *71*, 930-932.

Cohen, D., & Eisdorfer, C. (1986). *The loss of self: A family resource for the care of Alzheimer's disease and related disorders*. New York: Norton.

Cohen, D., & Eisdorfer, C. (1988). Depression in family members caring for a relative with Alzheimer's disease. *Journal of the American Geriatric Society, 36*, 885-889.

Cohen, J. (1982). Response of the health care system to the psychosocial aspects of cancer. In J. Cohen, J. Cullen, & L. Martin (Eds.), *Psychosocial aspects of cancer*. New York: Raven Press.

Cohen, J., Cullen, J., & Martin, L. (Eds.). (1982). *Psychosocial aspects of cancer*. New York: Raven Press.

Cohen, M. (1982a). In the presence of their absence. The treatment of older families with a cancer patient. *Psychotherapy: Theory, Research and Practice, 19*(4) 453-460.

Cohen, M. (1982b). Psychosocial morbidity in cancer: A clinical perspective. In J. Cohen, J. Cullen, & L. Martin (Eds.), *Psychosocial aspects of cancer* (pp. 117-127). New York: Raven Press.

Cohen, P., Dizenhuz, I., & Winget, C. (1977). Family adaptation to terminal illness and death of a parent. *Social Casework, 58,* 223-228.

Cohen, S. (1988). Psychosocial models of the role of social support in the etiology of physical disease. *Health Psychology, 7,* 269-297.

Cohler, B., Groves, L., Borden, W., & Lazarus, L. (1989). Caring for family members with Alzheimer's disease. In E. Light & B. Lebowitz (Eds.), *Alzheimer's disease treatment and family stress: Directions for research* (pp. 50-105). Washington, DC: National Institute of Mental Health.

Colditz, G. A., Martin, P., Stampfer, M. J., Willett, W. C., Sampson, L., Rosner, B., Hennekens, C. H., & Speizer, F. E. (1986). Validation of questionnaire information on risk factors and disease outcomes in a prospective cohort study of women. *American Journal of Epidemiology, 123,* 894-900.

Colerick, E. J., & George, L. K. (1986). Predictors of institutionalization among caregivers of patients with Alzheimer's disease. *Journal of the American Geriatric Society, 34,* 493-498.

Cone, J. (1985). *Coping strategies and marital support in the adjustment of cancer patients,* Unpublished doctoral dissertation, University of Pittsburgh.

Cooper, E. T. (1984). A pilot study on the effects of the diagnosis of lung cancer on family relationships. *Cancer Nursing, 7,* 301-308.

Coppel, D. B., Burton, C., Becker, J., & Fiore, J. (1985). The relationships of cognitions associated with coping reactions to depression in spousal caregivers of Alzheimer's disease patients. *Cognitive Therapy and Research, 9,* 253-266.

Coughlan, A. K., & Humphrey, M. (1982). Presenile stroke: Long-term outcome for patients and their families. *Rheumatology and Rehabilitation, 21,* 115-122.

Coulton, C. (1988). Prospective payment requires increased attention to quality of post hospital care. *Social Work in Health Care, 13*(4), 19-31.

Cozolino, L. J., & Nuechterlein, K. (1986). Pilot study of the impact of a family education program on relatives of recent-onset schizophrenic patients. In I. Hand, M. J. Goldstein, & K. Hahlweg (Eds.), *Family assessment and intervention* (pp. 129-144). Berlin: Springer-Verlag.

Craig, T. J., Hussey, P. A., Parsons, P. J., & Seamans, S. C. (1985). A family group program in a state psychiatric hospital. *Hospital & Community Psychiatry, 36*(12), 1317-1318.

Croake, J. W., & Kelly, F. D. (1985). Adlerian family therapy with schizophrenic and depressed patients. *Individual Psychology: Journal of Adlerian Theory, Research & Practice, 41*(3), 302-312.

Croog, S., & Levine, S. (1977). *The heart patient recovers: Social and psychological factors.* New York: Human Sciences Press.

Croog, S., & Levine, S. (1982). *Life after a heart attack: Social and psychological factors eight years later*. New York: Human Sciences Press.

Croog, S., Levine, S., & Lurie, Z. (1968). The heart patient and the recovery process: A review of the literature on social and psychological factors. *Social Science & Medicine, 2*, 111-164.

Crotty, P., & Kulys, R. (1985). Social support networks: The view of schizophrenic clients and their significant others. *Social Work*, 301-309.

Crotty, P., & Kulys, R. (1986). Are schizophrenics a burden to their families? Significant others' views. *Health and Social Work*, 173-188.

Davies, A. D. M. (1981). Neither wife nor widow: An intervention with the wife of a chronically handicapped man during hospital visits. *Behavior, Research and Therapy, 19*, 449-451.

Davis, A. E., Dinitz, S., & Pasaminick, B. (1974). *Schizophrenics in the new custodial community*. Columbus: Ohio State University Press.

DeJong, G., & Branch, L. G. (1982). Predicting the stroke patient's ability to live independently. *Stroke, 12*, 648-655.

Dhooper, S. (1983). Family coping with the crisis of heart attack. *Social Work in Health Care, 9*, 15-31.

Dhooper, S. (1984). Social networks and support during the crisis of heart attack. *Health and Social Work, 9*(4), 294-302.

Dincin, J. (1975). Psychiatric rehabilitation. *Schizophrenia Bulletin, 13*, 131-147.

Doehrman, S. R. (1977). Psycho-social aspects of recovery from coronary heart disease: A review. *Social Science & Medicine, 11*, 199-218.

Dohrenwend, B. P. (1980). Summary and conclusions. In B. S. D. Dohrenwend (Ed.), *Mental illness in the United States: Epidemiological estimates*. New York: Praeger.

Doll, W. (1975). Home is not sweet anymore. *MH (Mental Hygiene), 59*, 2204-2206.

Doll, W. (1976). Family coping with the mentally ill: An unanticipated problem of deinstitutionalization. *Hospital and Community Psychiatry, 27*(3), 183-185.

Doty, P. (1986). Family care of the elderly: The role of public policy. *The Milbank Memorial Fund Quarterly, 64*(1), 34-75.

Dovidio, J. F. (1984). Helping and altruism: An empirical and conceptual overview. In L. Berkowitz (Ed.), *Advances in experimental social psychology,* Vol. 17. New York: Academic Press.

Drinka, T. J., Smith, J., & Drinka, P. J. (1987). Correlates of depression and burden for informal caregivers of patients in a Geriatric referral clinic. *Journal of the American Geriatric Society, 35*, 522-525.

Dunkel-Schetter, C. (1984). Social support and cancer: Findings based on patient interviews and their implication. *Journal of Social Issues, 40*(4), 77-98.

Dunkel-Schetter, C., & Wortman, C. (1982). The interpersonal dynamics of cancer: Problems in social relationships and their impact on the patient. In H. Freeman & R. DiMatteo (Eds.), *Interpersonal issues in health care* (pp. 69-100). New York: Academic Press.

Dura, J. R., Haywood-Niler, E., & Kiecolt-Glaser, J. K. (in press). Alzheimer's and Parkinson's disease dementia caregivers: Effects of chronic stress. *The Gerontologist.*

Dura, J. R., Stukenberg, K. W., & Kiecolt-Glaser, J. K. (in press). Chronic stress and depressive disorders in older adults. *Journal of Abnormal Psychology.*

Eagles, J. M., Beattie, J. A. G., Blackwood, G. W., Restall, D. B., & Ashcroft, G. W. (1987). The mental health of elderly couples. I. The effects of a cognitively impaired spouse. *British Journal of Psychiatry, 150*, 299-303.

Elliott, G. R., & Eisdorfer, C. (Eds.). (1982). *Stress and human health.* New York: Springer.

Endicott, J., & Spitzer, R. L. (1978). A diagnostic interview: The schedule for affective disorders and schizophrenia. *Archives of General Psychiatry, 35*, 837-844.

Evans, D. A., Funkenstein, H. H., & Albert, M. S. (1989). Prevalence of Alzheimer's disease in a community population of older persons. *Journal of the American Medical Association, 262* (November 10), 2551-2556.

Evans, R. L., & Held, S. (1984). Evaluation of family stroke education. *International Journal of Rehabilitation Research, 7*(1), 47-51.

Evans, R. L., Matlock, A. L., Bishop, D. S., Stranahan, S., & Pederson, C. (1988). Family intervention after stroke: Does counseling or education help? *Stroke, 19*, 1243-1249.

Falloon, I. R. H. (1985). Plan of the study. In I. R. H. Falloon (Ed.), *Family management of schizophrenia: A study of clinical, social, family, and economic benefits* (pp. 38-68). Baltimore, MD: Johns Hopkins University Press.

Falloon, I. R. H. (1986). Behavioral family therapy for schizophrenia: Clinical, social, family, and economic benefits. In I. Hand, M. J. Goldstein, & K. Hahlweg (Eds.), *Treatment of schizophrenia: Family assessment and intervention.* (pp. 171-184). Berlin: Springer-Verlag.

Falloon, I. R. H., Boyd, J. L., & McGill, C. W. (1984). *Family care of schizophrenia: A problem solving approach to the treatment of mental illness.* New York: Guilford Press.

Falloon, I. R. H., Boyd, J. L., & McGill, C. W. (1985). Clinical outcome: Exacerbations, symptom patterns, and community tenure. In I. R. H. Falloon (Ed.), *Family management of schizophrenia: A study of clinical, social, family, and economic benefits* (pp. 69-84). Baltimore, MD: Johns Hopkins University Press.

Falloon, I. R. H., Boyd, J. L., McGill, C. W., Razani, J., Moss, H. B., & Gilderman, A. M. (1982). Family management in the prevention and exacerbation of schizophrenia. *New England Journal of Medicine, 306*(24), 1437-1440.

Falloon, I. R. H., Boyd, J. L., McGill, C. W., Strang, J. S., & Moss, H. B. (1981). Family management training in the community care of schizophrenia. In M. J. Goldstein (Ed.), *New developments in interventions with families of schizophrenic.* New Directions for Mental Health Services No. 12 (pp. 61-77). San Francisco: Jossey-Bass.

Falloon, I. R. H., Boyd, J. L., McGill, C. W., Williamson, M., Razani, J., Moss, H. B., Gildersman, A. M., & Simpson, G. M. (1985). Family management in the prevention of morbidity of schizophrenia. *Archives of General Psychiatry, 42*(9), 887-896.

Falloon, I. R. H., Boyd, J., Moss, H., Cardin, V., McGill, C., Razani, J., Pederson, J., & Doane, J. (1985). Behavioural family therapy for schizophrenia: A controlled two-year study. In P. Berner, P. Pichot, R. Wolf, & K. Thau (Eds.), *Psychiatry, the state of the art: Vol. 7. Epidemiology and community psychiatry* (pp. 481-485). New York: Plenum.

Falloon, I. R. H., & Liberman, R. P. (1983). Behavioral family intervention in the management of chronic schizophrenia. In W. R. McFarlane (Ed.), *Family therapy in schizophrenia* (pp. 117-137). New York: Guilford Press.

Falloon, I. R. H., Liberman, R. P., Lillie, F. J., & Vaughn, C. E. (1981). Family therapy of schizophrenics with high risk of relapse. *Family Process, 20*(2), 211-221.

Falloon, I. R. H., & Pederson, J. (1985). Family management in the prevention of morbidity of schizophrenia: The adjustment of the family unit. *British Journal of Psychiatry, 147*, 156-163.

Falloon, I. R. H., Pederson, J., & Al-Khayyal, M. (1986). Enhancement of health-giving family support versus treatment of family pathology. *Journal of Family Therapy, 8*(4), 339-350.

Feibel, J. H., & Springer, C. J. (1982). Depression and failure to resume social activities after stroke. *Archives of Physical Medicine and Rehabilitation, 63*, 276-278.

Feldman, F. (1982). Work and cancer health histories. In J. Cohen, J. Cullen, & L. Martin (Eds.), *Psychosocial aspects of cancer* (pp.198-208). New York: Raven Press.

Fengler, A. P., & Goodrich, N. (1979). Wives of elderly disabled men: The hidden patients. *The Gerontologist, 19*, 175-183.

Finlayson, H., & McEwen, J. (1977). *Coronary heart disease and patterns of living.* New York: Prodist.

Fiore, J., Becker, J., & Coppel, D. B. (1983). Social network interactions: A buffer or a stress? *American Journal of Community Psychology, 11*, 423-439.

Fitting, M., Rabins, P., Lucas, M. J., & Eastham, J. (1986). Caregivers of dementia patients: A comparison of husbands and wives. *The Gerontologist, 26*, 248-252.

Fobair, P., & Cordoba, C. (1982). Scope and magnitude of the cancer problem in psychosocial research. In J. Cohen, J. Cullen, & L. Martin (Eds.), *Psychosocial aspects of cancer* (pp. 9-15). New York: Raven Press.

Forsyth, D. R. (1987). *Social pyschology.* Monterey, CA.: Brooks/Cole.

Francell, C. G., Conn, V. S., Gray, D. P. (1988). Families' perception of burden for care for mentally ill relatives. *Hospital and Community Psychiatry, 39*(12), 1296-1300.

Freeman, H., & Simmons, O. (1963). *The mental patient comes home.* New York: John Wiley.

Freese, A. S. (1980). *Stroke: The new hope and the new help.* New York: Random House.

Freidenbergs, I., Gordon, W., Hubbard, M., Levine, L., Wolf, C., & Diller, L. (1981-1982). Psychosocial aspects of living with cancer: A review of the literature. *International Journal of Psychiatry in Medicine, 11*(4), 303-329.

Gallagher, D., Rose, J., Rivera, P., Lovett, S., & Thompson, L. W. (1989). Prevalence of depression in family caregivers. *The Gerontologist, 29*, 449-456.

Gallagher, D., Wrabetz, A., Lovett, S., Del Maestro, S., & Rose, J. (1989). Depression and other negative affects in family caregivers. In E. Light & B. D. Lebowitz (Eds.), *Alzheimer's disease treatment and family stress: Directions for research.* (DHHS Publication No. ADM89-1569). Rockville, MD.: National Institute of Mental Health.

Garraway, M. (1985). Stroke rehabilitation units: Concepts, evaluation, and unresolved issues. *Stroke, 16*, 178-181.

Garraway, W. M., Whisnant, J. P., & Drury, I. (1983). The continuing decline in the incidence of stroke. *Mayo Clinic Proceedings, 58*, 520-523.

Garraway, W. M., Whisnant, J. P., Kurland, L. T., & O'Fallon, W. M. (1979). Changing pattern of cerebral infarction, 1945-1974. *Stroke, 10*, 657-663.

Geiser, R., Hoche, L., & King, J. (1988). Respite care for mentally ill patients and their families. *Hospital and Community Psychiatry, 39*(3), 291-295.

George, L. (1980). *Role transitions in later life.* Monterey, CA: Brooks/Cole.

George, L. K., & Gwyther, L. P. (1986). Caregiver well-being: A multidimensional examination of family caregivers of demented adults. *The Gerontologist, 26,* 253-259.

Giacquinta, B. (1977). Helping families face the crisis of cancer. *American Journal of Nursing, 77,* 1585-1588.

Gilleard, C. J., Belford, H., Gilleard, E., Whittick, J. E., & Gledhill, K. (1984). Emotional distress amongst the supporters of the elderly mentally infirm. *British Journal of Psychiatry, 141,* 1467-1468.

Gilleard, C. J., Gilleard, E., & Whittick, J. E. (1984). Impact of psychogeriatric day hospital care on the patient's family. *British Journal of Psychiatry, 145,* 487-492.

Given, C. W., Collins, C. E., & Given, B. A. (1988). Sources of stress among families caring for relatives with Alzheimer's disease. *Nursing Clinics of North America, 23,* 69-82.

Glosser, G., & Wexler, D. (1985). Participants' evaluation of education/support groups for families of patients with Alzheimer's disease and other dementias. *The Gerontologist, 25*(3), 232-236.

Godkin, M. A., Krant, M. J., & Doster, N. J. (1983-1984). The impact of hospice care on families. *International Journal of Psychiatry in Medicine, 13*(2), 153-165.

Goldberg, D. P., Cooper, B., Eastwood, M. R., Kedward, H., & Shepherd, M. (1970). A standardized psychiatric interview suitable for use in community surveys. *British Journal of Preventive and Social Medicine, 24,* 18-23.

Goldberg, D. P., & Hillier, V. F. (1979). A scaled version of the General Health Questionnaire. *Psychological Medicine, 9,* 139-145.

Goldberg, R. , & Tull, R. (1983). *The psychosocial dimensions of cancer.* New York: Free Press.

Goldberg, R. J., & Wool, M. S. (1985). Psychotherapy for the spouses of lung cancer patients: Assessment of an intervention. *Psychotherapy and Psychosomatics, 43*(3), 141-150.

Goldman, H. H. (1982). Mental illness and family burden: A public health perspective. *Hospital and Community Psychiatry, 33*(7), 557-560.

Goldman, H. H. (1984). Epidemiology. In J. A. Talbott (Ed.), *The chronic mental patient: Five years later,* Orlando, FL: Grune & Stratton.

Goldman, H. H., Gattozzi, A. A., & Taube, C. A. (1981). Defining and counting the chronically mentally ill. *Hospital and Community Psychiatry, 32,* 22-27.

Goldman, H. H., & Manderscheid, R. W. (1987). Chronic mental disorders in the United States. In R. W. Manderscheid & S. A. Barrett (Eds.), *Mental health, United States, 1987* (pp. 1-13). Washington, DC: U.S. Government Printing Office.

Goldman, L. S., & Luchins, D. J. (1984). Depression in the spouses of demented patients. *American Journal of Psychiatry, 141,* 1467-1468.

Goldstein, E. G. (1987). Mental health and illness. *Encyclopedia of Social Work* (18th Ed.). Silver Spring, MD: National Association of Social Workers.

Goldstein, M. J. (1981a). *New developments in interventions with families of schizophrenics* No. 12. San Francisco: Jossey-Bass.

Goldstein, M. J. (1981b). Family therapy during the aftercare treatment of acute schizophrenia. In M. R. Lansky (Ed.), *Family therapy and major psychopathology.* (pp. 21-34). New York: Grune & Stratton.

Goldstein, M. J. (1987). Psychosocial issues. In D. Shore (Ed.), *Special Report: Schizophrenia 1987.* Reprinted from *Schizophrenia Bulletin, Vol. 13, No. 1.* Rockville,

MD: U.S. Department of Health and Human Services, Alcohol, Drugs, and Mental Health Administration.

Goldstein, M. J., & Kopeikin, H. S. (1981). Short- and long-term effects of combining drug and family therapy. In M. Goldstein (Ed.), *New developments in interventions with families of schizophrenics* No. 12 (pp. 5-26). San Francisco: Jossey-Bass.

Goldstein, M. J., Rodnick, E. H., Evans, J. R., May, P. R. A., & Steinberg, M. R. (1978). Drug and family therapy in the aftercare of acute schizophrenics. *Archives of General Psychiatry, 35*, 1169-1177.

Gonyea, J.G. (1989). Alzheimer's disease support groups: An analysis of their structure, format, and perceived benefits. *Social Work in Health Care, 14*(1), 61-72.

Googe, M., & Varricchio, C. (1981). A pilot investigation of home health care needs of cancer patients and their families. *Oncology Nursing Forum, 8*(4), 24-28.

Gordon, W. A., & Diller L. (1983). Stroke: Coping with a cognitive deficit. T. G. Burish & L. A. Bradley (Eds.), *Coping with chronic disease.* New York: Academic Press.

Gotay, C. (1984). The experience of cancer during early and advanced stages: The views of patients and their mates. *Social Science in Medicine, 18*(7), 605-613.

Grad, J., & Sainsbury, P. (1968). The effect that patients have on their families in a community care and a control psychiatric service: A two year follow-up. *British Journal of Psychiatry*, 114, 265-278.

Grad, J. P. D., & Sainsbury, P. M. D. (1963). Mental illness and the family. *Lancet, 1*, 544-547.

Grandstaff, N. W. (1976). The impact of breast cancer on the family. *Frontiers of Radiation Therapy and Oncology, ll*, 146-156.

Gray-Price, H., & Szczesny, S. (1985). Crisis intervention with families of cancer patients: A developmental approach. *Topics in Clinical Nursing, 11*, 58-70.

Greenberg, M. S. (1980). A theory of indebtedness. In K. J. Gergen, M. S. Greenberg, & R. H. Willis (Eds.), *Social exchange: Advances in theory and research* (pp. 3-26). New York: Plenum.

Greene, V. L., & Monahan, D. J. (1989). The effect of a support and education program on stress and burden among family caregivers to frail elderly persons. *The Gerontologist, 29*(4), 472-477.

Gresham, G. E., Fitzpatrick, T. E., Wolf, T. A., McNamara, P. M., Kannel, W. B., & Dawber, T. R. (1975). Residual disability in survivors of stroke—The Framingham study. *The New England Journal of Medicine, 293*, 954-956.

Grobe, M. E., Ilstrup, D., & Ahmann, D. (1981). Skills needed by family members to maintain the care of an advanced cancer patient. *Cancer Nursing, 4*(5), 371-375.

Group for the Advancement of Psychiatry. (1978). *The chronic mental patient in the community, 10*(102), 281-379.

Gulledge, A.D. (1979). Psychological aftermaths of myocardial infarction. In W. D. Gentry & R. Williams (Eds.), *Psychological aspects of myocardial infarction and coronary care* (pp.113-130). St. Louis: C. V. Mosby.

Gwyther, L. P., & Blazer, D. G. (1984). Family therapy and the dementia patient. *American Family Physician, 29*(5), 149-156.

Hackett, T., & Cassem, N. (1979). Psychological intervention in myocardial infarction. In W. D. Gentry & R. Williams (Eds.), *Psychological aspects of myocardial infarction and coronary care* (pp. 151-161). St. Louis: C. V. Mosby.

Hackett, T., & Cassem, N. (1984). Psychological aspects of rehabilitation after myocardial infarction and coronary artery bypass surgery. In N. Wenger & H. K. Hellerstein (Eds.), *Rehabilitation of the coronary patient* (pp.437-451). New York: John Wiley.

Hagnell, O. (1970). Disease expectancy and incidence of mental health among the aged. *Acta Psychiatric Association (1980) Diagnostic and Statistical Mannual* (3rd ed.). Washington, DC: Author.

Hagnell, O., Lanke, J., Rorsman, B., Ohman, R., & Ojesjo, L. (1983). Current trends in the incidence of senile and multi-infarct dementia. A prospective study of a total population followed over 25 years. The Lundby study. *Archiv für Psychiatrie und Nervenkrankheiten, 233*, 423-438.

Haley, J. & Ranson, D. C. (1976). Development of a theory: A history of a research project. In C. E. Sluzki & D. C. Ransom (Eds.), *Double bind: The foundation of the communication approach to the family.* New York: Grune & Stratton.

Haley, W. E. (1989). Group intervention for dementia family caregivers: A longitudinal perspective. *The Gerontologist, 29*(4), 478-480.

Haley, W. E., Brown, S. L., & Levine, E. G. (1987). Experimental evaluation of the effectiveness of group intervention for dementia caregivers. *The Gerontologist, 27*(3), 376-382.

Haley, W. E., Levine, E. G., Brown, S. L., & Bartolucci, A. A. (1987). Stress, appraisal, coping, and social support as predictors of adaptational outcome among dementia caregivers. *Psychology and Aging, 2*, 323-330.

Haley, W. E., Levine, E. G., Brown, S. L., Berry, J. W., & Hughes, G. H. (1987). Psychological, social, and health consequences of caring for a relative with senile dementia. *Journal of the American Geriatric Society, 35*, 405-411.

Hamilton, W. D. (1964). The genetical evolution of social behaviour, I and II. *Journal of Theoretical Biology, 7*, 1-52.

Hansen, D., & Hill, R. (1964). Families under stress. In H. Chistensen (Ed.), *Handbook of marriage and the family.* (pp. 782-819). Chicago: Rand-McNally.

Harrell, A. W. (1978). Physical attractiveness, self-disclosure, and helping behavior. *Journal of Social Psychology, 104*, 15-17.

Hart, K. (1986), Stress encountered by significant others of cancer patients receiving psychotherapy. *Omega Journal of Death and Dying, 17*(2) 151-169.

Hatfield, A. B. (1978). Psychological costs of schizophrenia to the family. *Social Work,* 355-359.

Hatfield, A. B. (1979a). The family as a partner in the treatment of mental illness. *Hospital and Community Psychiatry, 30*(5), 338-340.

Hatfield, A. B. (1979b). Help-seeking behavior in families of schizophrenics. *American Journal of Community Psychology, 7*, 563-569.

Hatfield, A. B. (1981). Coping effectiveness in families of the mentally ill: An exploratory study. *Journal of Psychiatric Treatment and Evaluation, 3*, 11-19.

Hatfield, A. B. (1987a). Coping and adaptation: A conceptual framework for understanding families. In A. B. Hatfield & H. P. Lefley (Eds.), *Families of the mentally ill: Coping and adaptation* (pp. 60-83). New York: Guilford Press.

Hatfield, A. B. (1987b). Families as caregivers: A historical perspective. In A. B. Hatfield & H. P. Lefley, (Eds.), *Families of the mentally ill: Coping and adaptation* (pp. 3-29). New York: Guilford Press.

Hatfield, A. B., Spaniol, L., & Zipple, A. M. (1985). *Expressed emotion: A family perspective.* Boston: Center for Rehabilitation Research and Training in Mental Health, Sargent College of Allied Health Professions, Boston University.

Hatfield, E., Walster, G. W., & Piliavin, J. A. (1978). Equity theory and helping relationships. In L. Wispe (Ed.), *Altruism, sympathy, and helping* (pp. 115-139). New York: Academic Press.

Heinrich, R. L., & Schag, C. C. (1985). Stress and activity management: Group treatment for cancer patients and spouses. *Journal of Consulting and Clinical Psychology, 53*(4), 439-446.

Herz, F. & McGoldrick, M. (1980). The impact of death and serious illness on the family life cycle. In E. Carter & M. McGoldrick (Eds.), *The family life cycle: A framework for family therapy* (pp. 223-240). New York: Gardner Press.

Herz, M., Endicott, G., & Spitzer, R. (1976). Brief versus standard hospitalization: The families. *American Journal of Psychiatry, 133*, 795-801.

Hill, R. (1949). *Families under stress.* Westport, CT: Greenwood Press.

Hinds, C. (1985). The needs of families who care for patients with cancer at home: Are we meeting them? *Journal of Advanced Nursing, 10*, 575-581.

Hinton, J. (1981). Sharing or withholding awareness of dying between husband and wife. *Journal of Psychosomatic Research, 25,* 337-343.

Hirsch, S., Platt, S., Knights, A., & Weyman, A. (1979). Shortening hospital stay for psychiatric care: Effect on patients and their families. *British Medical Journal, 1*, 442-446.

Hoenig, J., & Hamilton, M. (1966). The schizophrenic patient in the community and his effect on the household. *International Journal of Social Psychiatry, 12*, 165-176.

Hoenig, J., & Hamilton, M. (1969). *The desegregation of the mentally ill.* London: Rutledge & Kegan Paul.

Hoffman, M. L. (1982.). Development of prosocial motivation: Empathy and guilt. In N. Eisenberg (Ed.), *The development of prosocial behavior* (pp. 281-313). New York: Academic Press.

Holbrook, M. (1982). Stroke: Social and emotional outcome. *Journal of the Royal College of Physicians of London, 16*, 100-104.

Holden, D. F., & Lewine, R. R. J. (1982). How families evaluate mental health professionals, resources and effects of illness. *Schizophrenia Bulletin, 8*, 626-633.

Hooyman, N. R., & Lustbader, W. (1986). *Taking care: Supporting older people and their families.* New York: Free Press.

Horenstein, S. (1970). Effects of cerebrovascular disease on personality and emotionality. In A. L. Benton (Ed.), *Behavioral change in cerebrovascular disease.* New York: Harper & Row.

Horowitz, A. (1985). Family caregiving to the frail elderly. In M. P. Lawton & G. Maddox (Eds.), *Annual review of gerontology and Geriatric: Vol. 5.* (pp. 194-246). New York: Springer.

Horowitz, A., & Shindelman, L. (1983). Reciprocity and affection: Past influences on current caregiving. *Journal of Gerontological Social Work, 5*, 5-20.

Houpt, J. L., Orleans, C. S., George L. K., & Brodie H. K. H. (1979). *The importance of mental health to general health care.* Cambridge, MA: Ballinger.

Houpt, J. L., Orleans, C. S., George, L. K., & Brodie, H. K. H. (1980). The role of psychiatric and behavioral factors in the practice of medicine. *American Journal of Psychiatry, 137*, 37-47.

House, J. (1974). Occupational stress and coronary heart disease: A review and theoretical integration. *Journal of Health and Social Behavior, 15*, 12-27.

Hyman, M. D. (1971). The stigma of stroke. *Geriatric, 26*, 132-141.

Ingersoll-Dayton, B., Chapman, N., & Neal, M. (1990). A program for caregivers in the workplace. *The Gerontologist, 30*(1), 126-130.

Intagliata, J., & Willer, B. E. (1986). Role of the family in case management of the mentally ill. *Schizophrenia Bulletin, 12*(4), 699-708.

An interview with a parent of a chronic mentally ill daughter. (1986). *Community Mental Health Journal, 2*(3), 238-246.

Isaacs, B. (1982). The continuing needs of stroke patients. In F. C. Rose (Ed.), *Advances in stroke therapy.* New York: Raven Press.

Issacs, B., Neville, Y., & Rushford, I. (1976). The stricken: The social consequences of stroke. *Age and Aging, 5,* 188-192.

Jamison, K., Wellisch, D., & Pasnau, R. (1978). Psychosocial aspects of mastectomy: I. The woman's perspective. *American Journal of Psychiatry, 135*(4), 432-436.

Johnson, E. M., & Stark, D. E. (1980). A group program for cancer patients and their family members in an acute care teaching hospital. *Social Work and Health Care, 5*(4), 335-349.

Kahan, J., Kemp, B., Staples, F. R., & Brummel-Smith, K. (1985). Decreasing the burden in families caring for a relative with a dementing illness: A controlled study. *Journal of the American Geriatric Society, 33*(10), 664-670.

Kannel, W. (1984). Potential for prevention of myocardial reinfarction and cardiac death. In N. Wenger & H. Hellerstein (Eds.), *Rehabilitation of the coronary patient* (pp. 133-159). New York: John Wiley.

Kaplan, D. (1982). Intervention strategies for families. In J. Cohen, J. Cullen, & L. Martin (Eds.), *Psychosocial aspects of cancer* (pp. 221-233). New York: Raven Press.

Kasl, S. V., & Berkman, L. F. (1981). Some psychosocial influences on the health status of the elderly: The perspective of social epidemiology. In J. L. McGaugh & S. B. Kiesler (Eds.), *Aging: Biology and behavior* (pp. 345-377). New York: Academic Press.

Katon, W. (1985). Somatization in primary care. *Journal of Family Practice, 21,* 257-258.

Katschnig, H., Konieczna, T., & Sint, P. (1985). Helping the family to cope with schizophrenia: Professionally supported self-help. In P. Berner, P. Pichat, R. Wolf, & K. Thau (Eds.), *Psychiatry, the state of the art (Vol. 7): Epidemiology and community psychiatry* (pp. 487-493). New York: Plenum.

Keith, S. J., & Matthews, S. M. (1984). Research overview. In J.A. Talbott (Ed.), *The chronic mental patient: Five years later.* Orlando, FL: Grune & Stratton.

Kent, D. P. (1965). Aging—fact or fancy. *The Gerontologist, 5,* 2.

Kerns, R., & Turk, D. (1985). Behavioral medicine and the family: Historical perspectives and future directions. In D. Turk & R. Kerns (Eds.), *Health, illness and families: A life space perspective* (pp. 338-353). New York: John Wiley.

Kerson, T. S. (1985a). Cancer. In T. S. Kerson & W. L. Kerson (Eds.), *Understanding chronic illness: The medical and psychosocial dimension of nine diseases.* New York: Free Press.

Kerson, T. S. (1985b). Heart disease. In T. S. Kerson & W. L. Kerson (Eds.), *Understanding chronic illness: The medical and psychosocial dimension of nine diseases* (pp. 149-186). New York: Free Press.

Kiecolt-Glaser, J. K., Glaser, R., Shuttleworth, E. E., Dyer, C. S., Ogrocki, P., & Speicher, C. E. (1987). Chronic stress and immunity in family caregivers of Alzheimer's disease patients. *Psychosomatic Medicine, 49,* 523-535.

Kinney, J. M., & Stephens, M. A. P. (1989). Hassles and uplifts of giving care to a family member with dementia. *Psychology and Aging, 4,* 402-408.

Kinsella, G. J., & Duffy, F. D. (1979). Psychosocial readjustment in spouses of aphasic patients. *Scandinavian Journal of Rehabilitation Medicine, 11,* 129-132.

Kint, M. (1977). Problems for families vs. problem families. *Schizophrenia Bulletin, 3,* 355-356.

Kint, M. G. (1978). Schizophrenia as a family affair: Problems of families in coping with schizophrenia. *Journal of Orthomolecular Psychiatry, 7,* 236-246.

Kleinke, C. (1977). Compliance to requests made by gazing and touching experimenters in field settings. *Journal of Experimental Social Psychology, 13,* 218-223.

Kopeikin, H. S., Marshall, V., & Goldstein, M. J. (1983). Stages of impact of crisis oriented family therapy in the aftercare of acute schizophrenia. In W. R. McFarlane (Ed.), *Family therapy in schizophrenia* (pp. 69-97). New York: Guilford Press.

Kottgen, C., Sonnichsen, I., Mollenhauer, K., & Jurth, R. (1984). Group therapy with the families of schizophrenic patients: Results of the Hamburg Camberwell-Family-Interview study: III. *International Journal of Family Psychiatry, 5*(1), 83-94.

Krantz, D., & Deckel, A. W. (1983). Coping with coronary disease and stroke. In T. Burish & L. Bradley (Eds.), *Coping with chronic disease.* New York: Academic Press.

Kreisman, D., & Joy, V. D. (1974). Family response to the mental illness of a relative: A review of the literature. *Schizophrenia Bulletin, 10,* 34-57.

Kreisman, D., Simmons, S., & Joy, V. (1979). Rejecting the patient: Preliminary validation of a self-report scale. *Schizophrenia Bulletin, 5,* 220-222.

Kuipers, L., Berkowitz, R., & Leff, J. (1985). Helping families of schizophrenic patients: An eclectic approach. In P. Berner, P. Pichot, R. Wolf, & K. Thau (Eds.), *Psychiatry, the state of the art, Vol. 7. Epidemiology and community psychiatry* (pp. 509-515). New York: Plenum.

Kuller, L. H. (1978). Epidemiology of stroke. *Advances in Neurology, 19,* 281-311.

Labi, M. L. C., Phillips, T. F., & Gresham, G. E. (1980). Psychosocial disability in physically restored long-term stroke survivors. *Archives of Physical Medicine and Rehabilitation, 61,* 561-565.

Lamb, H. R. (1982). *Treating the long term mentally ill: Beyond deinstitutionalization.* San Francisco: Jossey-Bass.

Lamb, H. R., Hoffman, A., Hoffman, F., & Oliphant, E. (1986). Families of schizophrenics: A movement in jeopardy. *Hospital and Community Psychiatry, 37*(4), 353-357.

Lamb, H. R., & Oliphant, E. (1978). Schizophrenia through the eyes of families. *Hospital and Community Psychiatry, 29,* 803-806.

Latane, B., & Darley, J. M. (1970). *The unresponsive bystander: Why doesn't he help?* New York: Appleton-Century-Crofts.

Lawrence, L., & Christie, D. (1979). Quality of life after stroke: A three-year follow-up. *Age and Aging, 8,* 167-172.

Lawton, M. P., Brody, E. M., & Saperstein, A. R. (1989). A controlled study of respite service for caregivers of Alzheimer's patients. *The Gerontologist, 29*(1), 8-16.

Lazarus, L. W., Stafford, B., Cooper, K., Cohler, B., & Dysken, M. (1981). A pilot study of an Alzheimer's patients' relatives discussion group. *The Gerontologist,* 21 (4), 353-358.

Lazarus, R. S., & Folkman, S. (1984). *Stress, appraisal, and coping.* New York: Springer.

Leff, J. P. (1979). Developments in family treatment of schizophrenia. *Psychiatric Quarterly, 51,* 216-232.

Leff, J. P. (1983). The management of the family of the chronic psychiatric patient. In I. Barofsky & R. D. Budson (Eds.), *The chronic patient in the community: Principles of treatment.* New York: SP Medical & Scientific Books.

Leff, J. P., Kuipers, L., & Berkowitz, R. (1983). Intervention in families of schizophrenics and its effect on relapse rate. In W. R. McFarlane (Ed.), *Family therapy in schizophrenia* (pp. 173-188). New York: Guilford Press.

Leff, J. P., Kuipers, L., Berkowitz, R., Eberlein-Vries, R., & Sturgeon, D. (1982). A controlled trial of social intervention in the families of schizophrenic patients. *British Journal of Psychiatry, 141,* 121-134.

Leff, J. P., Kuipers, L., Berkowitz, R., Eberlein-Vries, R., & Sturgeon, D. (1986). Controlled trial of social intervention in the families of schizophrenic patients. In I. Hand, M. J. Goldstein, & K. Hahlweg (Eds.), *Treatment of schizophrenia: Family assessment and intervention* (pp. 153-165). Berlin: Springer-Verlag.

Leff, J. P., Kuipers, L., Berkowitz, R., & Sturgeon, D. (1985). A controlled trial of social intervention in the families of schizophrenic patients: Two year follow-up. *British Journal of Psychiatry, 146,* 594-600.

Lefley, H. P. (1985). Etiological and prevention views of clinicians with mentally ill relatives. *American Journal of Orthopsychiatry, 55*(3), 363-370.

Lefley, H. P. (1987). Behavioral manifestations of mental illness. In A. B. Hatfield & H. P. Lefley (Eds.), *Families of the mentally ill: Coping and adaptation* (pp. 107-127). New York: Guilford Press.

Leventhal, H., Leventhal, E.A., & Nguyen, T.V. (1985). Reactions of families to illness: Theoretical models and perspectives. D. C. Turk & R. D. Kerns (Eds.), *Health, illness and families: A life-span perspective* (pp. 108-145). New York: John Wiley.

Levy, N. (1979). The chronically ill patient. *Psychiatric Quarterly, 51*(3), 189-197.

Lewis, F. M. (1986). The impact of cancer on the family: A critical analysis of the research literature. *Patient Education and Counseling, 8*(3), 269-290.

Lewis, F. M., & Bloom, J. (1978-1979). Psychosocial adjustment to breast cancer: A review of selected literature. *International Journal of Psychiatry in Medicine, 9*(1), 1-17.

Lezak, M. D. (1978a). Living with the characterologically altered brain injured patient. *Journal of Clinical Psychiatry, 39,* 592-598.

Lezak, M. D. (1978b). Subtle sequelae of brain damage. *American Journal of Physical Medicine, 57,* 9-15.

Liberman, R. P., Falloon, I. R. H., & Aitchison, R. A. (1984). Multiple family therapy for schizophrenia: A behavioral, problem-solving approach. *Psychosocial Rehabilitation Journal, 7*(4), 60-77.

Liberman, R. P., Wallace, C. J., Vaughn, C. E., Snyder, K. S., & Rust, C. (1980). Social and family factors in the course of schizophrenia. In J. Strauss (Ed.), *The psychology of schizophrenia.* New York: Plenum.

Lichtman, R., Taylor, S., & Wood, J. (1987). Social support and marital adjustment after breast cancer. *Journal of Psychosocial Oncology, 5*(3), 47-74.

Lieber, L., Plumb, M., Gerstenzang, M., & Holland, J. (1976). The communication of affection between cancer patients and their spouses. *Psychosomatic Medicine, 38*(6), 379-389.

Linsk, N. L., Keigher, S. M., & Osterbusch, S. E. (1988). State policies regarding paid family caregiving. *The Gerontologist, 28*(2), 204-212.

Lovett, S., & Gallagher, D. (1988). Psychoeducational interventions for family caregivers: Preliminary efficacy data. *Behavior Therapy, 19*, 321-330.

Lubkin, I. M. (1986). *Chronic illness: Impact and interventions.* Boston: Jones and Bartlett Publishers.

Lundervold, D., & Lewin, L. M. (1987). Effects of in-home respite care on caregivers of family members with Alzheimer's disease. *Journal of Clinical and Experimental Gerontology, 9*(3), 201-214.

Lynch, J. J. (1977). *The broken heart: The medical consequences of loneliness.* New York: Basic Books.

MacCarthy, B., Kuipers, L., Hurry, J., Harper, R., & LeSage, A. (1989). Counseling the relatives of the long-term adult mentally ill: I. Evaluation of the impact on relatives and patients. *British Journal of Psychiatry, 154*, 768-775.

Mace, N., & Rabins, P. (1981). *The 36-hour day.* Baltimore, MD: Johns Hopkins University Press.

Mackay, A., & Nias, B. C. (1979). Strokes in the young and middle aged: Consequences to the family and to society. *Journal of the Royal College of Physicians of London, 13*, 106-112.

Maddox, G. L., & Douglass, E. B. (1973). Self-assessment of health: A longitudinal study of elderly subjects. *Journal of Health and Social Behavior, 14*, 87-93.

Mages, N., & Mendelsohn, G. (1979). Effects of cancer on patient's lives: A personological approach. In A. Hund, G. Stone, & F. Cohen (Eds.), *Health psychology* (pp.255-284). San Francisco: Jossey-Bass.

Mailick, M. (1979). The impact of severe illness on the individual and family: An overview. *Social Work in Health Care, 5*, 117-128.

Malone, R. L. (1969). Expressed attitudes of families of aphasics. *Journal of Speech and Hearing Disorders, 34*, 146-151.

Marcus, L. J. (1987). Health care financing. *Encyclopedia of social work* (18th Ed., Vol. 1), (pp. 697-709). Silver Spring, MD: National Association of Social Workers.

Marcus, L. M. (1977). Patterns of coping in families with psychotic (retarded) children. *American Journal of Orthopsychiatry, 47*, 388-399.

Martin, L. R. (1982). Overview of the psychosocial aspects of cancer. In J. Cohen, J. Cullen, & L. Martin (Eds.), *Psychosocial aspects of cancer* (pp. 1-8). New York: Raven Press.

Mayou, R., Foster, A., & Williamson, B. (1978a). Psychosocial adjustment in patients one year after myocardial infarction. *Journal of Psychosomatic Research, 22*, 447-453.

Mayou, R., Foster, A., & Williamson, B. (1978b). The psychological and social effects of myocardial infarction on wives. *British Medical Journal, 18*, 699-701.

Mayou, R., Williamson, B., & Foster, A. (1978). Outcome two months after myocardial infarction. *Journal of Psychosomatic Research, 22*, 439-445.

McCance, K. L., Eutropius, L., Jacobs, M. K., & Williams, R. R. (1985). Preventing coronary heart disease in high-risk families. *Research in Nursing and Health, 8*(4), 413-420.

McCubbin, H., & Patterson, J. (1982). Family adaptation to crisis. In H. McCubbin, A. E. Cauble, & J. Patterson (Eds.), *Family stress, coping, and social support* (pp. 26-47). Springfield, IL.: Charles C Thomas.

McGill, C. W., Falloon, I. R. H., Boyd, J. L., & Wood-Siverio, C. (1983). Family education intervention in the treatment of schizophrenia. *Hospital and Community Psychiatry*, *34*(10), 934-938.

Meyerowitz, B. (1980). Psychosocial correlates of breast cancer and its treatments. *Psychological Bulletin*, *87*(1), 108-131.

Meyerowitz, B., Heinrich, R., & Schag, C. (1983). A competency based approach to coping with cancer. In T. Burish & L. Bradley (Eds.), *Coping with chronic disease* (pp.137-157). New York: Academic Press.

Mills, P. D., Hansen, J. C., & Malakie, B. B. (1986). Psychoeducational family treatment for young adult chronically disturbed clients. *Family Therapy*, *13*(3), 275-285.

Minkhoff, K. (1978). A map of chronic mental patients. In J. A. Talbott (Ed.), *The chronic mental patient* (pp. 11-37). Washington, DC: American Psychiatric Association.

Minuchin, S. (1974). *Families and family therapy*. Cambridge, MA: Harvard University Press.

Mishel, M., & Braden, C. (1987). Uncertainty—a mediator between support and adjustment. *Western Journal of Nursing Research*, *9*(1), 43-57.

Montgomery, R. J. V., & Borgatta, E. F. (1989). The effects of alternative support strategies on family caregiving. *The Gerontologist*, *29*(4), 457-464.

Montgomery, R. J. V., Kosloski, K., & Borgatta, E. (1990). Service use and caregiving experience: Does Alzheimer's disease make a difference? In D. Biegel & A. Blum (Eds.), *Aging and caregiving: Theory, research and policy*. Newbury Park, CA: Sage.

Montgomery, R. J. V., Stull, D. E., & Borgatta, E. F. (1985). Measurement and the analysis of burden. *Research on Aging*, *7*, 137-152.

Mor, V., Guadagnoli, E., & Wool, M. (1987). An examination of the concrete service needs of advanced cancer patients. *Journal of Psychosocial Oncology*, *5*(1), 1-17.

Moritz, D. J., Kasl, S. V., & Berkman, L. F. (1989). The health impact of living with a cognitively impaired elderly spouse: Depressive symptoms and social functioning. *Journal of Gerontology: Social Sciences*, *44*, S17-27.

Moroney, R. (1976). *The family and the state: Considerations for social policy*. London: Longman Press.

Morra, M., & Potts, E. (1980). *Choices: Realistic alternatives in cancer treatment*. New York: Avon.

Morris, T., Greer, S., & White, P. (1977). Psychological and social adjustment to mastectomy. *Cancer*, *40*, 2381-2387.

Mortimer, J. A. (1988). The epidemiology of dementia: International comparisons. In J. A. Brody & G. L. Maddox (Eds.), *Epidemiology and aging* (pp. 150-167). New York: Springer.

Morycz, R. (1985). Caregiving strain and the desire to institutionalize family members with Alzheimer's disease. *Research on Aging*, *7*(3), 329-361.

Muurinen, J. (1986). The economics of informal care: Labor market effects of the national hospice study. *Medical Care*, *24*(11), 1007-1017.

Myers, J., & Bean, L. (1968). *A decade later: A follow-up of social class and mental illness*. New York: John Wiley.

National Center for Health Statistics. (1989). *Health/United States, 1988*. (DHHS Publication No. PHS 89-1232). Washington, DC: U.S. Government Printing Office.

Naughton, J. (1984). Vocational and avocational rehabilitation for coronary patients. In N. K. Wenger & H. K. Hellerstein (Eds.), *Rehabilitation of the coronary patient* (pp. 473-492). New York: John Wiley.

Neugarten, B. (Ed). (1968). *Middle age and aging: A reader in social psychology*. Chicago: University of Chicago Press.

New, P., Ruscio, A., Priest, R., Petritsi, D., & George, L. (1968). The support structure of heart and stroke patients. *Social Science and Medicine, 2*, 185-200.

Noelker, L. S., & Townsend, A. L. (1987). Perceived caregiving effectiveness. In T. H. Brubaker (Ed.), *Aging, health and family: Long-term care* (pp. 58-79). Newbury Park, CA: Sage.

Northouse, L. (1981). Mastectomy patients and the fear of cancer recurrence. *Cancer Nursing, 4*, 213-220.

Northouse, L. (1984). The impact of cancer on the family: An overview. *International Journal of Psychiatry in Medicine, 14*(3), 215-242.

Northouse, L. (1988) Social support in patients and husband's adjustment to breast cancer. *Nursing Research, 37*(2), 91-95.

Northouse, P., & Northouse, L. (1988). Communication and cancer: Issues confronting patients, health professionals and family members. *Journal of Psychosocial Oncology, 5*(3), 17-46.

Northouse, P., & Swain, M. (1987). Adjustment of patients and husbands to the initial impact of breast cancer. *Nursing Research, 36*(4), 221-225.

Oberst, M. T., & James, R. H. (1985). Going home: Patient and spouse adjustment following cancer surgery. *Topics in Clinical Nursing, 7*, 46-57.

Oberst, M. T., Thomas, S. E., Gass, K. A., & Ward, S. E. (1989). Caregiving demands and appraisal of stress among family caregivers. *Cancer Nursing, 12*(4), 209-215.

Oktay, J., & Palley, H. (1981). A national family policy for the chronically ill elderly. *Social welfare forum, 1980*. New York: Columbia University Press.

Older Women's League. (1989). *Failing America's caregivers: A status report on women who care*. Washington, DC: Author.

Pagel, M., Becker, J., & Coppel, D. (1985). Loss of control, self-blame, and depression: An investigation of spouse caretakers of Alzheimer's disease patients. *Journal of Abnormal Psychology, 94*, 169-182.

Palmore, E. (1976). Total chances of institutionalization among the aged. *The Gerontologist, 16*, 504-507.

Parsons, T., & Bales, R. (1955). *Family socialization and interaction*. Glencoe, IL: Free Press.

Pasaminick, B., Scarpetti, F., & Dinitz, S. (1967). *Schizophrenics in the community: An experimental study in the prevention of rehospitalization*. New York: Appleton-Century-Crofts.

Passamani, E., Frommer, P., & Levy, R. (1984). Coronary heart disease: An overview. In N. Wenger & H. Hellerstein (Eds.), *Rehabilitation of the coronary patient* (pp. 1-15). New York: John Wiley.

Pepper, B., & Ryglewicz, H. (1984). The young adult chronic patient: A new focus. *The chronic mental patient: Five years later*. Orlando, FL: Grune & Stratton.

Pfeiffer, E., Cairl, R., Middleton, L., Alexander, L., Kleine, E., & Elbare, J. (1989). *Alzheimer's disease: Caregiver practices, programs, and community-based strategies*. Tampa: Suncoast Gerontology Center, University of South Florida.

Philips, I. (1988). Problems of the present system of service delivery. In J. G. Looney (Ed.), *Chronic mental illness in children and adults*. Washington, DC: American Psychiatric Press.

Piliavin, I. M., Piliavin, J. A., & Rodin, J. (1975). Costs, diffusion, and the stigmatized victim. *Journal of Personality and Social Psychology, 32*, 429-438.

Pinkston, E. M., & Linsk, N. L. (1984). Behavioral family intervention with the impaired elderly. *The Gerontologist, 24*(6), 577-583.

Pinkston, E. M., Linsk, N. L., & Young, R. N. (1988). Home-based behavioral family treatment of the impaired elderly. *Behavior Therapy, 19*, 331-344.

Plant, H., Richardson, J., Stubbs, L., Lynch, D., Ellwood, J., Slevin, M., & DeHaes, H. (1987). Evaluation of a support group for cancer patients and their families and friends. *British Journal of Hospital Medicine (England), 38*(4), 317-322.

Platman, S. R. (1983). Family caretaking and expressed emotion: An evaluation. *Hospital and Community Psychiatry, 34*(10), 921-925.

Pohl, C. R. (1980). The "WTL" model of cancer care. *Journal of Religion and Health, 19*(4), 304-312.

Potaszynik, H., & Nelson, G. (1984). Stress and social support: The burden experienced by the family of a mentally ill person. *American Journal of Community Psychology, 12*(5), 589-607.

Poulshock, S. W., & Deimling, G. T. (1984). Families caring for elders in residence: Issues in the measurement of burden. *Journal of Gerontology, 39*, 230-239.

President's Commission on Mental Health. (1978). *Report to the President from the President's Commission on Mental Health.* Washington, DC: U.S. Government Printing Office.

Preston, S. H. (1984). Children and the elderly. *Scientific American, 250*(6), 44-49.

Pringle, J. (1973). *Schizophrenia: The family burden.* Surbiton, England: National Schizophrenia Fellowship.

Pruchno, R. A., & Potashnik, S. L. (1989). Caregiving spouses: Physical and mental health in perspective. *Journal of the American Geriatric Society, 37*, 697-705.

Pruchno, R. A., & Resch, N. L. (1989a). Aberrant behaviors and Alzheimer's disease: Mental health effects on spouse caregivers. *Journal of Gerontology, 44*, S177-182.

Pruchno, R. A., & Resch, N. L. (1989b). Husbands and wives as caregivers: Antecedents of depression and burden. *The Gerontologist, 29*, 159-165.

Pruchno, R. A., & Resch, N. L. (1989c). Mental health of caregiving spouses: Coping as mediator, moderator, or main effect. *Psychology and Aging, 4*, 454-463.

Quayhagen, M. P., & Quayhagen, M. (1989). Differential effects of family-based strategies on Alzheimer's disease. *The Gerontologist, 29*(2), 150-155.

Quinn, W., & Herndon, A. (1986). The family ecology of cancer. *Journal of Psychosocial Oncology, 4*(1/2), 45-49.

Rabins, P. V., Mace, N. L., & Lucas, M. J. (1982). The impact of dementia on the family. *Journal of the American Medical Association, 248*, 333-335.

Radloff, L. S. (1977). The CES-D scale: A self-report depression scale for research in the general population. *Applied Psychological Measurement, 1*, 385-401.

Raymond, M. E., Slaby, A. E., & Lieb, J. (1975). Familial responses to mental illness. *Social Casework, 56*, 492-498.

Razin, A. (1984). Coronary artery disease. In H. Roback (Ed.), *Helping patients and their families cope with medical problems* (pp. 216-250). San Francisco: Jossey-Bass.

Reifler, B. V., & Eisdorfer, C. (1980). A clinic for the impaired elderly and their families. *American Journal of Psychiatry, 137*(11), 1399-1403.

Reis, H. T., & Gruzen, J. (1976). On mediating equity, equality, and self-interest: The role of self-presentation in social exchange. *Journal of Experimental Social Psychology, 12,* 487-503.

Revenson, T., Wollman, C., & Felton, B. (1983). Social supports as stress buffers for adult cancer patients. *Psychosomatic Medicine, 45*(4), 321-331.

Rix, S. E. (1984). *Older women: The economics of aging.* Washington, DC: Women's Research and Education Institute of the Congressional Caucus for Women's Issues.

Roberts, R. E. , & Vernon, S. W. (1983). The Center for Epidemiologic Studies Depression Scale: Its use in a community sample. *American Journal of Psychiatry, 140,* 41-46.

Robins, M., & Baum, H. M. (1981). The national survey of stroke incidence. *Stroke, 12,* (Pt. 2, Suppl. 1), I-45-I-47.

Robinson, A. M. (1988). A social skills training program for adult caregivers. *Advanced Nursing Science, 10*(2), 59-72.

Robinson, B. C. (1983). Validation of a caregiver strain index. *Journal of Gerontology, 38,* 344-348.

Robinson, R. G., Bolduc, P. L., Kubos, K. L., Starr, L. B., & Price, T. R. (1985). Social functioning assessment in stroke patients. *Archives of Physical Medicine and Rehabilitation, 66,* 496-500.

Robinson, R. G., & Szetela, B. (1981). Mood change following left hemispheric brain injury. *Annals of Neurology, 9,* 447-453.

Rolland, J. S. (1988). A conceptual model of chronic and life threatening illness and its impact on families. In C. S. Chilman, E. W. Nunnally, & F. W. Cox (Eds.), *Chronic illness and disability.* Newbury Park, CA: Sage.

Rose, L., Finestone, K., & Bass, J. (1985). Group support for the families of psychiatric patients. *Journal of Psychosocial Nursing, 23*(12), 24-29.

Rosen, S. M., Fanshel, D., & Lutz, M. E. (Eds.). (1987). *Face of the nation, 1987. Statistical supplement to the 18th edition of the Encyclopedia of Social Work.* Silver Springs, MD: National Association of Social Workers.

Ross, H., & Kedward, H. (1977). Psychogeriatric hospital admissions from the community and institutions. *Journal of Gerontology, 32,* 420-427.

Rubenstein, E., & Federman, D. D. (Eds.). (1982). *Scientific American medicine.* New York: Scientific American.

Sacco, R. L., Wolf, P. A., Kannel, W. B., & McNamara, P. M. (1982). Survival and recurrence following stroke: The Framingham Study. *Stroke, 13,* 290-295.

Sainsbury, P., & Grad, J. C. (1962). Evaluation of treatment and services. In J. D. N. Hill, G. M. Carstairs, A. Cartwright, et al. (Eds.), *The burden on the community: The epidemiology of mental illness.* London: Oxford University Press.

Samerotte, G. C., & Harris, M. B. (1976). Some factors influencing helping: The effects of a handicap, responsibility and requesting help. *Journal of Social Psychology, 98,* 39-45.

Satariano, W., Minkler, M. A., & Langhauser, C. (1984). The significance of an ill spouse for assessing health differences in an elderly population. *Journal of the American Geriatric Society, 32,* 187-190.

Sayetta, R. B. (1986). Rates of senile dementia—Alzheimer's type in the Baltimore Longitudinal Study. *Journal of Chronic Disease, 39,* 271-286.

Schleifer, S. J., Keller, S. E., Camerino, M., Thornton, J. C., & Stein, M. (1983). Suppression of lymphocyte stimulation following bereavement. *Journal of the American Medical Association, 250,* 374-377.

Schnaper, N., Legg-McNamara, C., Dutcher, J., & Kellner, T. (1983). Emotional support of the patient and his survivors. In P. H. Wiernik (Ed.), *Supportive care of the cancer patient* (pp. 1-15). Mt. Kisco, NY: Futura Publishing.

Schulberg, H. C., McClelland, M., & Burns, B. J. (1987). Depression and physical illness: The prevalence, causation, and diagnosis of comorbidity. *Clinical Psychology Review, 7,* 145-167.

Schulz, R., Biegel, D., Morycz, R., & Visintainer, P. (1989). Current psychological paradigms for understanding caregiver well being and burden within the family context. In E. Light & B. Lebowitz (Eds.), *Alzheimer's disease treatment and family stress: Directions for research* (pp. 106-127). Washington, DC: National Institute of Mental Health.

Schulz, R., & Decker, S. (1985). Long-term adjustment to physical disability: The role of social support, perceived control, and self-blame. *Journal of Personality and Social Psychology, 48,* 1162-1172.

Schulz, R., Tompkins, C. A., & Rau, M. T. (1988). A longitudinal study of the psychosocial impact of stroke on primary support persons. *Psychology and Aging, 3,* 131-141.

Schulz, R., Tompkins, C. A., Wood, D., & Decker, S. (1987). The social psychology of caregiving: Physical and psychological costs to providing support to the disabled. *Journal of Applied Social Psychology, 17,* 401-428.

Schulz, R., Williamson, G. M., Morycz, R., & Biegel, D. E. (in press). A longitudinal study of the costs and benefits of providing care to Alzheimer's patients. In S. Oskamp & S. Spacapan (Eds.), *The social psychology of helping.* Newbury Park, CA: Sage.

Schulz, R., Visintainer, P., & Williamson, G. M. (1990). Psychiatric and physical morbidity effects of caregiving. *Journal of Gerontology, 45*(P), 181-191.

Schulz, S. C., House, J., & Andrews, M. B. (1986). Helping families in a schizophrenia program. In M. Z. Goldstein (Ed.), *Family involvement in the treatment of schizophrenia* (pp. 20-34). Washington, DC: American Psychiatric Association.

Segal, S. P. (1987). Deinstitutionalization. *Encyclopedia of social work.* (18th Ed.). Silver Spring, MD: National Association of Social Workers.

Selye, H. (1956). *The stress of life.* New York: McGraw-Hill.

Shanas, E. (1979). The family as a social support system in old age. *The Gerontologist, 9*(2), 169-174.

Shanas, E., & Maddox, G. (1976). Aging, health and organization of health resources. In R. Binstock & E. Shanas (Eds.), *Handbook of aging and the social sciences.* New York: Van Nostrand Reinhold.

Shapiro, R. M., Possidente, S. M., Plum, K. C., & Lehman, A. F. (1983). The evaluation of a support group for families of the chronic mentally ill. *Psychiatric Quarterly, 55*(4), 236-241.

Silliman, R. A. (1984, March). *Family caregivers and their frail elderly.* Paper presented at the annual meeting of the American Geriatric Society, Denver, CO.

Silver, L. B. (1988). The scope of the problem in children and adolescents. In J. G. Looney (Ed.), *Chronic mental illness in children and adults. Washington, D.C.: American Psychiatric Press.*

Singer, B. A. (1983). Psychosocial trauma, defense strategies and treatment considerations in cancer patients and their families. *American Journal of Family Therapy, 11*(3), 15-21.

Sistler, A. (1989). Adapative coping of older caregiving spouses. *Social Work,* 415-420.

Skelton, M., & Dominian, J., (1973). Psychological stress in wives of patients with myocardial infarction. *British Medical Journal, 2*, 101-103.

Skorupa, P., & Bohnet, N. (1982). Primary caregivers' perceptions of nursing behaviors that best met their needs in a home care hospice setting. *Cancer Nursing, 5*, 371-374.

Smith, J. V., & Birchwood, M. J. (1987). Specific and non-specific effects of educational intervention with families living with a schizophrenic relative. *British Journal of Psychiatry, 150*, 645-652.

Snyder, B., & Keefe, K. (1985). The unmet needs of family caregivers for frail and disabled adults. *Social Work in Health Care, 10*, 1-14.

Snyder, K. S., & Liberman, R. P. (1981). Family assessment and intervention with schizophrenics at risk for relapse. In M. J. Goldstein (Ed.), *New directions for mental health services: New developments in interventions with families of schizophrenics.* No. 12. (pp. 49-60). San Francisco: Jossey-Bass.

Soltero, I., Liu, K., Cooper, R., Stamler, J., & Garside, D. (1978). Trends in mortality from cerebrovascular disease in the United States, 1960-1975. *Stroke, 9*, 549-555.

Spaniol, L. (1987). Coping strategies of family caregivers. In A. B. Hatfield & H. P. Lefley (Eds.), *Families of the mentally ill: Coping and adaptation* (pp. 208-222). New York: Guilford Press.

Spaniol, L., & Jung, H. (1983). *Families as a central resource in the rehabilitation of the severely psychiatrically disabled.* Boston: Center for Rehabilitation Research and Training in Mental Health, Sargent College of Allied Health Professions, Boston University.

Spaniol, L., & Jung, H. (1987). Effective coping: A conceptual model. In A. B. Hatfield & H. P. Lefley (Eds.), *Families of the mentally ill: Coping and adaptation* (pp. 85-104). New York: Guilford Press.

Spaniol, L., Jung, H., Zipple, A. M., & Fitzgerald, S. (1987). Families as a resource in the rehabilitation of the severely psychiatrically disabled. In A. B. Hatfield & H. P. Lefley (Eds.), *Families of the mentally ill: Coping and adaptation* (pp. 167-190). New York: Guilford Press.

Spaniol, L., & Zipple, A. Current research on families that include a person with severe mental illness: A review of the findings.

Spaniol, L., Zipple, A., & Fitzgerald, S. (1984). How professionals can share power with families: Practice approaches to working with families of the mentally ill. *Psychosocial Rehabilitation Journal, 8*(2), 77-84.

Stallones, R. A., Dyken, M. L., Fang, H. C. H., Heyman, A., Seltser, R., & Stamler, J. (1972). Report of the Joint Committee for Stroke Facilities I. Epidemiology for stroke facilities planning. *Stroke, 3*, 360-371.

Stein, R. W., Hier, D. B., & Caplan, L. R. (1985). Cognitive and behavioral deficits after right hemisphere stroke. *Current Concepts of Cerebrovascular Disease—Stroke, 20*, 1-5.

Stephens, S. A., & Christianson, J. B. (1986). *Informal care of the elderly.* Lexington, MA: D.C. Heath.

Stern, M. (1984). Psychological rehabilitation following myocardial infarction and coronary bypass surgery. In N. K. Wenger & H. Hellerstein (Eds.), *Rehabilitation of the coronary patient* (pp. 453-471). New York: John Wiley.

Stetz, K. (1987). Caregiving demands during advanced cancer. *Cancer Nursing, 10*(5), 260-268.

Stewart, A., Greenfield, S., Hays, R., Wells, K., Rogers, W., Berry, S., McGlynn, E., & Ware, J. (1989). Functional status and well-being of patients with chronic conditions: Results from the medical outcomes study. *Journal of the American Medical Association, 262*(7), 907-913.

Stoller, E. P., & Pugliesi, K. L. (1989). Other roles of caregivers: Competing responsibilities or supportive resources. *Journal of Gerontology, 44,* S231-238.

Stone, R., Cafferata, G. L., & Sangl, J. (1987). Caregivers of the elderly: A national profile. *The Gerontologist, 27,* 616-626.

Strauss, A. L., Corbin, J., Fagerhaugh, S., Glaser, B. G., Maines, D., Suczek, B., & Wiener, C. L. (1984). *Chronic illness and the quality of life.* St. Louis: C.V. Mosby.

Strauss, J. C., Carpenter, W. T., & Bartko, J. J. (1974). Speculations on the processes that underlie schizophrenic signs and symptoms. *Schizophrenia Bulletin, 2,* 51-69.

Talbott, J. A. (1981). Successful treatment of the chronic mentally ill. *The chronic mental patient: Treatment, programs, systems.* New York: Human Sciences Press.

Talbott, J. A. (1988). The chronic adult mental patient: An overview. In J. G. Looney (Ed.), *Chronic mental illness in children and adults,* Washington, DC: American Psychiatric Press.

Taeuber, C. (1983). America in transition: An aging society. *Current population reports, Special Studies Series, P-23, No. 128.* Bureau of the Census. Washington, DC: U.S. Department of Commerce.

Terkelson, K. G. (1987a). The evolution of family responses to mental illness through time. In A. B. Hatfield & H. P. Lefley (Eds.), *Families of the mentally ill: Coping and adaptation* (pp. 151-166). New York: Guilford Press.

Terkelson, K. G. (1987b). The meaning of mental illness to the family. In A. B. Hatfield & H. P. Lefley (Eds.), *Families of the mentally ill: Coping and adaptation* (pp. 128-150). New York: Guilford Press.

Tessler, R. C., Goldman, H. H., & Associates. (1982). *The chronically mentally ill: Assessing community support programs.* Cambridge, MA: Ballinger.

Theorell T., Haggmark, C., & Eneroth, P. (1987). Psycho-endocrinological reactions in female relatives of cancer patients: Effects of an activation programme. *Acta Oncologica (Sweden), 26*(6), 419-424.

Thomas, S. G. (1978). Breast cancer: The psychosocial issues. *Cancer Nursing,* 53-60.

Thompson, J. E. H., & Doll, W. (1982). The burden of families coping with the mentally ill: An invisible crisis. *Family Relations, 31,* 379-388.

Thompson, S. C., Sobolew-Shubin, A., Graham, M. A., & Janigian, A. S. (1989). Psychosocial adjustment following a stroke. *Social Science and Medicine, 28,* 239-247.

Thornton, J. F., Plummer, E., Seeman, M. V., & Littmann, M. B. (1981). Schizophrenia: Group support for relatives. *Canadian Journal of Psychiatry, 26*(5), 341-344.

Tilden, V., & Galyen, R. (1987). Cost and conflict: The darker side of social support. *Western Journal of Nursing Research, 9*(1), 9-18.

Tompkins, C. A., Schulz, R., & Rau, M. T. (1988). Post-stroke depression in primary support persons: Predicting those at risk. *Journal of Consulting and Clinical Psychology, 56*(4), 502-508.

Toseland, R. W., Rossiter, C. M., & Labrecque, M. S. (1989). The effectiveness of peer-led and professionally led groups to support family caregivers. *The Gerontologist, 29*(4), 465-471.

Townsend, A. L., & Noelker, L. S. (1987). The impact of family relationships on caregiving effectiveness. In T. H. Brubaker (Ed.), *Aging, health, and family: Long-term care* (pp. 80-99). Newbury Park, CA.: Sage.

Treas, J. (1977). Family support systems for the aged: Some social and demographic considerations. *The Gerontologist, 17*, 486-491.

Treas, J. (1981). The great American fertility debate: Generational balance and support of the aged. *The Gerontologist, 21*, 98-103.

Trudel, L., Fabia, J., & Bouchard, J. P. (1984). Quality of life in 50 carotid endarterectomy survivors: A long-term follow-up study. *Archives of Physical Medicine and Rehabilitation, 65*, 310-312.

Unks, R. P. (1983). The relative influence of social, physical, and psychological factors on the morale and life satisfaction of elderly wives of stroke patients: A descriptive exploratory study (Doctoral dissertation, University of Washington, 1983). *Dissertation Abstracts International, 44* (SECA), 25-85.

U.S. Bureau of the Census. (1987). *Statistical abstract of the United States: 1988* (108th Ed.). Washington, DC: U.S. Government Printing Office.

U.S. Department of Commerce (1980). *Statistical abstract of the United States,* 101st Edition, Series P-25, Nos. 802-888. Washington, DC: U. S. Government Printing Office.

U.S. Department of Health and Human Services. (1980). *International classification of diseases, 9th Revision, 2nd Edition, Clinical Modification.* Washington, DC: U.S. Government Printing Office.

U.S. Department of Labor, Bureau of Labor Statistics. (1984). *Employment and earnings, 30*(1). Washington, DC: U.S. Government Printing Office.

U.S. Department of Health and Human Services. (1980). Report to the Secretary by the Department of Health and Human Services Steering Committee on the Chronically Mentally Ill. *Toward a national plan for the chronically mentally ill.* Washington, DC: U.S. Government Printing Office.

U.S. General Accounting Office (1977a). *Returning the mentally disabled to the community: The government needs to do more.* Washington, DC: U.S. Government Printing Office.

U.S. General Accounting Office. (1977b). *The well-being of older people in Cleveland, Ohio.* Doc. No. HRD-77-70. Washington, DC: U.S. Government Printing Office.

U. S. House of Representatives. (1987). *Exploding the myth: Caregiving in America.* (Select Committee on Aging Publication No. 99-611). Washington, DC: Government Printing Office.

U.S. National Institutes of Health, National Cancer Institute. (1988, January). *Annual Cancer Statistics Review.* Washington, DC: U.S. Government Printing Office.

Vachon, M. L. S., Freedman, A., Formo, A. Rogers, J., Lyall, W., & Freeman, S. (1977). The final illness in cancer: The widow's perspective. *Canadian Medical Association Journal, 117*, 1151-1154.

Vachon, M. L. S., Rogers, J., Lyall, A., Lancee, W., Sheldon, A., & Freeman, S. (1982). Predictors and correlates of adaptation to conjugal bereavement. *American Journal of Psychiatry, 139*(8), 998-1002.

Vannicelli, M., Washburn, S. L., & Scheff, B. J. (1980). Family attitudes toward mental illness: Immutable with respect to time, treatment setting, and outcome. *American Journal of Orthopsychiatry, 50*(1), 151-155.

Vaughn, C. (1982). Family factors in schizophrenic relapse: A replication. *Schizophrenia Bulletin, 8,* 425-426.

Vaughn, C., & Leff, J. (1976a). The influence of family and social factors on the course of psychiatric illness: A comparison of schizophrenic and depressed neurotic patients. *British Journal of Psychiatry, 129,* 125-137.

Vaughn, C., & Leff, J. (1976b). The measurement of expressed emotions in the families of psychiatric patients. *British Journal of Social and Clinical Psychology, 15,* 157-165.

Vaughn, C., & Leff, J. (1981a). Patterns of emotional response in relatives of schizophrenic patients. *Schizophrenia Bulletin, 7,* 43-45.

Vaughn, C., & Leff, J. (1981b). The role of maintenance therapy and relatives' expressed emotion in relapse of schizophrenia: A two-year follow-up. *British Journal of Psychiatry, 139,* 102-104.

Vaughn, C., Snyder, K. S., Freeman, W., Jones, S., Falloon, I. R. H., & Liberman, R. P. (1982). Family factors in schizophrenia relapse: A replication. *Schizophrenia Bulletin, 8,* 425-426.

Vess, J., Moreland, J., & Schwebel, A. (1985a). An empirical assessment of the effects of cancer on family role functioning. *Journal of Psychosocial Oncology, 3*(1), 1-16.

Vess, J., Moreland, J., & Schwebel, A. (1985b). A followup study of role functioning and the psychological environment of families of cancer patients. *Journal of Psychosocial Oncology, 3*(2), 1-14.

Vettese, J. (1981). Family stress and mediation in cancer. In P. Ahmed (Ed.), *Living and dying with cancer* (pp. 273-284). New York: Elsevier.

Vincente, L., Wiley, J. A., & Carrington, R. A. (1979). The risk of institutionalization before death. *The Gerontologist,* 361-367.

von Bertalanffy, L. (1968). *General systems theory.* New York: George Braziller.

Waldo, D. R., Levit, K. R., & Lazenby, H. (1986). National health expenditures, 1985. *Health Care Financing Review, 8*(1), 1-21.

Waters, M. A., & Northover, J. (1965). Rehabilitated long-stay schizophrenics in the community. *British Journal of Psychiatry, 111,* 258-267.

Webster, E. J. (1980). Home and family: Problems and payoffs. In R. Brookshire (Ed.), *Clinical Aphasiology Conference Proceedings, 1980.* Minneapolis, MN: BRK Publishers.

Webster, E. J., & Newhoff, M. (1981). Intervention with families of communicatively impaired adults. In D. S. Beasley & G. A. Davis (Eds.), *Aging: Communication processes and disorders.* New York: Grune & Stratton.

Weinfeld, F. D. (Ed.). (1981). The National Survey of Stroke. *Stroke, 12* (Part 2, Suppl. 1).

Weisman, A. (1979). *Coping with cancer.* New York: McGraw-Hill.

Weisman, A. (1984). A model for psychosocial phasing in cancer. In R. Moos (Ed.), *Coping with physical illness* (pp. 107-122). New York: Plenum.

Weisman, A., & Worden, J. W. (1976-7). The existential plight in cancer: Significance of the first 100 days. *International Journal of Psychiatry in Medicine, 7*(1), 1-15.

Weisman, A., & Worden, J. W. (1985-6). The emotional impact of recurrent cancer. *Journal of Psychosocial Oncology, 3*(4), 5-16.

Welch, D. (1981). Planning nursing interventions for family members of adult cancer patients. *Cancer Nursing, 4*(5), 365-369.

Wellisch, D. (1985). Family therapy and cancer: Keeping house in a foundation of quicksand. In M. Lansky (Ed.), *Family approaches to major psychiatric disorders.* Washington, DC: American Psychiatric Press.

Wellisch, D., Fawzy, F., Landsverk, J., Pasnau, R., & Wolcott, D. (1983). Evaluation of psychosocial problems of the home-bound cancer patient: The relationship of disease and the sociodemographic variables of patients to family problems. *Journal of Psychosocial Oncology, 1*(3), 1-15.

Wellisch, D., Jamison, K., & Pasnau, K. (1978). Psychosocial aspects of mastectomy: II. The man's perspective. *American Journal of Psychiatry, 135,* 543-546.

Wellisch, D., Wolcott, D., Pasnau, R., Fawzy, F., & Landsverk, J. (1989). An evaluation of the psychosocial problems of the homebound cancer patient: Relationship of patient adjustment to family problems. *Journal of Psychosocial Oncology, 7*(1/2), 55-75.

Wells, K., Stewart, A., Hays, R., Burnham, A., Rogers, W., Daniels, M., Berry, S., & Ware, J. (1989). The functioning and well-being of depressed patients: Results from the medical outcomes study. *Journal of the American Medical Association, 262*(7), 914-919.

Wenger, N., & Hellerstein, H. (1984). *Rehabilitation of the coronary patient.* New York: John Wiley.

Wikler, L. (1981). Chronic stresses of families of mentally retarded children. *Family Relations, 30,* 281-288.

Williams, P. A., & Williams, M. (1986). The treatment team. In A. I. Holleb (Ed.), *The American Cancer Society cancer book: Prevention, detection, diagnosis, treatment, rehabilitation, cure.* New York: Doubleday.

Williamson, G. M., & Schulz, R. (in press). Relationship orientation, quality of prior relationship, and distress among caregivers of Alzheimer's patients. *Psychology and Aging.*

Winogrond, I. R., Fisk, A. A., Kirsling, R. A., & Keyes, B. (1987). The relationship of caregiver burden and morale to Alzheimer's disease patient function in a therapeutic setting. *The Gerontologist, 27*(3), 336-339.

Worden, J. W., & Sobel, H. (1978). Ego strength and psychosocial adaptation to cancer. *Psychosomatic Medicine, 40*(8), 585-592.

Worden, J. W., & Weisman, A. (1977). The fallacy in postmastectomy depression. *American Journal of the Medical Sciences, 273*(21), 169-175.

Wortman, C. B. (1984). Social support and the cancer patient: Conceptual and method-ological issues. *Cancer, 53* (Suppl.), 2339-2359.

Yarrow, M. R., Schwartz, C. G., Murphy, H. S., & Deasy, L. (1955). The psychological meaning of mental illness in the family. *Journal of Social Issues, 11,* 12-24.

Yess, J. P. (1981). What families of the mentally ill want. *Community Support Service Journal, 2*(1), 1-3.

Young, R., & Kahana, E. (1987). Conceptualizing stress, coping and illness management in heart disease caregiving. *The Hospice Journal, 2*(3), 53-73.

Zarit, S. H., Anthony, C. R., & Boutselis, M. (1987). Interventions with caregivers of dementia patients: Comparison of two approaches. *Psychology and Aging, 2*(3), 225-232.

Zarit, S. H., Reever, K. E., & Bach-Peterson, J. (1980). Relatives of impaired elderly: Correlates of feelings of burden. *The Gerontologist, 20,* 649-655.

Index

About the Authors

David E. Biegel is the Henry L. Zucker Professor of Social Work Practice, and Co-Director, Practice Demonstration Program, Mandel School of Applied Social Sciences, Case Western Reserve University. He received his Ph.D. in Social Work from the School of Social Work and Community Planning, University of Maryland at Baltimore. He has been involved in research over the past fifteen years pertaining to factors affecting the delivery of services to hard to reach population groups and the relationship between informal and formal care.

Esther Sales is Associate Professor of Social Work at the University of Pittsburgh School of Social Work. She received her Ph.D. in Social Work and Social Psychology from the University of Michigan. Her interest in family caregivers emerges from prior published research addressing a variety of women's life course adjustment issues, including the mental health of working women, rape victims, and women re-entering school for graduate training. She is currently completing a comparative study of men and women involved in an educational program for dislocated workers.

Richard Schulz is Professor of Psychiatry and Director of Gerontology at the University of Pittsburgh. For the past decade he has been interested in psychosocial and behavioral dimensions of physically disabling conditions. His research has focused on diverse patient populations, including spinal-cord injured persons, amputees, stroke, and Alzheimer's disease patients. His work in this area is characterized by an interest in understanding individual functioning by examining the psychological representation of, and response to, physical disability as well as the social context in which it occurs.